THE

BLOOMSBURY

WENDY HITCHMOUGH

LOOK

YALE UNIVERSITY PRESS   NEW HAVEN AND LONDON

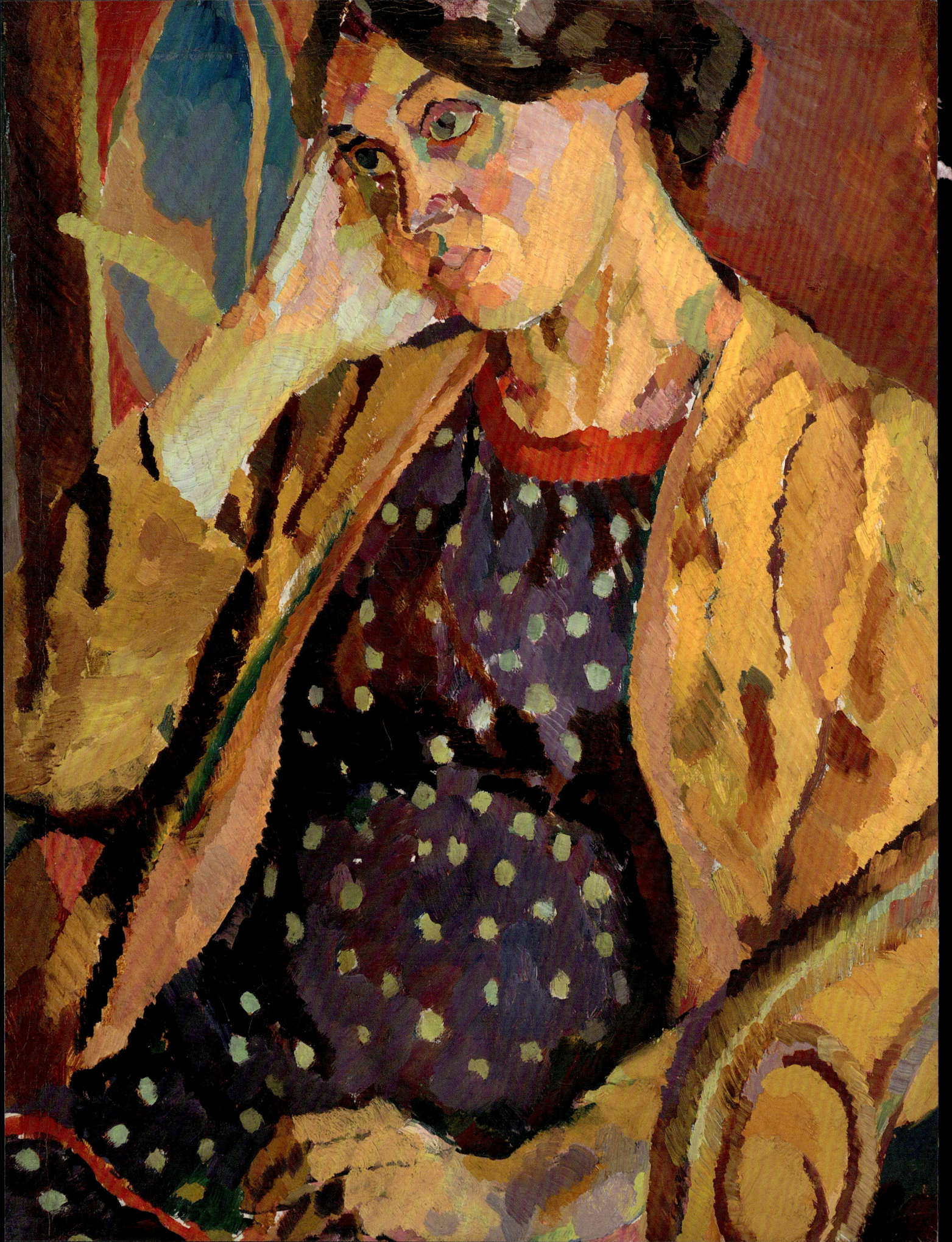

CONTENTS

INTRODUCTION	**BLOOMSBURY: IMAGE AND IDENTITY** 5
CHAPTER 1	**CURATING THE 'FAMILY' ALBUM** 23
CHAPTER 2	**EXPERIMENTS IN DRESS AND UNDRESS** 59
CHAPTER 3	**OMEGA DRESS** 91
CHAPTER 4	**EXHIBITING AND COLLECTING BLOOMSBURY** 131

ACKNOWLEDGEMENTS 154
ABBREVIATIONS 155
NOTES 155
BIBLIOGRAPHY 169
INDEX 178
PICTURE CREDITS 183

INTRODUCTION

BLOOMSBURY:

IMAGE

AND

IDENTITY

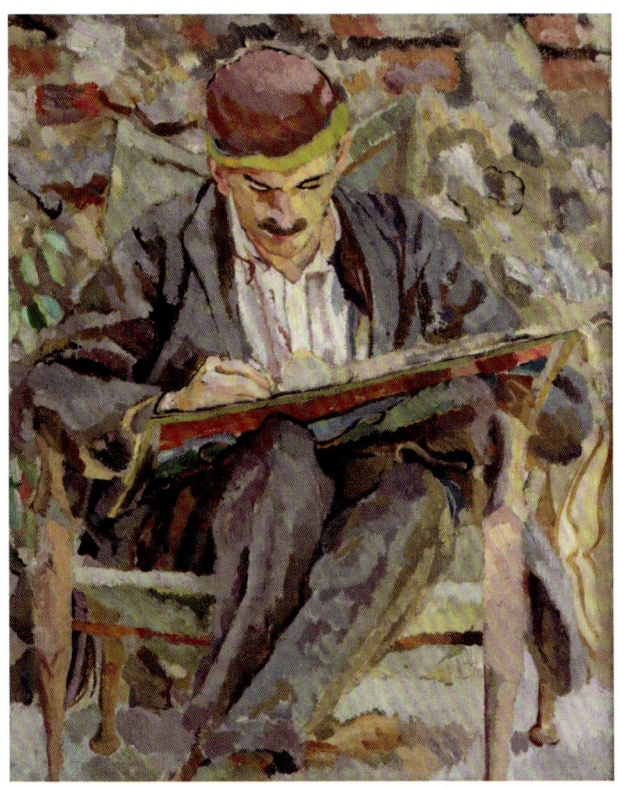

Sitting in a canvas chair in the walled garden of Charleston Farmhouse, East Sussex, as the First World War raged across Europe, the economist John Maynard Keynes drafted a telegram to America making the case for a loan that would finance Britain's military survival. Working with him in the garden, painting his portrait, were two fellow members of the Bloomsbury circle of friends, the critic and artist Roger Fry and the artist Duncan Grant. Their portraits capture the moment. They also characterize the ways in which Bloomsbury self-fashioned a visual identity that consolidated and promoted its position as an influential group of radicals. Keynes wears a loose grey suit and a collarless shirt that in Grant's portrait, the more intimate of the two, is unbuttoned at the neck (fig. 1). A red and gold cap, crocheted by the artist Vanessa Bell, identifies him with the vanguard of progressive British culture.[1] It was designed by Bell as part of an extraordinary dress collection for the Omega Workshops. With their showrooms at 33 Fitzroy Square in London's Bloomsbury, the Workshops, founded and co-directed by Fry, Bell, and Grant, provided a public platform for the Group and its aesthetic propositions. In the privacy of Charleston's garden, sheltered by the Sussex Downs, Keynes's unconventional headwear is indicative of a system of encoded references through which Bloomsbury members signalled their allegiances to the Group. This book explores Bloomsbury's public and private faces and the ways in which, as a group, it created a protective environment in which to test and explore experimental ideas and identities before presenting them to a wider public.

❈ ❈ ❈

Keynes shared the farmhouse with two of the Omega Workshops' co-founders, Bell and Grant, paying a third of the rent and receiving in return a refuge away from London and the intellectual and social constraints of his work at the Treasury. Charleston was one of a number of Bloomsbury homes in which the Group congregated to exchange ideas and to work, in close proximity, across the fields of literature, economics, politics, and the visual arts. Bloomsbury's boundaries were porous

1 Duncan Grant, *Portrait of John Maynard Keynes*, 1917. Oil on canvas, 565 × 463 mm. The Charleston Trust

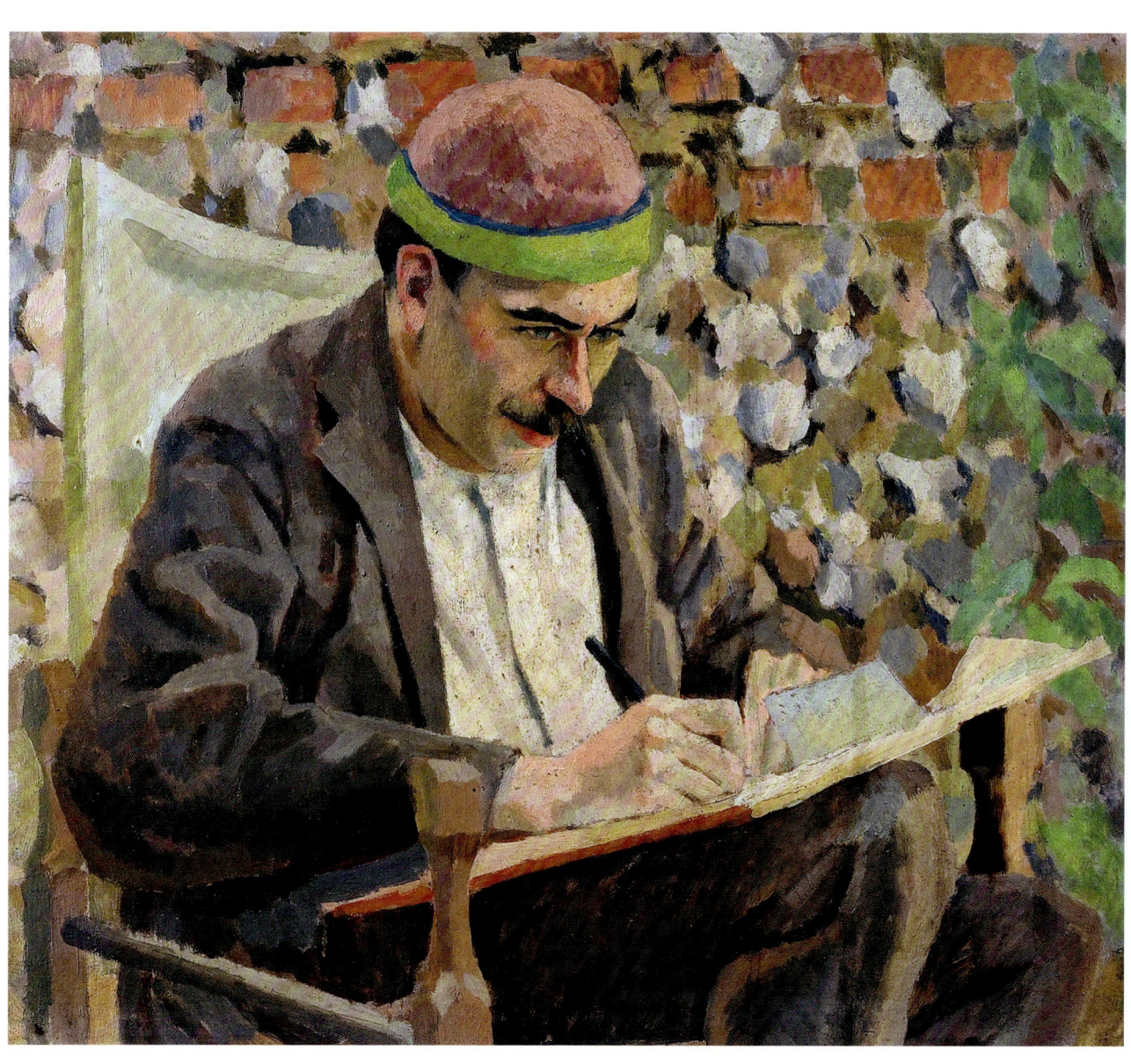

6 THE BLOOMSBURY LOOK

and elastic, capable of accommodating a range of perspectives. Charleston was an enclave for pacifism during the First World War, yet, as a Treasury official, Keynes and his work supported the war effort. This provoked criticism from his Bloomsbury friends, but he used his status to persuade a tribunal that Grant and his lover, the author David Garnett, should be exempt from conscription as conscientious objectors.[2] They moved to Charleston in October 1916 with Bell and her two young children so that Grant and Garnett could work on a neighbouring farm as labourers, thereby disrupting class boundaries as well as normative conventions of domesticity and sexuality.

Fry's portrait articulates the brilliant intensity of Keynes as an economist in the act of constructing his argument (fig. 2). He is hunched over his writing board, his expression self-absorbed, and the dappled sunshine highlights the knuckles of his right hand as he positions pen to paper. Grant's portrait is more abstracted and relaxed. The brick and flint details of the garden wall are loosely indicated by patches of colour, applied with broad brushstrokes. Bold outlines accentuate elements of the composition in a style adapted, as Bell was to note, from the Post-Impressionist portraits of Van Gogh and Matisse.[3] The quiet intimacy of Grant's portrait of Keynes reflects the nature of their relationship. They had been lovers for a period from 1908 and then shared rooms in an experimental household in Bloomsbury's Brunswick Square. The two portraits are emblematic of a moment in the Group's history. Keynes acquired the painting by Fry, endorsing his self-fashioning as a radical. Grant kept his portrait of his lifelong friend in his own private collection, stashed in the studio racks at Charleston, until the 1950s.

Bloomsbury's incursions into modernism were stimulated by the friendships and relationships within the Group. Its complex, shifting dynamics encouraged and enabled its members to step outside the conventions of their time and to innovate. The Group's subversive experiments with domesticity intensified its sense of its own separate values and identity. At Charleston, a copy of the *London Evening Standard* on the porch table on Friday evenings would mark Keynes's arrival for the weekend and a disturbance of the farmhouse community's rural isolation. Bell's son, Quentin, recalled it as 'a slightly astonishing thing for it looked so urban and remote in that primitive and countrified place'.[4] Keynes exchanged his habitual Treasury suit and starched collar and tie for tweeds, and with this change of clothes, this alternative setting, came a change in consciousness. It was possible to think and behave differently. He even insisted upon changing the clocks, for a period, to 'Charleston time' (an hour ahead of British Summer Time), which caused chaos. The kitchen clock was run down in protest, as the biographer Lytton Strachey noted, 'so that the servants have *no* time'.[5] Working in the company of artists and writers in the garden at Charleston or in his room there, sporting an Omega cap on occasion, Keynes developed his political and economic treatises. He wrote to Bell from Paris in June 1919 when he was obliged to represent the Treasury in punitive peace-treaty negotiations: 'I shall be back very soon indeed and in great need of Charleston. I shall want desperately to spend a good part of the summer with you, if I can, to recover my health and sanity.'[6] He wrote *The Economic Consequences of the Peace* at Charleston in August and September of that year.

Belonging within a stable and enduring framework has been identified by social psychologists as fundamental to human happiness. Bloomsbury's success and its longevity as a group relate directly to theories of 'belongingness'. Group membership satisfies a pervasive need for frequent and positive interactions with a small number of people – interactions which, psychologists claim, 'have multiple and strong effects on emotional patterns and cognitive processes'.[7] The need to belong is closely connected to needs for intimacy, for approval, and for achievements to be recognized and valued by others, all of which were met by the configuration of Bloomsbury as a group. Bloomsbury spanned over sixty years, from its original formation in the first years of the twentieth century, when many of its core members were students or recent graduates, until their deaths. It was uniquely successful and productive by comparison with other independent groups that forged new directions for

2 Roger Fry, *Portrait of John Maynard Keynes*, 1917. Oil on canvas, 520 × 610 mm. King's College, Cambridge

> Mr Sydney Turner
>
> Miss Vanessa Stephen,
> and
> Mr J. T. Stephen,
> At Home.
>
> 10 P.M.
> 46, Gordon Square,
> Bloomsbury.
>
> 1st Month
>
> 1905

twentieth-century culture and society. Its members continued to live and work in close proximity, to critique and promote one another's work, and to share initiatives even after their early rebellions had earned them positions within the establishment. Vanessa Bell's husband, the art critic Clive Bell, made his permanent home at Charleston during the Second World War, and he and Grant were still living together there as octogenarians after her death in 1961. The author, editor, and publisher Leonard Woolf remained nearby at Monk's House in Sussex, working on his autobiography throughout the 1960s and supporting the work of his nephew, Quentin Bell, who was writing the first biography of Leonard's late wife, Virginia Woolf. The scope and quantity of interconnected texts and material culture that Bloomsbury produced, together with its richly textured networks and the ways in which it operated professionally to effect change, would reward a sociological study. This book explores how Bloomsbury presented its evolution as a group through its displays of photographs and dress. It contextualizes Bloomsbury paintings and designs to examine their making, exhibition, and ownership as nuanced expressions within the political microcosm of the Group.

In addition to its domestic and intellectual benefits, Bloomsbury provided support in times of physical and emotional crisis. Research has shown that threatening events increase the strength and endurance of bonds within a group. Military veterans, for example, form and maintain relationships that are proportionate, in intensity, to the level of combat they have experienced together.[8] Bloomsbury traced its origins back to the University of Cambridge and the circle of friends who clustered around Thoby Stephen there. They joined his sisters, Vanessa and Virginia, for 'Thursday evenings' from the winter of 1904–5 at their home, 46 Gordon Square, in Bloomsbury (fig. 3). The Stephen siblings were already a close-knit group. Vanessa, Thoby, Virginia, and Adrian were aged 15, 14, 13, and 11 when their mother, Julia Stephen, died in 1895. Two years later their half-sister, Stella (a child of Julia's first marriage), also died suddenly, leaving the care of their father, the eminent editor, biographer, and mountaineer Leslie Stephen, and all domestic responsibilities to the teenage Vanessa. She was 25 when Leslie Stephen died in February 1904. With youthful determination she found 46 Gordon Square, away from the dark Victorian interiors, the well-meaning family friends

3 'At Home' invitation from Thoby and Vanessa Stephen to Saxon Sydney-Turner, 1906. Ink on card, 90 × 112 mm. The Charleston Trust

and relatives, and the respectability of 22 Hyde Park Gate in Kensington, where she and her sister had been born. It was to this new home, with stylish interiors arranged by Vanessa to suit herself and her three siblings, that Thoby brought his Cambridge friends. On a family expedition to Greece in the autumn of 1906, however, both Vanessa and Thoby became seriously ill. Thoby had contracted typhoid fever and soon after his return to London he died, at the age of 26. The trauma of his sudden death had a profound and enduring effect on the depth and nature of relationships within the Group. Clive Bell, Thoby's close friend, proposed marriage to Vanessa within two days of his death. She had refused his advances on two previous occasions but, perhaps distracted by grief, she accepted and they were married less than three months later, on 7 February 1907. Another of Thoby's Cambridge friends, Leonard Woolf, married Virginia in 1912. Even a decade later, Keynes wrote to Vanessa from 46 Gordon Square, where he was then living, that he was 'rather depressed yesterday because it was the tenth anniversary of Thoby's death'.[9]

In her autobiographical essay, 'Old Bloomsbury', Virginia recalled the prospect of marriage within the Group as 'a horrible necessity'. She paints a word-picture of Vanessa, one summer's afternoon in 1905, 'stretching her arms above her head with a gesture that was at once reluctant and yielding', observing herself in 'the great looking-glass' in 46 Gordon Square. Watched by Virginia and Adrian, she said to them, 'Of course, I can see that we shall all marry. It's bound to happen.' Thoby agreed with her prediction: 'That's the worst of Thursday evenings!'[10] Woolf locates the origins of Bloomsbury in its 'headquarters' at Gordon Square with forensic precision. 'Chapter One', she writes, was monastic and brief. It began with the move to Gordon Square and 'Thursday evenings'. Leonard Woolf, writing much later in his autobiography, contradicts his wife's memoir with an assertion that Bloomsbury originated in the masculine intellectual territory of Cambridge University, around the pivotal figure of the philosopher G. E. Moore and his *Principia ethica* (1903).[11] Whether it began in London or Cambridge, Bloomsbury brought together two kinds of group that loom large in 'belongingness' studies: siblings and undergraduate friends.

Living together or in close proximity has also been shown to be a powerful factor in developing relationships and group identities.[12] The Group colonized an area of Bloomsbury, living and working within a few minutes' walk of one another. When Vanessa and Clive married, Virginia and Adrian moved to 29 Fitzroy Square. Grant and Keynes rented rooms a few doors away at 21 Fitzroy Square from 1909. They set up an unconventional Bloomsbury household together at 38 Brunswick Square in 1911, occupying the ground-floor rooms with Adrian and Virginia, while the economist Gerald Shove and Leonard Woolf lived and worked on the floors above. Buildings were leased, and over the ensuing decades the circle of friends occupied rooms and set up studios in a succession of houses in and around Gordon Square, prompting the definition of 'Gloomsbury' in the popular 1928 novel *Fire Down Below* as 'a circle . . . composed of a few squares where all the couples are triangles'.[13] Keynes took over the lease to 46 Gordon Square when Bell moved her household (minus her husband) to Charleston, a move which, in turn, consolidated the grouping of a cluster of houses in Sussex where Bloomsbury gathered. Virginia leased Little Talland House in Firle as a country cottage in 1911. The following year she and Vanessa leased Asheham, nearby in the Sussex Downs. From there, Leonard and Virginia found Charleston and persuaded Vanessa to rent it as a suitable wartime base for her household with Grant and Garnett. After the lease to Asheham expired, Virginia and Leonard bought Monk's House in Rodmell, a walk or cycle ride of less than seven miles from Charleston. Alongside these country retreats, most of Bloomsbury's members also kept up houses, rooms, or studios in London.

Vanessa and Virginia held Bloomsbury together. Just as earlier Victorian women artists and writers had cut pathways into the male-dominated avant-garde as sisters and wives, so they exploited their core domestic relationships to develop and exert their agency. Thoby's friends gave them access to a masculine world of ideas, youthful ambition, and entitlement. After his death, the sisters filled a void within the circle. They confronted society's expectations of them as homemakers, as social facilitators, even as dressmakers, and they adapted these conventional roles to suit themselves. In doing so, they positioned themselves at the heart of a power base that both retained and subverted family values and transposed them onto Bloomsbury's configuration as a group. Vanessa's matriarchal position within the Stephen family, her responsibilities as a carer during Virginia's periods of mental illness, and the enduring closeness and sibling rivalry between the two sisters contributed to the fundamental loyalties that defined Bloomsbury and to the Group's structure, which was both loose and robust. Its inclusion of women and the centrality of Vanessa and Virginia, both leaders in their respective professions, differentiated Bloomsbury from other artists' groups in the early twentieth century, such as the Camden Town Group, while also aligning Bloomsbury with a wider public interest in women's independence and suffrage. Family ties fostered the breadth and tolerance that made the Group exceptional. Its interest in psychology and Sigmund Freud, for example, emanated from the work of Adrian Stephen and his wife, Karin, who were both psychoanalysts, and from Lytton Strachey's brother James, who, with his wife, Alix, translated Freud's complete works for publication by the Hogarth Press (which Virginia and Leonard owned and managed). The Group was intergenerational, tracing a web of creative connections from its parents' and grandparents' colonial and artistic networks, and drawing the Bell children into its midst. This 'extended family', however, through which Bloomsbury opened its ranks to artists and intellectuals as well as relations, was never fully inclusive. Strachey and Grant's cousin, Mary Hutchinson, who was Clive Bell's mistress for many years, wrote to Vanessa that Bloomsbury had 'literally made a circle' that she found impenetrable: 'Your circle is so intimate, and has been so for so many years . . . I feel far more of a stranger than I think you can imagine. I cannot take part in your reminiscences which are like those of a family – they are so much connected'.[14]

In 'Old Bloomsbury' Virginia Woolf describes the new candour and intimacy at Gordon Square that followed Vanessa and Clive's marriage as 'Chapter Two' in the Group's evolution. 'Thursday evenings', with their intellectual purity and austerity, moved with her and Adrian to Fitzroy Square. Gordon Square was redecorated and became a setting for unrestrained discussions about sex and sexuality. Virginia claimed that all barriers of reticence were demolished with a single word, 'semen', when Lytton Strachey queried a stain on Vanessa's dress. From that moment, she wrote, Bloomsbury 'discussed copulation with the same excitement and openness that we had discussed the nature of good'.[15] Yet although her text articulates Bloomsbury's evolution as a group, it was also written to entertain. She confessed that the semen anecdote may have been invented.[16] It was conceived as a performance, read aloud to Bloomsbury's own, self-reflecting Memoir Club in July 1928.[17] S. P. Rosenbaum has noted the significance of Woolf's timing.[18] 'Old Bloomsbury' was reinvented for its members within weeks of Woolf dispatching her groundbreaking fictional biography, *Orlando*, to the printer on 31 May, when she wrote in her diary, 'I rather like the idea of these Biographies of living people.'[19] The memoir triggered a succession of complementary accounts of Bloomsbury's beginnings, by the editor and journalist Desmond MacCarthy, by Clive Bell, and later by Vanessa Bell, Leonard Woolf, and Duncan Grant, all members of the Club. The playful and parodic character of Bloomsbury encouraged the embellishment of fact with fiction. Its memoirs, biographies, and autobiographies, influenced by Strachey's irreverence as a biographer, are symptomatic of the Group's self-fashioning. They emphasize Bloomsbury's enduring friendships and are conversational and anecdotal, undermining attempts to define the Group and its significance. Bloomsbury was naturally resistant to manifestos and official enrolments, so the Memoir Club, which was formed in 1920 and held its last meeting in 1956, offers only one approximation of its membership. Other lists were compiled in Bloomsbury memoirs and autobiographies, with varying degrees of consistency. They invariably reflect the interests of their authors.

The thirteen core members of 'Old Bloomsbury' in the Memoir Club, and this correlates with a definition of the Group in Leonard Woolf's autobiography, were Virginia and Leonard Woolf, Vanessa and Clive Bell, Lytton Strachey, E. M. Forster, John Maynard Keynes, Roger Fry, Duncan Grant, Adrian Stephen, Saxon Sydney-Turner (a civil servant and part of the Cambridge circle), and Molly and Desmond MacCarthy.[20] Membership of the Group fluctuated. Other possible candidates include further members of the Strachey family, Gerald Shove, Sydney

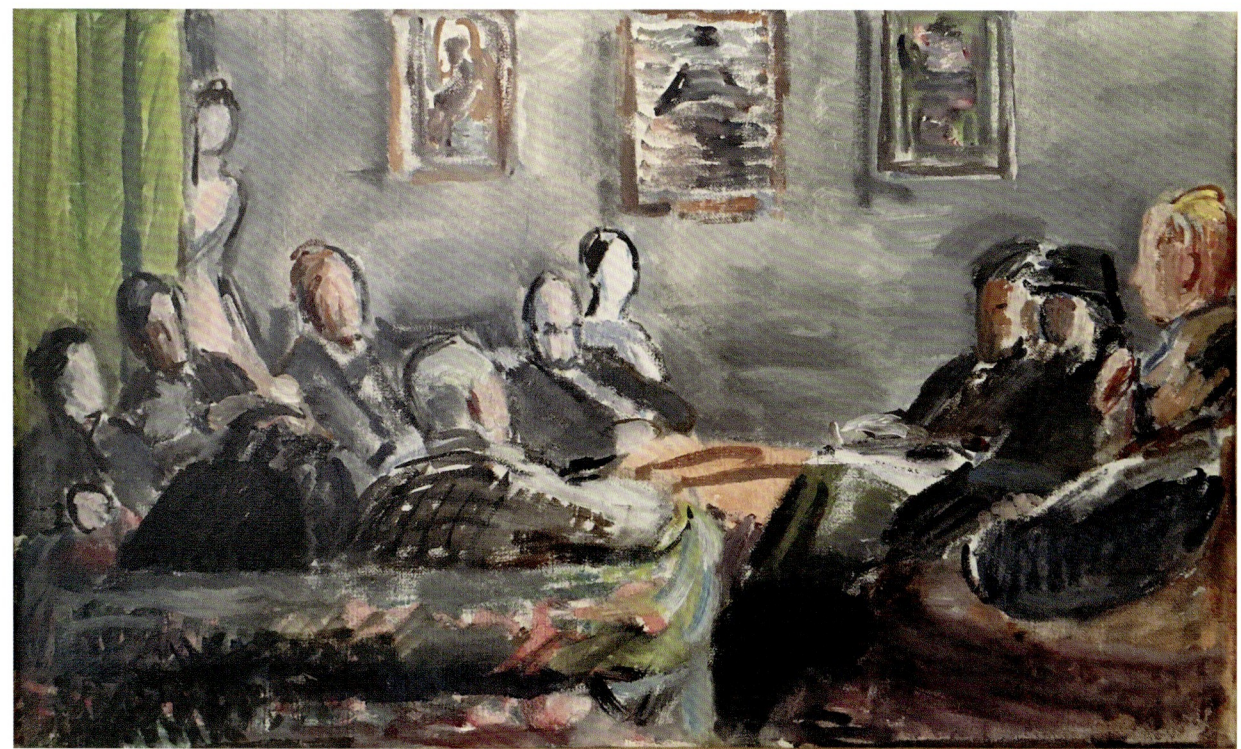

Waterlow, and H. T. J. Norton, all of whom were associated with Bloomsbury's early history. During the First World War the circle of friends was joined by David Garnett, Dora Carrington, Mary St John Hutchinson, Karin Costelloe, Barbara Hiles, Alix Sargant-Florence, Ralph Partridge, and Arthur Waley. By 1917 the Group had a sense of its own distinct identity, prompting Clive Bell to suggest to Fry that he paint 'a great historical portrait group of Bloomsbury'.[21] Fry reported the invitation to Vanessa Bell, musing that he might include the artist 'Walter Sickert coming in at the door and looking at us all with a kind of benevolent cynicism'. Vanessa Bell's gift for likenesses, he thought, might make her the better artist for the task; many years later, in 1943, when she painted her group portrait *The Memoir Club*, she included his idea of an interloper, introducing the figure of her own daughter, Angelica, into a doorway in the sketch for the painting (fig. 4).

❈ ❈ ❈

In-group favouritism and solidarity are endemic in the psychology of successful groups. For Bloomsbury this extended to the sharing of 'Bloomsbury status', described by Raymond Williams as 'eminence by association', with those on its peripheries.[22] The bolstering and complicating of Bloomsbury's ranks, depending upon who was defining its membership and when, is an indication of the Group's relatively open character. Studies have shown that even random and recently formed groups exhibit preferential treatment towards their members. This is not motivated by self-interest. It is automatic to the process of defining one's social identity and one's place in the world through affiliation to a group, and then positively differentiating that group from other, 'out-groups'.[23] Clive Bell and Roger Fry promoted each other's theories on aesthetics and reviewed the exhibitions of Vanessa Bell and Duncan Grant. Lytton Strachey, who with the publication of *Eminent Victorians* (1918) became one of the first in the Group to achieve critical acclaim, deployed both his influence and his affluence as a patron by buying one of the most innovative

4 Vanessa Bell, Sketch for *The Memoir Club*, c.1943. Oil on canvas, 300 × 500 mm. Private collection. (*Left to right*) Duncan Grant, Leonard Woolf, Angelica Garnett, Vanessa Bell, Clive Bell, David Garnett, Maynard and Lydia Keynes, Desmond and Molly MacCarthy, Quentin Bell, and E. M. Forster

paintings in Grant's first solo exhibition in 1920. Vanessa Bell's book jackets, woodcuts, and logo created a distinctive brand for the Hogarth Press, and photographs of her daughter, Angelica, dressed up as a Russian princess illustrated the first edition of *Orlando* (fig. 5).[24] Virginia Woolf underwrote her sister's joint exhibition with Grant at the Lefevre Galleries in 1932. She included the Society hostess Lady Ottoline Morrell in her plan to throw a 'quite ghastly party . . . to induce the rich to buy'. 'The rich', for Bloomsbury, were a necessary and familiar 'out-group', and Morrell was their intermediary. 'You are NOT to buy', Woolf wrote to her, 'what you're to do is to sacrifice yourself once more to the cause . . . and swim through the rooms trailing glory in your wake and entertain Margot [Asquith], Lord Sud[e]ley, Lord anybody – as you know how.'[25] For her pains, Morrell was promised 'a crack in a corner' with Woolf, a moment of 'in-group' conspiracy.

Bloomsbury's back-biting and bitchiness, even about its own friends and core members, are both entertaining and appalling. Woolf described T. S. Eliot as 'tight and shiny as a wood louse', and in a letter to her Strachey described Morrell 'after dinner in the lamplight, her cheek-pouches drooping with peppermints, a cigarette between her false teeth, and vast spectacles on her painted nose'.[26] The quantities of letters and diaries laying bare the Group's most private thoughts and feelings expose fickle and duplicitous behaviours that counterbalance its more worthy commitment to truth, beauty, and friendship. Until the 1960s and 1970s these were unpublished and therefore not explicitly known, though letters were often written with performance in mind, to be read aloud to assembled friends. The Group was flippantly disparaging about itself and everybody else from the outset. It was first named 'Bloomby' by Strachey in a diary entry in 1910 noting its absence from a gathering at Morrell's home. Two days later he called in at Gordon Square to dine with Clive and Vanessa Bell, intending that they should go on, together, to Fitzroy Square. He noted with some consternation that Clive 'refused to go to Fitzroy' on the grounds

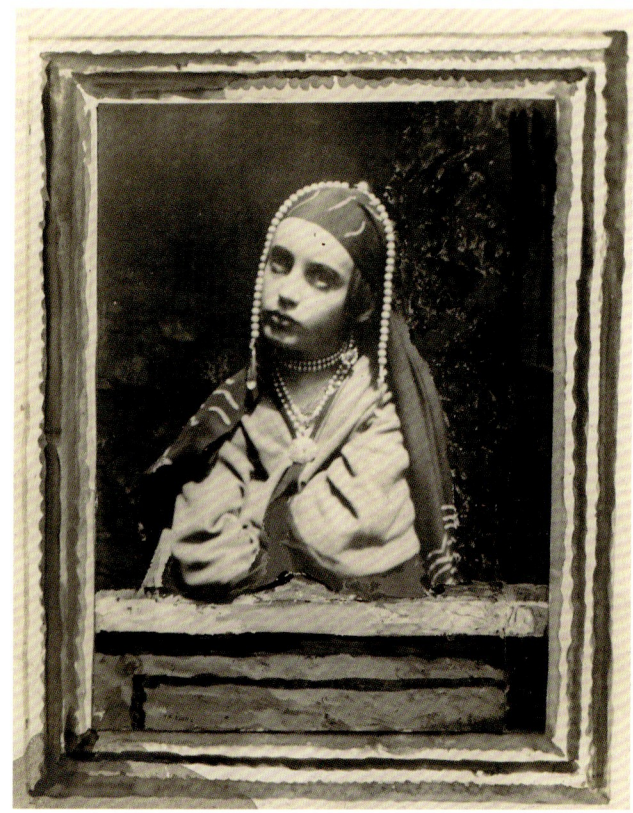

that 'collective affectation and dullness' had taken hold in the set: 'Everyone tries to make his individuality tell.'[27] This combination of assertive individuality and dissonance is critical to understanding the Group's complex self-fashioning. It is also one of the factors that make Bloomsbury so elusive.

As a group Bloomsbury courted controversy, and its powerful, if ambiguous, identity bolstered the daring and the resilience of its individual members. Even before it had made a name for itself, Bloomsbury's disregard for authority and social norms, and its reforming approach to social conventions, politics, economics, and the arts, invited censure. Vanessa noted the tone of disapproval when, 'at an ordinary conventional party', she was asked to account for the Group's Thursday evenings. 'Who were these young men' with whom she and her sister stayed up late, talking?[28] In 1910, when members of the Group participated in the *Dreadnought* hoax, it enjoyed a shared delight in the critical backlash they provoked.

5 Vanessa Bell, Angelica Bell as 'The Russian Princess as a Child', 1928. The Charleston Trust. This photograph illustrated the first edition of Virginia Woolf's novel *Orlando*

The hoax was planned by Adrian and Virginia's friend Horace de Vere Cole. It was a practical joke played against the navy in which Adrian and Virginia, together with Duncan Grant, joined a group of pranksters and successfully presented themselves as Abyssinian princes and their entourage to the Admiral and assembled forces on board HMS *Dreadnought*. The hoax was instrumental in shaping Bloomsbury's identity as a defiant and irreverent in-group, impervious to the critical reactions of the establishment forces that it undermined. It also tested the Group's capacity to accommodate dissent from within its ranks. Neither Clive Bell nor the Strachey family approved of the escapade.[29]

Press photographs by the Lafayette studios, one of the largest and most successful commercial photographers in London, which served the king and court as well as the military, were central to the success of the *Dreadnought* hoax. Cole employed an experienced theatrical costumier and arranged a sitting for the hoaxers before they boarded the train to Weymouth, where the battleship was anchored. The unlikely line-up of three men and a woman elaborately disguised as Abyssinian princes made the story front-page news in the *Daily Mirror*. Copies of the photograph, mounted and annotated, remained at Charleston with the Stephen family archive until after Vanessa's death (fig. 6). For Bloomsbury, they demonstrated the value of images in documenting and promoting otherwise ephemeral events. Over time the *Dreadnought* photographs served a multitude of purposes. Adrian used one as the cover image for his account of the event, published by the Hogarth Press in 1936.[30] Four years later Virginia presented a talk about it to her local Women's Institute in Rodmell; she later adapted it for the Memoir Club, leaving its members, according to E. M. Forster, 'helpless with laughter'.[31] Quentin Bell included the notes for Virginia's unpublished paper as an appendix to his biography of her, and illustrated his text with one of the *Dreadnought* photographs. Scholars have analysed the significance of the *Dreadnought* hoax as an attack on the imperialist and patriarchal bombast of the British Empire. They have also explored the ambivalence of Woolf's racial and sexual identity in the prank, where she appeared 'as an effeminized male and as a powerful African'.[32] The event was significant, too, in shaping Bloomsbury's engagement with the visual, and with material culture. It kindled a fascination with dressing up and with cross-dressing in order to embody alternative identities, and it informed Bloomsbury's image-making. In its drawings and paintings, the Group adopted the dress conventions of other cultures, whether a turban or a peasant headscarf, to contest boundaries. The *Dreadnought* hoax also instilled in the Group a sophisticated understanding of the potential of professional and amateur photographs to document and disseminate its public and private activities.

Bloomsbury courted controversy again later in 1910 with Fry's exhibition *Manet and the Post-Impressionists*, and revelled in the outcry it provoked. The Group's letters and diaries present versions of the exhibition very different from those in its memoirs and biographies. Virginia Woolf, for example, makes no mention of the first Post-Impressionist exhibition in her diaries and correspondence. She stayed in Studland, Dorset, with her sister, her new nephew Quentin, and his elder brother, Julian Bell, while Clive Bell, Roger Fry, Desmond MacCarthy, and Ottoline Morrell selected pictures for the exhibition in Paris. Vanessa Bell wrote to her husband, envious of 'that exciting atmosphere where people really seem to realise the existence of art'.[33] If the outrage the exhibition was to cause was unanticipated, however, it was certainly celebrated in Bloomsbury's later self-fashioning. Woolf devoted an entire chapter to *Manet and the Post-Impressionists* in her biography of Fry. She described its polarizing effects on an 'out-group', the press and public, who were 'thrown into paroxysms of rage and laughter' by the paintings of Matisse, Picasso, and Cézanne, and on an 'in-group' of progressive young English painters, many of whom were later to work at the Omega Workshops.[34] Woolf's vivid account of Fry examining the paintings before the exhibition's installation suggests that they may have been assembled at 46 Gordon Square, drawing European modernism into the very heart of Bloomsbury's 'headquarters': 'There they stood upon chairs – the pictures that were to be shown at the Grafton Gallery – bold, bright, impudent almost, in contrast with the Watts portrait of a beautiful Victorian lady that hung on the wall behind them.'[35] George Frederick Watts's portrait of Woolf's mother, the renowned beauty Julia Stephen, hung downstairs at 46 Gordon Square.[36]

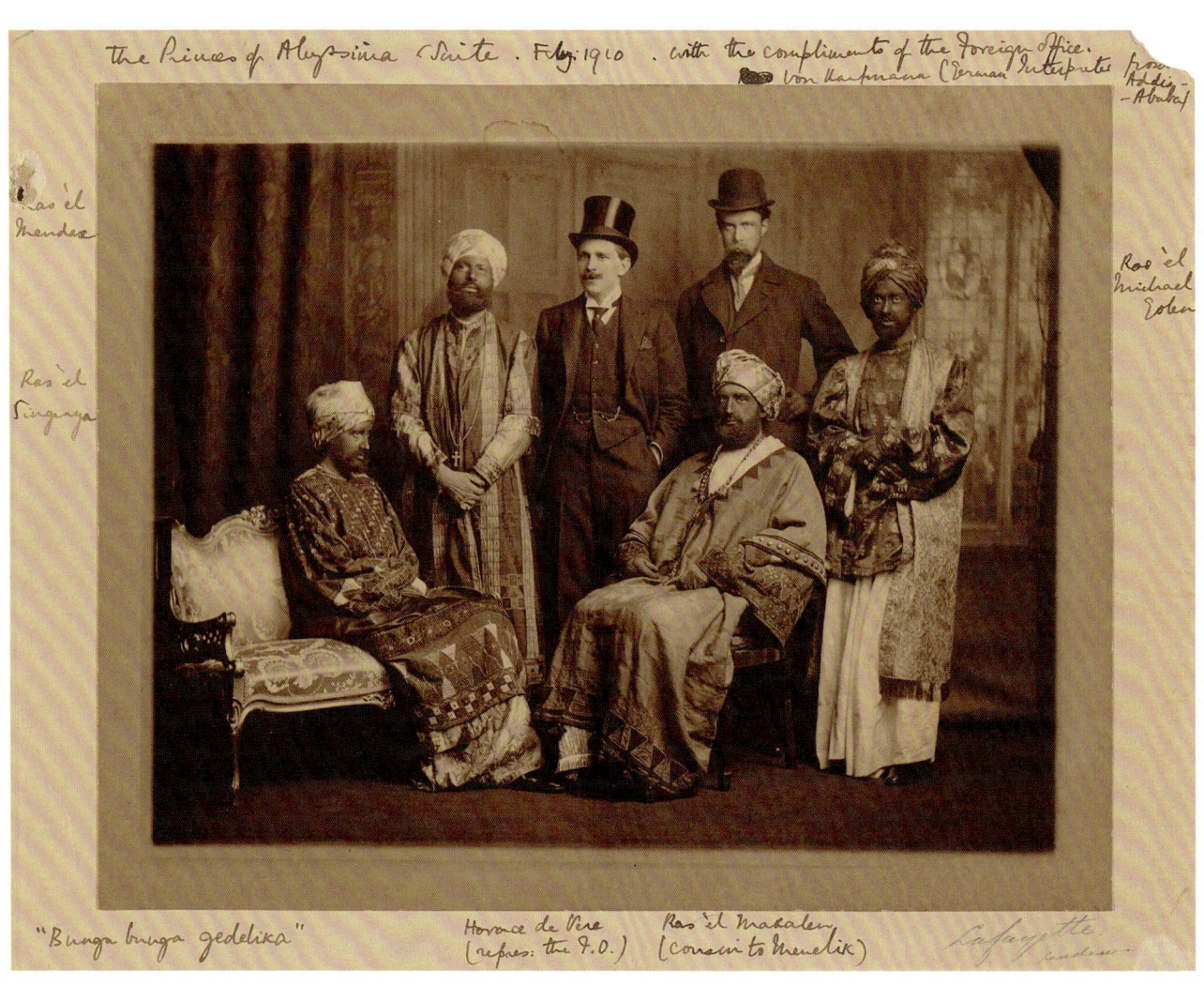

For Desmond MacCarthy, the exhibition's significance in establishing Bloomsbury's position in opposition to an outraged press and public outweighed its contribution to modernism. Appointed by Fry as the exhibition's secretary, he delighted in the crowds of curious visitors attracted by 'non-stop correspondence in the papers'. Bloomsbury memoirs often responded to one another, and MacCarthy's account, published after that of Woolf, elaborates on her description of a man so overcome by convulsions of laughter on seeing a Cézanne that he had to be taken outside and walked up and down by his companion.[37] Although, according to Woolf, MacCarthy was 'snatched from a sick-bed, revived with a bottle of champagne and assured that his real job in life was art criticism', his memoir is wittily constructed around a theme of profit rather than art.[38] It also subscribes to the literary conventions of 'the memoir', just as Bloomsbury letters, to some degree, are characteristic of their genre and period. Having been promised a small salary and a large share of what he was advised would be non-existent profits for his work as secretary, MacCarthy was delighted by the exhibition's financial success, through sales and admissions, as a consequence of its notoriety. His share of the profits, he wrote, was the largest lump sum he ever earned.

Vanessa Bell's 'Notes on Bloomsbury', given to the Memoir Club in 1951, conforms to this theme of 'rage and derision' in 1910 but also describes the new freedom and excitement of Post-Impressionism. She wrote, with evident satisfaction, that the exhibition 'caused even more dismay and disapproval than Bloomsbury itself'.[39] If the Group's image was strengthened by its propensity to shock, however, it was also associated with reform. In a memoir on Fry, Vanessa Bell wrote that artists in England at the beginning of the twentieth century, ignorant of the work of Cézanne, Van Gogh, Gauguin, and their contemporaries, 'needed rescue'. 'It is impossible', she wrote of *Manet and the Post-Impressionists*, 'that any other single exhibition can ever have had so much effect as did that on the rising generation.'[40] Bell described Post-Impressionism as a visual extension of Bloomsbury's intellectual values. As an artist, she wrote, 'it was as if one might say things one had always felt instead of trying to say things that other people told one to feel. Freedom was given one to be oneself.'[41]

The Group's identification with Post-Impressionism not only shaped its visual identity but also determined its adversarial position in relation to mainstream popular culture. Bloomsbury challenged the Anglocentric nature of British culture and heralded wider allegiances with the avant-garde in Europe, including Russia. With the Omega Workshops and its application of Post-Impressionist principles to dress and the decorative arts, these allegiances could be externalized and literally worn or inhabited. The 'explosion of public wrath' aroused by the Post-Impressionist exhibition enlivened Bloomsbury memoirs and contributed to its confidence as an in-group of pioneers.[42] The First World War, and the solidarity with which Bloomsbury upheld its vigorous commitment to pacifism in opposition to powerful social and political forces, also sharpened its identity as a group. Again, this contributed to prejudices against Bloomsbury, when: 'All the world was hostile close round one.'[43] Vanessa Bell noted that 'Bloomsbury was not destroyed as probably many other circles were destroyed by the departure of all its young men to the wars. Perhaps one reason for much of the later abuse was that many were Conscientious Objectors.'[44]

Keynes believed that Bloomsbury aroused suspicion and prejudice in 'the outer world' because it refused to obey general rules: 'We repudiated entirely customary morals, conventions and traditional wisdom. We were . . . immoralists.'[45] This culture of suspicion, he wrote, had a profound effect on the lives of Bloomsbury's members. The Group became robust in its responses to detractors who sneered at its work and made insinuations about the sexuality and lifestyles of its members. When Wyndham Lewis, one of the original Omega Workshops artists, denounced the Workshops in a 'Round Robin' letter to all its supporters, the Group rallied both in public and in private. Lewis denigrated Omega as 'this family party of strayed and Dissenting Aesthetes' and mockingly observed that, were it not for the contribution made by his own

---

6 Lafayette, 'The *Dreadnought* Hoax', 7 February 1910. National Portrait Gallery, London. (*Left to right*) Virginia Stephen, Guy Ridley, Horace De Vere Cole, Adrian Stephen, Anthony Buxton (*seated in front*), Duncan Grant

'rough and masculine work' and that of his modernist colleagues, the Workshops would have been incapable of rising above 'the level of a pleasant tea-party'.[46] He satirized the Group in his 1930 novel, *The Apes of God*. Aldous Huxley parodied Ottoline Morrell's Garsington gatherings in *Crome Yellow* (1921), and D. H. Lawrence, writing to Morrell and to David Garnett, condemned Bloomsbury as 'little swarming selves', likening them to beetles.[47] Christopher Reed has attributed this 'Bloomsbury Bashing' and the critical legacy that it engendered to a sexist and homophobic dismissal of Bloomsbury as part of 'a decadent and effeminate bourgeoisie'.[48] Queer scholarship continues to re-evaluate the Group's contribution to alternative heritages.[49]

❈ ❈ ❈

Bloomsbury might justifiably be criticized for the insularity and nepotism with which it determined its own historiography. The Woolfs' publishing house, the Hogarth Press, instilled in the Group a sense of editorial control over its own narratives. In addition to giving Virginia Woolf autonomy over the publication of her novels, in 1926 the Press published the first monograph on her great aunt, the photographer Julia Margaret Cameron, which was co-written by Woolf and Fry. After Fry's death, the Hogarth Press published Virginia Woolf's biography of him. Vanessa Bell wrote to Leonard Woolf in 1950 that if Bloomsbury was to be written about 'it must be by its own members'. She could not talk about her own generation, she wrote, 'except to my own family and friends'. Bell was dismissive of a Miss Benson, presumably a researcher, who had already approached Leonard Woolf and E. M. Forster before writing to her. 'I . . . told her that the Friday Club was a small society which didn't last very long, and implied that it was quite unimportant and that there never was such a thing as the "Bloomsbury Group."'[50] Her letter belies the fact, as Derek Ryan and Stephen Ross have noted, that she believed the opposite to be the case.[51] (The Friday Club was initiated by Bell in 1905 to discuss progressive art and art theory, and to organize exhibitions.)

Grace Brockington argues that Bloomsbury cultivated resistance to comprehensive definition as a group in order to deflect the attentions of its detractors. 'Critical baiting has made the beast of Bloomsbury shy, driving some of the Group's key contributors to question the accuracy and usefulness of a collective identity.'[52] Clive Bell complained that he had been 'stigmatized as "Bloomsbury"' in his 1956 memoir, *Old Friends*.[53] He challenged the 'grave historians' and 'pompous leader-writers' of Fleet Street to identify the Group's membership and summarize what it stood for. 'Beyond meaning something nasty,' he wrote, 'what do they mean by "Bloomsbury"?' Leonard Woolf, in his autobiography a few years later, reiterated Bell's insistence that Bloomsbury was 'fundamentally a group of friends' with its roots in the University of Cambridge: 'What came to be called Bloomsbury by the outside world never existed in the form given to it by the outside world.'[54]

Bloomsbury's legacy was shaped by the 1960s. It resonated with the sexual liberation, emerging feminism, gay liberation movement, pacifism, and vibrant pop culture that characterized that decade. Its historiography was tightly controlled, nevertheless, by Bloomsbury's sense of itself as a family. Leonard Woolf entertained prospective historians and biographers, he gave them lunch, but ultimately he charged Quentin with the commission to write his late wife's life. The first edition, published by the Hogarth Press, was illustrated with photographs from the Stephen family albums, professional portraits, and the amateur photographs through which Virginia and Vanessa, as children and young women, had projected their emerging identities. Quentin's biography of his aunt, in two volumes, coincided with his appointment to the new University of Sussex as Professor of History and Theory of Art in 1967. He described the challenges of addressing Woolf's reputation in the 1960s without appearing to provide merely a subjective 'nepotal offering': 'many people thought of her as a wealthy, precious, difficult and malicious snob'.[55] Leonard died in 1969 while the biography was a work in progress, and the papers he had made available to Quentin, together with interviews that Quentin recorded as part of his research, were gifted to the Special Collections at the University of Sussex. Its catalogue of the Woolfs' correspondents outlines the breadth of Bloomsbury's connections. Despite its identity as a group of radicals and outsiders, Bloomsbury exercised influence throughout and beyond the complex network of London's clubs and artists' groups. George Bernard Shaw, Rupert Brooke, Walter Sickert, Max Beerbohm, and Edith Sitwell are included among the Woolfs' correspondents, in addition to the leading thinkers and writers, from T. S. Eliot to Sigmund Freud, whose work they published through the Hogarth Press.

In *Bloomsbury Pie: The Making of the Bloomsbury Boom*, Regina Marler analyses the vested interests of a generation of Bloomsbury descendants in protecting and promoting their literary and artistic estates and 'the great divide in English and American evaluations of Bloomsbury'.[56] This was a generation of authors, artists, and publishers for whom the responsibilities of holding and protecting the copyright interests of their late siblings, spouses, parents, or grandparents weighed heavily. Michael Holroyd, an 'outsider' to Bloomsbury who nonetheless wrote a pioneering biography of Lytton Strachey, has described the crucial process of first earning the approval of Strachey's brother and literary executor, James Strachey, and that of James's wife, Alix. Without their support there could be no access to archive material, no permissions to quote from Strachey's texts, and, as the Bloomsbury diarist Frances Partridge intimated to him, very little in the way of co-operation from Lytton's former friends. (Frances Partridge was the second wife of Ralph Partridge, and had visited the home he shared with Lytton Strachey and his then-wife, Dora Carrington.) Holroyd visited the Stracheys at their home in Marlow Common, Buckinghamshire. After a testing lunch he was taken into a 'studio wilderness' in which his subject's entire archive had been stored for 30 years, forming 'a peculiar family museum with special emphasis on Lytton'.[57] Holroyd argued that Lytton's sex life should be given the same prominence in his biography as it had had in his life. He determined 'to trace its effect on his work, and to treat the whole subject of homosexuality without any artificial veils of decorum'.[58] Lytton's former friends and lovers, many of whom were now octogenarians, supported Holroyd's research and its publication, even though it jeopardized their own reputations. The first drafts of *Lytton Strachey: A Critical Biography* pre-dated the decriminalization of homosexuality in Britain. It promoted new understandings of Bloomsbury and it set a standard for future Bloomsbury biographers through its open engagement with sexuality and sexual relationships, and through its encyclopaedic approach to detail.

The Group's visual identity and the interweaving of its innovations and involvements in economics, dance, literature, politics, and the fine and decorative arts are captured in a short book that was published in the same year as the second volume of the Strachey biography, 1968. Quentin Bell's *Bloomsbury* responded to his mother's sense, almost two decades earlier, that only the Group's own members could fully understand and write about it. The book offers a snapshot definition of Bloomsbury and posits its visual milestones. Many of its illustrations are drawn from the Bell family archive, which Quentin and his half-sister, Angelica Garnett, had inherited after the deaths of Vanessa and Clive in 1961 and 1964. A section on 'Bloomsbury before 1914', for example, is illustrated with a full-page photograph of Quentin's uncle Thoby that had been safely preserved in both Vanessa's and Virginia's collections (fig. 7).[59] Bloomsbury's places are represented by the houses in which Quentin grew up: 46 Gordon Square, Asheham, and Charleston. Other Bloomsbury houses, such as Monk's House, Tilton, Tidmarsh, Hilton Hall, Keynes's rooms in Cambridge, and the Group's other homes and studios in Bloomsbury, go unmentioned. If this brief history is written from a Bell perspective, however, *Bloomsbury* yet encompasses the Group's visual legacy. It conveys the informality of snapshots and portraits that characterize Bloomsbury's self-fashioned image as a group relaxing and at work. Bell matches this spontaneity in his text, adopting the tone of a memoir and including anecdotes about the private lives as well as the work of his subjects. The Russian ballerina Lydia Lopokova, who married Keynes in 1925, for example, had been a friend and frequent visitor to Charleston, and Bell recalled her habit of walking over the South Downs, reciting the poetry of T. S. Eliot and discarding her clothes with the warmth of the exercise until she was naked.[60] Local boys would find them in the hedges and return them to Tilton.[61]

Domesticity became a vehicle for modernity in the lives and work of the Bloomsbury Group. Its houses and rooms, often accommodating unconventional households, projected the Group's self-constructed image. Their decorative schemes and collections relate to one another, reflecting a shared aesthetic.

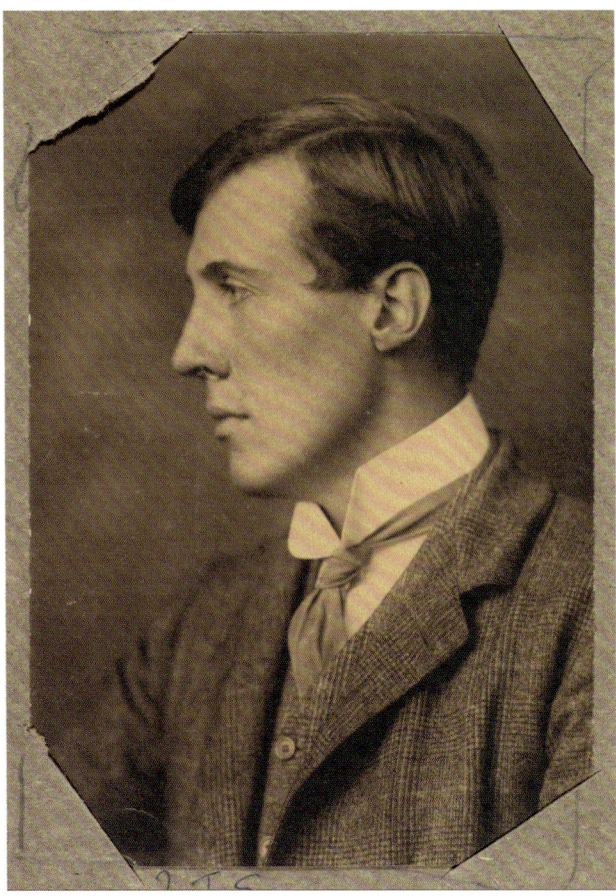

The provenances of pictures that were gifted within the Group or acquired at particular moments in its collective history are testaments to the longevity and nuances of the Group's existence. Bloomsbury painted its own interiors, which were photographed for publication. Fry's home, Durbins in Guildford, was featured in *Vogue* in 1918.[62] Bell and Grant's decorations for the Woolfs' apartment at 52 Tavistock Square and for Keynes's rooms at King's College, Cambridge, were featured in the same magazine in 1924 and 1925.[63] When *Bloomsbury* was published, the 'sister houses' of Charleston and Monk's House were still occupied by Duncan Grant and Leonard Woolf, respectively. Yet photographs of Charleston, its sitting room, and a gathering of Bloomsbury friends in its garden illustrate an account of its 'aesthetic comfort' and its 'adventurous' collection of Fauve and Cubist paintings, 'purchased when such things could be bought for a few pounds'.[64] Quentin took his art history students to visit Grant in his latter years at Charleston. After Grant's death in 1978, Quentin and his wife, Anne Olivier Bell, together with Angelica Garnett, were actively involved in restoring the house. Retaining some of its dilapidated character, they reconfigured its identity from the lived-in home of a 93-year-old artist to a house museum, representative of Bloomsbury in its heyday in the 1950s.

Grant had lived 'almost entirely in his studio' towards the end of his life. In an account very different from that of *Bloomsbury*, Bell outlined the restoration's challenges. Charleston, he wrote, had always been cold and damp, but by the time the Charleston Trust was founded, 'water was pouring in all over the place; the decorated wall surfaces mouldered . . . pictures decayed and, where they were painted on three-ply, became alive with woodworm'.[65] Charleston's contents were removed and conserved as part of the restoration process. The letters and photograph albums, the hoards of drawings and paintings that belonged in its attics, and the drawers of its cabinets and cupboards, were carefully sifted (fig. 8). In its early years, struggling for financial survival, the Charleston Trust was faced with difficult decisions. It lacked the resources to manage its own, dedicated archive and so Leslie Stephen's 'Mausoleum Book', Vanessa Bell's photograph albums, and the hundreds of Bloomsbury letters were gifted to institutions or sold to fund the purchase of the farmhouse, which hitherto had always been rented from the Firle Estate. The thousands of paintings and drawings that filled the racks and cupboards of working studios, but were never 'displayed' in the house in Bell and Grant's lifetimes, were taken to a dedicated London art store by the art dealer and family friend Anthony d'Offay. They formed a resource for a steady stream of beautifully curated exhibitions designed to rekindle Bell and Grant's reputations. Charleston may be thought of as a paradigm for Bloomsbury. Its contents and decoration were never fixed. It evolved over the decades in response to the changing interests and needs of the Group. Many of its best paintings were sold or given away during the artists' lifetimes and new work was always in progress. As a house museum it is intensely atmospheric, immersing visitors

7 George Beresford, Thoby Stephen, 1906. Houghton Library, Harvard University

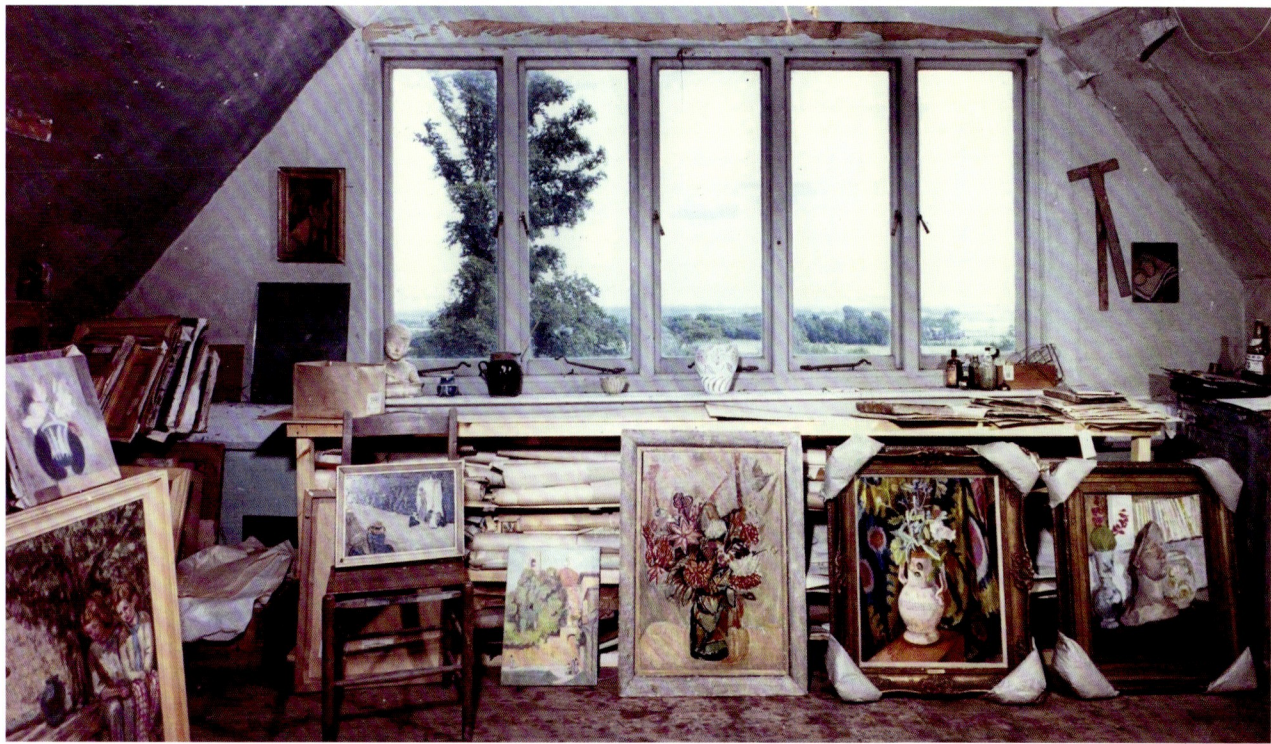

in the eclectic range of its contents. The values and work of its former occupants continue to resonate there in the twenty-first century.

Within walking distance of Charleston, Quentin and Anne Olivier Bell's home became a centre for Bloomsbury scholarship. The biographer Frances Spalding recalls that: 'To scholars of all nationalities, myself included, Quentin Bell offered availability and intelligence, patience and sternness, in an unremitting concern to make sure that the record was not falsified.'[66] Anne Olivier Bell continued to serve on Charleston's board of trustees and to maintain her particular standards for its presentation until 2013, when she was 97. She responded to scholarly enquiries and read and discussed every Bloomsbury publication until her death at the age of 102. Trickling through the filters of Bloomsbury heirs and collectors, material evidence for the Group has been gifted and sold to institutions around the world. Major holdings such as Tate, the National Portrait Gallery in London, King's College, Cambridge, and the Berg Collection in New York have benefited from astute collections policies that recognized the importance of the Group and its visual identity to twentieth-century culture and society. Important exhibitions, such as Richard Shone's *The Art of Bloomsbury* at Tate Britain and Sarah Milroy and Ian Dejardin's *Vanessa Bell* at Dulwich Picture Gallery, have reassessed the importance of Bloomsbury painting.

The chapters in this book recontextualize the material evidence for Bloomsbury's distinctive visual style. They consider the ways in which, consciously and intuitively, Bloomsbury used the conventional Victorian studio photographs, the cartes-de-visite, and the art photography of Julia Margaret Cameron that were its inheritance. Building on the work of Maggie Humm, they explore the Group's use of photography to shape its image and identity.[67] They trace the representations of Vanessa Bell and Virginia Woolf that emerge through their studio portraits and home-made photograph albums. They examine the narrative connotations of photographs arranged together in the family albums that the sisters inherited. Vanessa and Virginia's own albums are considered as part of their self-fashioning as young women, and then as Group representations of Bloomsbury and its friends. Bloomsbury is one of the earliest groups actively to assert its identity by

8 Unknown photographer, Vanessa Bell's attic studio at Charleston, 1970s.
The Charleston Trust

taking and exchanging photographs, and the chapters herein explore the currency of the Group's images in public and in private. Chapters on Bloomsbury nudity and dress interrogate photographs, paintings, and sketchbooks to understand the Group's complex relationship with fashion, conformity, and the avant-garde. The Bloomsbury artists asserted and established their identities by what they chose to exhibit, where, and with whom. Exhibitions were also important for Bloomsbury as a collective. The Group congregated at private views, and the deliberation with which it supported and contributed to contemporary art exhibitions as sitters, critics, and consumers, as well as artists, reveals a calculated self-fashioning. Finally, this book analyses transitions in the meaning and status of Bloomsbury's material culture when it is gifted, sold, and collected. It considers the passion with which Bloomsbury built and contested its own collections and the ways in which, then as now, the impact of a text or a dress or a portrait is inseparable from the circumstances in which it is encountered.

CHAPTER 1

CURATING THE 'FAMILY' ALBUM

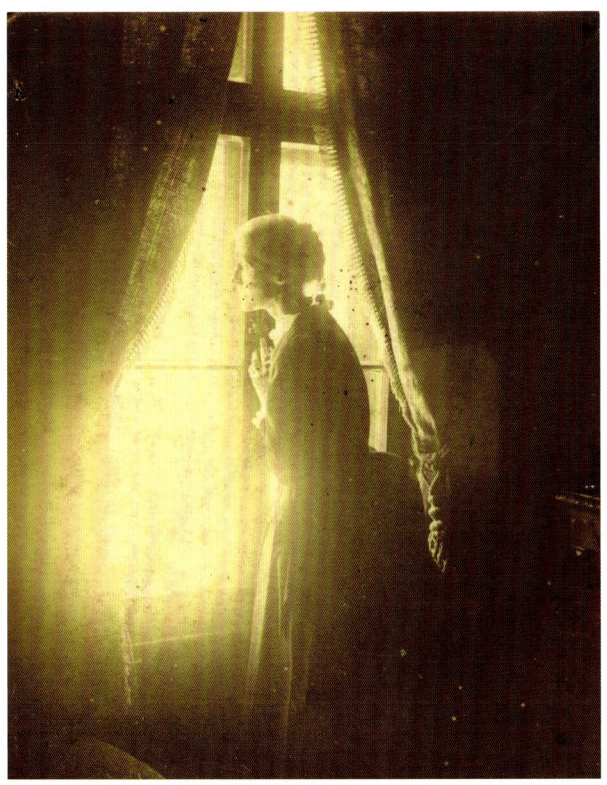

Deceived with Kindness by Angelica Garnett challenged comfortable Bloomsbury memoirs about 'old friends' and 'great friends'.[1] It was published in 1984, some years after the deaths of Garnett's parents, Vanessa Bell and Duncan Grant, and that of her husband, Grant's former lover, David Garnett. She had moved back to Charleston towards the end of Grant's life and became actively involved, together with Quentin and Anne Olivier Bell, in the restoration of the house after his death in 1978. For Garnett, however, Bloomsbury's powerful identity could overwhelm. She describes a photograph of her grandmother, Julia Stephen, in Deceived with Kindness and the merging of her sense of her own identity with that of her mother and grandmother: 'for me at least half its meaning lies in its resemblance to Vanessa herself. It is not so much the physical likeness as the resemblance of gesture and intention' (fig. 9).[2] She describes 'a hesitation in the hand raised towards the light, a doubt betrayed by the subtle and gracious lines of the pose, which links Julia and Vanessa close together. I know that I too sometimes take such poses.

❈ ❈ ❈

Garnett was raised to be acutely conscious of her physical likeness to her mother and a maternal ancestry that exemplified Victorian standards of beauty. Because she was illegitimate and brought up believing Clive Bell to be her father, this emphasis obscured a likeness to Grant that was obvious to everyone around her. It was never openly discussed. Numerous photographs of Angelica with her mother and her half-brothers locate her within the Bell family. Vanessa was one of Bloomsbury's most prolific amateur photographers and yet images of Angelica with her father, in which the facial resemblance is striking, are rare. The cover image for the American edition of Deceived with Kindness is a cut-out from a photograph by Vanessa of Angelica sitting confidently on her lap (fig. 10).[4] The image revolves around the relationship between their two faces side-by-side. Angelica looks straight at the camera while her mother's face is presented in profile, observing her daughter. There is a trace, perhaps, of The Three Ages of Man (1500–01) after Giorgione,

9 Gabriel Loppé, Julia Stephen at the Bear Hotel, Grindelwald, Switzerland, 1889. The Charleston Trust

CURATING THE 'FAMILY' ALBUM 23

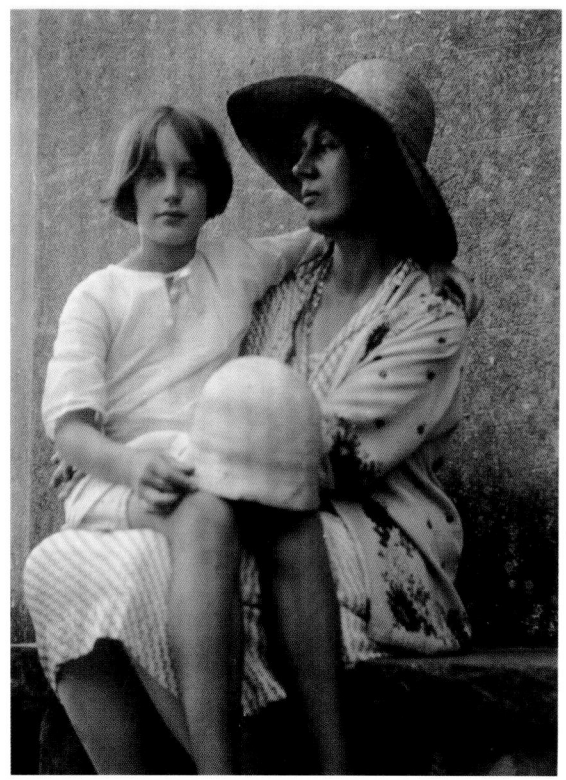

which Bell may have seen in Florence. As an artist and amateur photographer, Bell produced portraits that present a complex amalgamation of opportunism, art-historical references, and original composition. She could operate the camera shutter using a timer or a remote switch and her self-portraits, as a consequence, often present a moment of stillness after a rapid dash from setting up the camera and adopting a pose.[5] Bell's passive yet focused gaze, which features in many of her photographic self-portraits, emulates her own mother's work as the beautiful model and muse for Julia Margaret Cameron. Bell's eye is that of an artist, preoccupied with framing and fixing the image, but concurrently she makes an offering of her face for the camera.

Angelica's family resemblance to her mother and her grandmother is made explicit in another of the many photographs of her in Bell's collection. She lies on her stomach in Charleston's garden, cheek-to-cheek with a bust of her grandmother by Carlo Marochetti (fig. 11).[6] She is ten or eleven, around the same age that Julia Stephen (née Prinsep Jackson) had been when she modelled for the Victorian sculptor in 1856, and the likeness is striking. In a second photograph, taken at the same time, Quentin balances the bust on one knee and Angelica kneels at his side so that her face again aligns with that of her grandmother (fig. 12). These are not opportunistic snaps. They were arranged together in one of Bell's photograph albums and they document her determination to record a family resemblance, a line of beauty, from her own mother through to her daughter.[7] They demonstrate Bloomsbury's editorial use of photography, whether through repetition or omission (in the case of images of Angelica with her father), to emphasize relationships and articulate selected narratives. The bust was displayed on a pier outside the studio in Charleston's garden but its mnemonic function for the Charleston household was strictly limited.[8] Where photographs in the Stephen family albums served to memorialize Julia Stephen, consolidate familial identities, and preserve family memories of particular occasions, the use of the Marochetti bust at Charleston exemplifies an editorial process through which facts relating to the origin of an object, and memories associated with it, could be selectively discarded.

The bust was not conceived as a portrait. It was a study for a commission from Queen Victoria for a funerary monument to mark the grave of Elizabeth Stuart, who had been imprisoned at Carisbrooke Castle and died of pneumonia at the age of 14, soon after the execution of her father, Charles I. Reputedly, she died reading the bible that he had given her at their last meeting and, in Marochetti's effigy, the head rests on an open bible (fig. 13). The commission was to ornament a new church in Newport on the Isle of Wight, close to Osborne House. Queen Victoria went in her carriage to see the monument soon after it was completed, with two of her daughters, and recorded her impressions:

> It is a life size, recumbent figure, in marble, the head turned to the left reclining on her Bible, in which manner she was really found

10 Vanessa Bell, *Vanessa Bell with Angelica sitting on her knee*, undated. Tate, London

11 (*opposite, top left*) Vanessa Bell, *Angelica Bell in the garden at Charleston with Carlo Marochetti's bust of her grandmother, Julia Prinsep Jackson*, 1930. The Charleston Trust

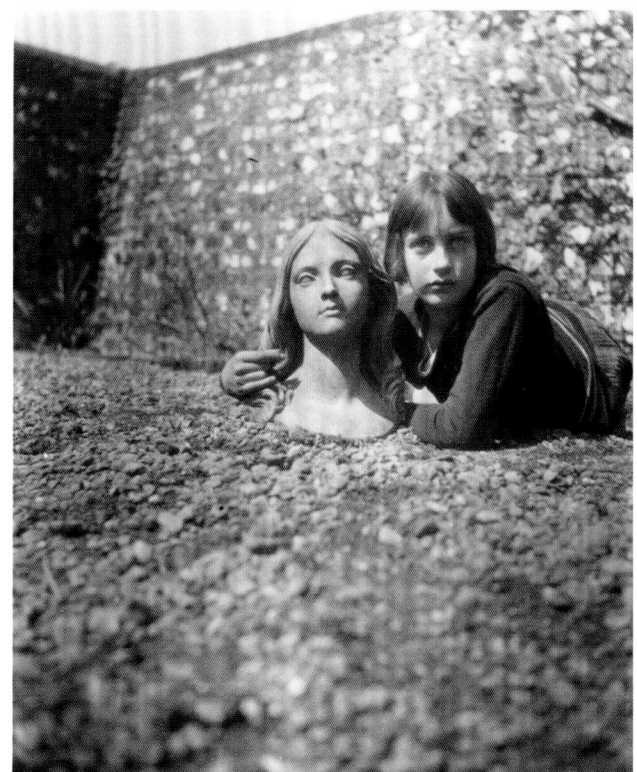
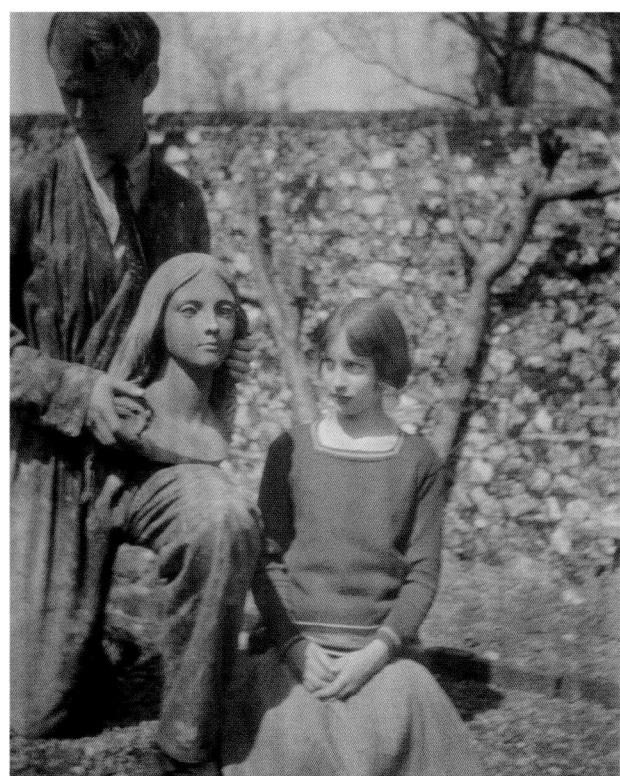

dead. . . . The face is beautiful with long curls, & the whole, is very touching. Poor young thing, I rejoice to think that I can pay a tardy tribute to her birth, youth, virtues and misfortunes!'[9]

In a memorial text to his wife, Leslie Stephen confuses the facts and, perhaps as a consequence of his atheism, omits the details of church and bible in a reductive account of the bust: 'Marochetti took her for a model, when she was fourteen or fifteen for a monument to the Princess Elizabeth. . . . He also made a bust at the same time.'[10] In fact, Julia Stephen was ten when she modelled for the head, and the 14-year-old Janet Duff Gordon was chosen as a model for the body. She had just recovered from scarlet fever and her own long hair had been cut off. 'I could not have believed', she wrote, 'that it was so tiring to lie flat on one's back for hours.'[11] The two girls were regular visitors to Little Holland House, where George Frederick Watts lived and worked, and shared experiences of sitting for him there.[12] (Little Holland House was the home of Julia's maternal aunt, Sara, and her husband, Thoby Prinsep, a politician and Indian civil servant, and the couple hosted an important salon there.) By coincidence, Marochetti also sculpted a bust of Leslie Stephen's father, Sir James Stephen, which was gifted to the National Portrait Gallery in the same year, 1896, that Sir Leslie became one of the Gallery's trustees.[13] This rich narrative, locating Julia Stephen within a

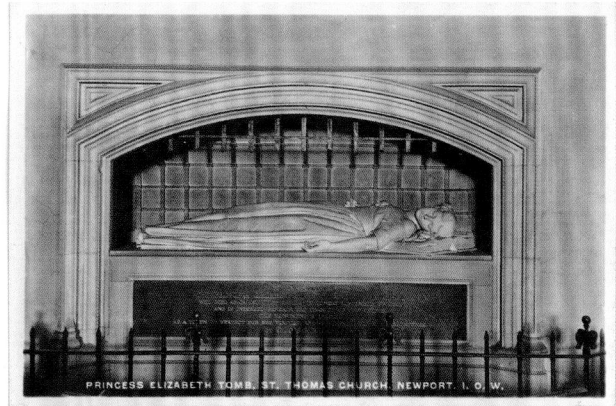

12 (*top right*) Vanessa Bell, Angelica and Quentin Bell in the garden at Charleston with Carlo Marochetti's bust of their grandmother, 1930. Tate, London

13 Postcard showing Carlo Marochetti's funerary monument of Princess Elizabeth Stuart at St Thomas's church, Newport, Isle of Wight, 1856. 90 × 140 mm. Private collection

CURATING THE 'FAMILY' ALBUM 25

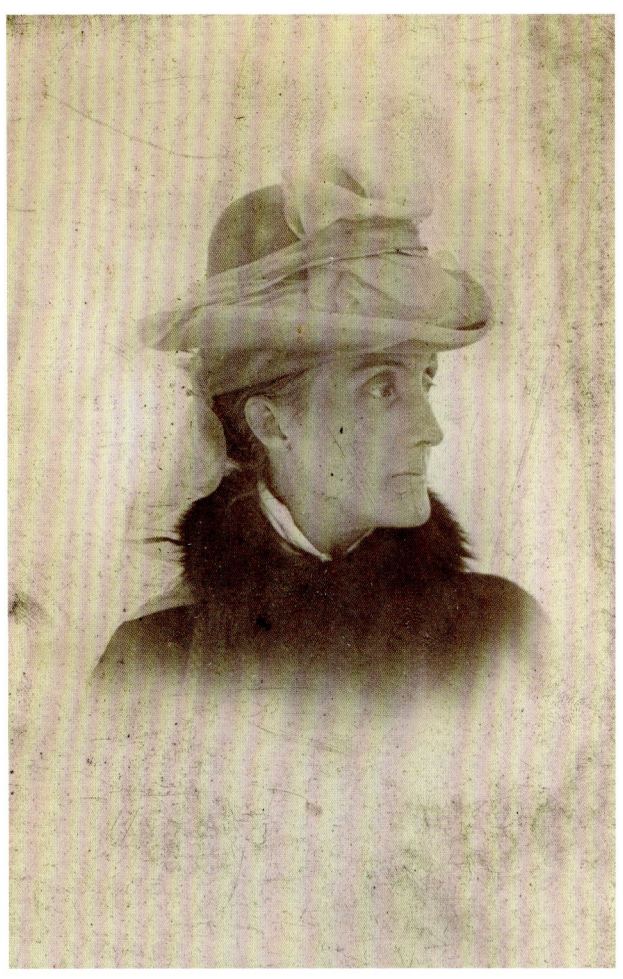

pious and sentimental context of royal commissions and Victorian representations of childhood innocence, illness, and mortality, became detached from the bust. By the time it was catalogued as part of the museum collection at Charleston, its early history in shaping her particular identity as a child model had been lost or obscured. While Bloomsbury discarded information and evidence that no longer served its changing self-fashioning as a group, however, its photograph albums, with their captions and juxtapositions of images, were fixed in the moment that each page was completed. They illuminate the processes of remembering and forgetting.

Context is critically important to understandings of the ways in which Bloomsbury used images to curate its identity. Because photographs exist in multiple copies they can recall shared experiences, or indeed different associations, in their arrangement in a number of photograph albums simultaneously. Their meanings also shift with time. The portrait of Julia Stephen with her hand raised towards the light that Garnett describes in *Deceived with Kindness* was taken by the French painter Gabriel Loppé at the Bear Hotel in the fashionable new winter resort of Grindelwald in Switzerland in 1889 (see fig. 9).[14] Loppé and Leslie Stephen were both mountaineers and fellow members of the Alpine Club. They became friends, and when Leslie and Julia took a three-week holiday in the Alps together, Loppé took a number of photographs of them. They are among the happiest surviving photographs of the pair, and are the most faded because they were displayed and exposed to light. Evidently they were circulated and fixed into the albums of friends as well as family (fig. 14).[15] Dame Janet Vaughan, for instance, later wrote that, 'asked about my memories of Bloomsbury I got out my mother's tattered old scrapbook'.[16] Her grandfather, John Addington Symonds, was one of Leslie Stephen's friends in Switzerland, her parents had first met at the Stephen family home in Hyde Park Gate, and her mother, Madge Vaughan, became a friend to the young Vanessa and Virginia. There are photographs of her in their albums.[17] She wrote:

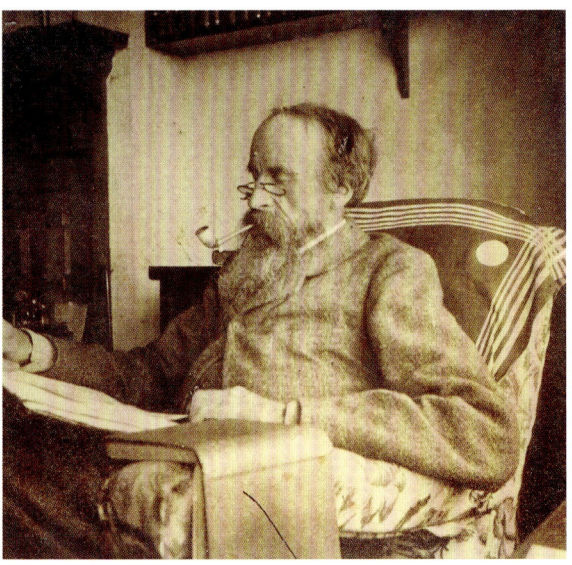

14 Unknown photographer, Julia Stephen, 1889. The Charleston Trust. In Leslie Stephen's album, this photograph is displayed with those captured by Loppé during the couple's holiday in the Alps

15 Unknown photographer, Leslie Stephen in his study at Hyde Park Gate, undated. The Charleston Trust

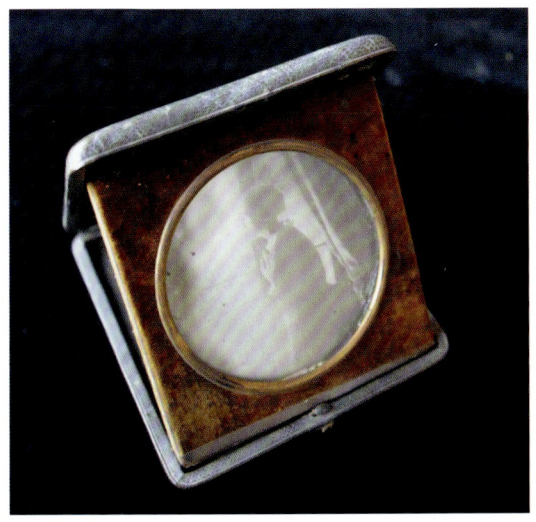 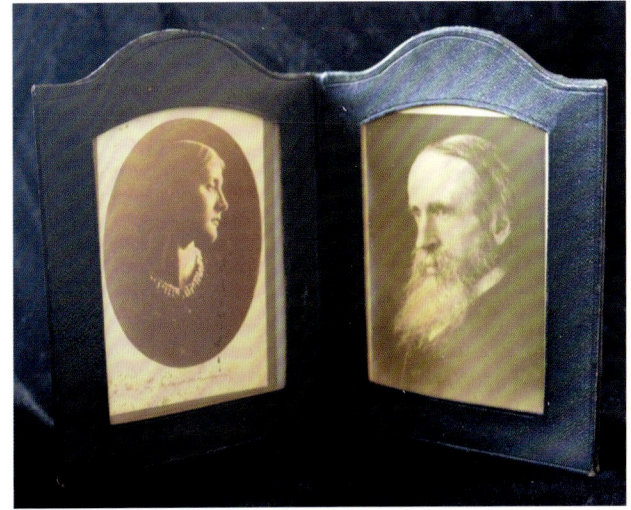

I found faded photographs of Leslie Stephen and Julia standing out in the snow at Davos ... there were photographs also of Leslie Stephen seated in his armchair in the Hyde Park study [fig. 15] and a very lovely one of Julia looking out of the same window as she pulled aside the curtain to let the light fall full on her face.

Vaughan's placing of the images at her family home in Davos and in Hyde Park Gate, thus relating them more closely to her own family history, may be mistaken; it is, however, indicative – as are the enduring currency of her mother's scrapbook, and her identification of the Swiss photographs as definitive for Bloomsbury – of the malleability of Bloomsbury's identity. After Julia's death in 1895, Leslie Stephen grouped five Loppé photographs together on the last page of an album dedicated to her memory (see fig. 25).[18] For her daughters, therefore, they became memorial images rather than holiday photographs.

In *Deceived with Kindness*, Garnett projects her own vulnerability onto the Loppé photograph of Julia, and, in the very sentence in which she claims entitlement to a legacy of beauty and fame, she also considers her own psychology as a state of mind passed down from mother to daughter. Exploring the pose rather than Loppé's innovative use of light, she writes: 'How far back do such inheritances go? Julia's mother for instance, one of the famous and beautiful Pattle sisters, did she also suffer from lack of self-confidence?'[19] This twisting of context was to take another turn in a small print of the same image that Vanessa kept in a green leather travelling case, embossed with her initials (fig. 16). Garnett wrote that the 'snapshot' always stood on her writing table: 'Because of its intimacy it held a special significance for Vanessa.'[20] Garnett moved to France before Charleston opened to the public in 1986, so the reconstruction of Vanessa Bell's bedroom with its writing table fell to Quentin and Anne Olivier Bell. After Vanessa's death in 1961 her bedroom, adjoining the studio, had been used by Grant and its contents moved or dispersed. For a time, Garnett herself had taken this bedroom when she moved back to Charleston. Anne Olivier, who had seldom had occasion to go into her mother-in-law's bedroom, did not believe that Bell would have had family photographs on her desk: 'too sentimental'.[21] In a museological concession to signposting Bloomsbury's complex relationships for visitors, however, she agreed to display archive photographs from Charleston's collection on Bell's writing table. She chose a portrait of Leslie Stephen by the photographer George Beresford, and a photograph of Julia Stephen taken

---

16 Leather travelling case embossed with Vanessa Bell's initials, containing a photograph of Julia Stephen taken by Loppé in 1889, case undated. 125 × 125 mm. The Charleston Trust

17 Julia Margaret Cameron, photograph of Julia Stephen, 1867 (*left*); George Beresford, photograph of Leslie Stephen, 1902 (*right*). The Charleston Trust. The photographs are now displayed together in Vanessa Bell's bedroom at Charleston

CURATING THE 'FAMILY' ALBUM   27

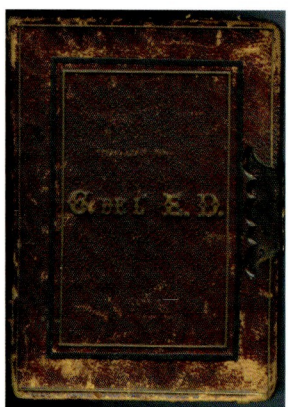 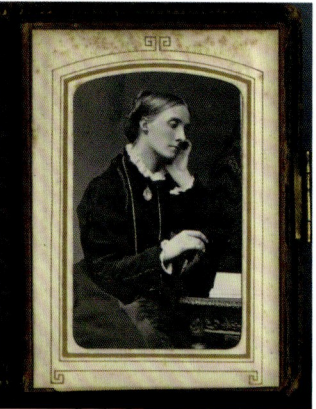

by Julia Margaret Cameron (fig. 17). The small, iconic object of the faded Loppé print in its green leather travelling case was mistakenly catalogued as an unknown woman by an anonymous photographer and relegated to Charleston's reserve collection for over twenty years. Its significance depended almost entirely upon context.

Before they were categorized as collections, archives, and resources for publications, Bloomsbury photographs were part of the apparatus through which the Group constructed and curated its own image. Virginia and Vanessa learnt from their father how to use photographs to position themselves within the family and to project their identities. He had created a massive photograph album accompanied by a separate autobiographical text immediately after their mother's sudden death to contain the outpouring of his grief. It was dubbed 'The Mausoleum Book'. Both volumes were bound in green leather. The album immortalized Julia Stephen's beauty through photographs taken by her aunt, Julia Margaret Cameron. Stephen described this beauty as 'the very essence of her nature . . . absolutely faultless'.[22] The Cameron photographs would 'remain to give an impression to her children of what she really was'.[23] Additional snapshots and professional portraits were carefully arranged and fixed to the album's pages to record the chronology and relationships that shaped her life. Stephen concluded his text on the birthday that Vanessa shared with her half-sister, Stella Duckworth, within a month of their mother's death. 'I have given to Stella a chain which I gave to her mother upon our marriage', he wrote, 'and to Vanessa a photograph by Mrs Cameron which, as I think, shows her mother's beauty better than any other. We will cling to each other.'[24]

As editor of the *Dictionary of National Biography*, Stephen understood the value of a well-organized archive in reconstructing a life. He dated his original manuscript for the Mausoleum Book, made four fair copies for Vanessa, Thoby, Virginia, and Adrian, and archived the correspondence 'between my own darling and me' on which it was based.[25] This provided an invaluable resource, as he may have anticipated, for his own biography, *The Life and Letters of Leslie Stephen*, written by his friend Frederic William Maitland.[26] It was published two years after his death in 1904 by his stepson, Gerald Duckworth. When Quentin was commissioned to write Woolf's biography, the two leather-bound volumes, stored in Charleston's attic, were again mined for both factual evidence and images. Anne Olivier recalled the photograph album as a huge, heavy book with the covers becoming detached. Charleston and Monk's House remained, at this time, repositories for the Stephen family archive and, still housed together within their domestic environments, the albums, the envelopes filled with loose photographs and negatives, the framed prints, and the small leather folding frames and cases retained their context as personal possessions. They were objects of memory, arrested in time but still caught within the fabric of everyday lives. Charleston's attic contained Gerald Duckworth's book of cartes-de-visite, fastened like a prayer book with a metal clasp and embossed with his full initials, G. de L.' E. D. (Gerald de L'Etang Duckworth) (figs 18 and 19). Filled almost exclusively with photographs of his mother, Julia, it is rubbed and worn at the edges and small enough to fit into a pocket or a desk drawer.[27] The photographs that Angelica and Quentin inherited, not catalogued as we know them today, but stuffed into cupboards and drawers and piled up in albums as a family archive in Charleston's attic, spoke to the same complex issues of identity that Angelica explored in *Deceived with Kindness*. A photograph, discoloured around the edges, of an engraving by Watts of Julia's mother, Maria Jackson, for example, can be matched to a framed picture on

18 (*above left*) Gerald Duckworth's book of cartes-de-visite, undated. Embossed leather and metal. The Charleston Trust

19 (*above right*) Interior of Gerald Duckworth's book of cartes-de-visite, showing a photograph of his mother, Julia Stephen. The Charleston Trust

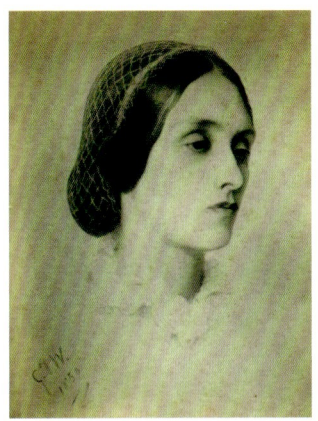 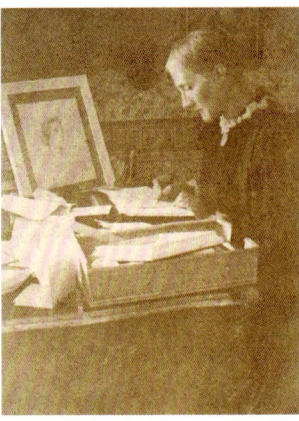

Julia's desk in a faded snapshot of her writing (figs 20 and 21). A drawing of Maria Jackson by Watts hung in the corridor at Charleston outside the door to Vanessa Bell's bedroom (fig. 22). They describe a continuum as each generation of Pattle/Duckworth/Stephen/Bell women was likened to its predecessors.

The material associations of Bloomsbury's photographs as artefacts, integrated into the cultures of family histories and households, altered in the 1980s when their archival importance was recognized. Virginia and Leonard Woolf had compiled six photograph albums that were named and numbered after their home, the Monk's House Albums.[28] Ten photograph albums by Vanessa Bell were identified in date order after their place in Charleston's attic.[29] This rudimentary cataloguing enabled Anne Olivier to keep a meticulous record of photographs loaned out to Bloomsbury's early biographers.[30] Leonard Woolf borrowed a George Beresford photograph of Vanessa, for example, for the first volume of his autobiography, *Sowing*. It was never returned and its place in Bell's album next to the now-famous Beresford image of her sister is marked with a note: 'Lent to Leonard Woolf Nov 1959'.[31] He raided the Monk's House albums, too, to illustrate George Spater and Ian Parsons's biography, *A Marriage of True Minds* (1977).[32] As Quentin and Anne Olivier Bell's family kitchen became a place of pilgrimage for Bloomsbury scholars, they loaned photographs for books and articles. From time to time, even after the albums and photographs were deposited with archives and museum collections, an original print would be unearthed from a drawer in their kitchen dresser and given to the Charleston Trust or sold to the National Portrait Gallery to raise money for one of the Trust's campaigns. Bloomsbury photographs often relate directly to the letters and diary entries with which they are contemporary; detached from their album settings, they have been used extensively to illustrate these texts, and are complemented by them. Quentin and Angelica compiled the first publication dedicated to their mother's photographs, *Vanessa Bell's Family Album*, in 1981.[33] In its extended captions it adopts the conversational style of the memoirs from the 1950s and 1960s, in which some of the photographs had already been published, reinforcing this relationship between text, image, and Bloomsbury's identity as a group.

The albums were not recognized as complex constructions of identity in their own right until Maggie Humm contextualized them within the modernist projections of their time.[34] They did,

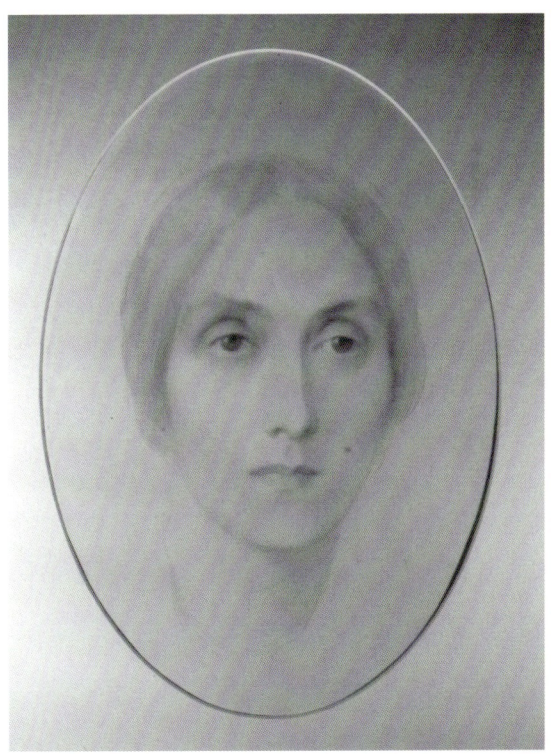

20 (*top left*) Unknown photographer, photograph of an engraving of Maria Jackson by George Frederick Watts, undated. The Charleston Trust
21 (*top right*) Unknown photographer, Julia Stephen at her writing desk, undated. The Charleston Trust

22 George Frederick Watts, *Portrait of Maria Jackson*, c.1845–50. Pencil on paper, 340 × 240 mm. The Charleston Trust. The portrait still hangs in its historic location outside Vanessa Bell's bedroom at Charleston

CURATING THE 'FAMILY' ALBUM   29

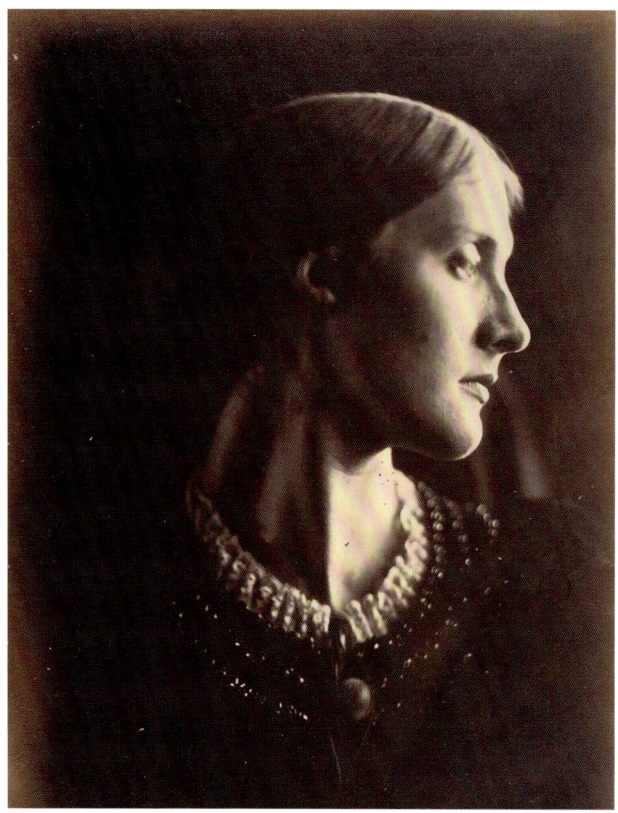

however, remain substantially complete. The Monk's House albums were purchased and presented to the Houghton Library at Harvard University. Angelica Garnett gave the Charleston albums and negatives to the Tate Archive. The Mausoleum Book was given to the London Library in response to an appeal, and was then sold to the British Museum.[35] In 1984 the remains of Leslie Stephen's photograph album were auctioned at Sotheby's and acquired by Smith College in Northampton, Massachusetts.[36] Only 16 of its original 39 leaves were intact at the time of sale. Its leather covers were missing and the photographs by Cameron that had filled its first 15 leaves had been repurposed, sold or given away.[37] In combination, these extraordinary albums describe the foundations for Bloomsbury's visual identity as a group. Their leaves draw boundaries around particular relationships and events.

Leslie Stephen's photograph album opened with 15 pages of Cameron photographs of Julia (fig. 23). This *tour de force* was to be replicated some years later when Vanessa Bell lined up Cameron's photographs of her mother in the entrance to 46 Gordon Square. Julia Stephen was named after her aunt, Julia Margaret Cameron, and was her favourite model. Leslie Stephen's album, in its format and organization, also provided a model for the albums his daughters were to compile throughout their lives. He was fastidious. His hand-written contents page corresponds with hand-written pagination on each of the leaves. It sets out the arrangement of photographs in family groups: early images of Julia's family, the Jacksons; of his own Stephen family friends and relations; photographs relating to Julia's first marriage, to Herbert Duckworth; and to his own first marriage, to Minny Thackeray. The final three sections of the album are devoted to Leslie's marriage and family with Julia. They include photographs of 'Julia with the 4 younger children', Vanessa, Thoby, Virginia, and Adrian.[38] Family photographs taken 'At St Ives' are grouped together and described in the Mausoleum Book as 'little snap-photographs taken by Georgy and Stella' (fig. 24).[39] The album concludes with the Loppé images 'In the Alps' (fig. 25).[40] Captions in Stephen's autograph identify the sitters and subjects, 'St Ives from Stella's window', for example, but not the photographers.

Stella Duckworth was responsible for some of the photographs in the album and may have had a hand in its construction. Several of her own albums containing family photographs survive, and she is the missing person in a number of family-group photographs taken at the family's holiday home in St Ives, Talland House, suggesting that she was behind the camera.[41] In these, the four Stephen siblings are lined up solidly together, taking lessons with their mother indoors, or grouped outside with their parents and half-brothers, Gerald and George Duckworth. They fulfil Stephen's aspiration, 'deeply fixed at the very core of my heart', to create a memorial to his wife that would help her children 'to keep close together, always remembering her'.[42] Leslie Stephen's photograph album exerts a pull from the past, an insistence upon the importance of family and its infrastructures that was to co-exist in the next generation of Bloomsbury albums with modernist and transgressive explorations.

23 Julia Margaret Cameron, 'Mrs Herbert Duckworth', 1867. Metropolitan Museum of Art, New York

24 (p. 32) Leslie Stephen, album page headed 'At St Ives', c.1895. Mortimer Rare Book Collection, Smith College, Northampton, MA

❈ ❈ ❈

In *Modernist Women and Visual Cultures*, Maggie Humm argues that Vanessa and Virginia experimented with domestic photography and created sequences of images in their albums that subverted masculine canons of modernity.[43] Engaging with the relatively new technology of photography, she writes, enabled the production 'of new representations of cognition, of new ways of seeing and knowing the world' that was the shared concern of modernist artists and writers.[44] Vanessa and Virginia adapted the visual narratives of Leslie Stephen's photograph album to articulate their own stories. On leaf 36 of Stephen's album, for example, albumen prints of the infant Stephen siblings and their mother, differing in size and composition, are meticulously arranged in a pattern around a much larger and more striking platinum print of Julia with Virginia on her lap by Henry H. H. Cameron (fig. 26). The names of sitters are hand-written beneath each print. A studio photograph of the infant Thoby on this page is one of many prints that are duplicated between Stephen's album and those of Stella, Vanessa, and Virginia, each time contributing to a different narrative context. In Virginia's album, the photograph of her elder brother is paired with another studio shot of the infant Vanessa (fig. 27).[45] The arrangement of just two portraits, side by side on the page, is a straightforward representation of Virginia's own position in the family, setting out her two older siblings. Hand-written initials, 'V.B.' and 'J.T.S.', indicate that these may have been written later, after Vanessa's marriage, and that the album, like that of their father, was designed to be shared with others.

Vanessa and Virginia began to construct visual narratives around their domestic lives while still in their teens. They were enthusiastic photographers throughout their lives. Many of the photographs in the early Stephen family albums are cartes-de-visite; these could be combined with larger cabinet photographs and snapshots to create album pages that structured and contained perceptions of the past and of relationships. Cartes-de-visite had opened up the practice of routinely disseminating studio portraits in place of visiting cards from the 1850s. Charles Dickens, writing in 1862, describes 'this thriving business of photography' and its appeal: 'you have the opportunity of distributing yourself among your friends, and letting them see you in your favourite attitude, and with your favourite expression. And then you get into those wonderful books which everybody possesses, and strangers see you there in good society.'[46] Cartes-de-visite were small, affordable photographs pasted onto a card backing. They were patented by a French photographer, Alphonse Disdéri, in 1854, and a collecting craze, 'cartomania', quickly spread across Europe. Dickens notes the prevalence of cartes-de-visite in small frames on drawing-room tables. The first commercially produced photograph albums were designed for their display, and he describes their superiority to the 'long cherished card-basket' in which visitors would leave their calling cards. Although the basket, Dickens writes, 'was a good thing to leave on the table that your morning-caller . . . might see what distinguished company you kept', it came with the disadvantage that less treasured cards, from 'Mrs Brown of Peckam', for example, could rise from the depths to which they had been consigned. Albums enabled their owners to curate the presentation of their callers. 'You place it in your friend's hands, saying, "This only contains my special favourites, mind," and there is her ladyship staring them in the face the next moment. "Who is this sweet person?" says the visitor. "Oh, that is dear Lady Puddicombe," you reply carelessly. Delicious moment!'[47]

Dickens tells his readers how to compose their features to achieve the right image. 'I have myself sat on two occasions for one of these portraits', he writes. 'On the first I was simply occupied in keeping still and presenting a tolerably favourable view of my features and limbs to the fatal lens; but the result was so tame and unimposing a picture that I determined on the next occasion to throw more intellect into the thing.' The pose had to be held for 30 seconds. Dickens fixed his gaze on a curtain-tassel: 'I gave it a look of such piercing scrutiny, and so withered and blasted it with the energy of my regard, that I almost wonder it did not sink beneath the trial.' His carte-de-visite, as a

---

25 (p. 33) Leslie Stephen, album page headed 'In Switzerland', c.1895. Mortimer Rare Book Collection, Smith College, Northampton, MA

26 (p. 34) Leslie Stephen, album page headed 'Julia', c.1895. Mortimer Rare Book Collection, Smith College, Northampton, MA

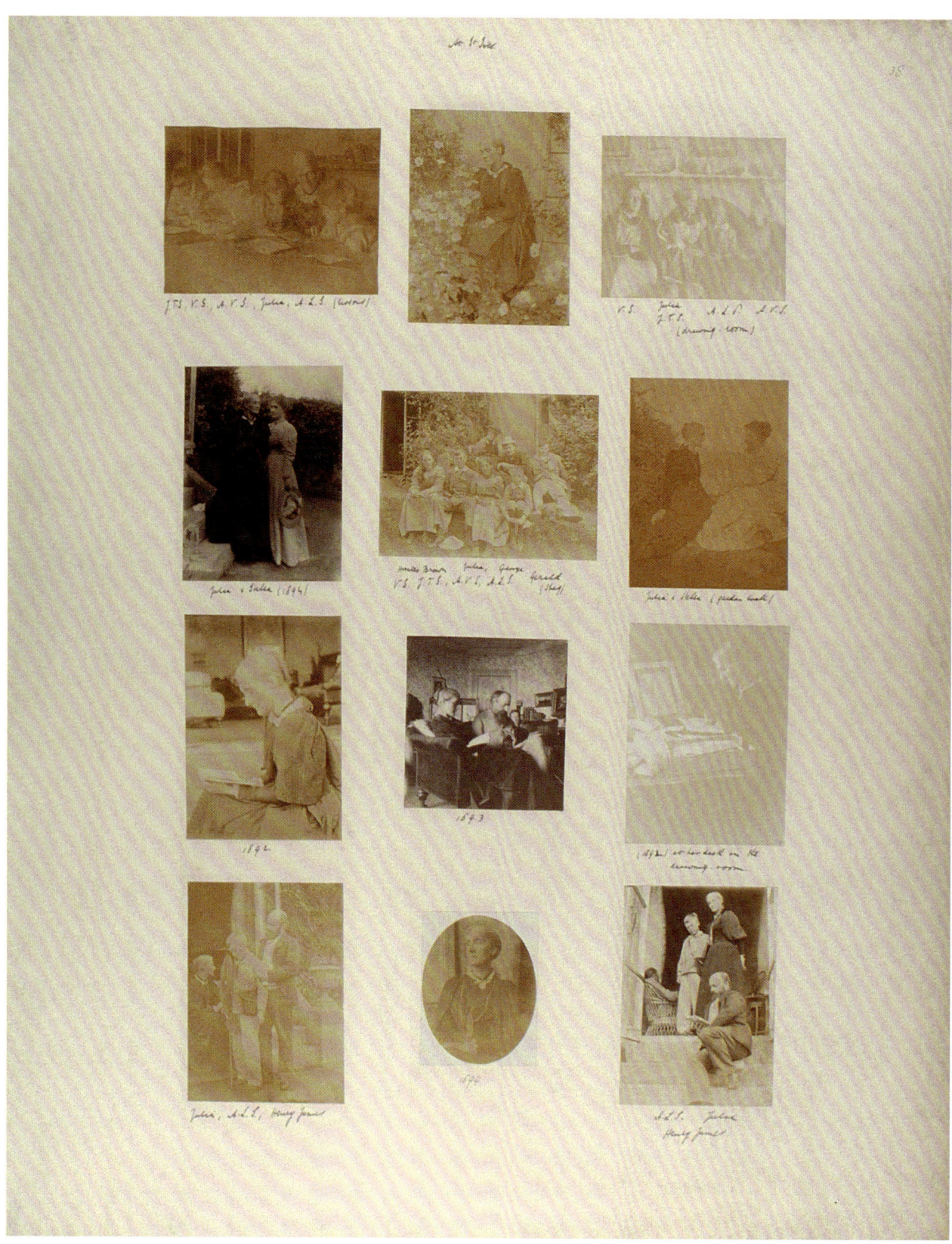

32 THE BLOOMSBURY LOOK

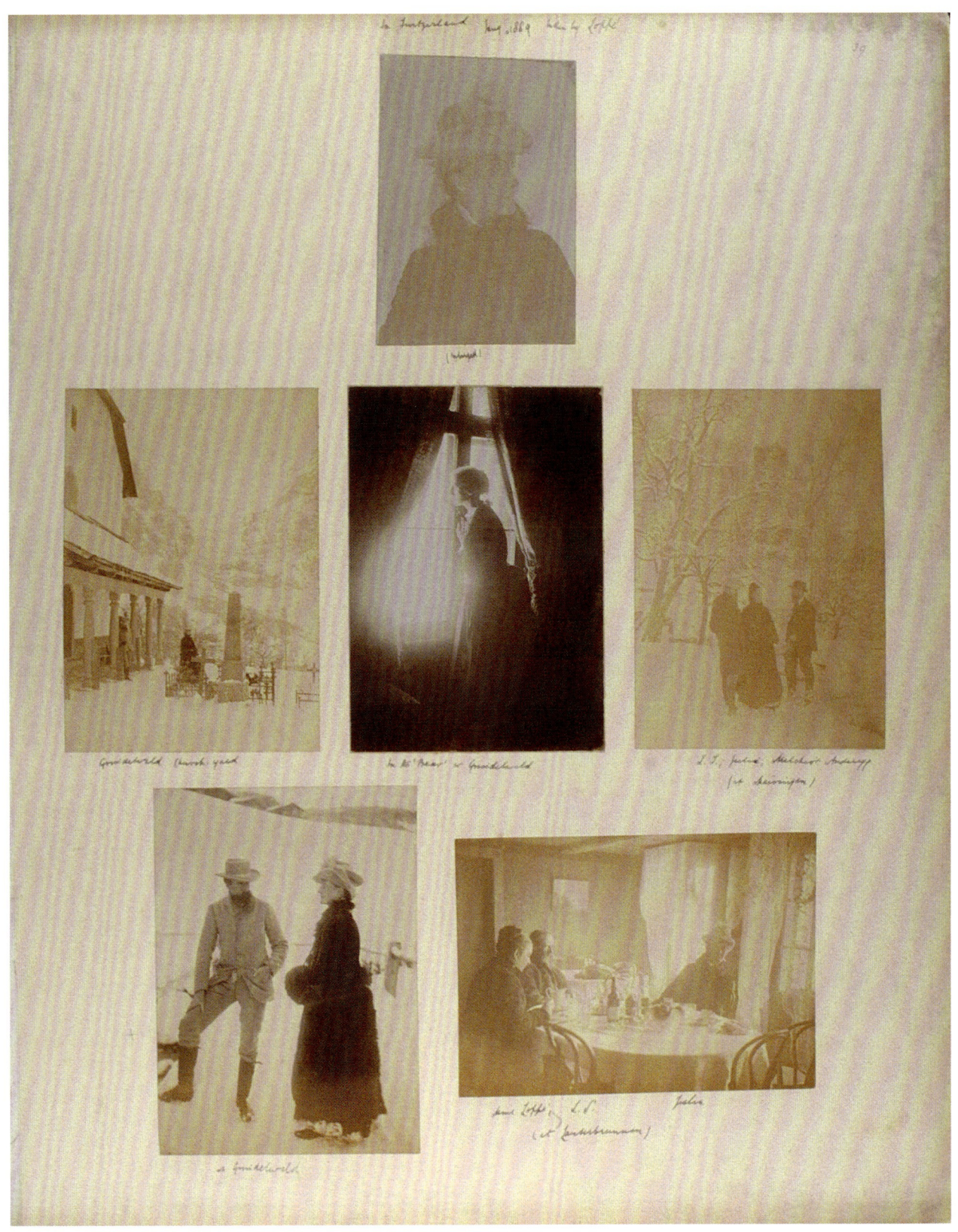

CURATING THE 'FAMILY' ALBUM

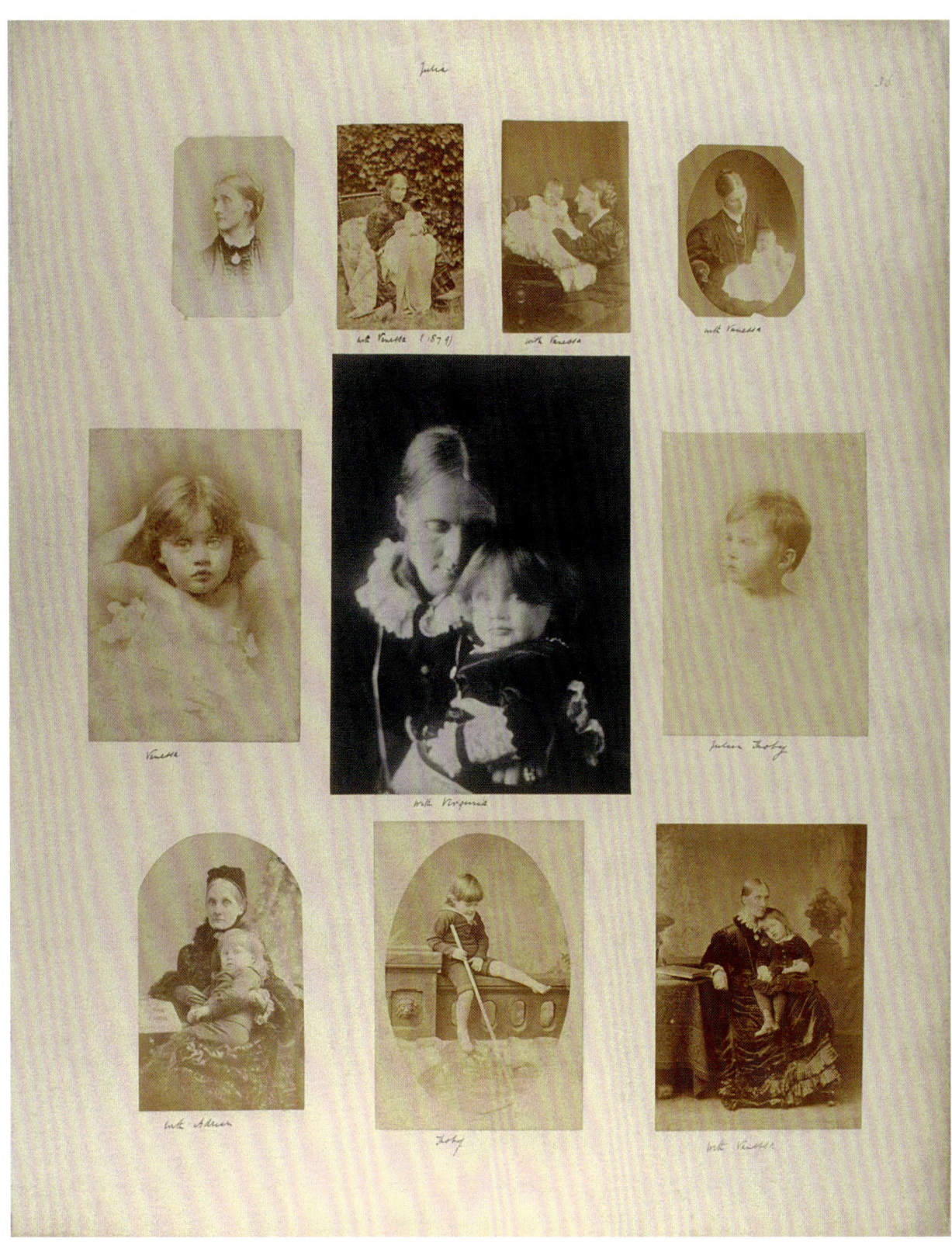

34 THE BLOOMSBURY LOOK

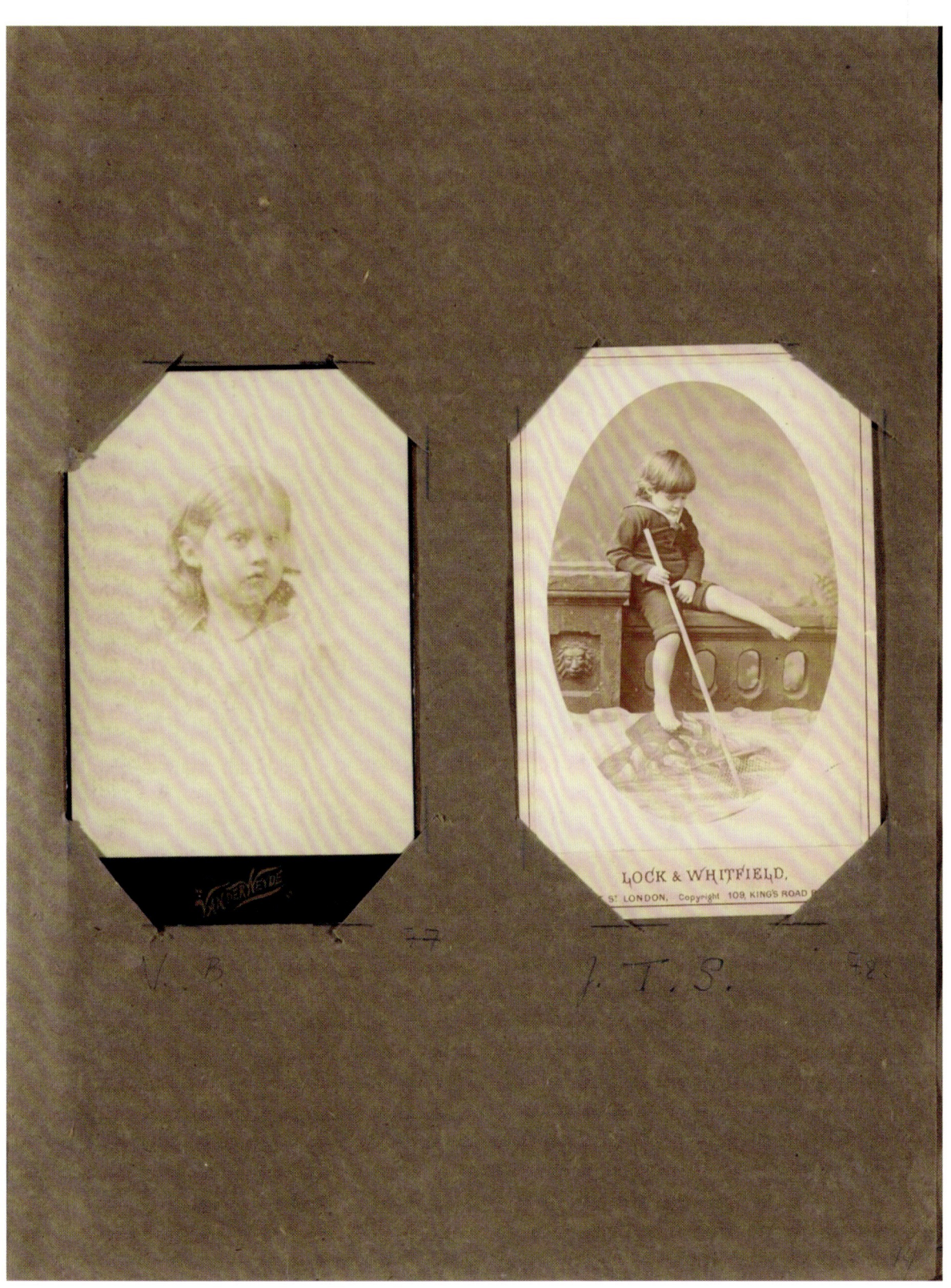

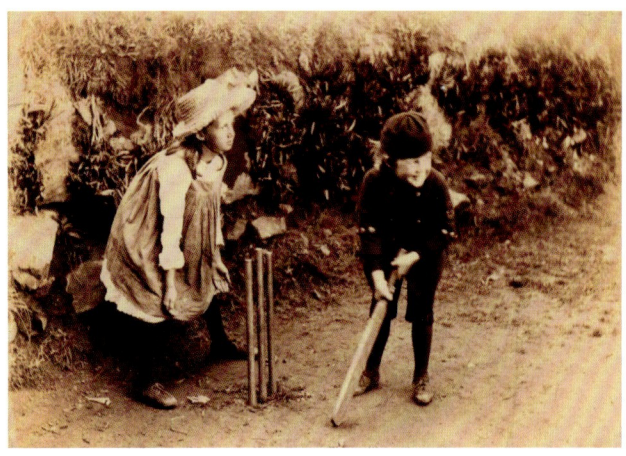

consequence, aptly conveyed 'immense penetration, great energy and strength of character, and a keen and piercing wit'.[48] Cartes-de-visite for famous men and women, including the royal family, writers, artists, actors, and politicians, were sold commercially by printsellers, enabling collectors to line up their own family photographs alongside images of the celebrities they admired. Virginia's earliest surviving photograph albums are complex psychological constructions of this kind. The first 13 pages of Monk's House Album 1 are dedicated entirely to cartes-de-visite. They are neatly aligned, combining family and friends with famous figures in arrangements that presumably codified a narrative of associations for her. On the first page the campaigning politician and husband of Millicent Fawcett, Henry Fawcett, who had been at Trinity Hall, Cambridge with Leslie Stephen, is aligned with Virginia's half-brother George Duckworth and Prince Albert. The larger, cabinet photographs of Vanessa and Thoby on leaf 14 of this album, duplicating those in Leslie Stephen's album, break the series of cartes-de-visite. In the album's subsequent pages, amateur family photographs are introduced and combined with professional studio prints. Several such photographs provide visual links between the related 'image narratives' of several family members. A picture of Virginia and Adrian playing cricket in St Ives, for example, appears in the albums of Virginia, Vanessa, and Leslie Stephen (fig. 28).[49] Similarly, a photograph by Vanessa of her parents reading at Talland House, in which Virginia's small face appears at her father's shoulder, is cropped to fit into Gerald Duckworth's case of cartes-de-visite and is also displayed in the albums of his stepfather, his half-sisters Vanessa and Virginia, and his sister Stella (fig. 29). For Virginia, the relative significance of this image is indicated by its presentation: mounted on card, it stands alone on the second page of Monk's House Album 3, immediately following the photograph of Julia Stephen with which the album opens.[50] In Bell's collection of loose photographs, a version of the print has been

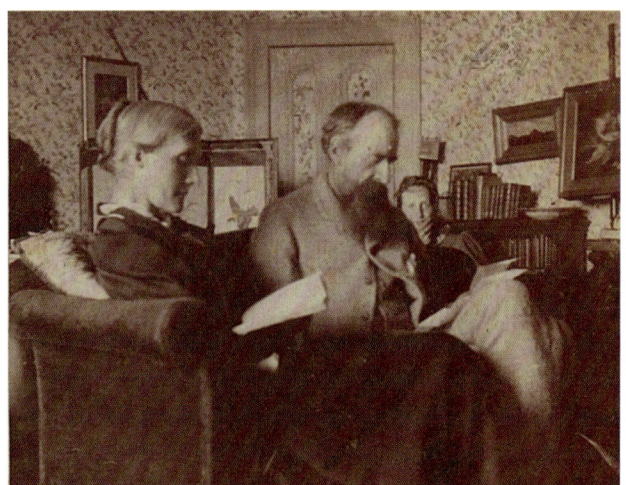
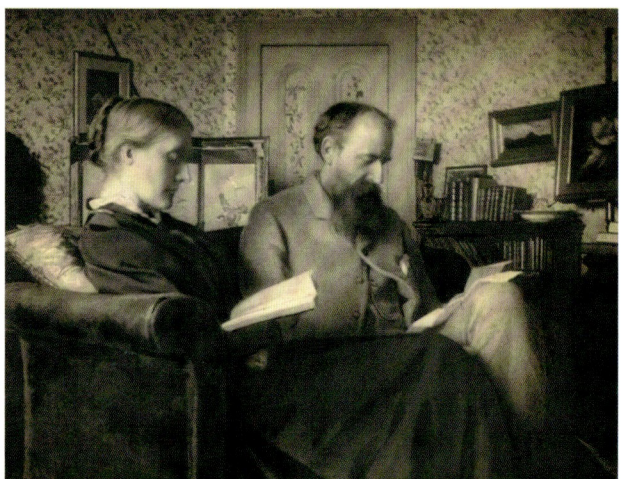

27 (p. 35) Van der Weyde, Vanessa Stephen as a young child, c.1880 (left), and Lock & Whitfield, Thoby Stephen as a young boy, c.1883 (right), displayed together in Virginia Woolf's Monk's House Photograph Album 1. Houghton Library, Harvard University

28 (top left) Unknown photographer, Virginia Woolf and Adrian Stephen playing cricket at St Ives, 1888. Houghton Library, Harvard University
29 (above left) Vanessa Bell, Julia and Leslie Stephen at Talland House, St Ives, with Virginia sitting behind, 1892. Houghton Library, Harvard University

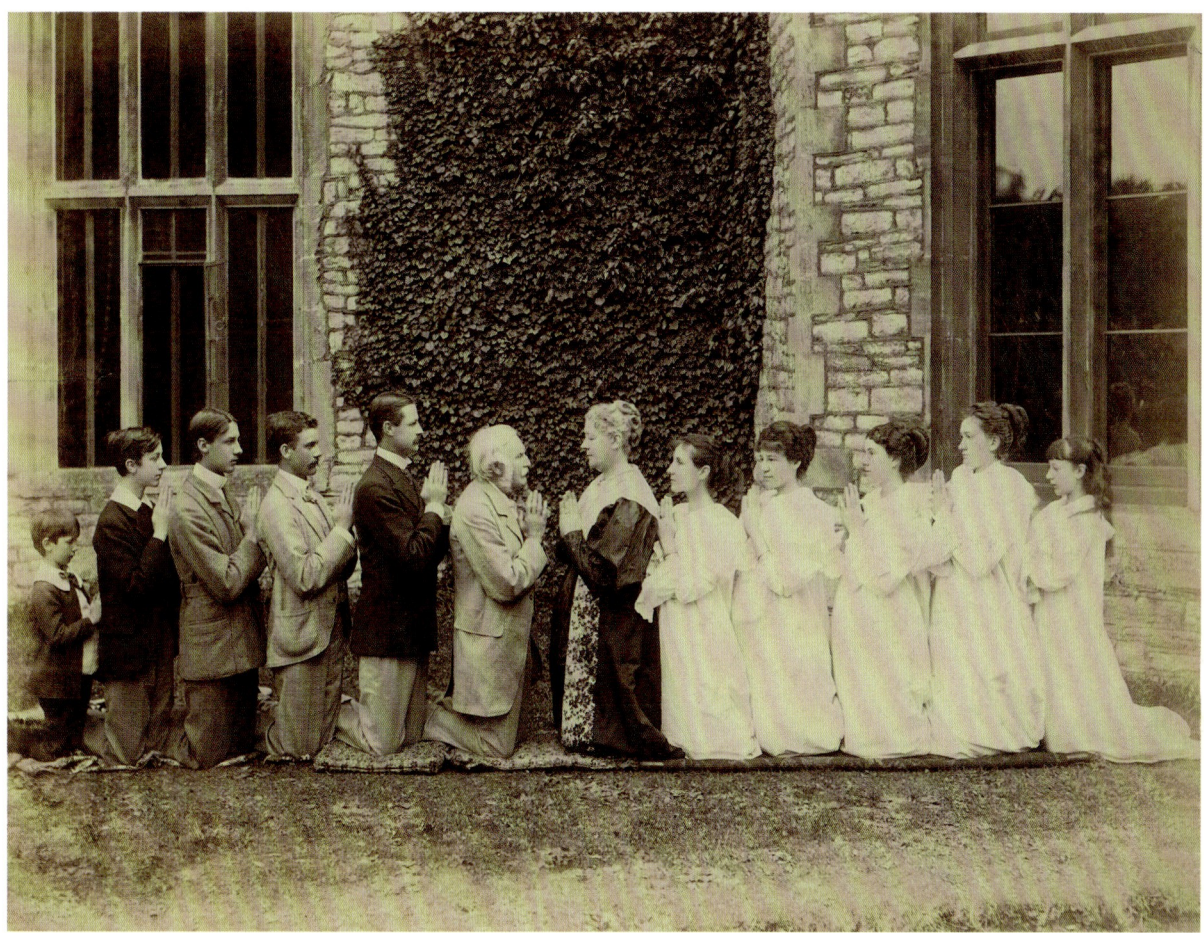

professionally enlarged and Virginia's face painted out, transforming the snapshot into a more formal portrait of their celebrated parents (fig. 30).

Bloomsbury family photographs record those families' extensive connections to British colonialism as senior administrators and soldiers. Working in the colonies could separate husbands from their wives for years at a time, and children were sent to boarding school. The photographs and letters that maintained their relationships during this time carried particular significance. Bloomsbury texts, from Lytton Strachey's *Eminent Victorians* to Virginia Woolf's monograph on Julia Margaret Cameron, are irreverent towards their colonial ancestry but it was one of the factors that bound them together as a group. Cameron's father, James Pattle, was a drunk and 'the biggest liar in India', according to Woolf.[51] Julia Margaret herself and her sister Maria (Woolf's grandmother) were both born in India and, although they were sent home to England for their health, six of these Pattle sisters married successful men in India. Woolf's mother, likewise, was born in Calcutta and was two years old before she moved to England. Similarly, Strachey family photographs include prints from the 1860s of Lytton's uncle, Sir John Strachey, in his capacity as Administrator to the Viceroy of India. He is included in a group photograph of the Supreme Indian Council at Simla, and when the Prince of Wales made his tour of India in 1875–6, Strachey was lined up under canvas to be photographed with the future king.[52] Lytton's father, Sir Richard, was also a powerful figure in India and commissioned photographs of his family outside

30 (*opposite, bottom right*) Vanessa Bell, Julia and Leslie Stephen at Talland House, St Ives, 1892. The Charleston Trust. Virginia Woolf's face has been touched out of this professional enlargement of the print, which has a sticker on the reverse for 'Messrs Bassano, 25 Old Bond Street, London'

31 Graystone Bird, 'The Strachey Family', c.1893. National Portrait Gallery, London. (*Left to right*) James, Lytton, Oliver, Ralph, Richard John, Sir Richard, Lady Jane Maria (née Grant), Elinor Rendel (née Strachey), Dorothy Bussy (née Strachey), Pippa, Pernel, and Marjorie Strachey

CURATING THE 'FAMILY' ALBUM   37

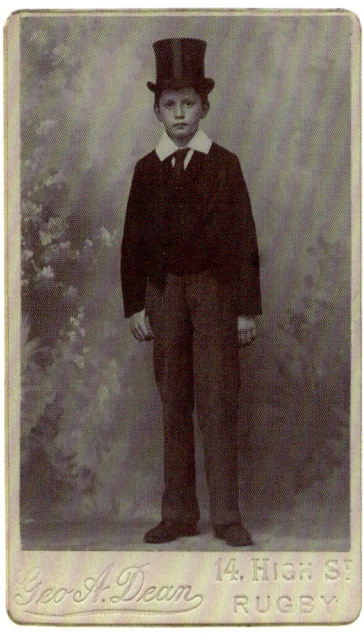 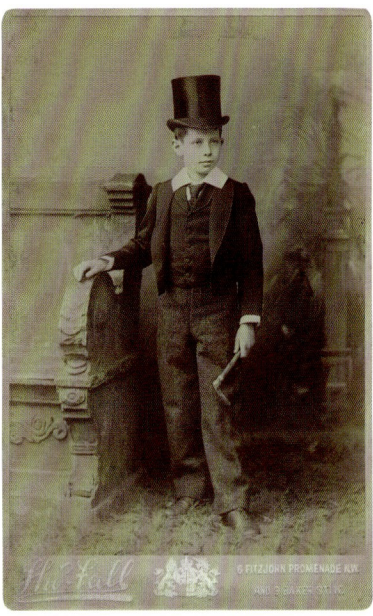 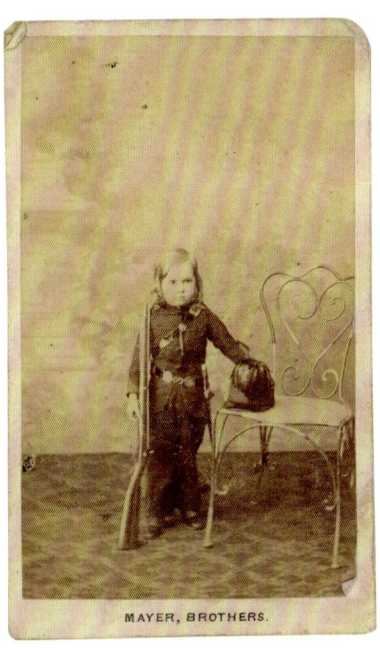

their country house, Sutton Court in Somerset, c.1893. On their knees as if in prayer, the five boys are lined up behind their father, and the five girls behind their mother, in descending order of age, in a witty representation of Strachey fecundity (fig. 31).

Individually, Lytton and his siblings posed from an early age and at a variety of studios for cabinet photographs and prints to mark the milestones of their childhood. An early carte-de-visite of Lytton was taken when he was around three years old.[53] Similarly, his younger brother James was photographed as a little boy in his new school uniform, complete with top hat, at a studio in Rugby where he attended Hillbrow preparatory school with Rupert Brooke and Duncan Grant (fig. 32). Strachey and Grant were cousins, and a matching photograph of Grant describes their shared identity (fig. 33). Grant's grandfather, John Peter Grant, was a member of the Supreme Council in Calcutta and set up a government in Benares with Richard Strachey, who subsequently married his daughter, Jane Maria Grant. Duncan Grant's grandmother, again from an eminent Anglo-Indian family, lived in India for 26 years but settled back in England before the birth of Grant's father, Bartle,

in 1856. Her husband remained in India for another six years, so photographs of Bartle as a little boy in Duncan Grant's collection are likely to duplicate images that were sent out to him in India. A carte-de-visite shows Bartle dressed up at the age of three or four as a soldier with a toy rifle and helmet (fig. 34). A miniature of him as a schoolboy, hand-coloured to emulate painted miniatures, was small enough to be worn or kept in a pocket.[54]

Duncan Grant lived with his parents in India and Burma until he was nine years old. Again, his collection of photographs offers insights into the colonial world of his childhood and adolescence. Portrait photographs of his father in military uniform and of his mother were prominently displayed at Charleston and it is likely that these travelled with him when he left his parents in Rangoon to attend preparatory school in Rugby.[55] One photograph of Grant in school uniform is in an Indian or Burmese metal frame, which suggests that it belonged to his mother in Rangoon (fig. 35). Rolled up in Grant's collection and retained to the end of his life, mid-nineteenth-century photographs of the historic buildings and landscapes of India by Samuel Bourne describe the scenery and colonialism of his

---

32 (*above left*) George Augustus Dean Jr, James Strachey in school uniform, c.1895. National Portrait Gallery, London

33 (*above middle*) Thomas Fall, Duncan Grant in school uniform, c.1895. National Portrait Gallery, London

34 (*above right*) Mayer Brothers, Bartle Grant dressed as a soldier, c.1860. The Charleston Trust

childhood.[56] Grant kept a cabinet photograph of his cousin, Pippa Strachey, in India in his collection, a testament to the shared frame of colonial references that bound Bloomsbury together (fig. 36). A snapshot of his parents reclining in a Burmese rickshaw also describes the privilege and racial inequality of the Group's colonial backgrounds (fig. 37). These images of empire underpinning Grant's sense of identity were not openly displayed. When interviewed about his life, however, Grant began with an exotic fantasy of entitlement, recalling his early life in Chakrata in the Himalayas.[57]

Bloomsbury embraced amateur photography to self-fashion its identity as a group in much the same way that its parents' and grandparents' generations had enjoyed the novelty and fashionable currency of cartes-de-visite and cabinet photographs. As amateur photographers, however, the Bloomsbury friends were able to operate on both sides of the lens. Without the formalities of photographic studios and professional photographers, they used photography to frame and to share private, uninhibited identities. Amateur photography had been a relatively elite hobby until the 1880s. Then, like cycling, it became a mark of emancipation for women and the Stephen sisters embraced modernity when they acquired

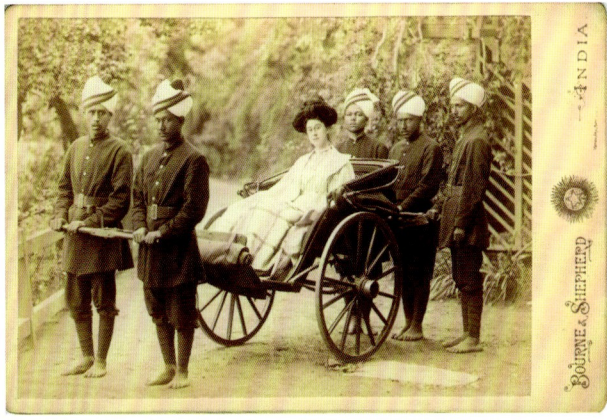

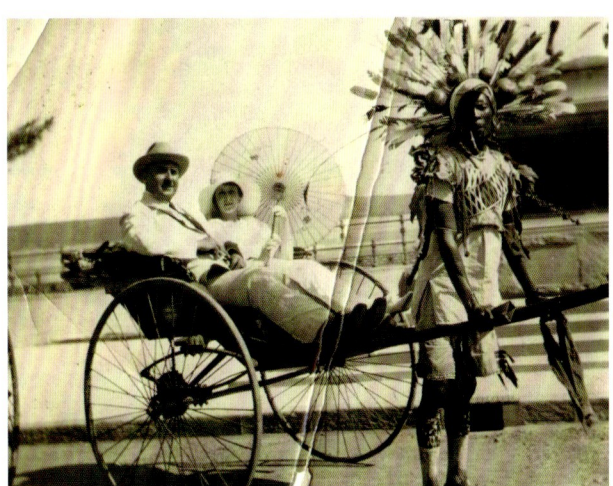

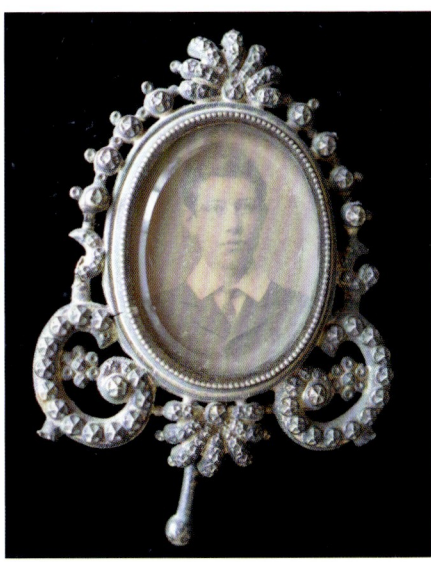

their first cameras as teenagers in the 1890s. They also joined a growing number of young women who made photography a means of self-expression. Humm has outlined the ways in which their early experiments and album constructions coincided with a rapid growth in the popularity of photography as an amateur activity for women in the last decades of the nineteenth century. She quotes the editor of *Amateur Photographer* in its first issue in 1884, encouraging 'amateur photographers of either sex', and his observation that, with their small hands, 'ladies make excellent manipulators'.[58] By 1905 there were an estimated four million amateur photographers in Britain. The processes of taking and developing pictures were collaborative among the Stephen siblings, and photographic equipment and prints were shared.

35 Unknown photographer, photograph of Duncan Grant in an Indian or Burmese frame, c.1900. Metal alloy frame, 75 × 62 mm. The Charleston Trust

36 (*top*) Bourne & Shepherd, Pippa Strachey in India, c.1900. The Charleston Trust

37 (*bottom*) Unknown photographer, Major Bartle and Ethel Grant in Burma, undated. The Charleston Trust

In an early journal reference to photography, Virginia noted that, left alone with one of Stella's visitors, she and Vanessa photographed his dog. 'Simon was photographed in a fur coat and hat and pipe; but at a second photograph we discovered that our Frend was broken.'[59] The dog's name was Simon and the make of their camera was a 'Frena', a box camera manufactured by R. & J. Beck Ltd. that Virginia consistently referred to as a 'Frend'.

Within a week the camera was repaired and sent to Bognor, where the three sisters with Stella's fiancé, Jack Hills, spent a disastrous few days on holiday.[60] Virginia wrote: 'The Frend arrived from Becks, in a new box, all rubbed up and beautiful.'[61] Vanessa was given responsibility for loading the films but clearly she was supported in this technical challenge by her sisters. Virginia consistently uses 'we' in her journal notes on photography:

> We tried shutting Nessa up in the cupboard to put in the films, but there were too many chinks. Then she suggested being covered by her quilt, and everything else that I could lay hands on – She was accordingly, buried in dresses and dressing gowns, till no light could penetrate. Soon she emerged almost stifled having forgotten how to put the film in.[62]

The Frena could hold 40 individually cut films in an internal mechanism. Used film would slide to the back of the camera after each exposure, where it was stored until it could be developed. Within hours of loading the films, Virginia wrote, 'We took 2 photographs of S and J on the sands, but the light was bad and I do not know whether they will come out.'[63] Plans to extend this February break were abandoned: 'Thank Goodness!' Virginia wrote. 'Another week of drizzle in that muddy misty flat utterly stupid Bognor (the name suits it) would have driven me to the end of the pier and into the dirty yellow sea beneath.'[64] They took the train back to London and the following day, Sunday 14 February, Simon was persuaded to pose for six more canine photographs with coat and pipe. 'After tea', Virginia wrote, 'Nessa and I developed in the night nursery. One very good one of Stella and Jack on the sands, the others all dim and under exposed.'[65]

The first of Vanessa Bell's surviving photograph albums includes two snapshots of Stella and Jack on the sands matching this description and, immediately below them, four photographs of Simon (from a different sitting) (fig. 38).[66] Their original context engaged common themes of amateur photography, holiday, and romance. The winter break in Bognor had cast Virginia and Vanessa in the roles of chaperones to enable Stella and Jack to spend time together. 'Jack has lodgings at an hotel near here', Virginia was careful to note, 'but comes always for meals'. Her journal entries record a fascination with their courtship. After cycling on the sands with Vanessa, she wrote: 'We soon went in and read, leaving Stella and Jack to wander about arm in arm'; later, on the pier, 'Stella and Jack made a pretence of walking on with us, but soon turned and went back alone'.[67] The couple were married three months later. In Bell's album the prints, captioned 'S.D. J.W.H. Bognor', follow directly after two visual 'holiday narratives' composed the previous year. The album presents an orderly record of family holidays, as if to assert a semblance of normality after Julia Stephen's death. George Duckworth still wears a mourning armband in the first photographs, captioned 'Hindhead House. Haslemere. September 1896.'[68] Two months later, 'A week in France. November 1896' heads up a succession of snapshots depicting another break. 'We took a lot of photographs', Vanessa wrote to Thoby.[69] The record begins with a snapshot of their boat, 'Mary Beatrice', paired with 'The Harbour Boulogne'.[70] After two leaves of French fisherwomen and townscapes, this visual journal concludes with a snapshot of Vanessa and George tucked up in a blanket on deck: 'G.H.D. V.S. On the way home' (fig. 39).[71] As with Leslie Stephen's photograph album, the prints are meticulously captioned. In general, initials are used for family and their closest friends, though dogs are given their full names. A photograph of Virginia and Thoby with their dogs, Spy and Shag, for example, is labelled 'A.V.S. Spy. J.T.S. Shag.' Even though it was her own album, Vanessa captions herself 'V.S.'

This first photograph album was homemade using heavy cream paper, cut to take the corners of Vanessa's snapshots. Patterned paper was pasted onto the front and back covers. The leaves are numbered 1 to 100 and the prints are arranged chronologically, with the year, beginning with 1896, hand-written at the top

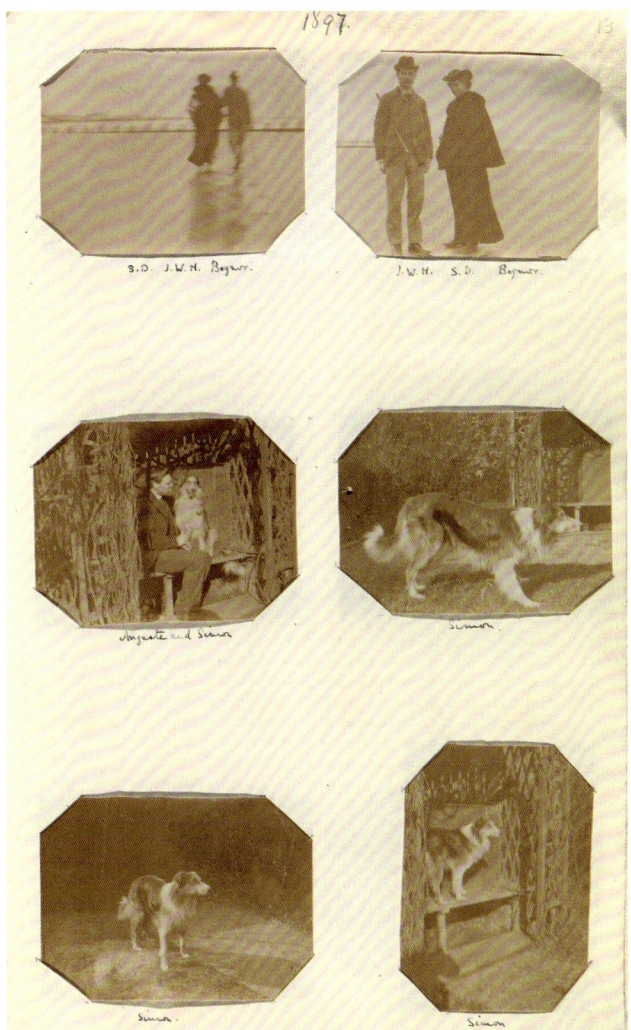 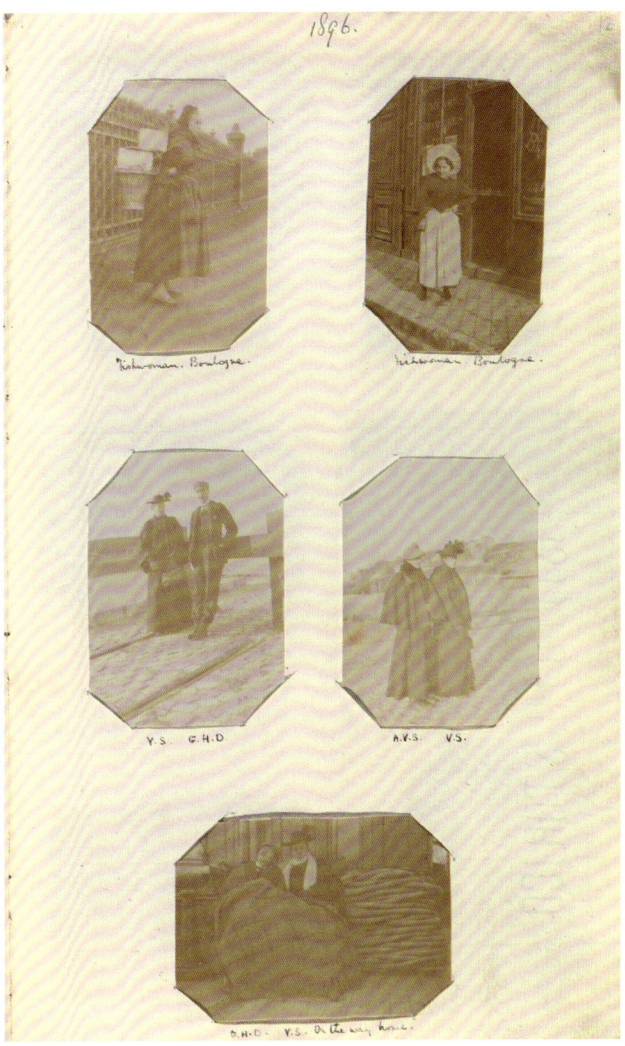

of each page. As the years progress the prints become slightly larger and less faded, but the album was abandoned before the final leaves were filled. The last photographs are of Virginia with Violet Dickinson, and of Leslie Stephen in 1902, followed by photographs, on leaf 92, of pigs and geese 'On Fritham Plain'. Leslie Stephen was diagnosed with abdominal cancer in the spring of 1902 and Dickinson then became Virginia's most intimate confidante.[72] She joined the Stephens for a family holiday at Fritham, near Lyndhurst in Hampshire, in August or September 1902, and Virginia later wrote a fictional biography and tribute to her.[73] Dickinson had become a maternal figure in the lives of Virginia and Vanessa after their mother's death. Her inclusion in one of the last photographs in the album reinforces its coherence in recording a passage in Stephen family life between the deaths of Julia and Leslie Stephen.

Before the first album was completed, Vanessa embarked upon a second family album that she designed, overtly, as a memorial to Stella. Three months after her marriage to Jack, Stella was suddenly taken ill and died. Bell's second photograph album bears a yellow sticker inside the cover showing that it was purchased from 'H. J. Ryman, Stationer', whose first store had opened on Great Portland Street, London, in 1893.[74] (Photograph albums had by this point become commercially available to cater to a growing demand from amateur photographers.) A sheet of black watered-silk paper, however, has been

---

38 Vanessa Bell, album page showing photographs of Stella Duckworth, Jack Hills, and Simon the dog in Bognor, 1897. Tate, London

39 Vanessa Bell, album page recording a family trip to Boulogne, 1896. Tate, London

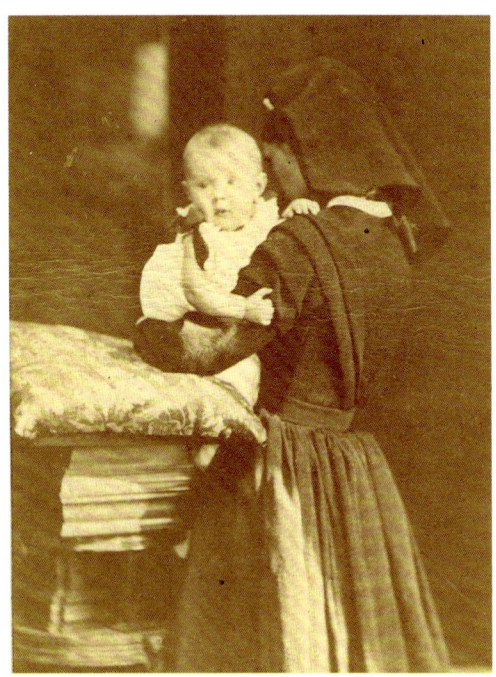

pasted over the album's brown card cover to reflect its sombre content. Black watered silk was commonly made up into mourning garments. The first pages of the album locate Stella within the Duckworth family, following the conventions of Leslie Stephen's photograph album and replicating some of its images. Studio photographs of Stella with her siblings are arranged four to a page and, on the second leaf, two photographs of her as a small child are set beneath cartes-de-visite of her mother turning her back to the camera to show the infant Gerald Duckworth (fig. 40).[75] He was born six weeks after his father's death. The cartes-de-visite are captioned 'Gerald & Mrs Herbert Duckworth' and 'G.D. & Mrs H.D.' Cartes-de-visite from the same series are included in Leslie and Virginia's albums. Vanessa introduces her own image as a baby in Stella Duckworth's arms on leaf 6 of the album and, again following her father's example, this page brings the Duckworth and Stephen families together (fig. 41). It includes a print of Leslie Stephen's daughter from his first marriage, Laura, and photographs of two of Vanessa's great aunts, 'Mrs Cameron' and 'Minna Duckworth'.[76]

✤ ✤ ✤

Cameron photographs are notably absent from Vanessa Bell's albums but the influence of her photographs of Julia Stephen and her assertive, creative originality cannot be overestimated in shaping Vanessa and Virginia's sense of their own identity. After their father's death, when they moved to Gordon Square, Vanessa wrote to Virginia describing her strikingly original arrangements for their new interiors. 'I have been hanging pictures in the hall . . . on the right-hand side as you come in I have put a row of celebrities.' These included their father, Darwin, Tennyson, and Browning. 'Then on the opposite side I have put five of the best Aunt Julia photographs of Mother.'[77] Cameron's photographs continued to resonate for both sisters throughout their lives. There are intriguing references to them in their letters. Bell wrote to Grant from Charleston in August 1921, 'If it's not too difficult, will you bring Aunt Julia's portrait . . .'; and an early letter from Virginia Woolf to Vita Sackville-West invites her to dine at Gordon Square, where Vanessa would be able to show her the Cameron photographs.[78] Sackville-West had recently published *Knole and the Sackvilles* and Woolf's response – 'There is nothing I enjoy more than family histories, so I am falling upon Knole the first moment I get' – was to proffer Cameron as part of her own creative heritage.[79] 'I hope you'll come and look at my great aunt's photographs of Tennyson and other people some time', she wrote to Sackville-West. 'My sister has many of them at her house.'[80] Lisa Tickner has noted the coincidence of Woolf's fictional portrait of her mother as Mrs Ramsay in *To the Lighthouse* and her co-authorship of the first monograph on Julia Margaret Cameron, which she wrote collaboratively with Fry in 1926.[81] The first biographical summary of Cameron had been written by Julia Stephen and published in the *Dictionary of National Biography* 40 years earlier.[82] In *Victorian Photographs of Famous Men and Fair Women* Woolf described Cameron's life and character in a spirited essay and Fry wrote a critical analysis of her work, positioning her as a Victorian portraitist and photographer. He noted the 'strong individualism' of the 1860s and 1870s and the self-conscious 'cult of beauty' encouraged by the Pre-Raphaelite movement.

40 Oscar Gustave Rejlander, 'Gerald & Mrs Herbert Duckworth', 1871. The Charleston Trust

41 (*opposite*) Vanessa Bell, album page representing the 'marriage' of the Duckworth and Stephen families, undated. Tate, London

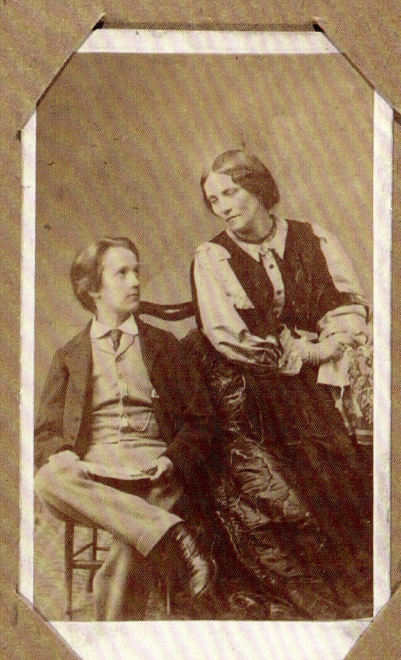
Mr Bailey (?)

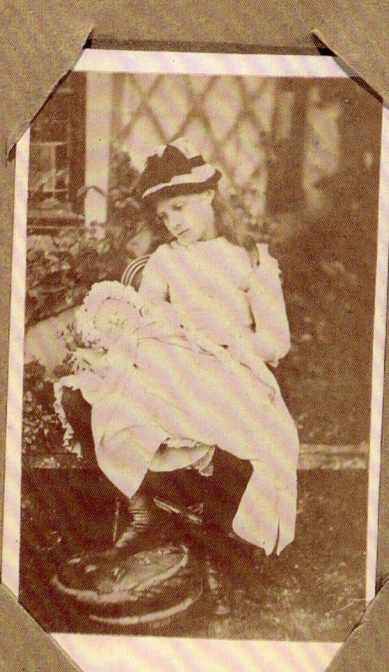
Stella Duckworth
Vanessa Stephen

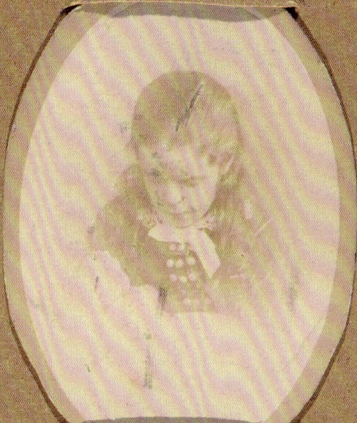
Laura Stephen

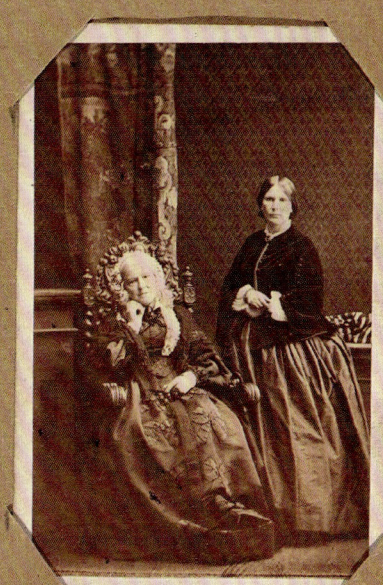
Lady Stephen C E Stephen
Mr Duckworth Minna Duckworth

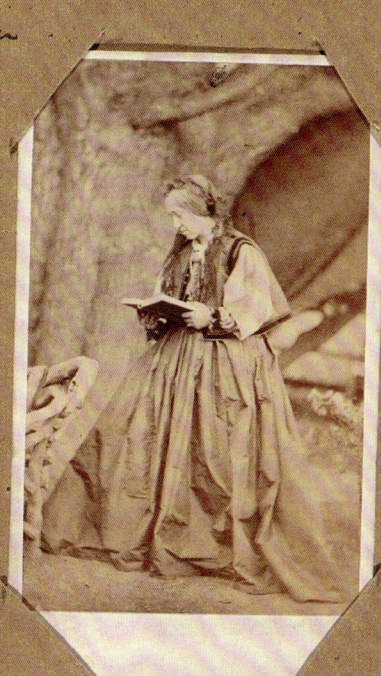
Mrs Cameron

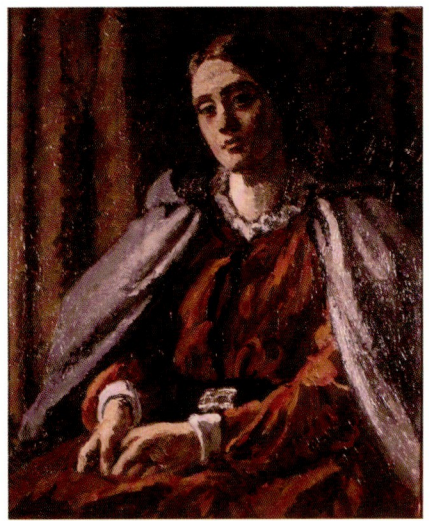 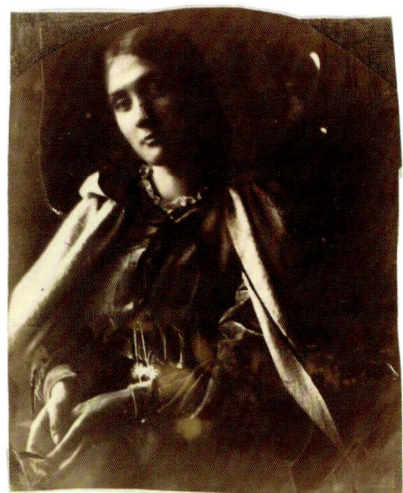 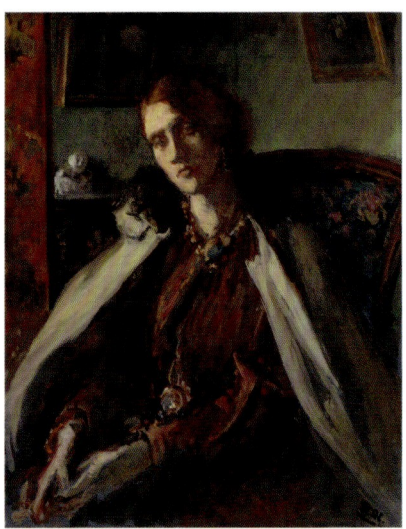

Making the case for photography as an art form he concluded that Cameron's portraits would 'outlive most of the works of the artists who were her contemporaries'.[83] Several of the photographs from Gordon Square were lavishly reproduced as plates in *Victorian Photographs of Famous Men and Fair Women*, and three years later, partly in response, Vanessa Bell based a painting, *The Red Dress*, on one of them. Somewhere between portrait and self-portrait, *The Red Dress* renders Vanessa's features and those of her mother indistinguishable (figs 42 and 43). A similar, undated portrait was produced by Jacques-Emile Blanche, under whom Grant had studied in Paris. Again the family identities overlap, as in 1959 it was purchased by the Ministry of Works as a portrait of Virginia Woolf (fig. 44).

Tickner argues that Cameron served as an 'elective' maternal figure for Bell and Woolf, enabling them, in Woolf's words, to 'think back through our mothers' without the encumbrance of Julia Stephen's self-sacrificing character.[84] Cameron offered 'a specifically matrilineal artistic heritage'.[85] She was also, at times, the butt of their humour. Woolf's play *Freshwater* satirized Cameron and her circle. Her photographs of Julia Stephen, nevertheless, served as psychologically complex templates for Stella, Vanessa, and Virginia when they sat for their own studio portraits and were represented as the next generation of Stephen family beauties. The placing of these later prints in their albums and interiors resonates with mnemonic references to Cameron's photographs in the opening pages of Leslie Stephen's album. One such print was taken of Stella in a studio in Rome. Bearing a

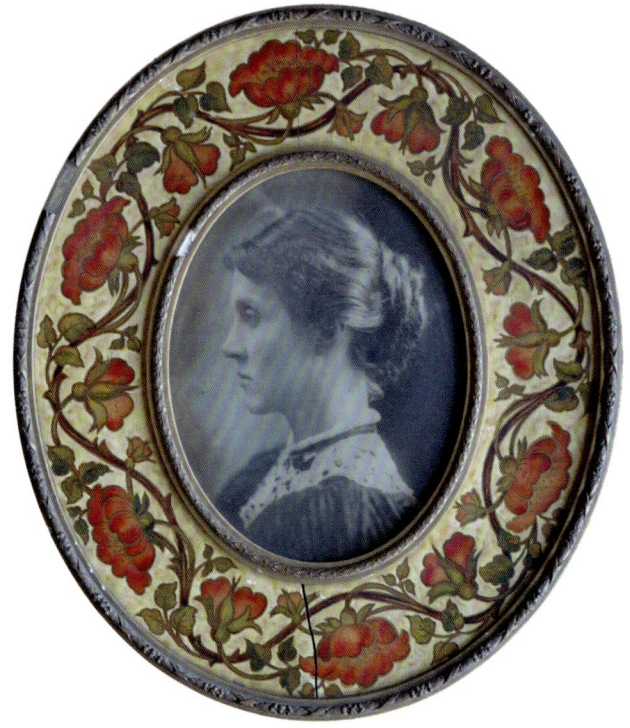

42 (*top left*) Vanessa Bell, *The Red Dress*, 1929. Oil on canvas, 733 × 605 mm. The Royal Pavilion and Museums, Brighton and Hove
43 (*top middle*) Julia Margaret Cameron, *Julia Jackson*, 1864. Victoria and Albert Museum, London

44 (*top right*) Jacques-Emile Blanche, *Julia Prinsep Stephen*, undated. Oil on canvas, 925 × 735 mm. UK Government Art Collection
45 (*above*) Unknown photographer, profile portrait of Stella Duckworth in a painted frame, *c*.1890. Studio photograph, wood, and paint, 410 × 370 mm (including frame). The Charleston Trust

44 THE BLOOMSBURY LOOK

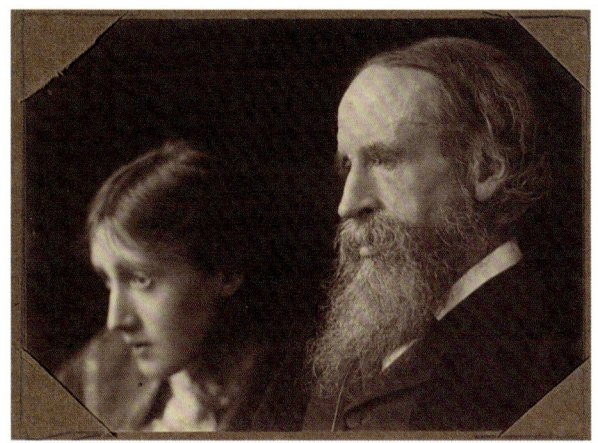

striking resemblance to Cameron's head-and-shoulders profile portraits of her mother, this image was given a full page in Monk's House Album 1.[86] A version of the print also remained in Vanessa Bell's collection to the end of her life. It was framed in a painted, late-nineteenth-century oval frame that would have been compatible with the William Morris-style interiors at 22 Hyde Park Gate (fig. 45).[87]

A narrative context can often be ascribed to the arrangement of individual pages in the Monk's House Albums. A photograph of Stella is paired with one of Violet Dickinson, for example, perhaps reflecting their related roles as maternal surrogates. But the pages themselves play havoc with chronological expectations. In Monk's House Album 1, for instance, 16 pages of Leonard Woolf's photographs from Ceylon are inexplicably grouped between early photographs of the Stephen family and their friends, and photographs of Julian and Quentin Bell playing at Asheham House. Victorian photographs resume in the ensuing leaves. Humm aligns this with 'Woolf's refusal of narrative realism in her fiction'.[88] It is evidence, she suggests, of the intertextuality, for Woolf, of past and present.[89] Subsequently in the album, however, images are juxtaposed with obvious connections. Three portraits of Virginia with her father, all by George Beresford, are arranged together on a page to accentuate a family likeness that was central to Virginia's sense of her own heredity as a writer and intellectual (fig. 46).[90] On the following page, four photographs of Thoby, in

profile and full face, again by Beresford, evidence what Leonard Woolf was later to describe as the 'magnificent and monumental simplicity' of his beauty (fig. 47).[91] Two pages further on, a snapshot of Thoby and Leslie Stephen together is set next to three more Beresford photographs of father and son. The portraits have a particular poignancy because Leslie Stephen's final illness had already been diagnosed, and he was awaiting surgery when he and Virginia sat for Beresford in 1902. Four years later the photographs of Thoby were taken just weeks before his death. Virginia wrote to Madge Vaughan, 'It was a most happy chance that you asked Thoby for a photograph: he was taken by Beresford the week he left England. I will send you one when they come; they are good – but not very much when you think of him.'[92] These leaves in the Monk's House album serve to memorialize Woolf's father and brother.

George Beresford set up his studio in Yeomans Row

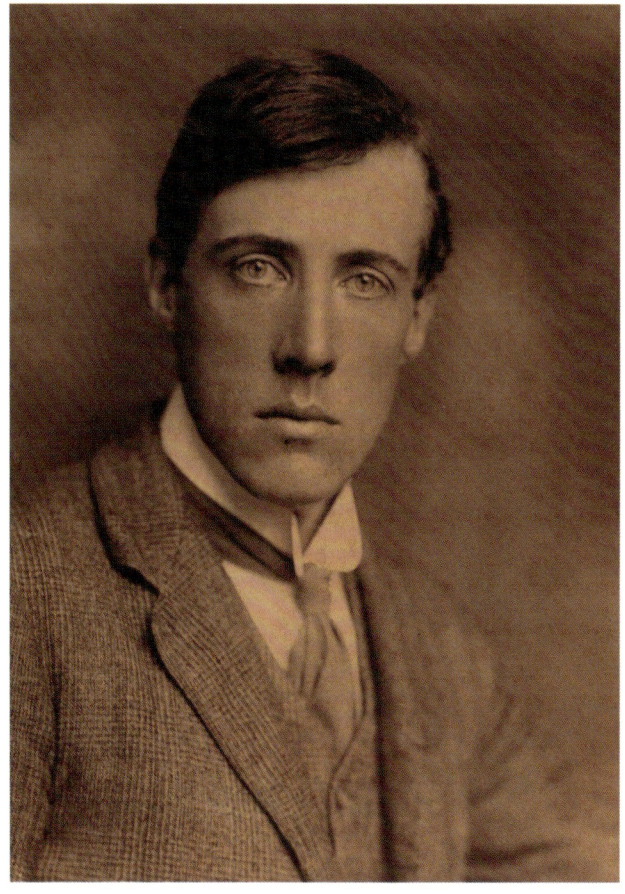

46 George Beresford, Virginia and Sir Leslie Stephen, 1902. Houghton Library, Harvard University

47 George Beresford, Thoby Stephen, 1906. The Charleston Trust. This photograph is one of four of Thoby that appear together on a page of Virginia Woolf's Monk's House Photograph Album 1

off the Brompton Road in South Kensington, hardly more than a mile away from the Stephen family home in Hyde Park Gate, in 1902. Virginia first sat for him in July of that year. Beresford had trained at the Slade after an early career in India. He and Rudyard Kipling had been school friends at the United Services College at Westward Ho! and Beresford was the inspiration for Kipling's character of M'Turk in *Stalky and Co*. A brief career as a civil engineer in Bombay was curtailed, possibly by malaria, when he was 24 and he returned to England in 1888 to study and work in the still-emerging field of portrait photography. Just as Jacques-Emile Blanche made a living in Paris and Dieppe painting portraits of famous artists and writers, for which there was an open market, so Beresford specialized in photographs of artists and writers, drawing on his friendships and contacts from the Slade. These could then be sold to the *Illustrated London News*, *Tatler*, *Sketch*, and other papers and periodicals.

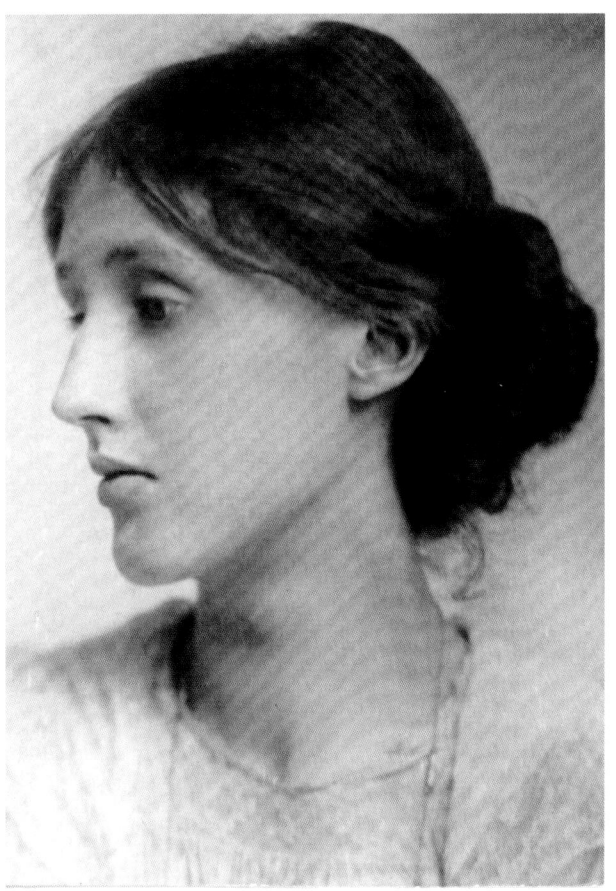

He was prolific. In his first year alone his sitters included Auguste Rodin, Augustus John, Alphonse Legros, Henry Tonks, J. M. Barrie, and David Lloyd George, as well as the Stephen family. Beresford is likely to have been aware of Cameron's portraits of Leslie and Julia Stephen and, as an eminent literary figure nearing the end of his life, Sir Leslie Stephen would have been an appealing subject. He had been awarded a knighthood in the coronation honours list in June 1902. Where Cameron's photographs capture Stephen's vigour and intensity, Beresford's portraits, taken 30 years later, reveal his frailty. His famous 'bright-red beard, radiating in fan-shape' was now thin and grizzled, and his once piercing blue eyes betray a haunted anxiety and melancholy.[93] There are two surviving versions of the double portrait with Virginia and in both she is the background figure, slightly out of focus. In one, father and daughter incline their heads slightly towards each other, as if in conversation.[94] In the print that Virginia selected for her photograph album, however, she is leaning towards her father and twisting to present her profile at an angle that replicates his. The shot is designed to accentuate their likeness.

Virginia was 20 and unpublished when Beresford produced the iconic portrait that most frequently represents her (fig. 48). It is one of the National Portrait Gallery's best-selling postcards.[95] Again, it is one of a series of related images created at a single sitting and it appears to have been commissioned by her half-brother, George Duckworth. She wrote to Violet Dickinson from Fritham early in August:

> I'm afraid Nessa raised your hopes too high, and you will be very much disappointed – but the man hasnt sent the photographs yet – and they mayn't do me justice – indeed I dont expect they will. If you are very kind to me, and spoil me thoroughly, and behave in every way tenderly you shall have one when you come here. (They belong to George.)[96]

Vanessa Bell was also given at least two prints. A large photograph was captioned 'Adeline Virginia Stephen'

48 George Beresford, Virginia Woolf, 1902. National Portrait Gallery, London

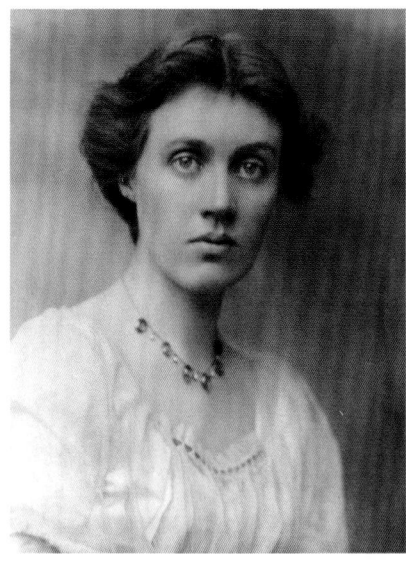
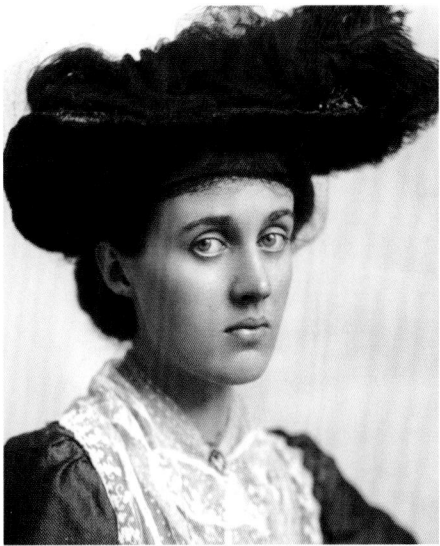
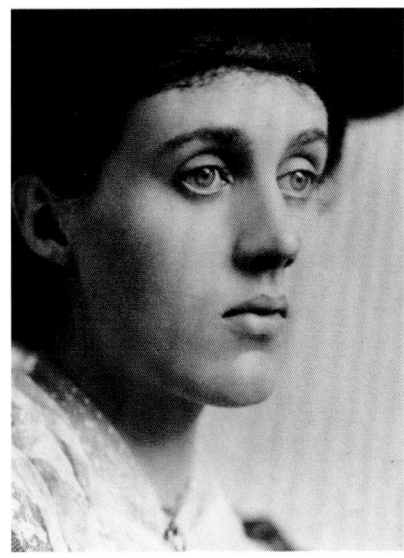

and given its own leaf in one of her albums, and a few pages further on a smaller print was grouped with later photographs of Bell and her children.[97] It is mistakenly dated 'A.V.S. 1903'. Beresford's book of sitters records that 14 photographs were taken of Virginia in July 1902 together with an unspecified number of Vanessa and six portraits of their father at the same sitting. As the family gathered around Sir Leslie in anticipation of his operation, George Duckworth may well have organized the session. It is also plausible, given the responsibility he assumed for his sisters' 'coming out' into fashionable society, that he was anxious to have portraits of them in their chaste white lace in anticipation of a period of mourning, if their father's operation was unsuccessful, that would necessitate their withdrawal from the balls and events where husbands might be secured for them. This may explain Virginia's anxiety in her letter to Violet Dickinson.

Beresford portrays the sisters as classic beauties (fig. 49). They offer their faces to the camera as their mother had done nearly forty years earlier, and replicate her expressions of wistful composure. Beresford's technical brilliance softens their features, the aquiline perfection of their noses, their large eyes, and the expressive and yet ambiguous curves of their lips. Their faces almost fill the frame, set against pale backgrounds. In his portraits of Virginia the tonal range is restrained, accentuating the delicacy of her pale skin, offset by lustrous dark hair that escapes in wisps from its elaborate knot. He photographed Vanessa again, five years later, around the time of her engagement and marriage (figs 50 and 51). In these photographs the lighting is more dramatic. Her face is lit to create deep shadows and highlights and, although cropped out of the print that most frequently represents her, she is dressed in a large, fashionable hat, resplendent with feathers. She is in mourning for Thoby, perhaps dressed for her own wedding, and the hat's black netting has been lifted away from her face. A heart-shaped locket rests on the lace bib that covers the neckline of her dark dress. It is ironic that these conventional images of the Stephen sisters' innocence and feminine beauty co-existed, throughout their lives, with the images that represented their modernity. When Mabel Selwood, Quentin's nurse, left Charleston to be married, Vanessa gave her a Beresford print as a memento and, as a wedding gift, she was invited to choose a painting. In addition to a Post-Impressionist landscape of Bosham church by Grant, she took a recent, and experimental, portrait by Grant of Bell (fig. 52).

The cropped version of Beresford's portrait of Bell, on a card mount but unframed, was propped up in

---

49 (*above left*) George Beresford, Vanessa Bell, 1902. The Charleston Trust
50 (*above middle*) George Beresford, Vanessa Bell in mourning for her brother Thoby, 1907. Getty Images

51 (*above right*) George Beresford, Vanessa Bell, 1907. The Charleston Trust. This iconic image is a cropped version of a photograph taken during the same sitting as figure 50, when Vanessa was in mourning for her brother Thoby

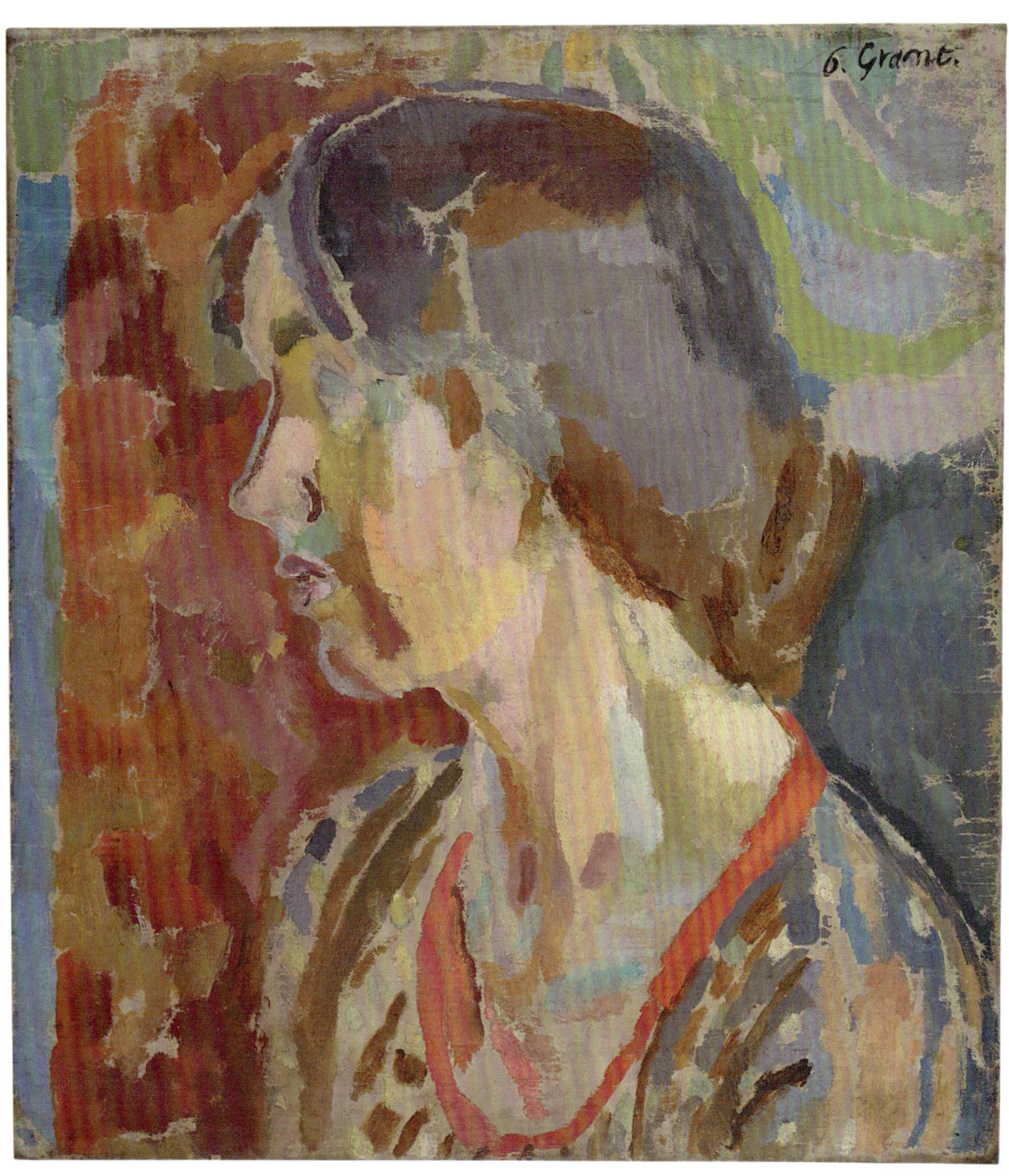

the studio at Charleston in later years (fig. 53).[98] It is impossible to know how these prints were displayed or stored in various locations over time but Bell refers to it in passing, in a letter to Grant, when she writes that she has been 'going through old Kodak films' and found 'a Beresford photograph of myself', perhaps indicating a shared familiarity with the series of prints.[99] Again, the Beresford was destined to be given to one of the servants, on this occasion Grace Higgens: 'as Grace was in the room I gave it to her'. It was also a mnemonic device, in Bell's letter, to draw Grant into a shared reflection upon beauty and heredity. Grace, she wrote, 'told me I must have been a great beauty! But Angelica thought at first it was of Virginia & then of my mother! Finally she admitted it had some likeness to me.' Grant would have been aware of Angelica's sharing in his own beauty as well as Bell's and, in London for New Year's Eve while Bell was at Charleston with their daughter and servants, her own plans for a party that evening 'having completely fallen through', he was being reminded of family ties.

Both Bell and Woolf, in their albums, continued to cluster their own photographs of family and friends together to describe and consolidate Bloomsbury's unconventional relationships and activities. Their amateur photographs of Group members, in their later albums, are arranged together to evoke occasions or complex associations. They apply an internalized logic to the protocols that had been learnt in adolescence for family photograph albums as manifestations of memory, biography, and identity. The pages of Bell's memorial album to Stella turn from images of the family and their friends in St Ives (Stella with Madge Vaughan, and the cricket-playing Virginia and Adrian Stephen), to cabinet photographs of Clive Bell as an undergraduate at Cambridge, and then to the Beresford photographs of Thoby. There are no studio photographs or snapshots in the album documenting the Bells' wedding. Rather, Vanessa appears to relate the confluence of mourning the deaths of Stella and Thoby in these pages to her marriage, evoking the complex working of memory and association across time. There is a revealing subjectivity in Bell's pairing of her

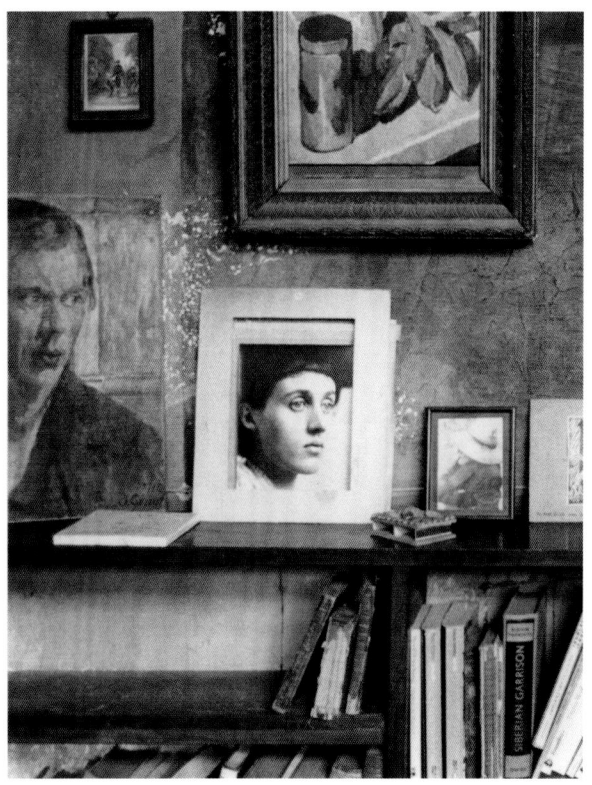

own 1907 portrait by Beresford, recording both her mourning and her marriage, with his now-famous 1902 print of Virginia on the page following the Beresford photographs of their brother. She does not place her own photograph next to that of her new husband even though, beneath these two prints, are three images of Vanessa Bell and her first born, Julian, describing a new chapter in the narrative.

The album closes with photographs of Bloomsbury Group gatherings at Studland beach, Dorset, in 1910 and 1911. A total of nine leaves are devoted to these. The photographs are connected to Bell's practice as an artist. Tickner argues that her iconic painting *Studland Beach* (c.1912) conflates the memories and imagery associated with these photographs of Bloomsbury and those of Stephen family holidays at Talland House. She contends that the painting abstracts and distils Bell's perceptions of her mother and of Stella as a surrogate mother.[100] The photographs also reconcile Bell's role as a young mother with her position as an artist within a group of radicals. Within the context of her photograph

52 (*opposite*) Duncan Grant, *Portrait of Vanessa Bell*, c.1915. Oil on canvas, 510 × 460 mm. The Charleston Trust

53 Belinda Parsons, photograph of a bookshelf in the studio at Charleston with the famous Beresford photograph of Vanessa Bell, undated. The Charleston Trust

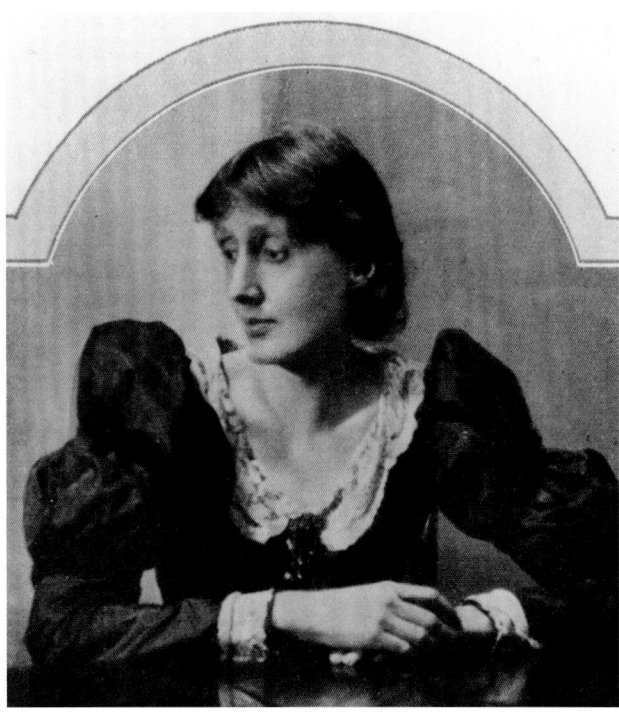

album, with its black watered-silk cover and opening leaves memorializing Stella, the fusion of figures in the Studland photographs with the taut composition of *Studland Beach* may be seen to complete the album's narrative arc.

Bloomsbury was exceptional among its contemporaries in its use of the emerging technologies of amateur and professional photography to self-fashion a distinctive Group image and identity. The domestic nature of its snapshots and photograph albums is a reflection of its sense of itself as a network of family and friends. Its album pages encapsulate the memories and narratives that inspired many of its literary texts. Holidays, special events, and visits that are documented in the Group's letters and diaries often also occasioned the taking of photographs. Inevitably, this has led to the use of Bloomsbury photographs as text illustrations, and Bloomsbury texts as captions. Bloomsbury snapshots characterize the irreverent informality of the Group. It was sophisticated, however, in controlling the circulation of photographs that were to define its image. The relationship between loose prints and those inserted into albums or arranged even more publicly on display describes the complex levels of access to the Group's intimate and more public manifestations of identity. Many of Bloomsbury's nude photographs, discussed in the next chapter, were excluded from its albums and they were held back, initially, from archival deposits.[101] They document collusions, within the Group and its wider circle, in reframing the imaging of women and sexuality.

Photographs contributed to the creative processes of writing and painting, but Bloomsbury's experiments as amateur photographers and casual sitters also affected its attitude to the camera. Later studio portraits, by Cecil Beaton of Ottoline Morrell and Mary Hutchinson, for example, demonstrate the sophistication with which they 'owned' their representations even when playing to society's expectations.[102] As individuals and as a group, Bloomsbury understood the commercial value of photographs for press and publicity purposes. British *Vogue*'s general editor, Dorothy Todd, and its fashion editor, her lover Madge Garland, were among its wider social circle. As Bloomsbury's identity as a leading group of British modernists became established, Todd and Garland were keen to craft a connection between fashion and the avant-garde. 'As well as articles of literary importance,' Garland later claimed, '*Vogue* contained photographs of the authors, of their houses and of their friends.'[103] She emphasized the 'eminence by association' of Todd's involvement with the Group: 'In those early days many of her friends – most of them members of the Bloomsbury Group – were also writing for *Vogue*: I particularly remember articles by Lytton Strachey and Roger Fry . . . Clive Bell was our art critic.'[104] Woolf, by contrast, in her letters to literary friends found it necessary to distance herself from the 'vulgarity, which is open and shameless, of *Vogue*', while at the same time defending the magazine when she published an article with them.[105] When she and the sculptor Stephen Tomlin were 'nominated' for its 'Hall of Fame' she decided against fashionable dress and chose instead to reference the artistic heritage of Cameron's images of her mother. Woolf was photographed for the feature, which claimed

54 Maurice Beck and Helen MacGregor, Virginia Woolf wearing one of her mother's dresses. *Vogue*, late May 1924, p. 49

55 (*opposite*) Unknown photographer, the sitting room at 52 Tavistock Square (residence of Virginia and Leonard Woolf), decorated by Vanessa Bell and Duncan Grant. *Vogue*, early November 1924, p. 43

her as 'the most brilliant novelist of the younger generation', in one of Julia Stephen's dresses, toying with the Victorian stereotypes of beauty that would continue to plague her niece, Angelica (fig. 54).[106]

British *Vogue* published photographs of Bloomsbury interiors, paintings, and applied arts, documenting the convergence of the Group's public and private lives. Fry wrote an article about the house that he designed for himself, Durbins in Guildford, for the magazine, and *Vogue* commissioned photographs of its main, double-height living space, which housed his Bloomsbury collection (see figs 150 and 151).[107] In 1919, and again in 1924 and 1925, *Vogue* published photographs of Bell and Grant's decorations for Mary Hutchinson at her home in Hammersmith, River House. *Vogue*'s numerous features on Bloomsbury applied arts in 1924 and 1925 included photographs of Bell and Grant's interiors for Keynes at King's College, Cambridge, and for Leonard and Virginia Woolf at 52 Tavistock Square in Bloomsbury.[108] Though the Woolfs had moved to Hogarth House in Paradise Road, Richmond, in 1915, they returned to Bloomsbury in 1924, installing the Hogarth Press in the building's basement and their domestic spaces in the top two floors ('a grimy solicitors office' occupied the ground and first floors).[109] Christopher Reed has analysed their sitting room, and the modernity of its decorations by Bell and Grant, relating them specifically to Woolf's urbanity, as a semi-public statement of identity (fig. 55).[110] He describes the continuity, in style and subject matter, between Bell and Grant's painted panels and Bell's book jackets and illustrations for Woolf's novels. As publishers, living above the Press, the Woolfs' sitting room reflected their professional as well as their private identities. It was used for meetings and for press purposes, providing a distinctive setting for photographs of Virginia and Leonard. Reed argues that it asserted a confluence between Bloomsbury's production of art and literature that positioned the Group in the history of modernism.[111] Its dissemination through *Vogue*, as Reed also notes, exemplified Bloomsbury's engagement with popular

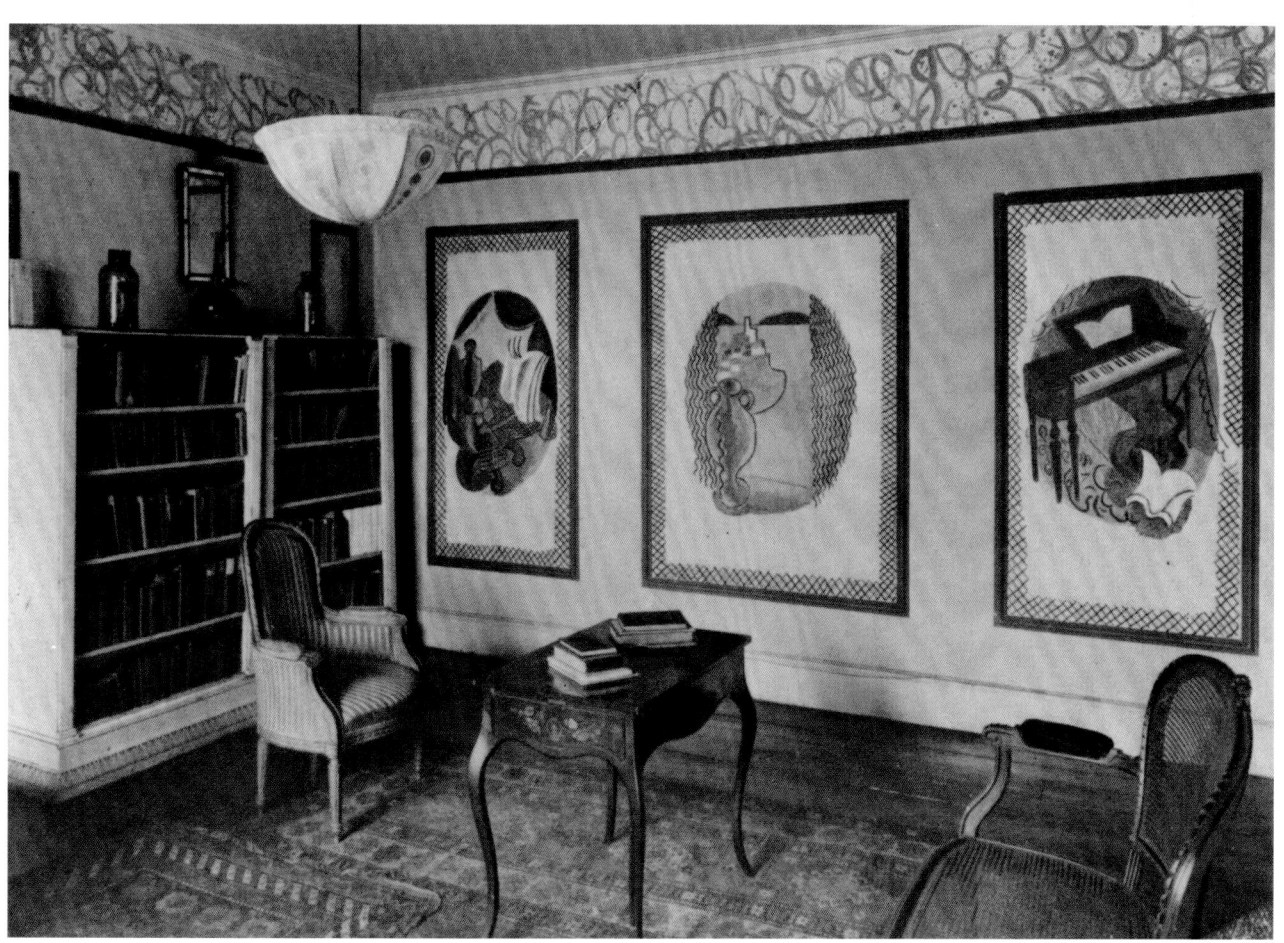

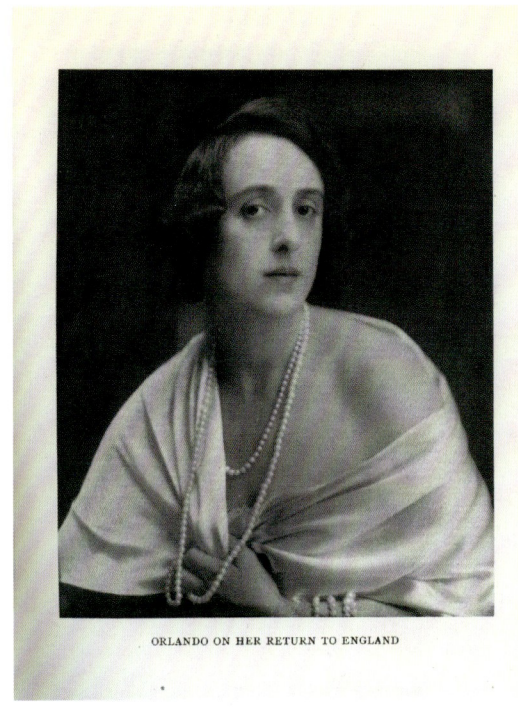

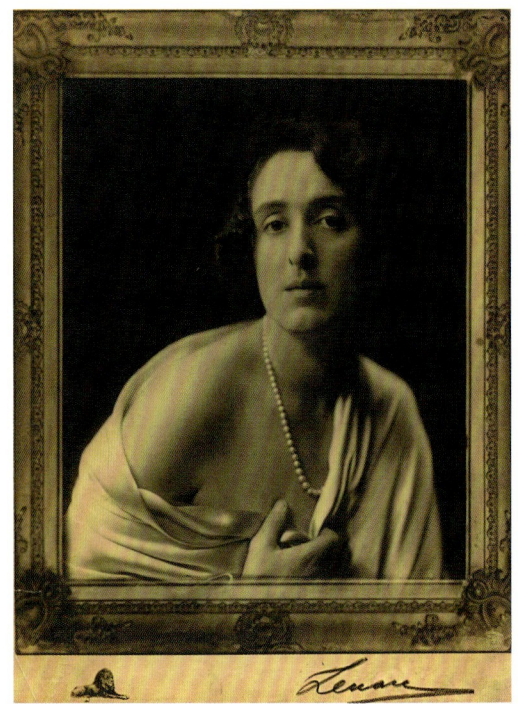

culture and with that magazine's ambiguous sexual non-conformity under Todd's editorial direction.[112]

As a publisher, Woolf had some control over the circulation of her own image and photographs of her authors for public and private purposes. Studio portraits of her and of Vita Sackville-West by the fashionable photographer Lenare describe the sophistication with which images were exchanged in a visual dialogue between the two women, negotiating the interface between their personal and professional lives. Woolf invited Bell and Grant to style and photograph the portraits of Sackville-West in character that would illustrate her novel *Orlando*. The image of Orlando in the twentieth century, however, captioned in the novel 'Orlando on Her Return to England', was a recent publicity photograph of Sackville-West by Lenare, taken when she was awarded the Hawthornden Prize. Woolf playfully merged the official and fictional identities when she asked Sackville-West to supply a copy of the print, writing to her, '*Bring photograph of Orlando*.'[113] She published it as a recognizable tribute to Sackville-West as a fellow author in *Orlando* and used it on posters to promote the book (fig. 56).[114] Woolf's private collection of photographs includes a more provocative version of the Lenare portrait, presumably a gift from Sackville-West (fig. 57).[115] She commissioned Lenare to take her own portrait, perhaps deliberately mirroring her lover's press photograph, promising Sackville-West: 'I've got some rather nice photographs of Virginia; but can't send them at the moment' (fig. 58).[116] When Woolf did give a copy of her own Lenare portrait to Sackville-West, it was framed and displayed conspicuously on the writing desk at Sackville-West's Kent home, Sissinghurst Castle. For Sackville-West, the image documented her relationship with the author of *Orlando*. It was integral to the professional personas of both women. It was also widely distributed to promote *A Room of One's Own* (1929) and Woolf's other publications. She sent a copy to her American publisher, writing to them: 'It is considerably later than the one you have, and we are using it over here.'[117] It was published in *Life* magazine. The exchange of Lenare photographs as tokens in the competitive and complex romantic and professional

---

56 (*above left*) Lenare, 'Orlando on Her Return to England', in Virginia Woolf, *Orlando* (London: Hogarth Press, 1928). The image was originally a publicity photograph of Vita Sackville-West, taken on the occasion of her winning the Hawthornden Prize in 1927

57 (*above right*) Lenare, Vita Sackville-West, 1927. Houghton Library, Harvard University

58 (*opposite*) Lenare, publicity photograph of Virginia Woolf, c.1929. Houghton Library, Harvard University

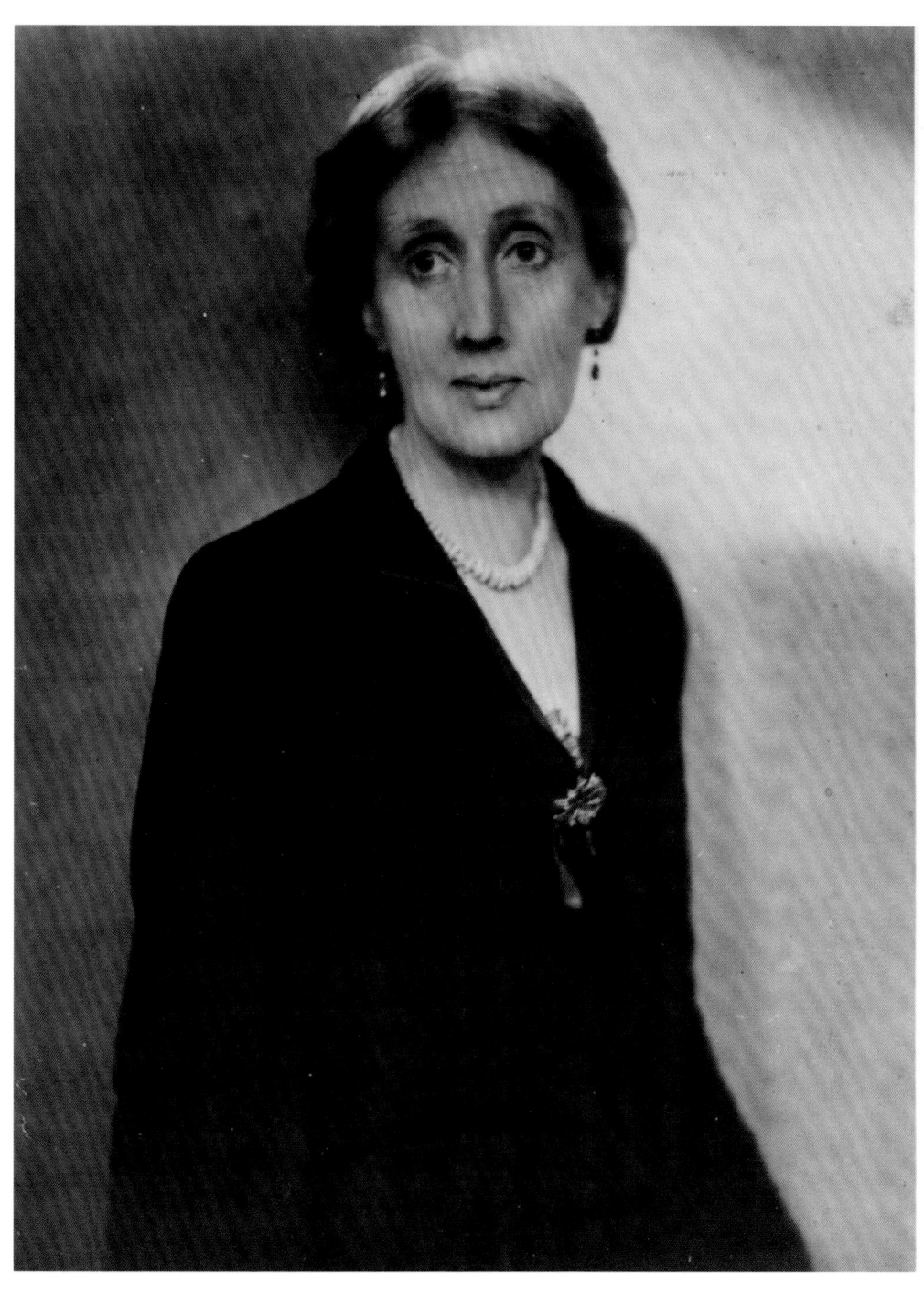

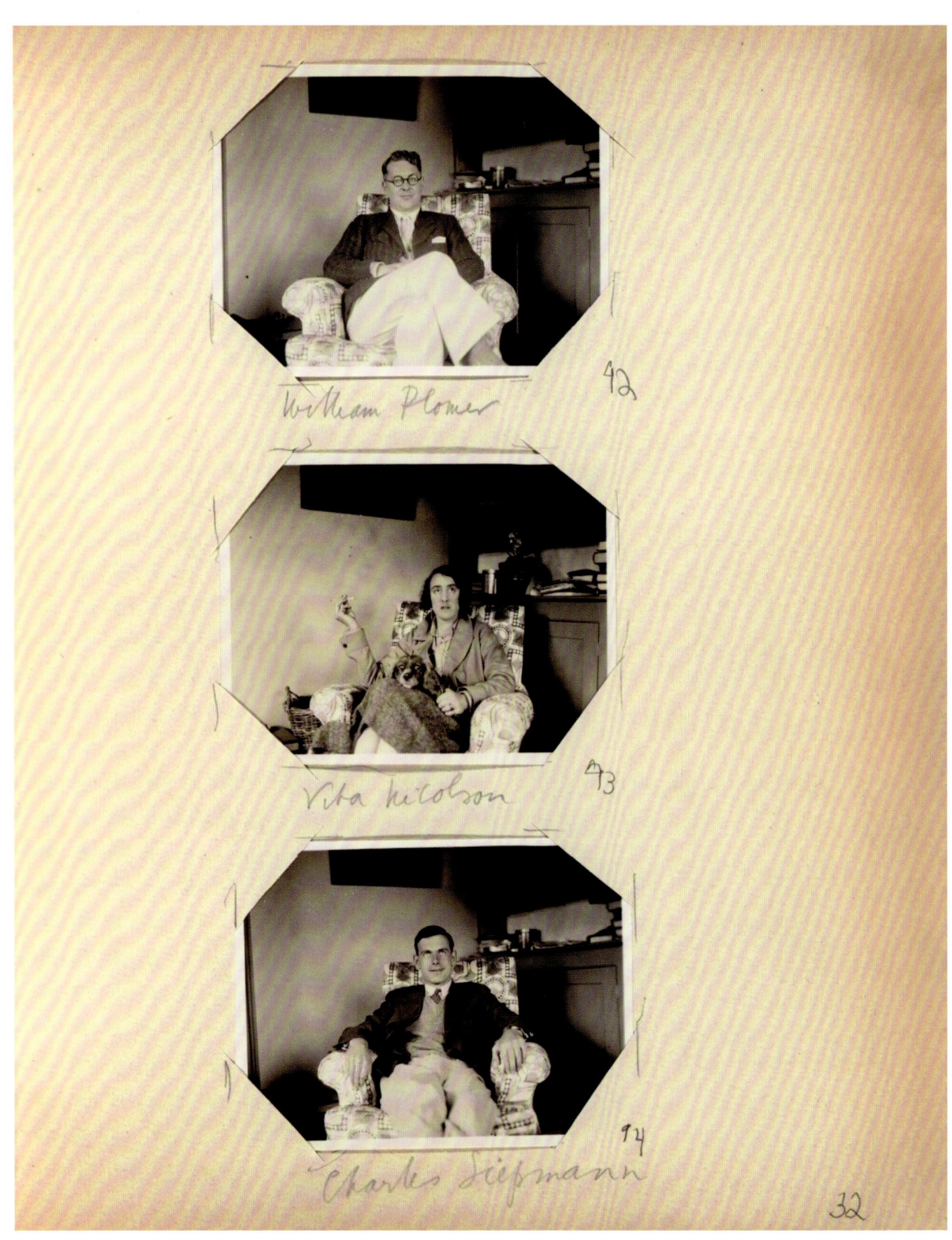

relationship between Woolf and Sackville-West was given a final twist when Woolf asked to borrow her print back. By this time her affair with Sackville-West was over and she wrote nonchalantly that a portrait was needed for a study of her own work: 'that devil Holtby wants one for her book in a hurry, and this might do. They'd return it . . . but doubtless now, with your other attachment, its down the coal hole. Oh alas.'[118] This self-assured dealing out and reeling in of image and identity was fragile, however. When Holtby's publishers selected a photograph by Leonard Woolf as the frontispiece for *Virginia Woolf* instead of the intended Lenare, she had a minor crisis of confidence: 'I feel that my privacy is invaded; my legs show; & I am revealed to the world (1,000 at most) as a plain dowdy old woman. . . . I sent the photographs off with some compunction about being too late. Now I'm all of a quiver.'[119]

Leonard Woolf's photograph belonged to the Woolfs' private self-fashioning. Maggie Humm has noted the repetition, in their Monk's House Album 3, of distinctive settings at their Rodmell cottage, and the presentation of their friends and fellow authors, posed within them as if in a photographer's studio. She describes the assertive presentation of four photographs of Maynard and Lydia Keynes, arranged together on a page, and the temporal associations of their taking it in turns to sit in the same chair, as if 'performing themselves'. Humm categorizes the images as 'agents of memory framing' and connects them with Woolf's use of photography to reconstitute the continuity of life in the face of oblivion and death.[120] The armchair in Leonard Woolf's photograph was one of two that had been covered earlier that year with a striking new textile, *Abstract*, designed by Vanessa Bell. An armchair covered with the same textile in the ground-floor sitting room bears, lined up in a column on one of the album's pages, Sackville-West, William Plomer, and Charles Siepmann, who worked for the BBC as Director of Talks (fig. 59).[121] Upstairs, in the sitting room at Monk's House, Virginia posed for Leonard in a larger, deeper armchair, again covered with *Abstract*, tucked under the slope of the cottage roof next to a dormer window. The series of photographs demonstrates that these were not snapshots but images exploring Woolf's identity for publication, in which she performs the role of author and publisher. Among them are the 'dowdy' photographs, showing her legs, that she complained about (fig. 60).[122] In the version published in Holtby's book and elsewhere, however, Woolf's legs are cropped out of the frame and she turns in her chair towards the light from the window, as if absorbed in thought (fig. 61).[123] The prints describe a transition in the Woolfs' use of amateur photography. They are rooted in the traditions of Bloomsbury family photographs.

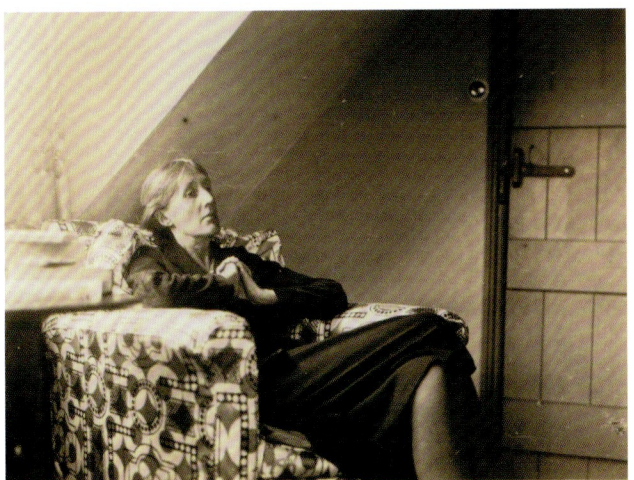
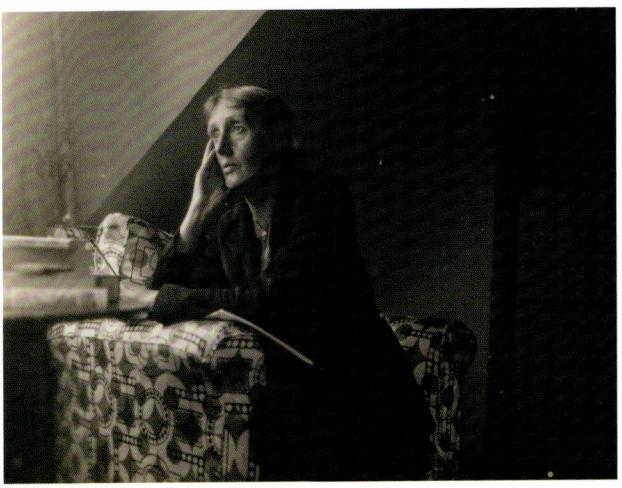

59 (*opposite*) Virginia Woolf, album page showing photographs of (*top to bottom*) William Plomer, Vita Nicolson (Sackville-West), and Charles Siepmann at Monk's House, 1932. Houghton Library, Harvard University

60 (*above left*) Leonard Woolf, Virginia Woolf at Monk's House, 1932. Houghton Library, Harvard University

61 (*above right*) Leonard Woolf, Virginia Woolf at Monk's House, 1932. Houghton Library, Harvard University

The turn of Woolf's head to accentuate her renowned beauty, and her abstracted gaze with the light from the window falling on her face, echo photographs of her mother by Cameron and Loppé. The staging of her cottage environment, however, suggests a writer's attic through the angle of the roof, the simple batten-and-ledge door, the pile of books out of focus in the foreground, and the presence of her sister's creative identity literally wrapped around her in the distinctive upholstery of her chair. These deliberately constructed elements evidence Woolf's collusion as a maker and consumer of photographs, supported by her Bloomsbury family in cultivating her own distinctive image. Two years later, when she sat for Man Ray in 1934, she projected an image that combined modernity with authority. Ray's photograph, used for the cover of *Time* magazine, is uncompromising. It captures Woolf's fragile confidence and her status as an eminent and successful author and publisher (fig. 62).[124]

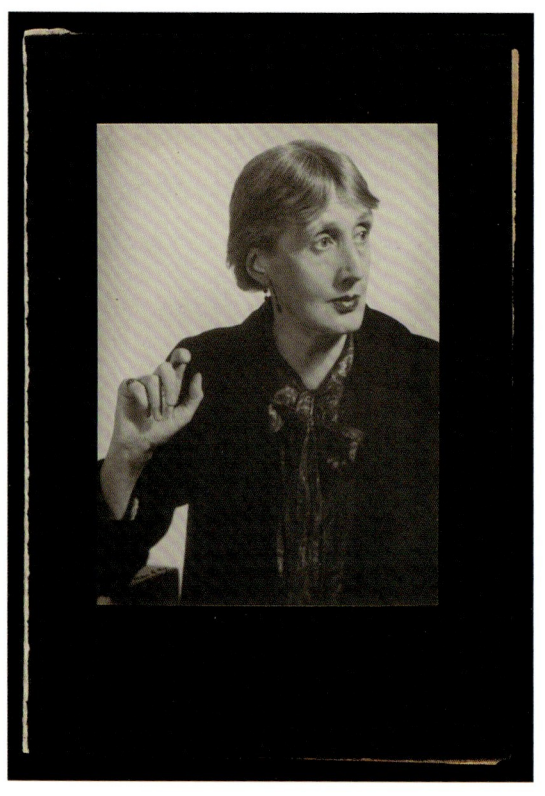

62 Man Ray, Virginia Woolf, 27 November 1934. Houghton Library, Harvard University

CHAPTER 2

EXPERIMENTS IN

DRESS

AND

UNDRESS

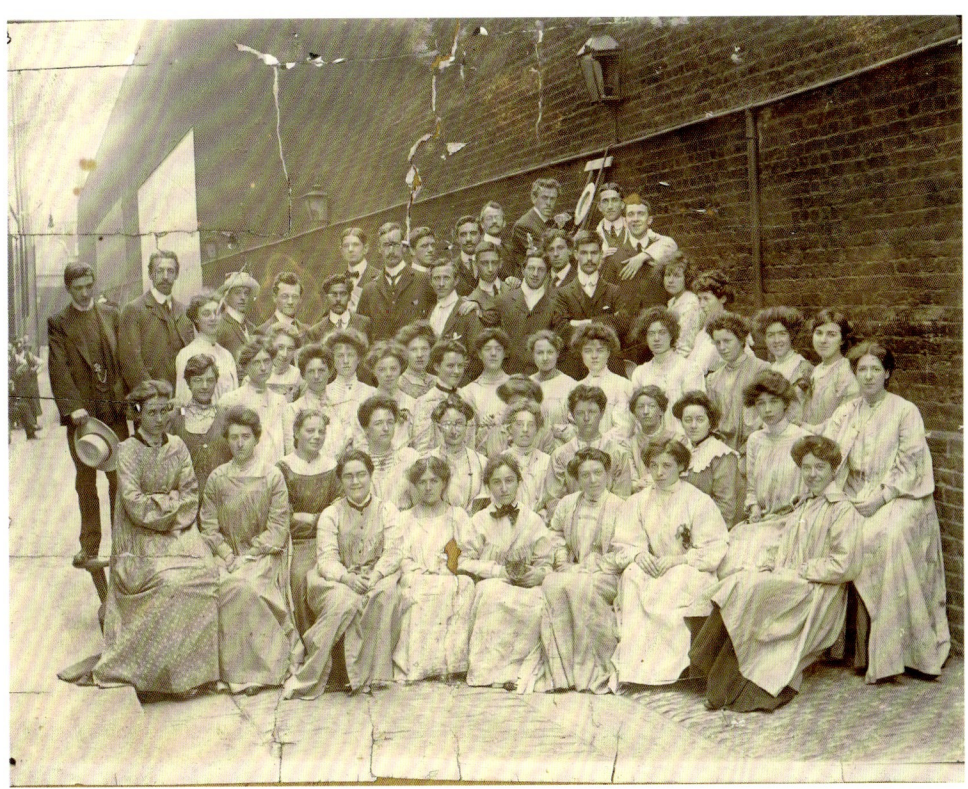

In his nineties the barrister Jeremy Hutchinson still recalled his mother's Omega Workshops dress as an acute embarrassment. The dress itself, full-length, red, and painted by Bell or Grant with large abstract shapes, was less problematic than the fact that she wore it to walk him and his sister to school. Local children in the relatively deprived area between their home in London's Upper Mall, Hammersmith, and the school would mock, pointing at her and calling out, ''ere comes the Queen of Sheba!'[1] Mary Hutchinson was intimately involved with Omega as a patron and a close associate of the Bloomsbury Group. She was stylish and fashionable. Appearing in Bloomsbury photographs with her lover, Clive Bell, her dress is often conspicuous as more elaborate or more *couture* than that of her friends. A Cubist dress designed and hand-painted or appliquéd by the Omega artists would have been striking, even in the artists' studios and salons that Bloomsbury frequented. On a weekday morning in the back streets of Hammersmith it was a provocation.

Understanding Bloomsbury's approach to dress and undress as an expression of its identity is complicated by issues of context, conformity, and social class. Their family backgrounds instilled in the Group's individual members a keen understanding of dress as a signifier of wealth, status, style, and a sliding scale of respectability. In their matriculation and art school photographs the Group's intellectuals and artists are inconspicuous. The colour and pattern of Vanessa Stephen's painting overall may have been a minor statement of individuality among her fellow students at the Royal Academy Schools in 1901, but she 'belongs' to her peer group (fig. 63). Bloomsbury adapted its dress to meet the demands of particular occasions. In private, however, it abandoned clothing altogether or experimented with the distinguishing features of other groups with which it felt an affinity, such as the Neo-Pagans, until it arrived at a distinctive code of references that it could call its own.

✤ ✤ ✤

---

63 Unknown photographer, Vanessa Stephen with her class at the Royal Academy Schools, *c*.1901. The Charleston Trust. Vanessa is at the far left of the front row, in a patterned smock

EXPERIMENTS IN DRESS AND UNDRESS

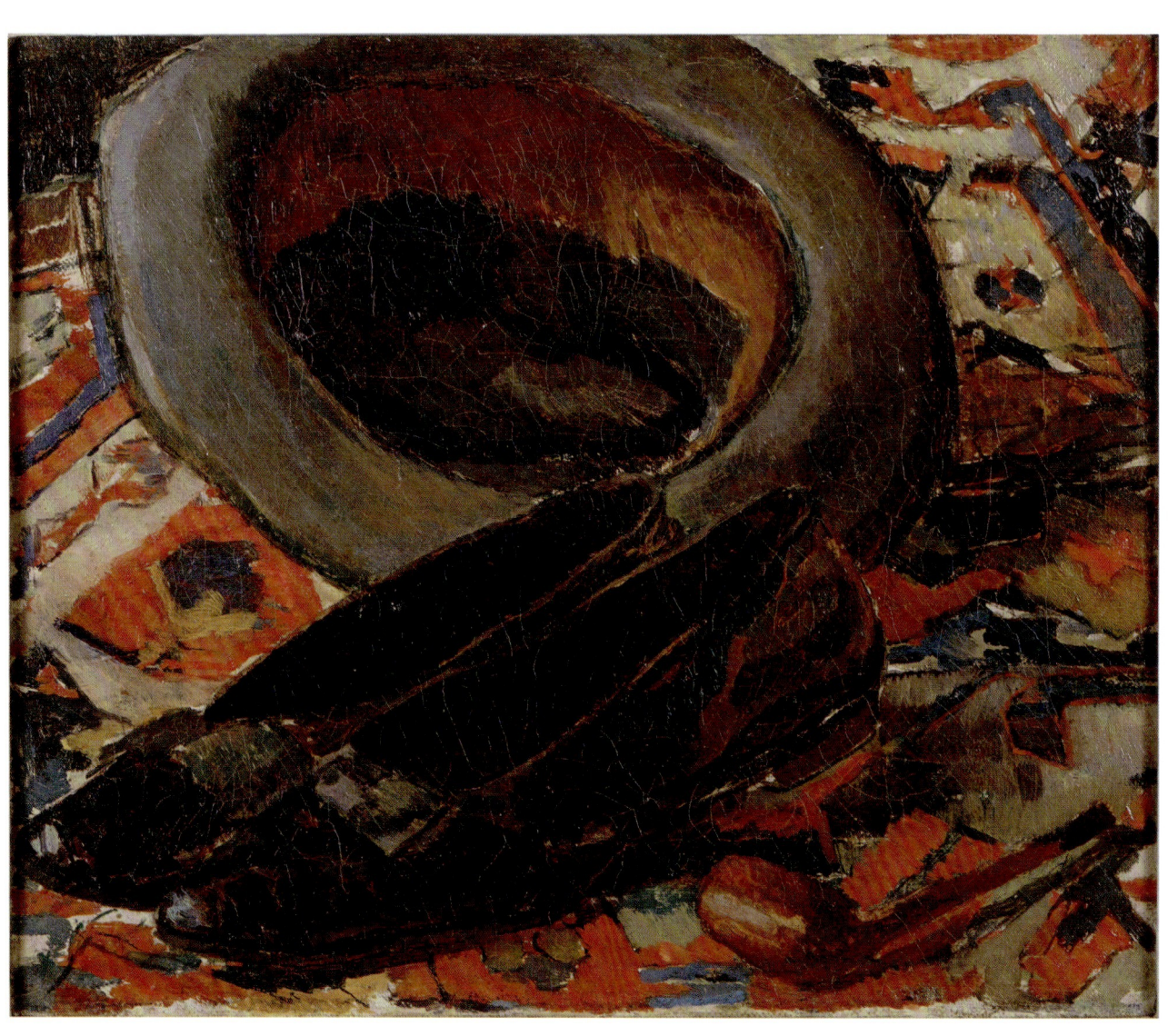

This chapter explores Bloomsbury's early experiments as a group with dress and undress. As an expression of identity, a means of standing out or fitting in, dress mattered to Bloomsbury. Vanessa and Virginia, as teenage girls, had been obliged to acquiesce to Victorian dress conventions in order to comply with George Duckworth's ambitions for them in society. Dress, for them, was aspirational but it was also a façade. Virginia recalled that:

> Vanessa in her white satin dress made by Mrs Young, wearing a single flawless amethyst round her neck, and a blue enamel butterfly in her hair . . . beautiful, motherless, aged only eighteen, was a touching spectacle, an ornament for any dinner table, a potential peeress, anything might be made of such precious material.[2]

At the same time, she wrote, her sister had a single desire, 'for paint and turpentine, for turpentine and paint'.[3] The dress that most aptly expressed Vanessa's sense of identity and potential at this time would have been her painting overall.

After Leslie Stephen's death and the move to Gordon Square, Vanessa and Virginia continued to dress with elaborate conformity. For Leonard Woolf, recalling his first encounter with them when they visited Thoby in Cambridge, their identity was inseparable from the starched white cotton and lace that announced their social class and eligibility as Edwardian young ladies: 'In white dresses and large hats, with parasols in their hands, their beauty literally took one's breath away.'[4] This description in the first volume of his autobiography is illustrated by the Beresford photographs. Memories and photographs informed one another. Leonard Woolf's autobiography also articulates an acute awareness of social and racial difference. He observes that the Stephens were deeply rooted in 'the upper levels of the professional middle class and county families'.[5] He notes the social connections of the Stephens, the Duckworths, and the Stracheys 'stretching far and wide', while he identified as an outsider. Although he and his parents, he writes,

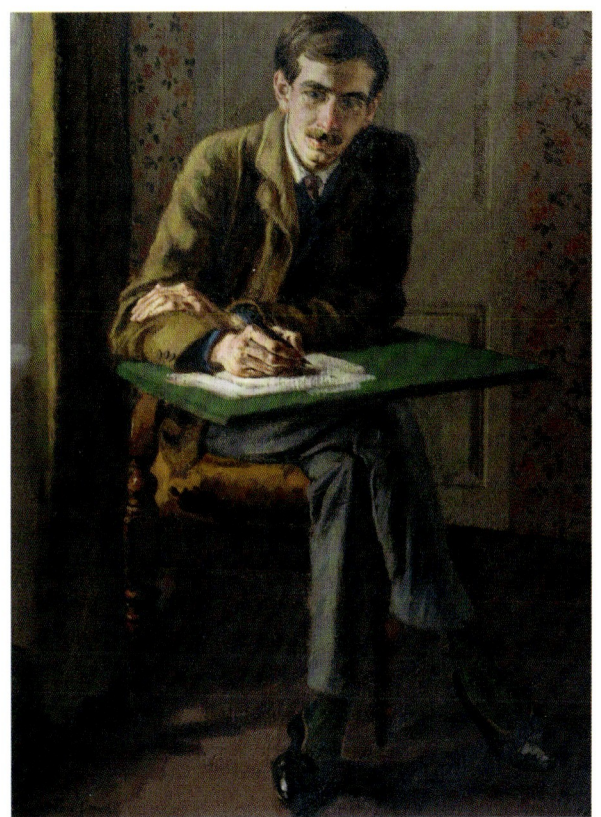

belonged to the professional middle class, 'we had only recently struggled up into it from the stratum of Jewish shopkeepers'.[6] Woolf never drew attention to himself through his dress.

A still life of Keynes's hat, pipe, and patent-leather opera pumps by Grant may be read as a commentary upon dress and social class (fig. 64). Opera slippers, with their elegant form and grosgrain bows, were the correct footwear for black tie. They were also worn with velvet or brocade smoking jackets by gentlemen entertaining at home in the early 1900s, and on more private occasions as slippers. Grant spent much of his youth in England staying with the Strachey family, where patent-leather pumps were routinely worn about the house. A portrait of his cousin James Strachey, reading, shows him wearing such slippers, one dangling idly from his toe.[7] The small study of Keynes's hat and shoes, painted early in their relationship, is an exercise in form and texture. Grant evidently enjoyed the reflective qualities of the pumps, placed in parallel with the stem of the pipe

---

64 (opposite) Duncan Grant, *John Maynard Keynes's Hat, Shoes and Pipe*, c.1908. Oil on canvas, 228 × 280 mm. Private collection

65 Duncan Grant, *John Maynard Keynes*, 1908. Oil on canvas, 800 × 595 mm. King's College, Cambridge

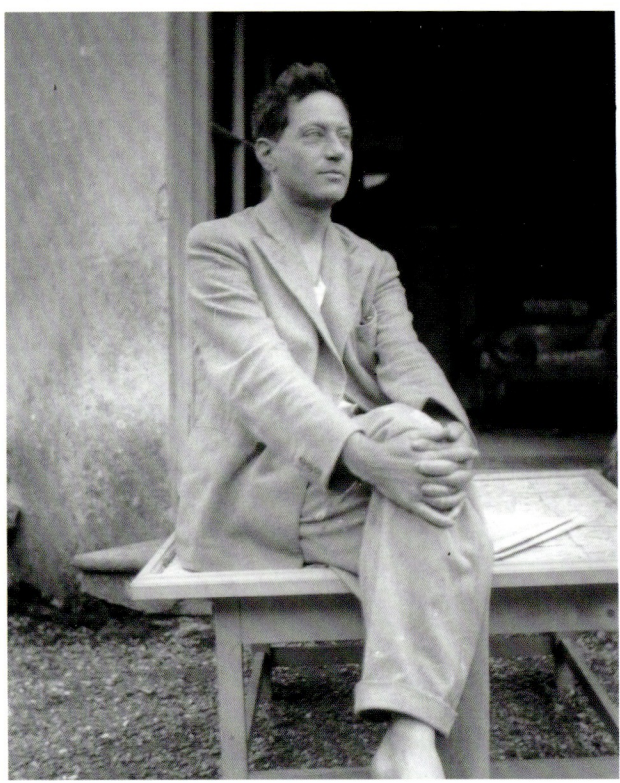 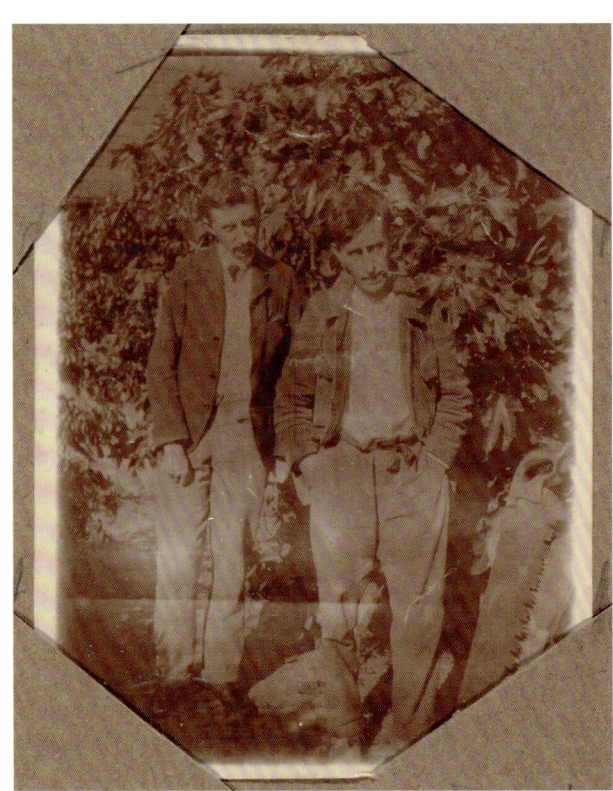

on the richly patterned oriental carpet. The challenge of grounding them next to the ellipses and the soft textures of the upturned hat is not entirely mastered. The heel of the right shoe appears to float. But the painting also suggests absence. The void of the hat's bowl and the worn shoes placed so precisely together imply an intimate relationship with their wearer and a fascination, perhaps, with these indicators of lifestyle and elite identity. Keynes was studying for a fellowship at King's College, Cambridge, when the two men first met in 1905. Grant painted him on a holiday that they shared on the island of Hoy in Orkney in September 1908 and here he is correctly dressed for the country in a tweed jacket, collar and tie, blue pullover, and grey flannel trousers (fig. 65). It is one of the earliest of many painted portraits of the Bloomsbury friends engrossed in their work. Keynes leans forward over a green writing board balanced across one knee and the arm of his chair, in his characteristic writing pose. His expression is absorbed in the process of revising his dissertation for the fellowship. Even indoors the jacket and jumper are necessary for warmth. Keynes wears his slippers, and the composition, tightly cropped around his figure, is enlivened by their highlights, drawing attention to the elongated elegance of his ankles.

Grant was ridiculed, in Bloomsbury memoirs, for his makeshift and erratic dress. Photographs of him in Sussex often show him without a tie, sometimes without socks, and in random jackets and trousers, where the men in his company dress with relative formality in country suits or sports jackets and flannels (fig. 66). It was considered improper, in the first half of the twentieth century, for a man to venture out in public without a tie. Grant was teased for wearing ties to hold up his borrowed trousers, but in photographs taken at Charleston and La Bergère (a house Bell rented in Cassis, France) he has often emerged from the studio and is dressed in old clothes for painting. Victorian etiquette manuals allowed that, in his own home and in the mornings, a man might 'wear out his old clothes', and Grant took this ruling to extremes.[8] Even Leonard Woolf, however, in a photograph taken at Monk's House with E. M. Forster, wears baggy

66 Unknown photographer, Duncan Grant outside the garden room at Charleston, c.1933. The Charleston Trust

67 Virginia Woolf, E. M. Forster (*left*) and Leonard Woolf (*right*) at Monk's House, c.1922. Houghton Library, Harvard University

trousers tied together (fig. 67).⁹ A large handsaw at his side affords an explanation: he is dressed for gardening.

Bloomsbury men generally adhered to Victorian and Edwardian etiquette guidelines that masculine dress should be appropriate to the occasion and that each article should be perfectly clean. A man should take care to present himself immaculately 'from the curl of your hair to the tip of your boot' at the moment of dressing, 'but as soon as you have left your mirror, forget your dress'.¹⁰ Any extravagance calling attention to a man's dress was considered the height of bad taste. Artists and writers, however, were to some extent special cases. Their creativity could be expressed, as George Beresford's portfolio demonstrates, in unruly beards, longer hair, and flamboyant ties. It was fashionable in the first decades of the twentieth century for men to be clean-shaven or to sport trim moustaches, and to wear their hair short with a side or centre parting. E. M. Forster exemplified this look. Lytton Strachey, by contrast, cultivated a long beard and an eccentric, almost Renaissance, hairstyle in defiance of the trend. His Bloomsbury friends supported this assertion of individuality. On at least one occasion Vanessa Bell trimmed his hair at Asheham while Duncan Grant, Clive Bell, and Roger Fry gathered round to watch; the event was considered worthy of a series of photographs (fig. 68).¹¹ She cut Grant's hair, too, writing to him in 1915, 'Has your hair grown to a decent length since I cut it so badly?'¹²

Women's hairstyles could signal their sexuality, social class, and modernity. Bell's letters describe the class consciousness with which she used her skills as an impromptu hairdresser to subvert boundaries. She wrote to Keynes from Sussex: 'This evening I cut the children's hair & then Mabel's too! She is now short-haired & more fit for the drawing room than ever – more fit for the bed room perhaps you'll think.' The exclamation mark highlights the irony of a 'mistress' cutting her servant's hair. Mabel Selwood was maid and governess in Bell's household and the progressive, cropped cut likened her to assertively independent young art students, such as Dora Carrington. 'Mabel', Bell wrote, 'will no doubt set the fashion for domestic

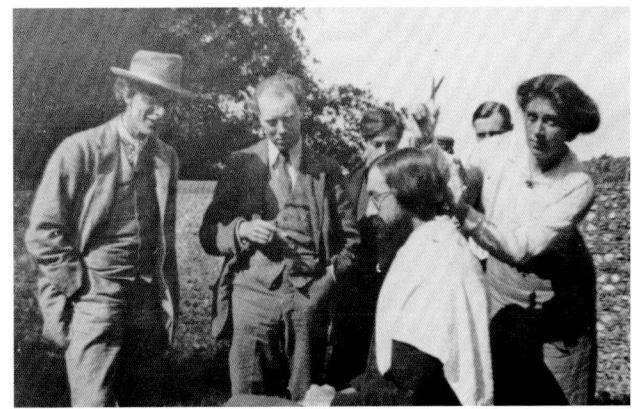

servants.'¹³ When Virginia Woolf had her hair shingled, nearly twelve years later, she wrote ironically in her diary that Clive Bell thought it 'the most important event in my life since marriage'.¹⁴ It signalled a turning point in her sexual and professional identity. Her novel *To the Lighthouse*, laying the ghosts of her parents to rest, was just completed, she had been offered a passage to New York to write for the *New York Herald Tribune*, and she was involved in an affair with the shingled Vita Sackville-West. She described the event as a seduction in a letter to Sackville-West:

> There's nothing I wouldn't do for you, dearest Honey. It's true, the other night, I did take a glass too much. . . . And then Bobo Mayor is a great seducer in her way. She has gipsy blood in her: she's rather violent and highly coloured, sinuous too, with a boneless body, and thin hands; all the things I like. So, being a little tipsy about twelve o'clock at night, I let her do it. She cut my hair off. I'm shingled.¹⁵

Woolf dramatizes the haircut as a sudden act of allegiance, a shift in image inseparable from her sexual interest in Sackville-West and the attractions of provocative women in their circle, such as the writer and dramatist Beatrice Mayor. 'It's off; its in the kitchen bucket: my hairpins have been offered up like crutches . . . at the high altar.' The 'Bobo shingle' had to be followed up with a visit to a professional hairdresser on

68 Unknown photographer, Vanessa Bell cutting Lytton Strachey's hair in the garden at Asheham with (*left to right*) Roger Fry, Clive Bell, Duncan Grant, and Saxon Sydney-Turner, 1913. National Portrait Gallery, London

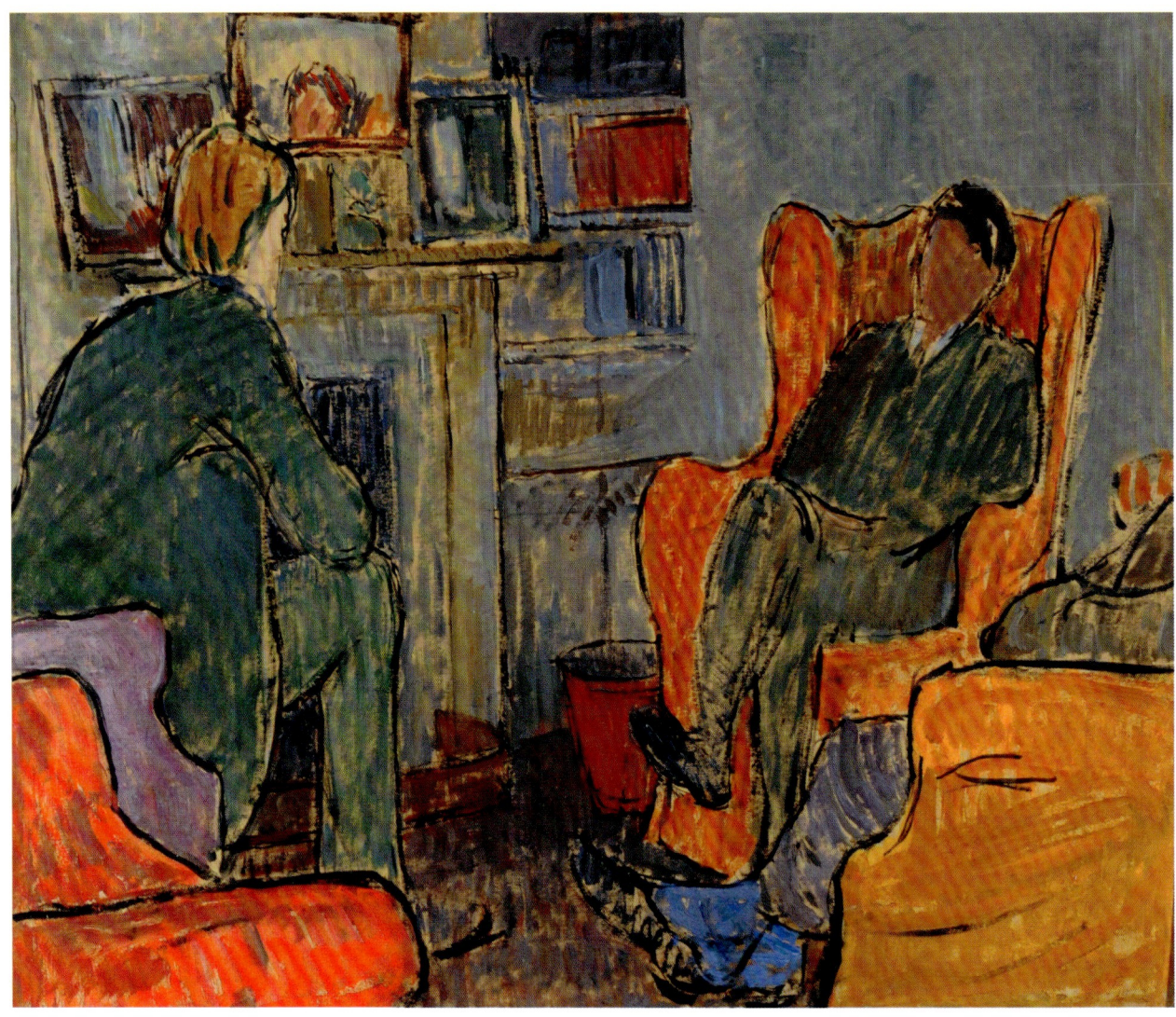

the Tottenham Court Road.[16] In her playful letter to Sackville-West, Woolf exaggerates her sister's 'wild fury': 'Vita's at the bottom of your shingling I know.'[17] But in her diary, and in Vanessa's letters to her, the practicalities rather than the sexual and political implications of short hair are articulated. Woolf regarded the haircut as a release from the 'claims to beauty. . . . Every morning I go to take up brush & twist that old coil round my finger & fix it with hairpins & then start with joy, no I needn't. . . . This robs dining out of half its terrors.'[18] Vanessa, not in the least furious, wrote to Virginia that Clive Bell thought her new haircut made her look young and neat: 'My hair has been coming down all the evening and I feel sorely tempted', she wrote. 'I have always thought neatness was the quality to aim at in middle age.'[19] Both sisters, however, were capable of duplicity in their letters. Bell wrote to Keynes that she was not quite reconciled to Woolf's shingled head, that when she had 'threatened to be done' Angelica had cried and Grant had said he would disown her. She urged him: 'Don't let Lydia be done.' (Keynes had married the ballerina Lydia Lopokova in 1925.)[20] Woolf, on the other hand, flirted and flattered Sackville-West with the qualities and sexual overtones she associated with their shared appearance: 'Darling Honey, if anything could make me say Vita's a villain it is that you didn't tell me, you'll be happier, wiser, serener,

69 Vanessa Bell, *Conversation Piece*, 1912. Oil on board, 675 × 800 mm. University of Hull Art Collection

cleverer a thousand times shingled than haired.'²¹ Her letter concludes: 'You shall ruffle my hair in May, Honey: its as short as a partridges rump.'

Even small departures from normative dress codes and hairstyles would have been glaring in their day. A century on, however, they are often inconspicuous. Strachey's hair and beard were strikingly unconventional. Clive Bell's hair, too, was at times allowed to curl over his ears and the back of his collar. Among conservative men this was still considered effeminate and unkempt even into the 1950s. A photograph of Clive in Vanessa's album from the early years of their marriage shows him with longer hair, a coloured shirt, and an artistic tie, trying out his image as a critic and connoisseur of contemporary art; his hair, although thinning a little, waves and curls in a drawing by Henry Lamb from about the same time.²² Clive's socks, too, were a challenge to propriety. They are almost the only part of him represented in Vanessa Bell's ambitious painting *Conversation Piece*, and they are a brilliant blue (fig. 69). The Strachey and Bell families both had substantial country houses and Clive made an outward display of his credentials as a country gentleman. Thoby described him as 'a sort of mixture between Shelley and a sporting country squire'.²³ He was proud of having possessed a game-licence from the age of 16 'and walked with the guns since I was a child'.²⁴ At Charleston he identified with the local gentry, regularly wearing plus fours to go out shooting. Strachey, more inclined to walk in the country than to shoot, cut a romantic, ambiguous figure and this reflects, in part, the very different ways in which the two men wished to engage with locals. Bell did not want to be mistaken for a poacher, while Strachey fantasized about intimate encounters with young postmen and blacksmiths' boys.²⁵ These public identities were transient, however, and easily adapted to circumstances with a haircut and a change of clothes. Even in its early years, beards were trimmed, hair was oiled into place, and Bloomsbury 'dressed up' for Lady Ottoline Morrell's gatherings at Garsington Manor, Oxfordshire, and this is documented in her photograph albums.

✼ ✼ ✼

Nudity was an important factor in Bloomsbury's sense of itself as an 'in-group', intimately bound together, and its radicalized culture of sexual ethics. Nevertheless, the Group self-censored nudity out of many of the texts and images that record its evolution. Christopher Reed has analysed the culture surrounding homosexuality at the University of Cambridge during Bloomsbury's embryonic years there and the currency of nude male photographs.²⁶ He describes the association of homoerotic desires with allusions to a classicized golden age and the circulation of pictures by the German photographer Wilhelm von Gloeden of nude Sicilian boys outdoors in their native landscape.²⁷ Reed speculates that Grant may have used these photographs as an alternative to the expense of hiring models. He posed in his studio for photographs that may also have had this dual purpose of artistic reference and homoerotica, and Keynes photographed him naked.²⁸ On holiday together in

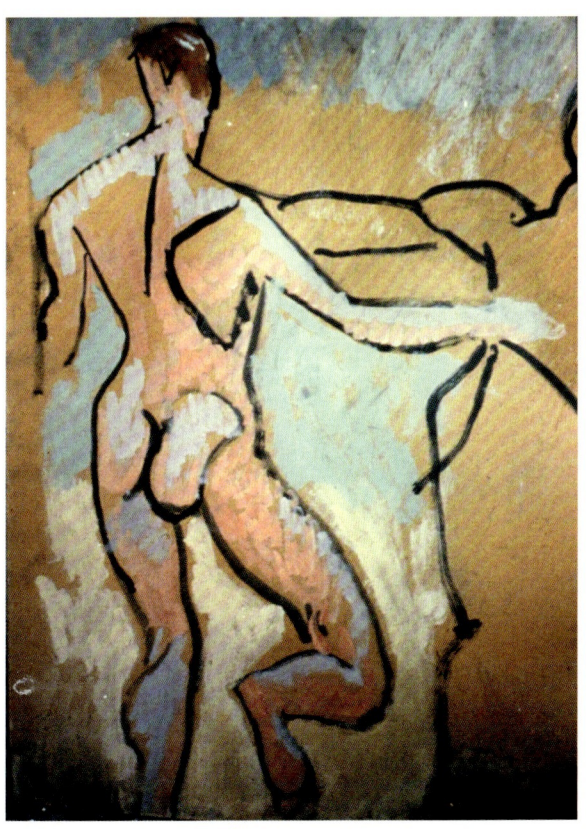

70 Duncan Grant, study for mural in Keynes's rooms at King's College, Cambridge, 1910. Medium and dimensions unknown. Private collection

EXPERIMENTS IN DRESS AND UNDRESS 65

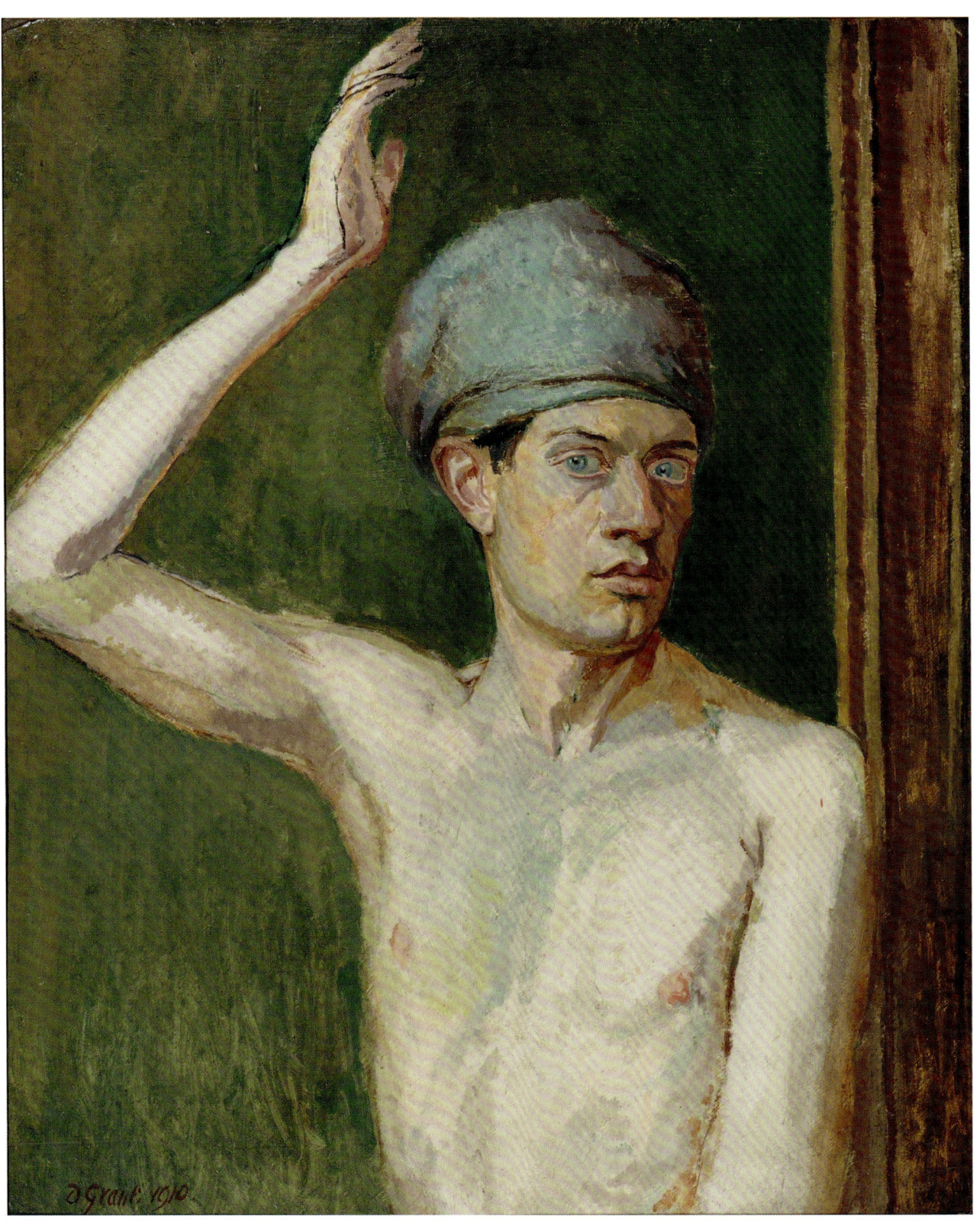

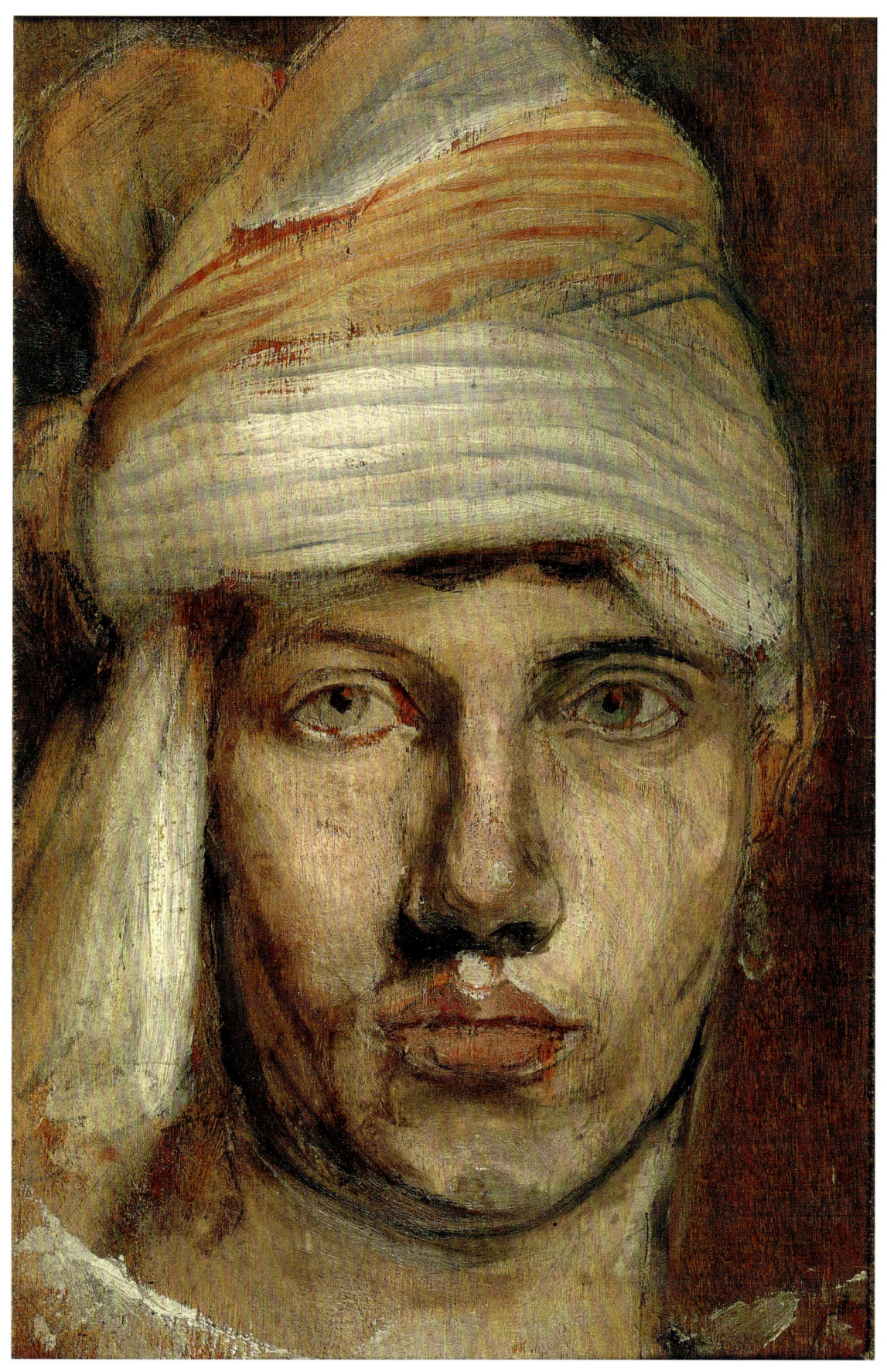

Greece in March 1910, Keynes and Grant likened their remote, rural setting to that of Arcadia. On their return, Keynes wrote to Grant, 'I developed Apollo in his temple at Bassae yesterday and printed him to-day. He is *lovely* . . . It will be quite unnecessary to take in the *Sportszeitung* anymore.'[29] Grant agreed that Keynes might share these images of him in classical guise with selected friends in Cambridge, provided that his anonymity was preserved: 'you must say that it was a shepherd or something and that no-one wears clothes in Arcadia'.[30] Keynes was apparently keen to photograph his friends naked in the English countryside, too. A few months later, before Grant joined him at a house he had rented for the summer in Burford, he teased him: 'when I'm at Burford everyone who stays with me will be forced to have their photographs taken naked'.[31]

Surviving photographs of Bloomsbury and its friends posing in the artists' studios, naked in the South Downs, and in the gardens of its rural retreats indicate that nude photographs were exchanged as tokens of intimacy within sexual relationships but that nudity was also integral to the sexual candour and the alternative values that Bloomsbury advanced. Grant painted a mural in Keynes's rooms at King's College, Cambridge, in 1910 exploring the boundaries between Arcadian ideals, homoerotica, and the avant-garde (fig. 70).[32] His forthright representation of nearly life-sized naked male dancers painted onto the walls of Keynes's living room referenced Matisse, but they also championed the intellectual modernism and the progressive values at Cambridge. Grant explored his own individual identity, unclothed, in *Self-Portrait in a Turban*, which he painted at around the same time (fig. 71). Again, the painting draws on a shared repository of cultural references: Bloomsbury's identification with colonialism. Grant's naked torso and arms are unidealized in this portrait and his expression is searching. In the painting's first iteration his raised hand supported a basket, overlaying his own identity onto a series of his other paintings: *The Lemon Gatherers*, *Two Nudes on a Beach*, and the Keynes mural, which all featured male or female canephoroe (figures bearing baskets on their heads).[33] Grant over-painted the basket, exchanging it for a turban, and in doing so he revised the frame of references. A turban had been part of his recent disguise for the *Dreadnought* hoax. It also identified him with the colonial family backgrounds that he shared with other members of the Group. In this self-portrait, however, and in a second, smaller *Self-Portrait in a Turban*, Grant's interpretation of his colonial past is transgressive (fig. 72). The two paintings articulate a sexual availability. They appropriate the visual language of 'oriental' photographs and paintings of women and boys, eroticized as 'other'. In doing so, Grant usurps racial and gender stereotypes to challenge the canon of Western, male self-portraiture.

Vanessa Bell's disregard for inhibitions was also initially tested within the safe confines of the Group's private spaces and encounters. After giving birth to Julian Bell in 1908, when it was customary for new mothers to be confined to bed for a month, she and Clive entertained in their bedroom.[34] Keynes was among their visitors, and Quentin later recalled that his mother's disdain for Edwardian decorum extended, within a few years, to Keynes sitting in the bathroom at 46 Gordon Square and chatting with her while she was in the bath. For Bell, personal and artistic freedoms from convention were interwoven. In 1911 she embarked on an affair with Roger Fry. Exploring her own audacity, she wrote to him describing an unorthodox sequence of events that, she proposed, had set 'a useful precedent' within the Group. It is a teasing account of the transition from a respectable 'tea' with Grant at 46 Gordon Square to 'inventing a new art' together, decorating boxes with 'a most beautiful lacquer of different colours and painted with figures'.[35] Grant then asked Bell to sit for him. In her letter to Fry she suggested that he might paint her at the same time:

> And then – what do you think happened? I had my bath in his presence! You see he wanted to shave and I wanted to have my bath (he stayed to dinner) and he didn't see why he should move and I didn't see why I should remain dirty, and Clive was there and didn't object – and so!

---

71 (p. 66) Duncan Grant, *Study for Composition (Self-Portrait in a Turban)*, 1910. Oil on board, 760 × 635 mm. Private collection

72 (p. 67) Duncan Grant, *Self-Portrait in a Turban*, c.1909–10. Oil on panel, 420 × 270 mm. The Charleston Trust

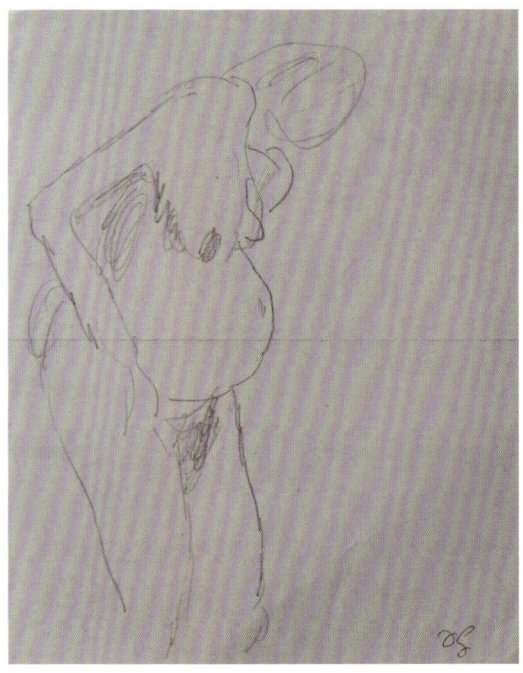 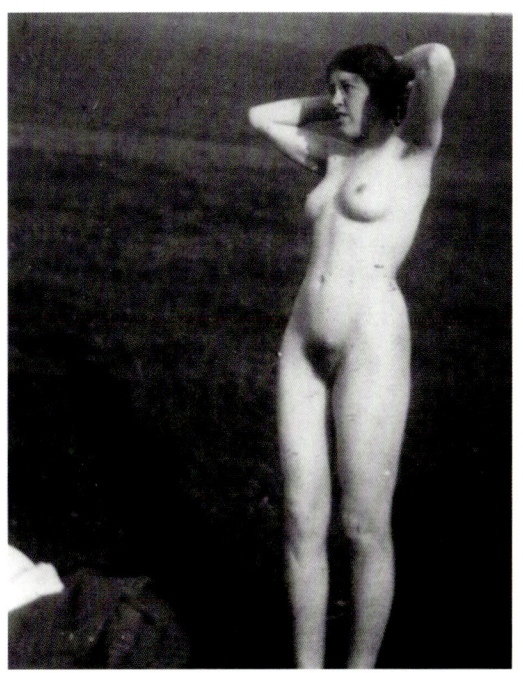

The letter is intended to sharpen Fry's sexual interest: 'Roger – aren't you jealous[?]' But it also asserts Bell's agency and her modernity as a woman and an artist, challenging restrictive boundaries of conventional behaviour. Bell did pose for Grant, clothed and in the nude. He would later make a series of drawings of her pregnant with their daughter, Angelica, that express the most intimate contract between the two artists and their subversive transgression of heteronormative family infrastructures (fig. 73).

Bell and Grant were opportunistic about using their friends as models, but Bloomsbury was also closely connected to the Neo-Pagans and shared their interest in naturism. Their Neo-Pagan friend Ka Cox, for example, posed nude for Bell in the Sussex landscape, and Bell incorporated a sketch of her into a letter to Grant from Asheham: 'Ka got naked on the downs & I took some photographs of her. She is very fine naked. Not so fat as one would expect, and with very good legs . . . I think we might get her to sit naked pretty easily' (fig. 74).[36] Bell complained to her sister that, at the Hutchinsons' new Sussex retreat at West Wittering, Eleanor House, 'The garden is on the road, so all that goes on in it must be irreproachably respectable – no posing naked as at Asheham' (fig. 75).[37] Soon after her sister moved to Charleston, Woolf wrote that 'Nessa seems to have slipped civilization off her back, and splashes about entirely nude, without shame, and enormous spirit'.[38] Clive, she wrote, 'now takes up the line that she has ceased to be a presentable lady'.[39] At Garsington, photographs by Ottoline Morrell of Dora Carrington climbing one of the garden statues suggest a playful flaunting of nudity as symptomatic

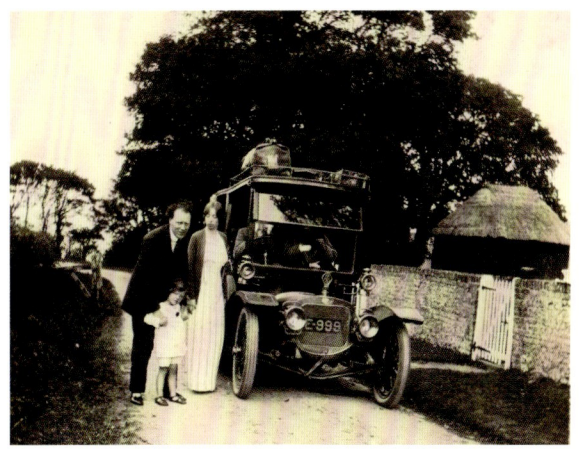

73 Duncan Grant, sketch of Vanessa Bell when pregnant, 1918. Pencil on paper, 450 × 390 mm. The Charleston Trust

74 (*top*) Vanessa Bell, Ka Cox nude on the South Downs, c.1913. The Charleston Trust

75 (*bottom*) Vanessa Bell, Clive Bell and Mary Hutchinson outside Eleanor House in West Wittering, c.1915. The Charleston Trust

EXPERIMENTS IN DRESS AND UNDRESS

of the disregard for social conventions that Morrell encouraged in her artist guests.[40] Through to the 1960s and 1970s Lydia Lopokova was to be found naked among the raspberry canes at Tilton (the Keyneses' home across the fields from Charleston), and Duncan Grant sunbathed naked, even in his eighties, in Charleston's Folly Garden.[41]

As artists, Bell and Grant were engaged in modernist revisions of the pastoral and the nude. Post-Impressionist paintings by Manet, Degas, Cézanne, Picasso, and Matisse were in their minds' eye as they framed their own responses to these classic art historical themes. Their work as artists legitimized nudity among their family and friends, and their photographs, drawings, and paintings describe an interface between art and life. Humm has analysed the fusion of maternal devotion, art historical referencing, and erotic pleasure in Bell's photographs of her sons, Quentin and Julian, at Asheham.[42] In a letter to Grant, Bell used the image of naked boys as an enticement:

> I'm very sorry you cant come today . . . As it is a divine day here & the quiet most conducive to work . . . It is so hot & delicious here that I have been photographing the children naked. They loved being naked & jumped about in delight. Julian has a great idea of posing & placed himself in what he considered to be good poses. Of course Quentin is simply an Old Master.[43]

The letter locates photographs by Bell of her sons, such as one back view of Julian leaning, arms and legs outstretched, into the closed French windows at Asheham, within her complex relationship with Grant.[44] Modern sensibilities find the erotic connotations of these images troubling, but both Bell and Woolf thought them innocent enough for display in their albums.

Bell and Grant used photographs as inspiration and aids for their paintings. Vanessa Bell, Molly MacCarthy, and Marjorie Strachey (Lytton Strachey's sister) posed for the camera in the studio at 46 Gordon Square. The unidealized reality of their naked bodies is juxtaposed against a monumental painting by Bell, immediately behind them, of two nude bathers (figs 76–80).[45] Assuming that Bell is the photographer, this series of images self-constructs a layered identity of artist, sitter, and activist. Life drawing was still a contested subject when Bell began her studies at the Royal Academy Schools in 1901. Women had won their campaign for equality to study from the nude there less than a decade earlier. Some semblance of the academic respectability of nineteenth-century paintings of a 'Venus' or 'Diana' is assumed in the pose that Bell and MacCarthy adopt together, but the photograph shows their clothing and underwear discarded at their feet (see fig. 79). Strachey and MacCarthy adopt unabashedly contemporary positions. Strachey surveys the camera wearing only her glasses, with a hand resting on her ribcage. She and MacCarthy stretch to the floor or up towards the ceiling in energetic poses that reference Mikhail Fokine's choreography for the Ballets Russes. The photographs are playful, but they describe an anarchic exploration into the ways in which women might requisition modernity in representations of the female form.

The Ballets Russes became a touchstone for Bloomsbury's sense of identity as a group. Founded in Paris by Sergei Diaghilev in 1909, it took London by storm with its first season at Covent Garden in 1911. Eight years later, when Picasso came to London with *El sombrero de tres picos*, for which he had designed the sets and costumes, he was taken to the Omega Workshops, and Clive Bell and Maynard Keynes hosted a supper for him at 46 Gordon Square. Keynes married the Ballets Russes dancer Lydia Lopokova in 1925, and the Group's letters describe their shared enthusiasm for the composers and designers who worked with Diaghilev. In Paris, Clive delighted in reading aloud a letter from Vanessa declaring *Parade* the best production she had ever seen to the assembled company of Picasso, Erik Satie, and Jean Cocteau.[46] Grant's collection of photographs included a rare gelatin silver print by Eugène Druet of Vaslav Nijinsky from *Les orientales*, and

---

(*opposite, clockwise from top left*) 76 Marjorie Strachey standing nude in Vanessa Bell's studio, c.1914; 77 Molly MacCarthy posing nude in the studio, c.1914; 78 Marjorie Strachey posing nude and reaching upwards in the studio, c.1914; 79 Vanessa Bell and Molly MacCarthy posing nude in the studio; 80 Marjorie Strachey posing nude and holding up a vase in the studio, c.1914. Photographs by Vanessa Bell. The Charleston Trust

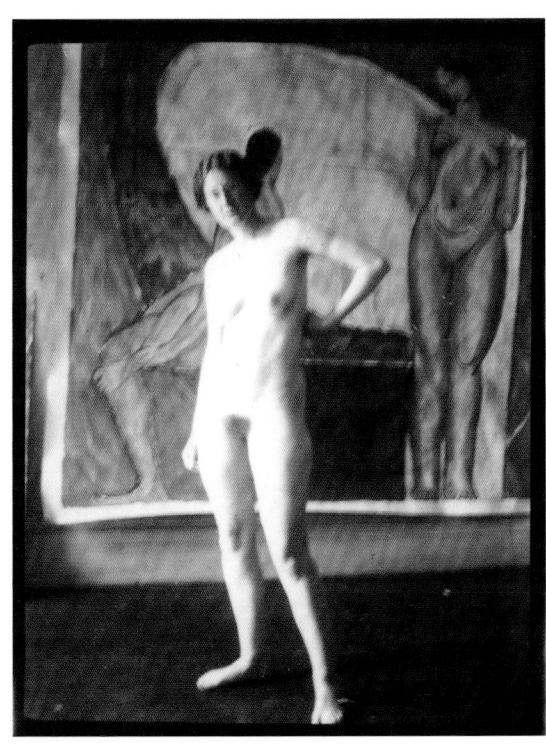
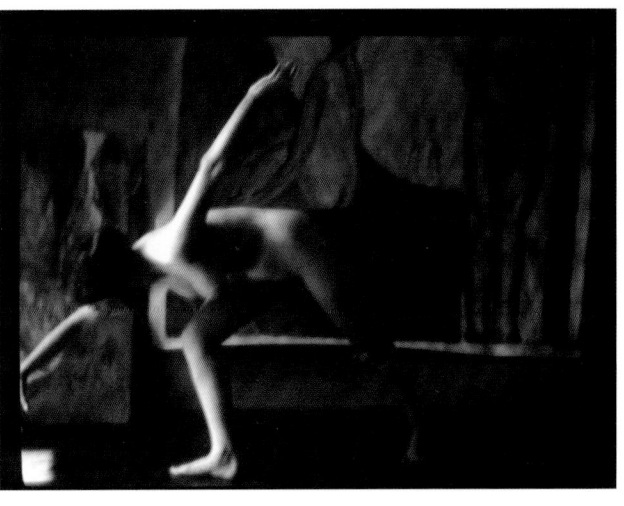
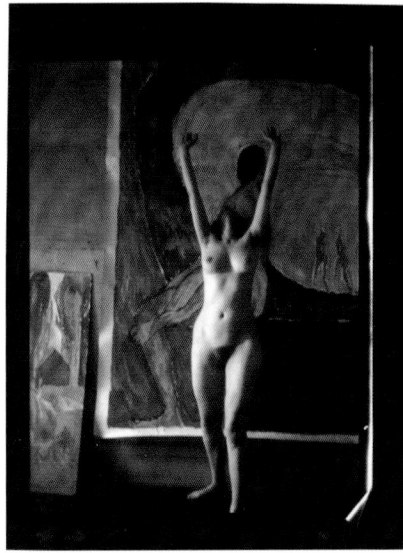
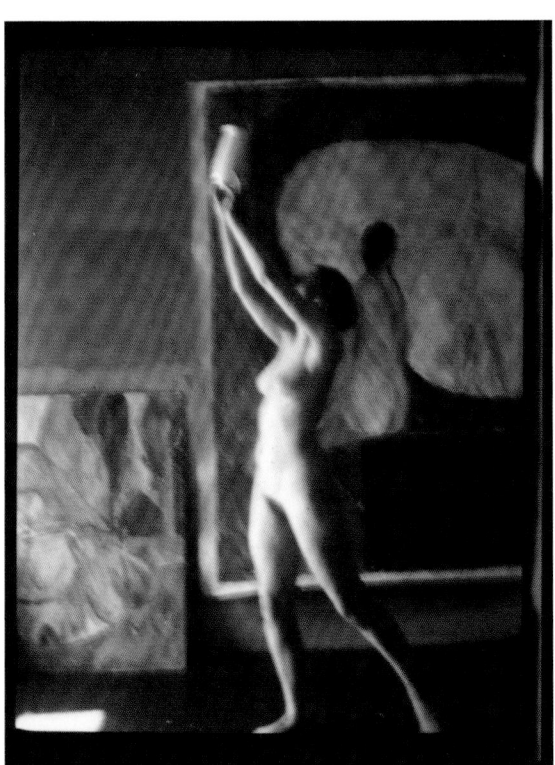
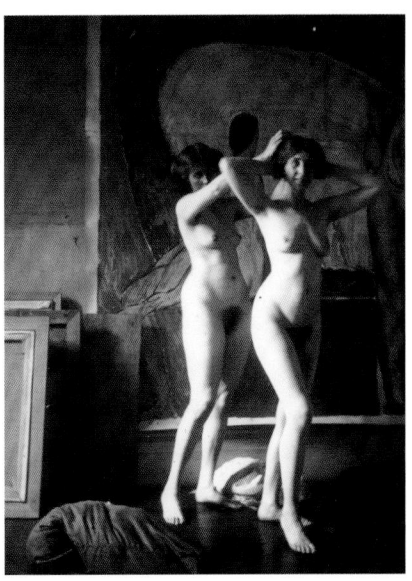

EXPERIMENTS IN DRESS AND UNDRESS 71

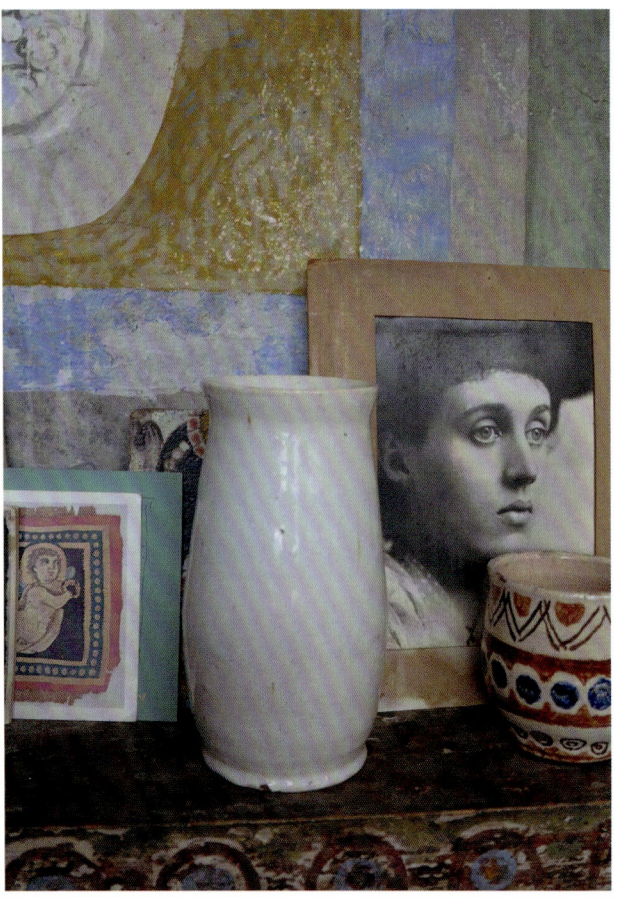

he met Nijinsky on several occasions at the home of Ottoline Morrell in Bedford Square.[47] Reputedly, the costumes and set designs for *Jeux* were inspired by the sight of Grant playing tennis there in 1912, observed by Léon Bakst and Nijinsky.[48] Grant, in turn, produced a *Tennis Player* design for the Omega Workshops after seeing this ballet in 1913.[49] This synchronicity between photographs, progressive performance, and design is reiterated in Bell's photographs of herself, Strachey, and MacCarthy. Although amateur snapshots, slightly out of focus and with feet sometimes cropped out of the frame, they reference Druet's ability to record 'stills' of a dancer in motion. The series conveys the movement of Strachey and MacCarthy's dance and relates directly to the Omega Workshops and its Post-Impressionist designs. Figures in a design for a folding screen, *Adam and Eve*, produced by Bell for the Workshops, correspond to the angular poses, and in particular to Bell's photograph of MacCarthy with one arm twisted upwards behind her while reaching down towards the floor (see fig. 77).[50] Wittily, Strachey holds an Omega Workshops vase aloft in another of Bell's photographs (see fig. 80), perhaps emulating Mikhail Fokine's choreography for *Le spectre de la rose* in which Nijinsky personified the spirit of a rose given to a young girl. The vase (fig. 81), substituted for a rose in Strachey's hands, dates Bell's photographs. They are likely to have been taken soon after Fry began to produce pottery for the Workshops in 1913. The vase also features in the first portrait that Grant painted of Bell after they moved to Charleston in 1916.[51]

In the background to the Bell and MacCarthy photograph and to nude photographs of MacCarthy with her hair down, canvases are stacked up facing the wall (see fig. 79).[52] In the Strachey and MacCarthy photographs, a painted landscape at Asheham faces outwards (see figs 77, 78, and 80). There were, perhaps, two separate sittings. But in all of the photographs, Bell and her subjects invite comparisons with the larger-than-life painted nudes in the vast canvas pinned to the studio wall behind them. These massive, distorted figures position Bell in the vanguard of artists engaged in reimagining the female nude for the twentieth century. The painting, now lost, relates to a study by Bell, squared up and previously thought to have been for a decorative design – a fireplace mural.[53] Reed has noted that one of the voluptuous figures appears to sit casually on the actual fire surround.[54] The photographs show the painting to have been on canvas with unpainted borders at the base and sides, however, ready to be stretched onto a frame. The dark painted rectangle within the composition is unlikely to have been cut out for a fireplace. It was designed not as a decoration but as an ambitious painting. A succession of tilted, painted ovals or egg shapes binds the composition together, framing a standing and a seated nude without containing them. The form relates to another monumental painting by Bell, *The Tub* (see fig. 135) for which Clive Bell's mistress, Mary Hutchinson, modelled, but in this instance the intersecting ovals are more likely to represent a dew pond. These were artificial pools, still being made in the Sussex Downs using an ancient technique

81 Roger Fry, Omega vase, c.1913. Tin-glazed ceramic, 205 × 95 mm. The Charleston Trust

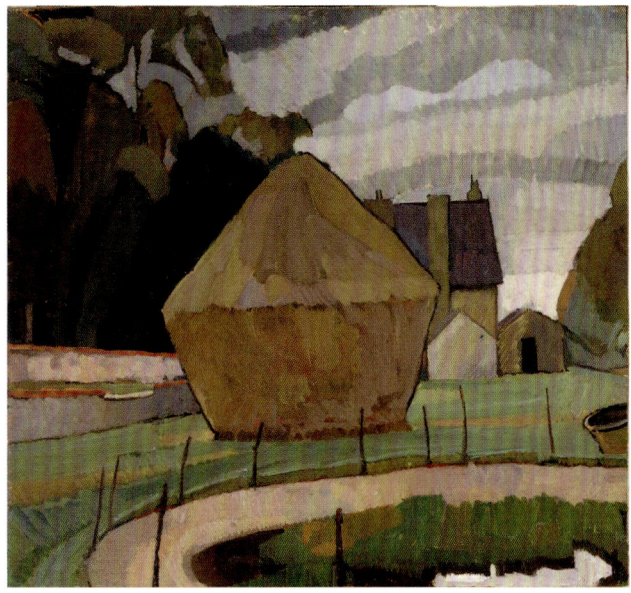
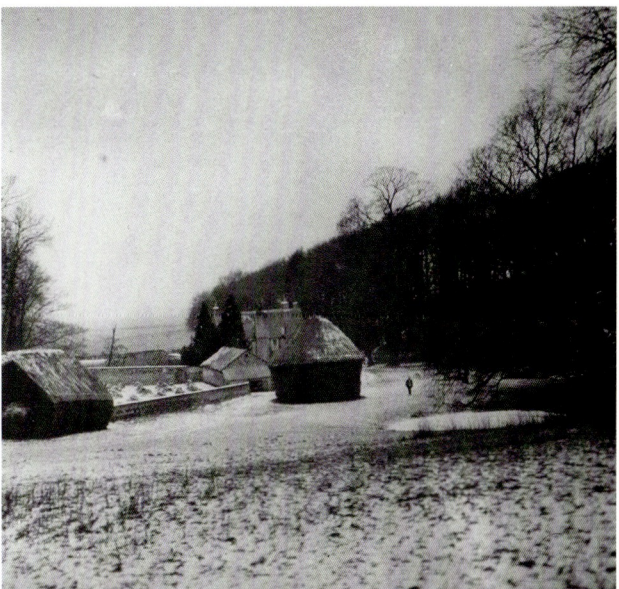

to grind and puddle chalk linings until they set as hard as cement to contain rain water and dew.[55] Bell painted the curve of the dew pond at Asheham in the foreground to her *Landscape with Haystack, Asheham* in 1912, and later there was a dew pond in the grounds to Monk's House (figs 82 and 83).

Nudity at Asheham, naturalized within the Sussex countryside, was not unusual during Bloomsbury gatherings there. Oliver Strachey was photographed naked next to his bed on one visit, and Grant stripped off on the South Downs in a series of photographs that bear witness to his intimacy with Bell (fig. 84).[56] In her painting pinned to the wall of the Gordon Square studio, the standing nude is positioned in the extreme foreground, facing the viewer, while the seated figure has turned her back and looks towards the pool behind her. Two disproportionately small figures at the pool's edge appear to dance. Their stylized forms are reminiscent of work by Matisse and of nudes in Omega Workshops designs. Within Bell's London studio this painting of women and their stylized forms has the solemnity and grandeur of an alternative Arcadia. It suggests fecundity. As Asheham was leased to Virginia and she spent the first night of her married life there with Leonard in 1912, the painting's subject may have related to Bell's changing relationship with her sister. Together with Bell's landscape paintings of Asheham it describes the potency of this rural retreat as a creative source, and its currency in Bell's imagination – the visual equivalent of Woolf's intertextuality between past and present, between town and country – within the urban setting of Bell's Gordon Square studio.

Bell's photographs of her Bloomsbury family and friends, naked and clothed, document an integral

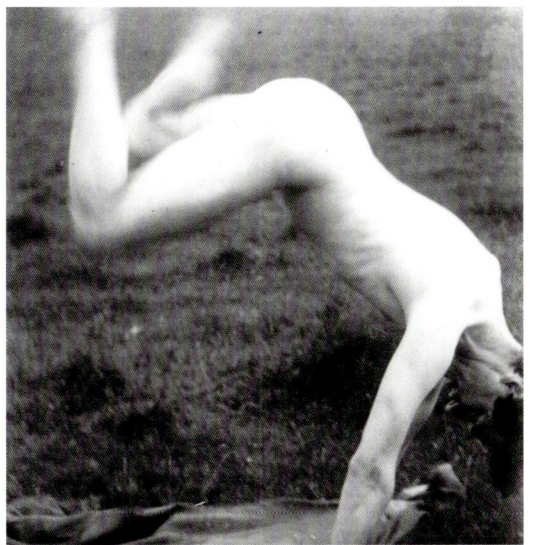

82 (*top left*) Vanessa Bell, *Landscape with Haystack, Asheham*, 1912. Oil on board, 603 × 657 mm. Smith College Museum of Art, Northampton, MA
83 (*top right*) Vanessa Bell, dew pond and haystack at Asheham (detail), undated. The Charleston Trust

84 (*bottom left*) Vanessa Bell, Duncan Grant attempting a handstand on the South Downs (detail), near Asheham, *c.*1913–14. The Charleston Trust

EXPERIMENTS IN DRESS AND UNDRESS

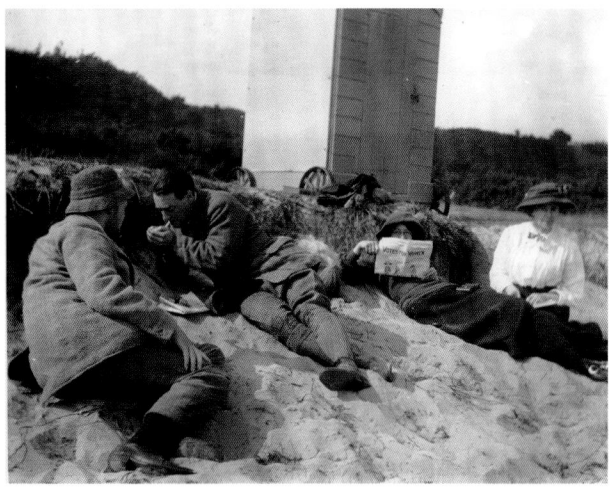

relationship between her lived experience as a free-thinking, twentieth-century woman, and her incursions into modernism through painting and the decorative arts. Her snapshots with MacCarthy and Strachey naked in the studio offer insights into a collegiality, perhaps what we might think of today as a feminist solidarity, among the women in the Group, and a commitment to modernism that could be made manifest in many forms. The audacity of posing naked for these private images is contextualized by the modesty of the women's dress in the more public-facing album pages. Even on the beach at Studland, for example, Marjorie Strachey, holding up her paper with its headline, 'Votes for Women', exposes only her hands and part of her face to the elements (fig. 85).[57]

✿ ✿ ✿

Bloomsbury's early experiments with dress describe catholic interests in mainstream fashion, Bohemian latitude, and the capacity of dress to signal alternative values. Bell evidently took pleasure in clothes, while for Woolf, as Lisa Cohen has described, fashion and dress could be enjoyed but were also complex investments in artifice and self-expression that provoked anxiety and required analysis.[58]

There is a clear trajectory in both sisters' dress from the conventional and relatively elaborate lace collars and cuffs in photographs taken at Studland Beach in 1910, to the more practical, simple dresses, skirts, and jackets in photographs taken at Asheham in 1912.[59] Bell wrote to Fry in June 1912, unsure that he would approve of a new coat: 'I have got myself a new coat, a long blue cloth one for everyday wear, with a large white triangle in front.'[60] It is likely to have been one of the fitted, full-length over-garments that were fashionable that summer. She painted it in a self-portrait, and it may also be the garment that Fry painted her asleep in, layered with a different collar, a blue-grey dress or skirt, and green stockings (fig. 86).[61] A white 'V' painted on the sole of her elegant black shoe affectionately references her name. Bell's sexual relationship with Fry coincided with a period of intense creative innovation during which her own personal experiments with dress and appearance became increasingly distinctive. In one of her most sensuous photographs, taken either as a self-portrait or by Fry at his home, Durbins, in 1911, she abandons her passive mode as a model to gaze directly at the camera with lips slightly parted (fig. 87).[62] Her fashionable summer hat and fine cotton-and-lace dress are combined with the first trappings of the style that she was to develop – a crumpled shawl is draped around her shoulders and beads are wound haphazardly and repeatedly around her neck. Undoubtedly there were clothes for London, aligned to current trends, and there were other clothes that signalled increasingly experimental approaches to dress and the fashioning of alternative identities. Bell experimented with the Edwardian fashion for masculine ties worn with blouses and skirts. A photograph shows her exploring this assertive image of the working woman at Durbins. The look is idiosyncratically completed with a headscarf, loosely tied at the nape of the neck (fig. 88).[63]

Headscarves, and dresses that reduced the need for restrictive underwear, were associated in the Edwardian consciousness with artistic freedom but

85 (*above*) Vanessa Bell, (*left to right*) Clive Bell, Desmond MacCarthy, Marjorie Strachey, and Molly MacCarthy on the beach at Studland, 1910. The Charleston Trust
86 (*opposite, top left*) Roger Fry, *Portrait of Vanessa Bell*, c.1912. Oil and pastel on paper, 196 × 250 mm. Private collection
87 (*opposite, top right*) Attributed to Roger Fry, Vanessa Bell at Durbins, Guildford, 1911. The Charleston Trust
88 (*opposite, bottom right*) Unknown photographer, Vanessa Bell by the pond at Durbins, Guildford, 1914. The Charleston Trust
89 (*opposite, bottom left*) Augustus John, *Dorelia*, 1909. Graphite and watercolour on paper, 445 × 368 mm. Tate, London

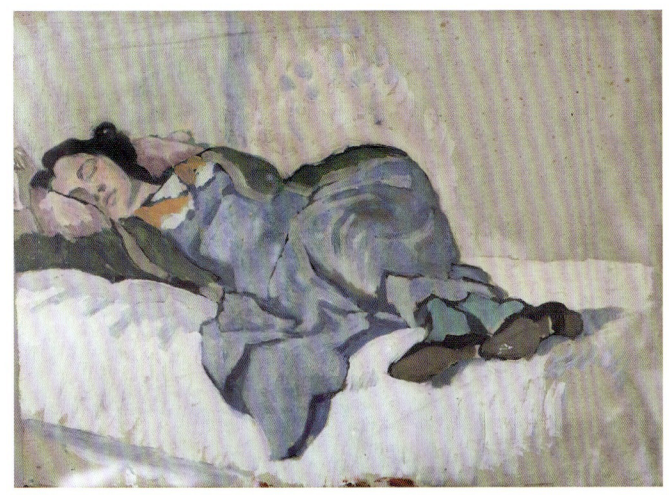
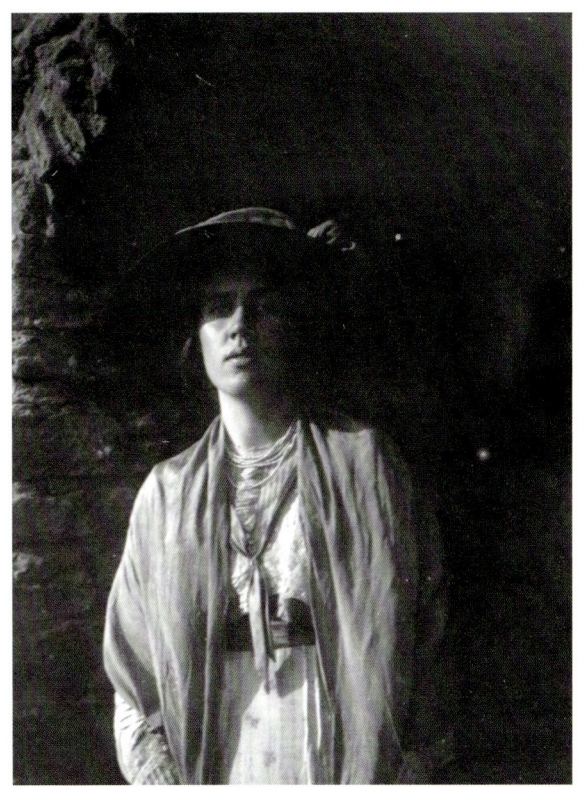
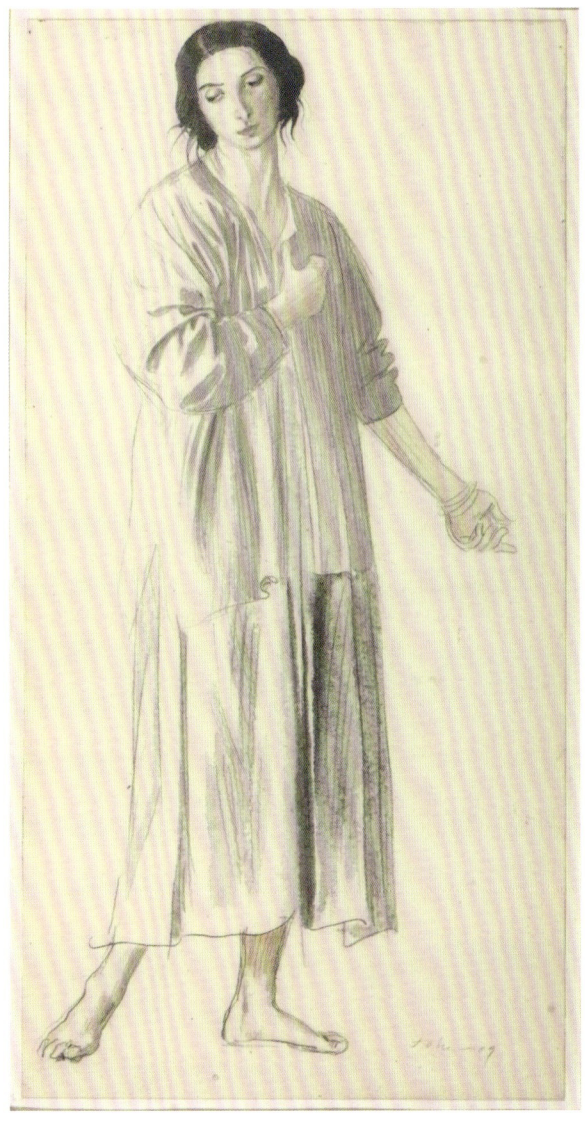
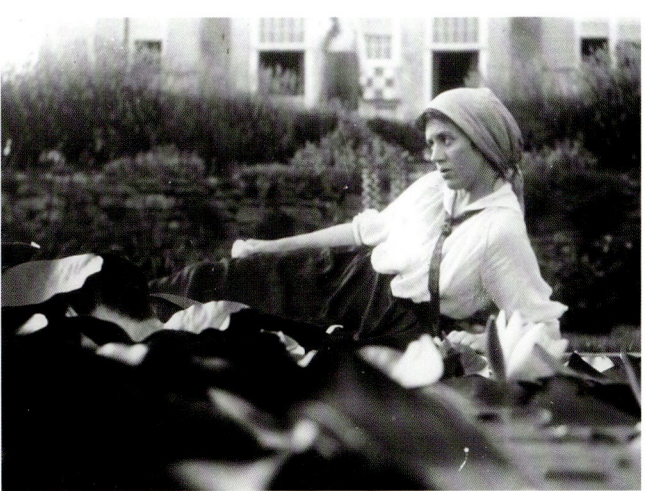

EXPERIMENTS IN DRESS AND UNDRESS

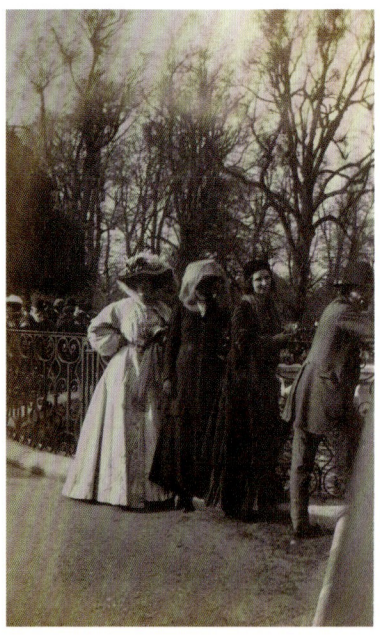 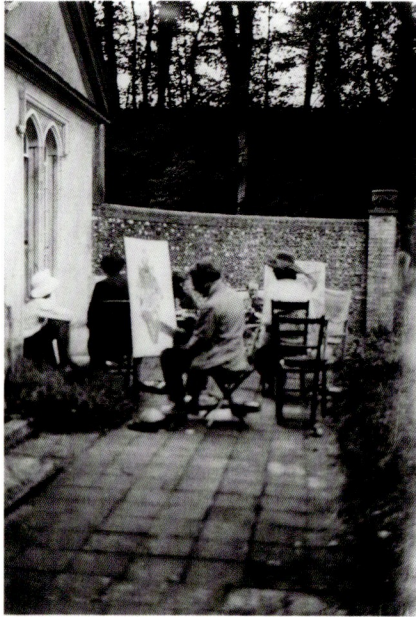 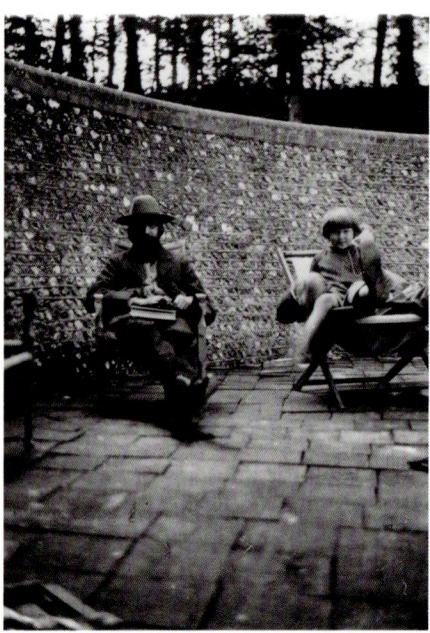

also with moral latitude. Augustus John's portraits of Dorelia McNeill with her hair bound up in a scarf and unconventional dresses and tunics, open at the neck, play to these preconceptions (fig. 89).[64] McNeill also exemplified, at least superficially, a contemporary simplicity combined with a dash of gypsy rebelliousness that Bloomsbury women aspired to. It was replicated in other artists' studios in London and Paris that Bell visited with her husband and with Fry. When Morrell sat for Augustus John in his Fitzroy Street studio in 1909, she described McNeill's graceful movements and her nonchalance and dignity as 'of a peasant from a foreign land'.[65] She met Clive and Vanessa Bell for the first time there, but her own, theatrical appearance did not succumb to the simple lines combined with the rich colours and textures of Dorelia McNeill's style. Photographs of her with John and McNeill at Hampton Court Palace in May 1909 document extreme differences between McNeill's sense of appropriate dress for the occasion and that of Lady Ottoline (fig. 90).

Vanessa Bell and Roger Fry understood the characteristic dress of 'peasants from a foreign land' from recent experience. They travelled across Turkey with Clive Bell and Harry Norton in April 1911, sketching local people and places. Vanessa became seriously ill in Broussa following a miscarriage and it was there, as Roger nursed her back to health, that the nature of their relationship became intimate. Roger brought textiles, rugs, and silks that he had bought at the bazaar to her room. Later, when they co-founded the Omega Workshops, their shared passion for artisan textiles, ceramics, and jewellery informed a range of imports that they sold alongside products designed by the Omega artists. As a dressmaker, Vanessa Bell drew on a stock of Turkish fabrics for several years, and she kept a richly embroidered bedspread from Broussa to the end of her life.[66] It is likely that the headscarf, beads, and shawl that she was photographed wearing on her visits to Fry's home in 1911, while she was recuperating after her return from Turkey, reference their time together there.

Evidence for Bloomsbury's interest in dress, as witnessed in paintings, photographs, texts, and surviving items of clothing, is invariably subjective. In portraits by the Bloomsbury artists, dress is rarely

90 (*above left*) Attributed to Philip Edward Morrell, Lady Ottoline Morrell at Hampton Court Palace with (*left to right*) Emily Chadbourne, Dorelia McNeill, and Augustus John, 1909. National Portrait Gallery, London

91 (*above middle*) Vanessa Bell, Lytton Strachey sitting for Vanessa Bell, Duncan Grant, and Roger Fry in the garden at Asheham, 1913. The Charleston Trust

92 (*above right*) Vanessa Bell, Lytton Strachey sitting for his portrait, with Clive and Julian Bell in a deckchair, in the garden at Asheham, 1913. The Charleston Trust

detailed for its decorative qualities, or as a signifier of status or character, as it is in the work of painters such as John Singer Sargent and William Nicholson. Clothing is blocked in with loose brushwork. Its lines and colours are subject to artistic licence. Lytton Strachey, for example, sat for Bell, Grant, and Fry together in the garden at Asheham House in 1913 (figs 91 and 92).[67] In Grant's portrait, Strachey's hat is brown and his jacket is painted a greyish green with conventional notched lapels, corresponding in form with photographs that document the occasion (fig. 93). In Bell's portrait, the same jacket is a bold emerald green, the hat is grey with a broad brim, and its form, together with that of Strachey's spectacles and collar, is not constrained by the bounds of literal representation (fig. 94).

Nevertheless, dress is significant in Bell's portraits and it relates to her perceptions of her sitters. Her sister wears the same elegant grey jacket in three portraits by Bell, a portrait by Fry, and a number of photographs taken at Asheham House, all dating from

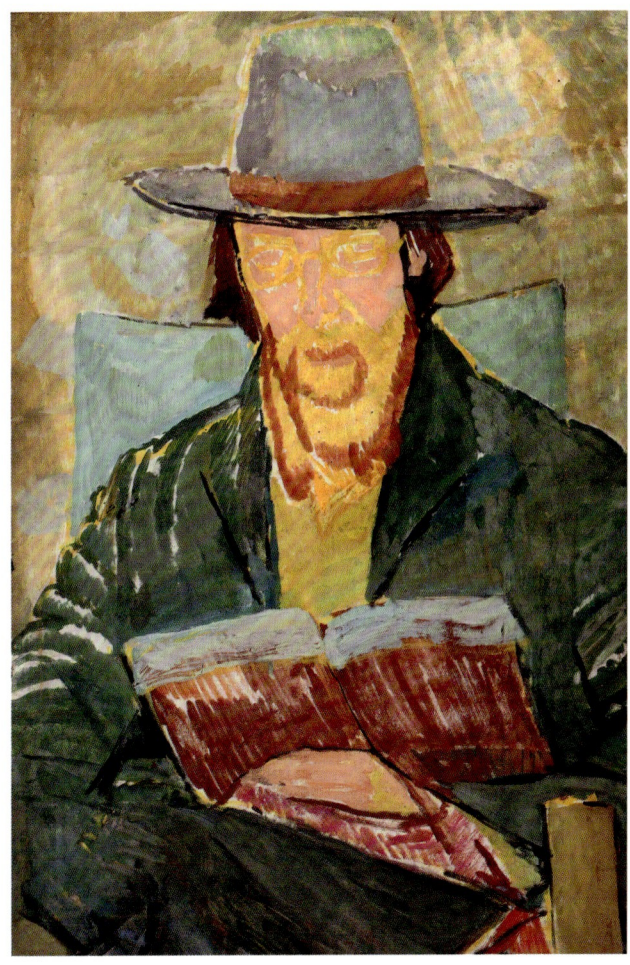

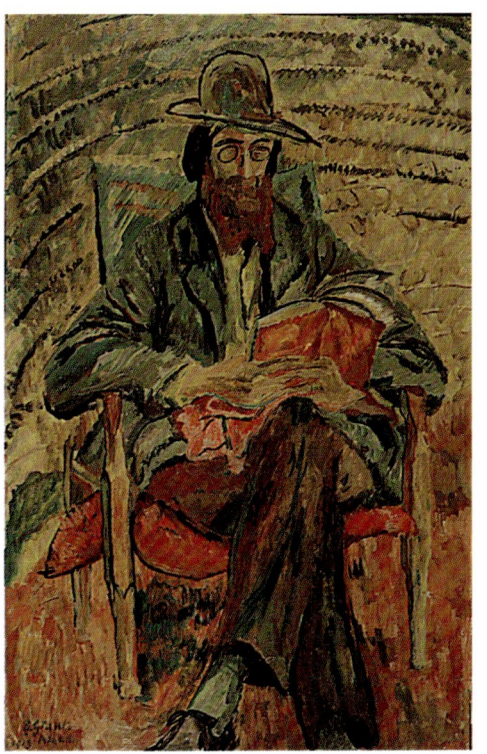

around 1912 (fig. 95).[68] The jacket has three-quarter-length sleeves with contrasting dark green cuffs and a matching banded neckline and front opening. The hemline angles down towards the front, and in photographs Woolf wears the jacket with a full, ankle-length skirt (fig. 96).[69] In all the paintings and photographs, it is worn over coloured scarves, fastened at the neck. Items of clothing can be emblematic and the jacket may have embodied a particular significance for Woolf relating to the transition between single and married life in the months surrounding her wedding. It appears in a photograph that she enclosed with a letter to Leonard effectively agreeing to marry him, and other photographs of her wearing it record their relationship (fig. 97).[70] For Bell's purposes as a

93 (*above*) Duncan Grant, *Lytton Strachey in the Garden at Asheham*, 1913. Oil on plywood, 910 × 590 mm. The Charleston Trust
94 (*top right*) Vanessa Bell, *Lytton Strachey*, 1913. Oil on board, 915 × 610 mm. Ivor Braka Collection

95 (*p. 78*) Vanessa Bell, *Virginia Woolf*, c.1912. Oil on paperboard, 368 × 304 mm. Smith College Museum of Art, Northampton, MA
96 (*p. 79*) Unknown photographer, Virginia (*right*) and Leonard Woolf at Asheham with Vanessa Bell, 1912. Houghton Library, Harvard University

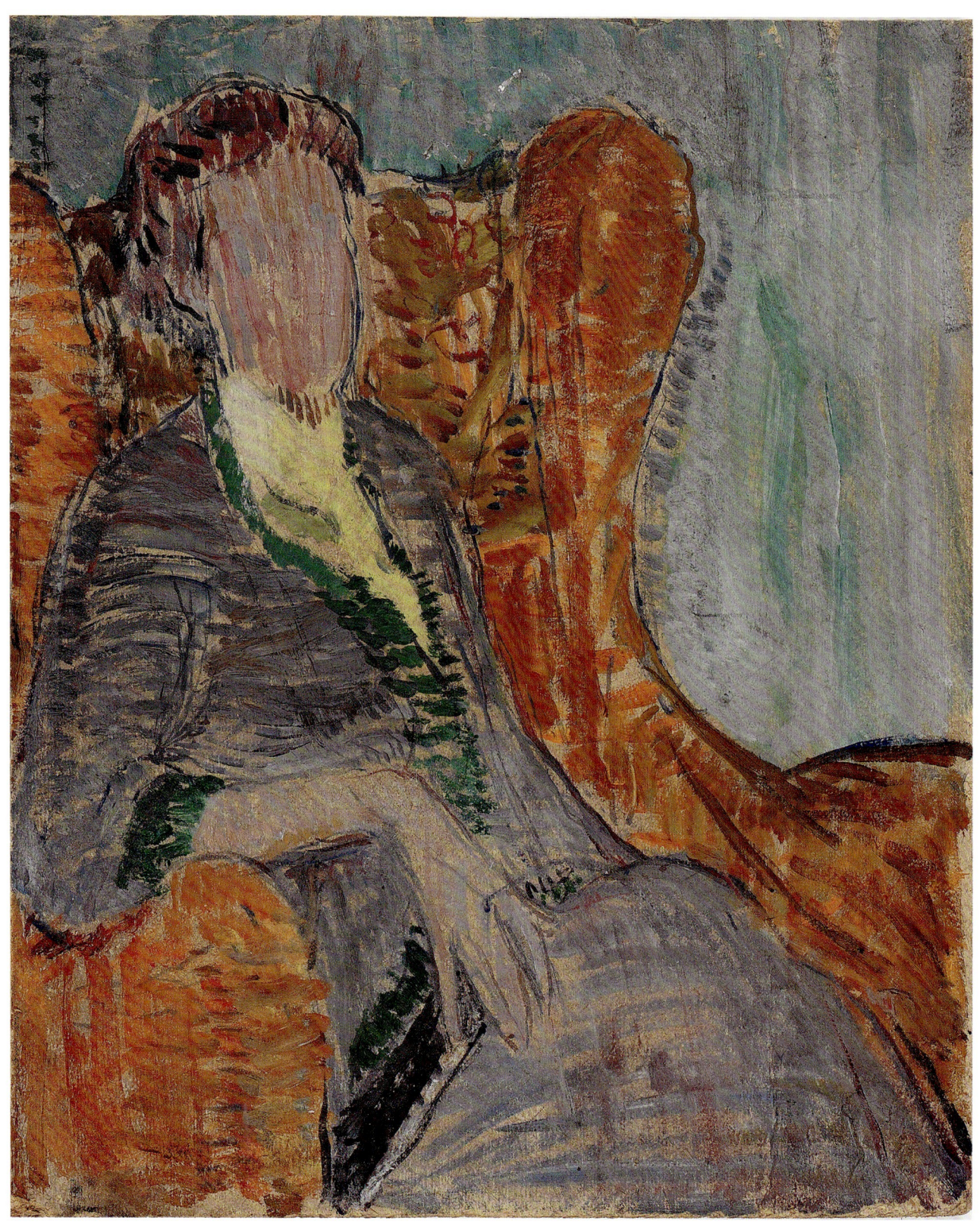

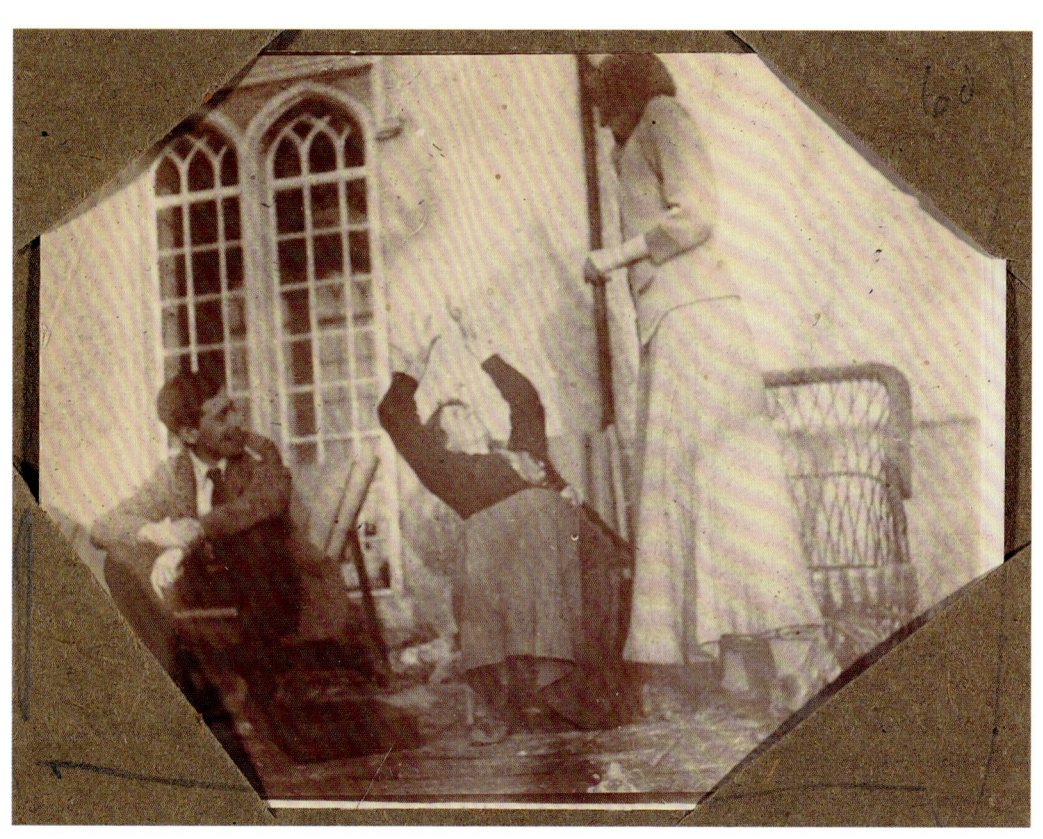

painter, the distinctive jacket identifies her sister in two of the portraits, as she explores the effects of a minimal handling of facial features. The linear qualities of its dark-green, banded neckline and cuffs add colour and movement to her compositions and bind them together.

Both Bell and Woolf were acutely observant of other women's appearances, though Woolf's written accounts, like her sister's paintings, were more often concerned with capturing vivid and original impressions than with the details of dress. When Ka Cox visited Asheham in 1912, she was photographed with Woolf, documenting the disparities between the conventional elegance of Woolf's familiar jacket and fashionable hat and the bold simplicity of Cox's 'Neo-Pagan' patterned dress, worn with large beads and a headscarf (fig. 98).[71] Photographs of Cox visiting Asheham with Margery and Sydney Waterlow also show her alternative dress and Margery Waterlow's disregard for conventions, walking on the Downs with her skirt hitched up and her hat tied down (figs 99 and 100). Duncan Grant painted Cox's portrait, capturing a monumental simplicity appropriate to the values

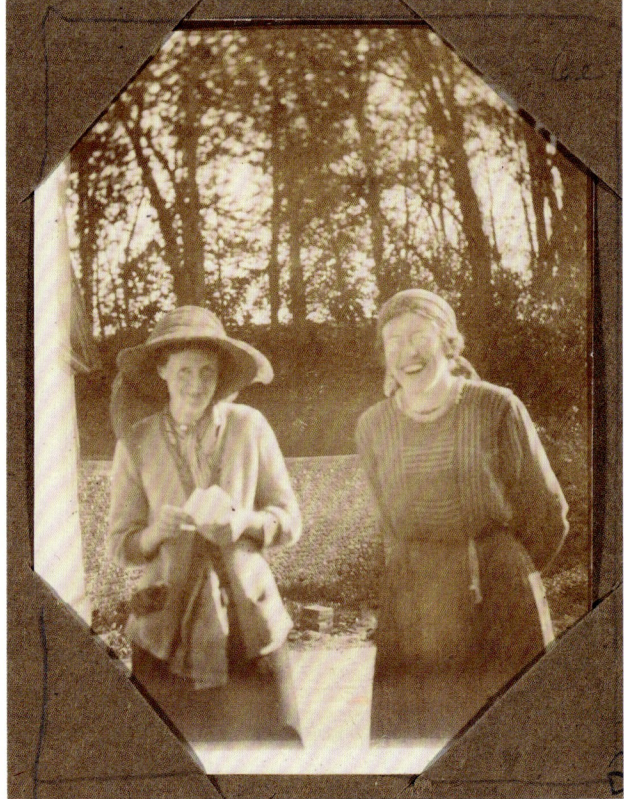

that she and her circle espoused. He exhibited it as *Seated Woman* in the *Second Post-Impressionist Exhibition* at the Grafton Galleries in 1912 and it was illustrated in the catalogue (see fig. 148).[72] Cox was a few years younger than Bell and Woolf, and she had attended Bell's Friday Club in 1906. She was a committed Fabian with a circle of friends that included Gwen Darwin, Jacques Raverat, and Geoffrey Keynes. As an undergraduate at Cambridge University she had formed a close relationship with Rupert Brooke. She made shirts for him as well as her own clothes. In her diary, immediately following Cox's early death in 1938, Woolf recalled a conversation about her with Brooke: 'Bruin I called her, at the Vienna Café one day with Rupert – Bruin oaring her way – with a beavers tail, & short clumsy paws. He liked the image. It conveyed her thickness, breadth. She was very broad cheeked; & her face was long drawn out.'[73] Woolf also recalled her distinctive dress. 'She chose bright pure colours for her clothes; wore a coloured handkerchief round her hair; often stuck it with a silver pin: an individual

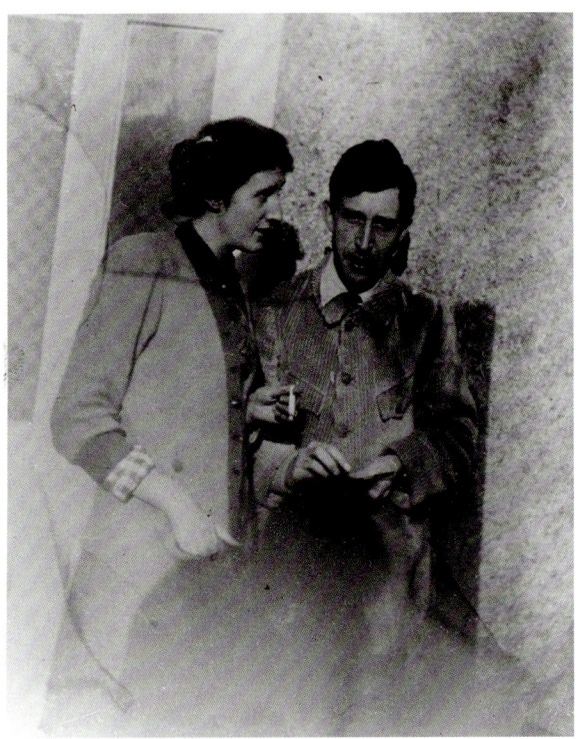

97 Vanessa Bell, Virginia and Leonard Woolf at Asheham, *c*.1912. The Charleston Trust

98 Vanessa Bell, Virginia Woolf (*left*) and Ka Cox (*right*) at Asheham, 1912. Houghton Library, Harvard University

looking woman; derived partly from a John painting.'[74]

Woolf's first account of meeting Ka Cox was written to entertain Clive Bell and focused, as a consequence, on Cox's Cambridge connections rather than her appearance. 'Miss Cox is one of the younger Newnhamites, and it is said that she will marry either a Keynes or a Brook. . . . She is a bright, intelligent, nice creature.'[75] Within a few months Woolf invented the epithet 'Neo Pagan' in another letter to Clive Bell: 'At any moment my Neo Pagan Cox may descend.'[76] She planned to make a trip to France with Cox and her friends: 'I mean to throw myself into youth, sunshine, nature, primitive art. Cakes with sugar on the top, love, lust, paganism, general bawdiness, for a fortnight at least; and not write a line.'[77] An account of Ka Cox's appearance was reserved for Vanessa Bell in a letter written the following day: 'Ka came striding along the road . . . with a knapsack on her back, a row of red beads, and daisies stuck in her coat. Her innocent face was brown.'[78] This 'peasant' or 'pagan' dress style was part of the visual language of modernity. Vanessa Bell described her excitement at painting Cox in a letter to Roger Fry in March 1912, and Grant completed another portrait of her the following year wearing her red beads and a long red headscarf (fig. 101).[79] Woolf, too, was persuaded to sit for a portrait in which dress was synonymous with the alternative aesthetics of Post-Impressionist modernism. She wrote to Molly MacCarthy, 'I have to dress up again as a South Sea Savage, to figure in a picture. It's an awful bore!'[80] She defended her 'savage' credentials as a modernist a few months later in an exchange with Vanessa Bell. Woolf wrote: 'Oh how I'm damned by Roger! Refinement! and we in a Post Impressionist age. You don't deserve any compliments for sending me that one.'[81]

In August 1911 Woolf visited Rupert Brooke at the Old Vicarage in Grantchester, and is reputed to have boasted that she swam with him in the river there, 'quite naked'.[82] In her essay 'Rupert Brooke', written three years after his death in 1918, she described him as 'consciously and defiantly pagan' during his time at Grantchester: 'his feet were permanently bare; he disdained tobacco and butcher's meat; and he lived all day, and perhaps slept all night, in the open air'.[83]

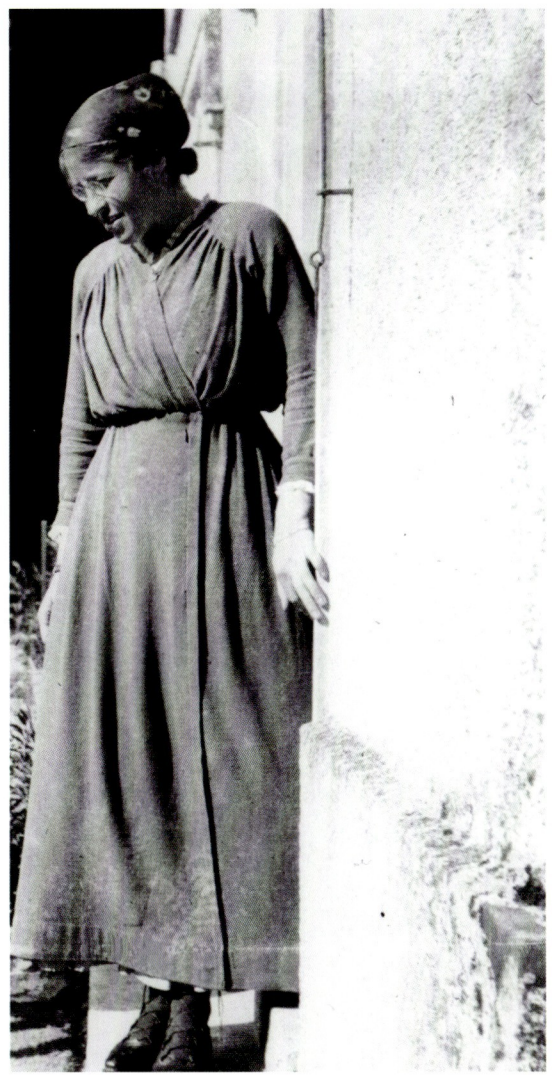

99 Vanessa Bell or Virginia Woolf, Ka Cox at Asheham, c.1914. The Charleston Trust

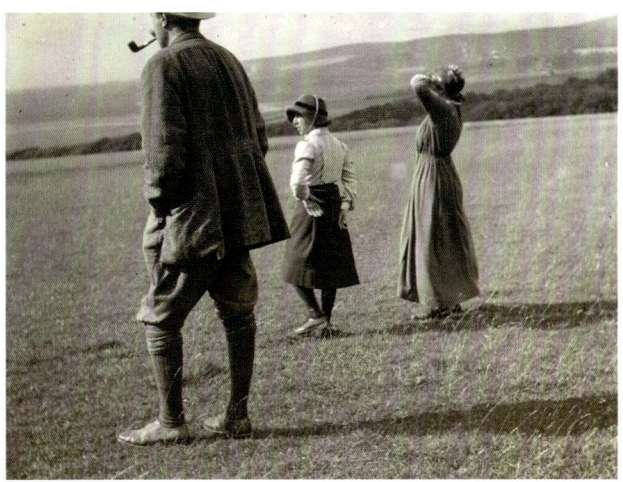

100 Vanessa Bell, Ka Cox (right) with Sydney and Margery Waterlow on the Downs near Asheham, c.1914. The Charleston Trust.

EXPERIMENTS IN DRESS AND UNDRESS

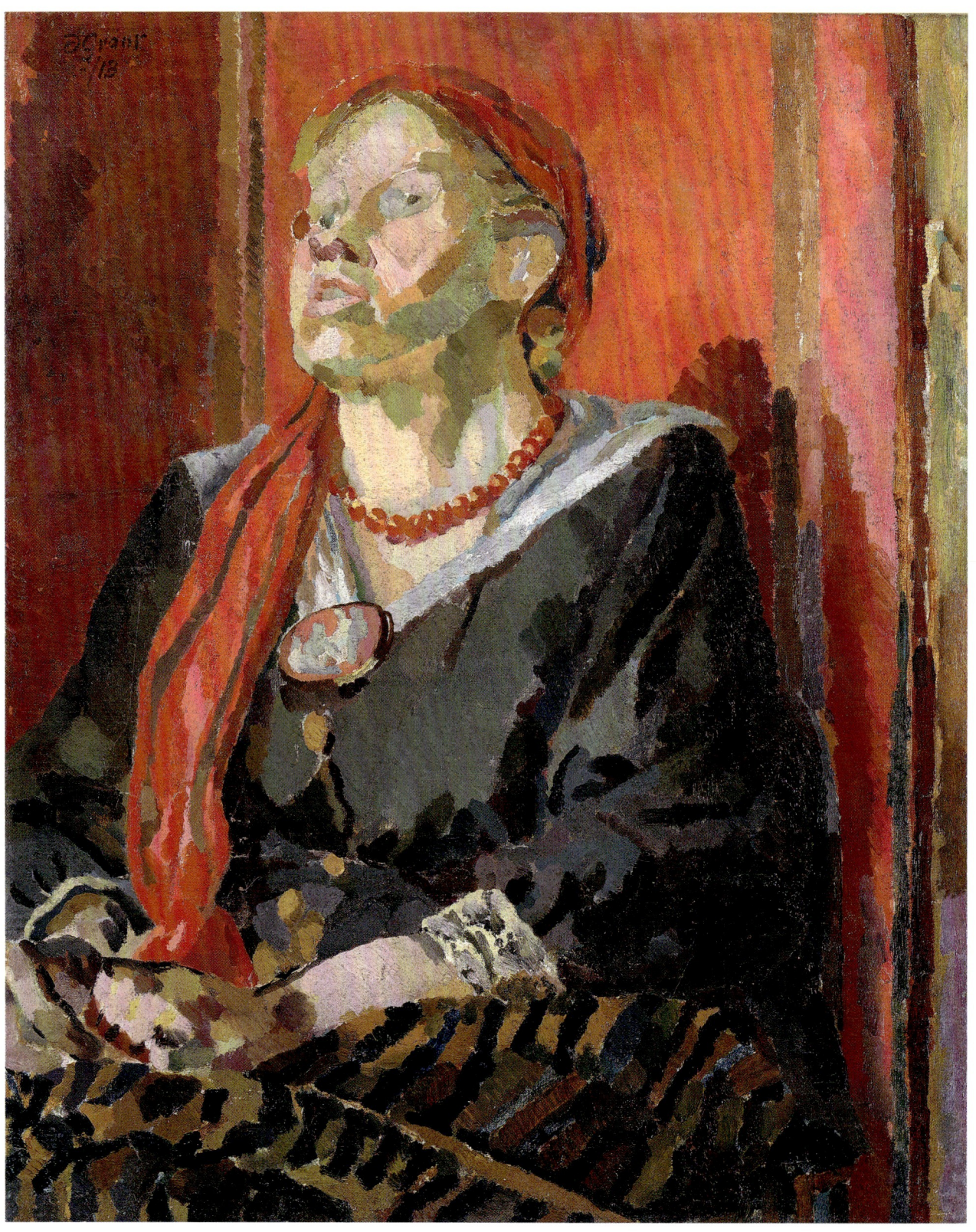

She described his charismatic leadership: 'Under his influence the country near Cambridge was full of young men and women walking barefoot, sharing his passion for bathing and fish diet'.[84] A photograph of Woolf herself, taken in 1911, with Rupert Brooke, Noel Olivier (with whom he was in love) and Maitland Radford shows her assimilating the dress code of a Neo-Pagan in a blouse and skirt with a long headscarf tied at the nape of her neck (fig. 102).[85] She was not entirely taken in by the Neo-Pagans, however, describing Brooke as 'self-conscious in the highest degree'. 'It was an amusing disguise . . . a game played for the fun of it, an experiment in living by one keenly inquisitive and incessantly fastidious . . . which had to live side by side with highly sophisticated tastes.'[86] Her insights are revealing because they reflect her own self-conscious experiments with appearances and identity.

Woolf's early friendships with the Neo-Pagans coincided with her move to the country. Before moving to Asheham she rented a semi-detached cottage in the Sussex village of Firle from January 1911 and immediately invited her friends to stay. Within weeks of taking the lease she wrote to Morrell, 'I've got to go down and make curtains and move beds at the cottage, having been so rash as to ask 5 people to stay the week after. Nessa is bringing a sewing machine.'[87] 'Dressing' this rural retreat in the heart of the South Downs was part of establishing her own identity, and although her sister was the more experienced designer and decorator, Woolf wrote to Violet Dickinson in the singular about the excitement of 'furnishing my cottage, and staining the floors the colour of the Atlantic in a storm'.[88] Molly MacCarthy gave her a comfortable chair and she wrote to thank her, describing the cottage as a 'villa' and 'inconceivably ugly' but 'done up in patches of post-impressionist colour'.[89] It was a relatively new house, half-timbered in accordance with Edwardian suburban fashions, and Woolf used the term 'villa' sardonically. 'It's right underneath the downs,' she wrote, 'and though itself an eyesore, still that dont matter when one's inside.' Bell's group portrait *Conversation Piece* represents the first-floor sitting room at the cottage, named 'Little Talland House' by Woolf after their childhood holiday home in Cornwall (see fig. 69).[90] In her painting, pictures are balanced on the mantel shelf on either side of the mirror, the floor is a dark grey, tinged with brown and mauve in Bell's brushwork, and some of the Post-Impressionist patches of colour are provided by red, orange, and mauve loose covers for an assortment of chairs. One of these, an Edwardian wing-backed chair, also features in Bell's portraits of Woolf. There is further evidence for Woolf taking ownership of the decorative scheme. She concluded her letter to Clive Bell anticipating the arrival of 'Neo Pagan Cox' in April 1911, 'This house has been turned into a very comfortable villa. . . . The tailor having refused to make chair covers, I have persuaded the dressmaker.'[91]

Ka Cox shared an interest with the Bloomsbury Group in textiles and interiors. She gave the Woolfs embroideries as a wedding present in 1912, to decorate their rooms in London. Virginia described fastening them 'first to a table, then a sofa, finally to our 2 arm chairs'.[92] She wrote to Leonard, describing one of

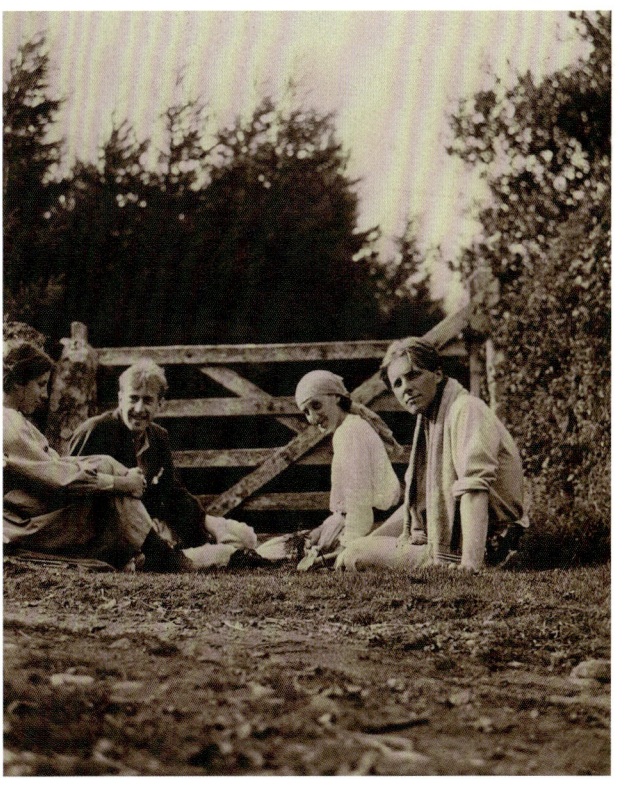

101 (*opposite*) Duncan Grant, *Katherine Cox*, 1913. Oil on canvas, 759 × 627 mm. National Museum of Wales, Cardiff

102 Unknown photographer, (*left to right*) Noel Olivier, Maitland Radford, Virginia Woolf, and Rupert Brooke, 1911. National Portrait Gallery, London

EXPERIMENTS IN DRESS AND UNDRESS

Cox's visits to Asheham soon afterwards: 'Ka and I stitch, gossip, grumble, as you can imagine.'[93] Woolf's letters and diaries describe her pleasure in the colours and textures of fabrics, and her encouragement of Bloomsbury's most striking experiments in dress. She became a regular customer at the Omega Workshops. Part of the appeal of Sussex for Woolf, however, was the freedom not to think about her appearance. When she wrote to Leonard confirming the arrangements for his first visit to Firle in September 1911, she concluded 'Please bring no clothes', meaning that there was no dress code.[94] 'It would be nice to leave all ones clothes in a great box in London', she wrote to Violet Dickinson the following year after she had exchanged Little Talland House for Asheham, 'and turn into a kind of muddy turnip root.'[95] Her photographs are seldom composed to show off a dress, and her albums, together with those of her sister, describe a limited wardrobe with the same outfit worn again and again. The 1912 jacket, for example, appears in photographs with Vanessa Bell, Leonard Woolf, and Roger Fry at Asheham, and in a photograph with Ka Cox, worn with muddy brogues and a knitted hood. The jacket was still in service on a holiday to Cornwall four years later.[96]

For conventional Edwardian women, dress was an expression of resources as well as social status and personal style. It was usual, before the First World War, for affluent women to change several times a day for different activities and to keep servants who would launder and maintain their elaborate wardrobes. Ottoline Morrell's photograph albums evidence a seemingly limitless wardrobe of extravagant clothes that are testaments to her affluence as well as her passion for dress and dressing up. Bloomsbury and their Neo-Pagan friends were less privileged than Lady Ottoline, whose half-brother was the 6th Duke of Portland. Nevertheless, their experiments with dress, and their alternative self-fashioning, undermined the hierarchies of class. Ka Cox with her knapsack and beads was mistaken for 'an old Trampwoman . . . with her bundle on her back' by the locals at Asheham.[97]

Photographs of one of the Neo-Pagan camping expeditions, a summer camp at Brandon in Norfolk, also describe the ways in which disregard for dress conventions could signal intellectual and creative freedoms. The images evidence shared values and fluid boundaries between Bloomsbury and the Neo-Pagans. The camp became a springboard for new work. It was organized by the Olivier sisters, Brynhild, Margery, Noel, and Daphne, and over the course of 12 days Keynes, Fry, Grant, Cox, Adrian Stephen, Clive and Vanessa Bell, Molly MacCarthy, and Gerald Shove all stayed for various lengths of time. Photographs grouped together in one of Bell's albums under the heading 'Brandon Camp August 1913' describe a liberation from conventions of dress and behaviour (fig. 103).[98] Noel Olivier is photographed sitting outside her tent and lying outdoors, wrapped up in a blanket, wearing a chequered headscarf and a loose, spotted dress. Bell sits on the grass with a garment – a heavy, button-through skirt or a jacket – pulled over her bare legs and her hair poking out from beneath a lopsided headscarf decorated with a single flower motif. In her album page, the photographs capture the camp's freedom from rules. Her own photograph is paired with an image of Fry in a collarless shirt, and both artists are completely unguarded in their facial expressions and body language. In a letter to Rupert Brooke, Noel Olivier described Bell and Grant sketching in the fields and Keynes writing.[99] Bell wrote to Keynes, describing him as the 'figure head of Brandon Camp' on her return to London, and recalled 'all those exquisite creatures flitting about on the grass'. She wrote that she had 'seldom or never spent such a happy week'.[100] She painted a small, exploratory study, *Seated Figure*, at the camp, depicting a seated woman in a loose green dress with her arms clasped around her knees (fig. 104). A sketch on the back was worked up into her painting *Summer Camp* (fig. 105), and Bell abstracted the key elements of this composition for one of her most iconic designs for the Omega Workshops, the screen *Bathers in a Landscape* (fig. 106).[101] The Workshops had opened in July 1913, just weeks before its three co-founders, Fry, Bell,

---

103 (*opposite*) Vanessa Bell, album page of photographs taken during Brandon Camp, 1913. Tate, London

104 (*p. 86*) Vanessa Bell, *Seated Figure*, 1913. Oil on board, 370 × 520 mm. Philip Mould & Company, London

105 (*p. 87*) Vanessa Bell, *Summer Camp*, 1913. Oil on board, 787 × 838 mm. Collection of Bryan Ferry

Brandon Camp
August 1913.

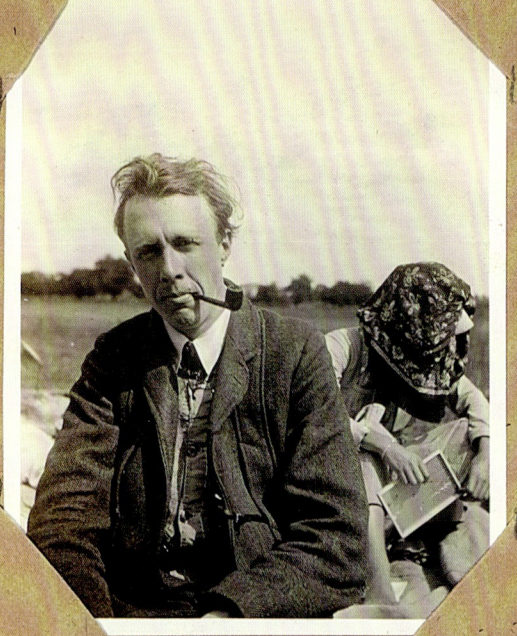
Adrian Stephen. Daphne Olivier.

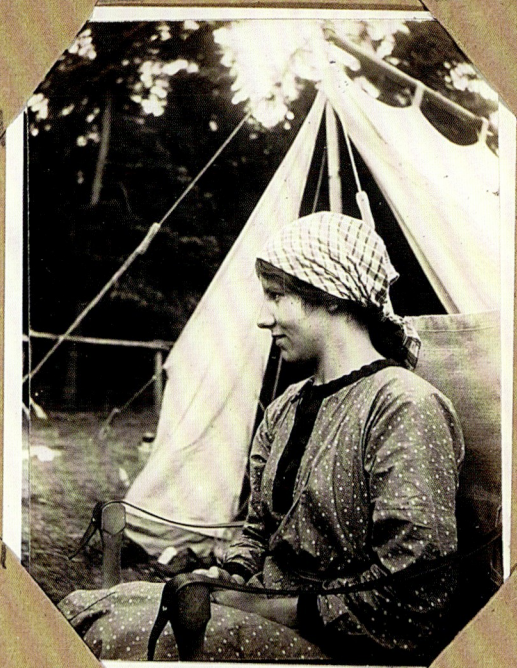
Noel Olivier

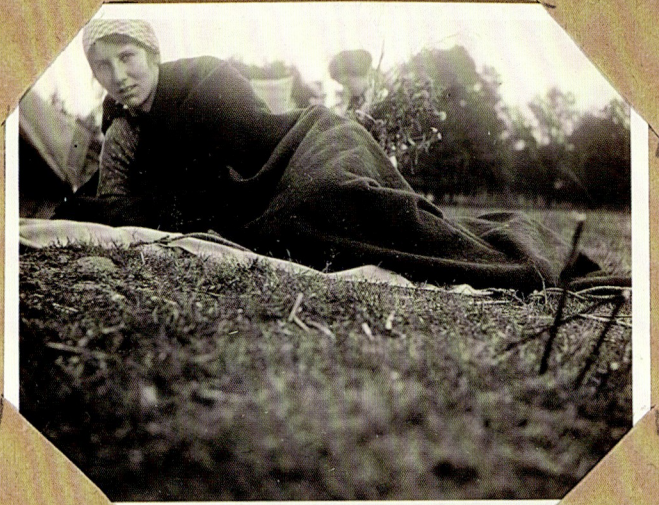
Noel Olivier

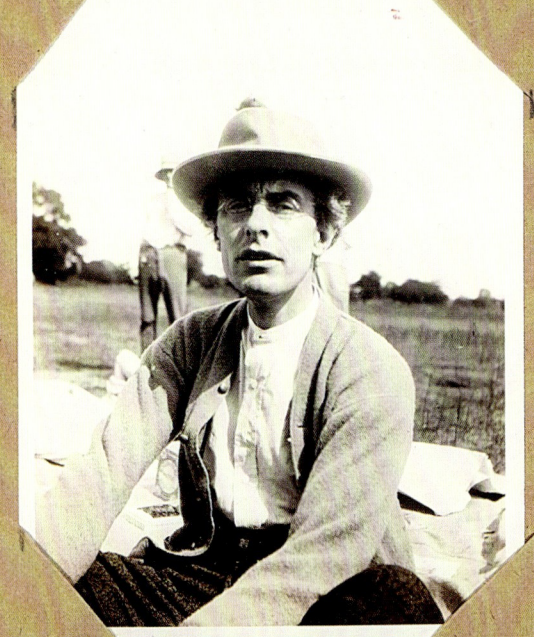

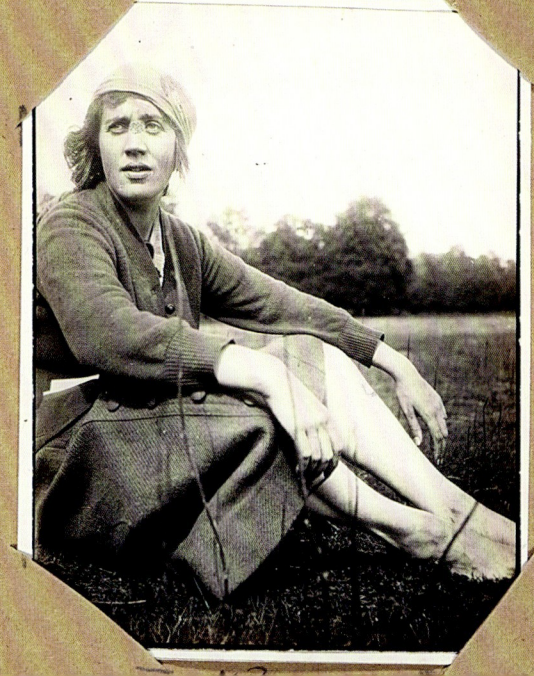

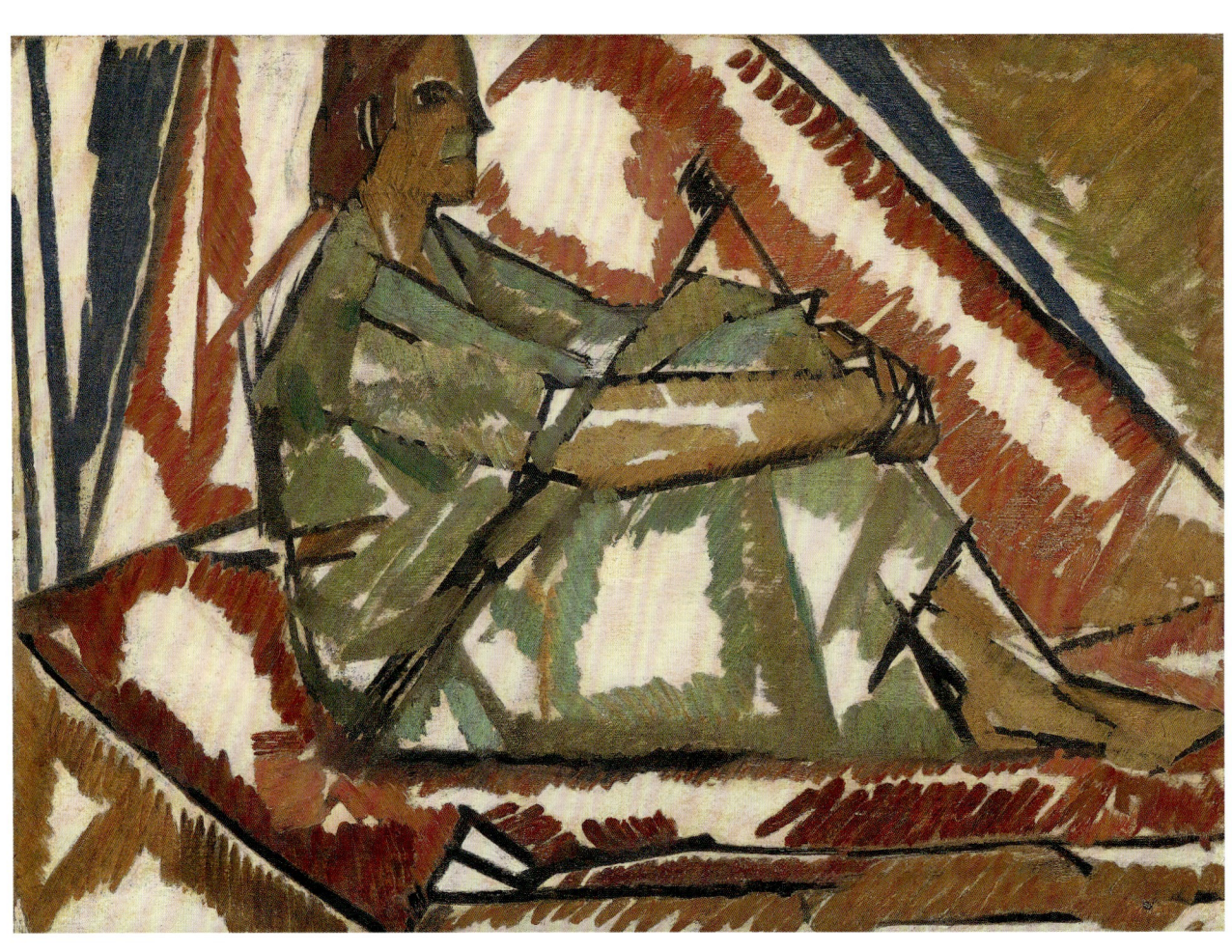

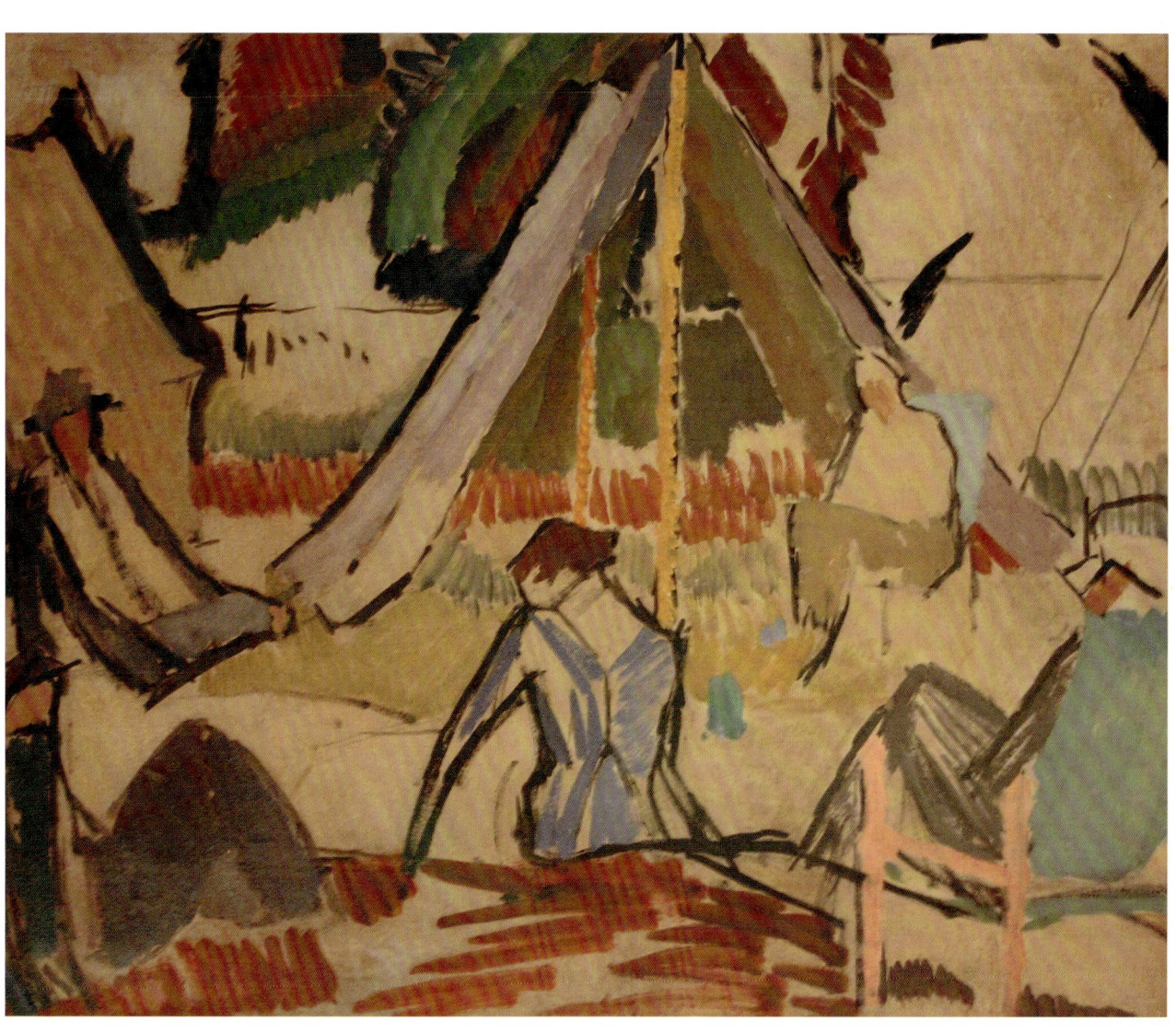

and Grant, all joined the camp. In the design for her screen, Bell retains the compositional structure of tent poles and angles of canvas. She refines the form and placing of three out of the five figures in her *Summer Camp* painting. Art historians have noted the influence of Cézanne, Derain, and Matisse in her substitution of the clothed figures in the painting, at least two of which are presumed to have been male, for four stylized female nudes in the screen.[102] They are painted green. The four Olivier sisters might also have inspired these nudes. Although letters from Brandon make no reference to nudity, Noel Olivier describes diving from one of the weirs near the camp.[103] The sisters were known for 'wild swimming' and were photographed naked together after swimming in Cornwall the following year.[104]

Bloomsbury's early experiments with turbans and headscarves, with the fabrics and beads that they collected abroad, and their fusion of Post-Impressionist painted surfaces with the earthiness of the everyday were to mature into a distinctive style with the formation of the Omega Workshops. Virginia Woolf's Post-Impressionist patches of colour at Little Talland House, as early as 1911, and the versatility shown by her instructing her dressmaker to apply her skills to upholstery, found fruition in the Workshops' repurposing of upholstery fabrics for tunics and waistcoats. Bloomsbury's easy acceptance of nudity and sexuality were to have a liberating effect on the evolution of a dress range for the Workshops. Its Post-Impressionist paintings, distorting and monumentalizing the human form, prefigured a dress profile that was assertively plain and comfortable but sharply detailed. The Omega Workshops capitalized on Bloomsbury's early reputation as a group and its extended network of influential friends and relations. With its showrooms in Bloomsbury's Fitzroy Square and working studios on the floor above, it created spaces in which customers and influential guests were invited to meet the Omega artists and makers and emulate their style. As a co-founder, Bell was to find herself at least partly responsible for refining the alternative, anti-fashion identity that distinguished Bloomsbury's private experiments with appearances into a brand that was both radical and inclusive.

106 Vanessa Bell, *Bathers in a Landscape*, 1913. Omega Workshops screen, distemper on paper mounted on canvas, painted softwood frame, 1784 × 523 × 18 mm (outer measurements). Victoria and Albert Museum, London

CHAPTER 3

OMEGA

DRESS

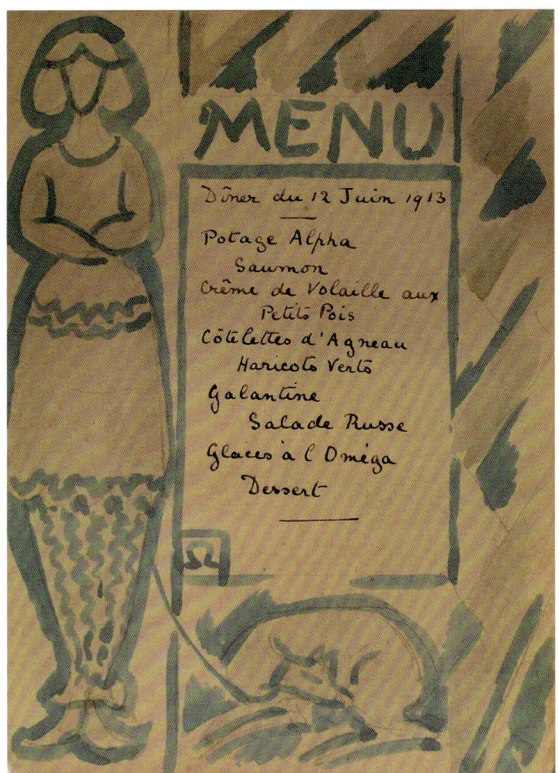

'Will Clive tell you I wonder', Vanessa Bell wrote to Roger Fry in February 1913, 'of our great scheme for a combined dinner to you and advertisement of the group?'[1] She proposed a 'Bohemian dinner' in Fry's honour to launch the Omega Workshops:

> given by all the grateful young artists . . . We should get all your disreputable and some of your aristocratic friends to come, and after dinner we should repair to Fitzroy Sq., where would be seen decorated furniture, painted walls, etc. There we should all get drunk and dance and kiss. Orders would flow in and the aristocrats would feel sure they were really in the thick of things.[2]

The design of decorated menus for the dinner, which included 'Salade Russe' and 'Glaces à l Oméga', indicate the importance of dress and the influence of the Ballets Russes at the Workshops from the outset (fig. 107).[3] Bell wrote to Fry again a few weeks later to make arrangements for painting Omega chairs with Grant, and to assert her authority in the business. 'It is true that the centre of this blessed business has got to be outside this house but it wont get on without me & I shall poke my nose into all the details & give you advice of all kinds wherever you establish yourself.'[4]

✤ ✤ ✤

The Omega Workshops opened in July 1913 at 33 Fitzroy Square, less than a fifteen-minute walk from Bloomsbury's Gordon Square 'headquarters' (fig. 108). Winifred Gill, who was employed by the Workshops from its inception, recalled that the artists 'went in and started working there in around January or February and got enough stuff together for opening in July'.[5] The Workshops was a separate entity from Bloomsbury as a group. It showcased Bloomsbury's aesthetics and provided a public platform for its

---

107 Vanessa Bell or Duncan Grant, menu card for a dinner to launch the Omega Workshops, 1913. Gouache on card, 150 × 115 mm. The Charleston Trust

OMEGA DRESS   91

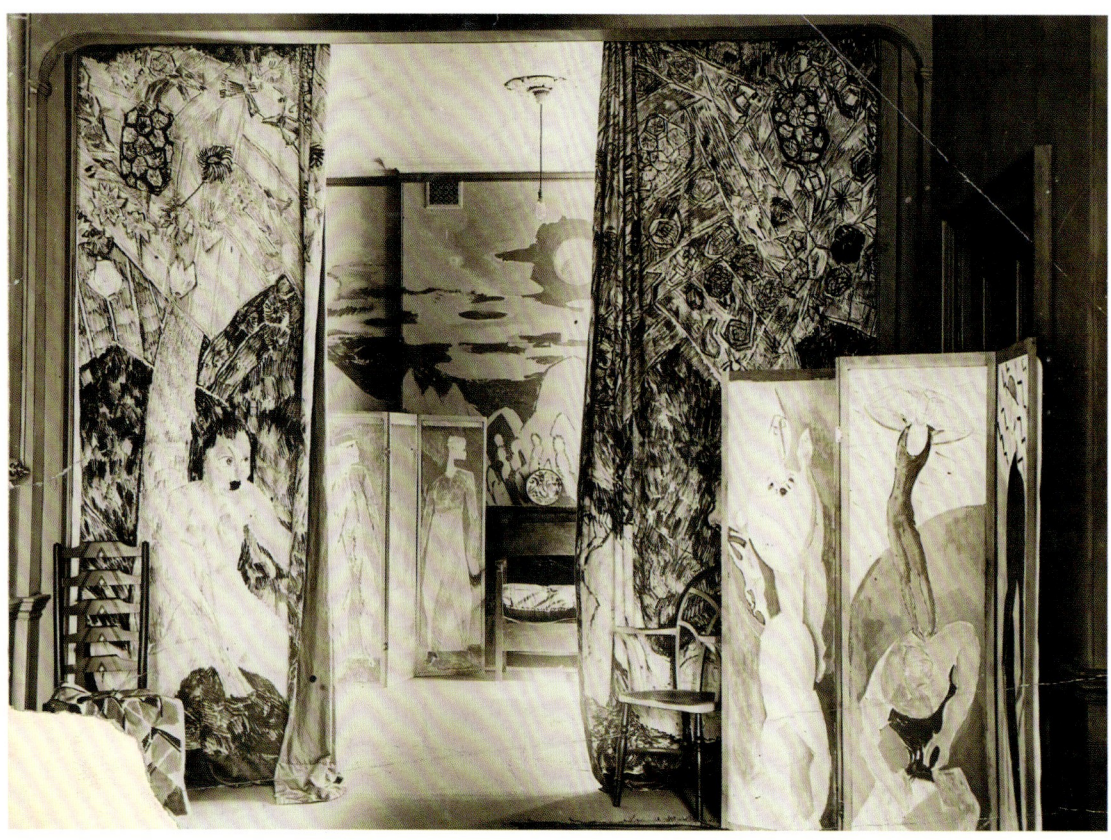

values and ideals. With the Group at its core, it was founded to champion and expand the principles of Post-Impressionism and to engage a wider circle of artists, intellectuals, and patrons. Bell's letter was sent a few days after the *Second Post-Impressionist Exhibition* closed on 31 January. The Bohemian dinner was intended to consolidate Bloomsbury's position within a European, modernist vanguard, but it was also conceived as an interface between the aspirations of an in-group of artists and activists, and an out-group of wealthy potential patrons. Omega exploited the Group's credentials as Bohemians for commercial and reputational purposes. It perpetuated a determination, initiated by William Morris and the Arts and Crafts movement, to challenge boundaries between the fine and decorative arts. The Workshops applied the principles of Post-Impressionism to the design of interiors and products for everyday use. It supported the work of contemporary artists and, although its workforce was divided and members were lost to internal disputes and the First World War,

Henri Gaudier-Brzeska, Wyndham Lewis, Edward Wadsworth, Paul and Christine Nash, Frederick and Jessie Etchells, and Nina Hamnett all contributed to the Omega Workshops' unique aesthetic. Artists were paid 30 shillings for three and a half days a week, providing them with a basic income and time to dedicate to their own work. Gill recalled, however, that initially: 'The artists were never employed by the week. They came and went just as they liked. They were free as air . . . when they wanted money they could come in and put in a day, or half a day's work and be paid on the spot.'[6]

Printed and painted textiles were among the Workshops' most striking products, and all three of its co-directors, Vanessa Bell, Roger Fry, and Duncan Grant, designed Omega printed linens. A catalogue published in autumn 1914 lists the designs: *Pamela*, for example, named after Fry's daughter, at three shillings and three pence per yard (fig. 109); and *Maud*, probably named for the influential society hostess Maud Cunard, priced at three shillings.[7] 'Ladies Linen Tunics made to

108 Unknown photographer, press photograph for the opening of the Omega Workshops, 33 Fitzroy Square, 1913. The Charleston Trust

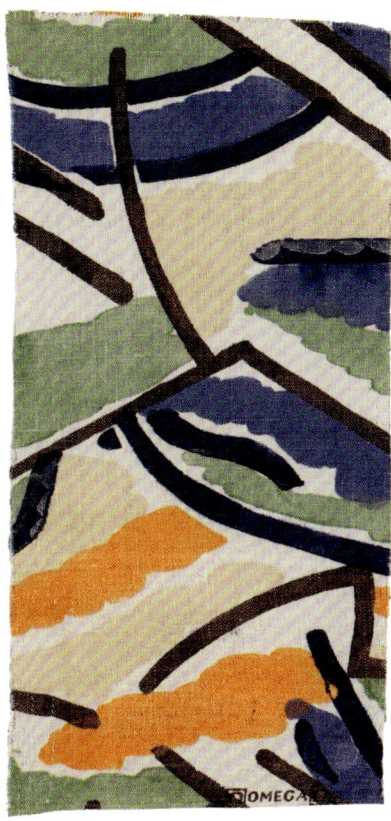

measure' are offered on the same catalogue page from 15 shillings, and these became part of the Workshops' distinctive identity, worn by assistants, co-directors, and customers alike. Joy Brown, who was to run the dressmaking department, recalled that the first tunic was made for one of the Omega showroom assistants, her cousin, May Layton, and that when she arrived in it, Clive Bell seized her hands and said, 'Look Roger, she's wearing it.'[8] In a letter to Roger in August 1914 Vanessa wrote 'I hope my tunic is coming soon', and Virginia Woolf complained that when she visited the Workshops to buy a shawl for her friend, Janet Case, she was served by 'a foolish young woman in a Post-Impressionist tunic'.[9] Press photographs and an early photograph of Fry and two of his female co-workers in the studio above the showroom show a variety of linen tunics and long painting smocks worn by the women (fig. 110). In one of these, the artist Nina Hamnett is wearing an Omega tunic and holds up another patterned with the *Margery* design (see fig. 125). The combination of loose tunic and skirt is comparable to Dorelia McNeill's Bohemian style in Augustus John's drawings of her (see fig. 89). For Omega artists and their customers it embodied creative and intellectual freedom.[10]

Winifred Gill describes her dress during the day, working at the Omega in 'overalls . . . liberally stained with paint and dye'. These were long painting smocks, worn over her own clothes. She describes one, comparable to the long smocks in the press photographs. It was made of Russian handwoven linen, 'put together in straight pieces, like a peasant's smock with square gussets under the arms. The pieces were joined together with a decorative stitch with additional pattern at the corners of the yoke.'[11] For evening events, such as the 'Art Circle' evenings that were staged by the Workshops for its more 'distinguished' customers, she changed into an Omega tunic with a makeshift skirt.[12] 'I took a spare length of plain material used as lining for curtains, folded it round me with a good overlap and safety-pinned it to my waist. over [sic] this I wore a tunic of Omega linen.'[13]

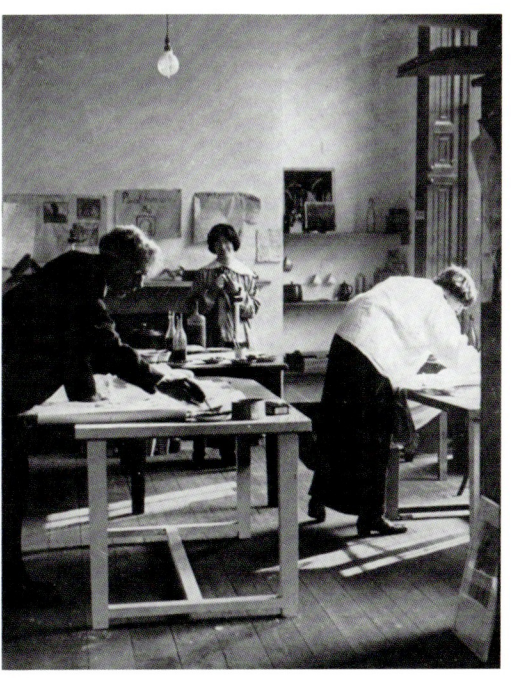

109 Vanessa Bell and Duncan Grant, *Pamela*, 1913. Omega Workshops printed linen. Victoria and Albert Museum, London

110 Unknown photographer, Roger Fry with artists at work in the Omega Workshops studio, c.1913. From Richard Shone, *The Art of Bloomsbury: Roger Fry, Vanessa Bell and Duncan Grant*, exh. cat. (Tate Gallery, London, 1999), fig. 98, p. 137

OMEGA DRESS 93

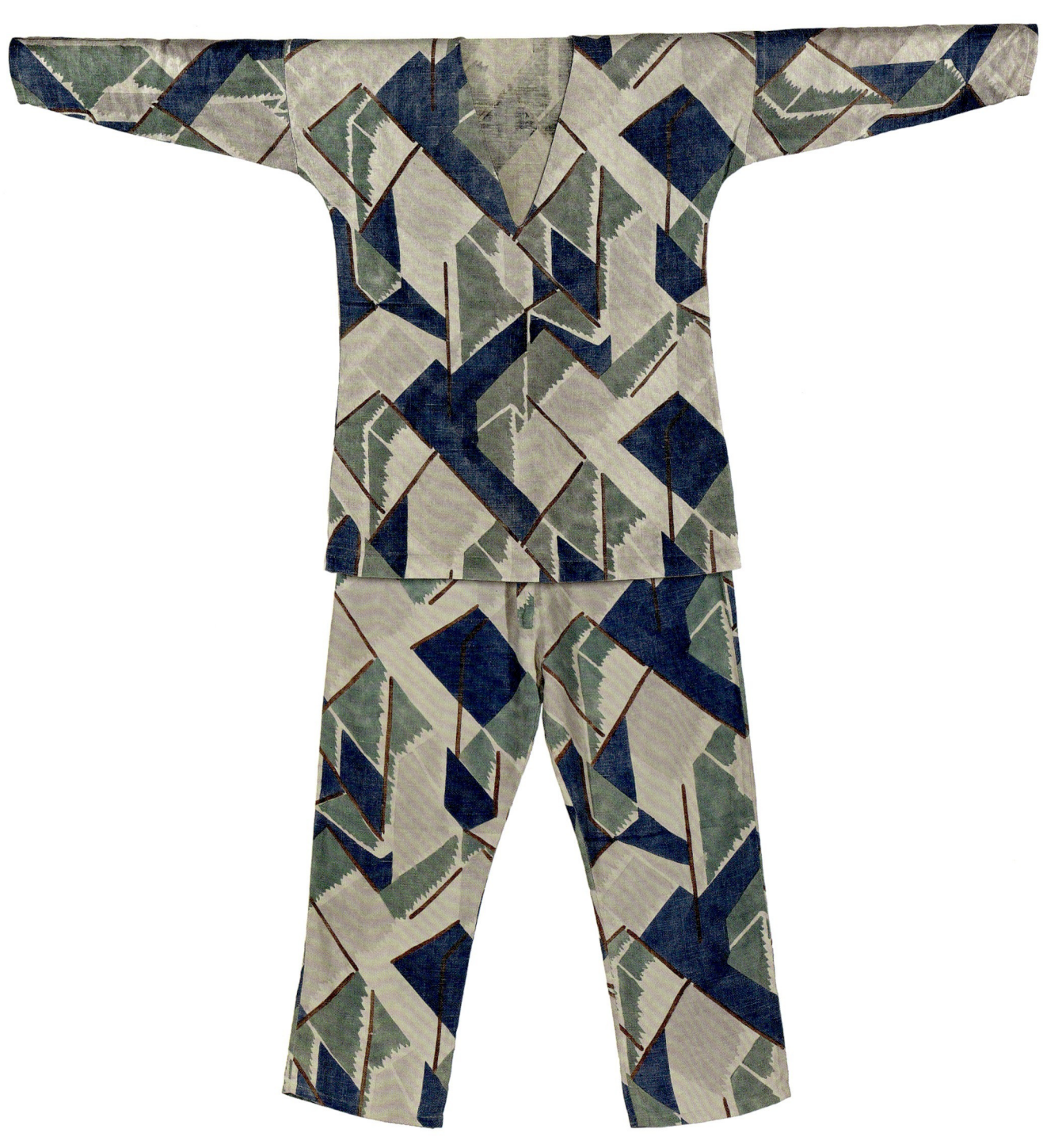

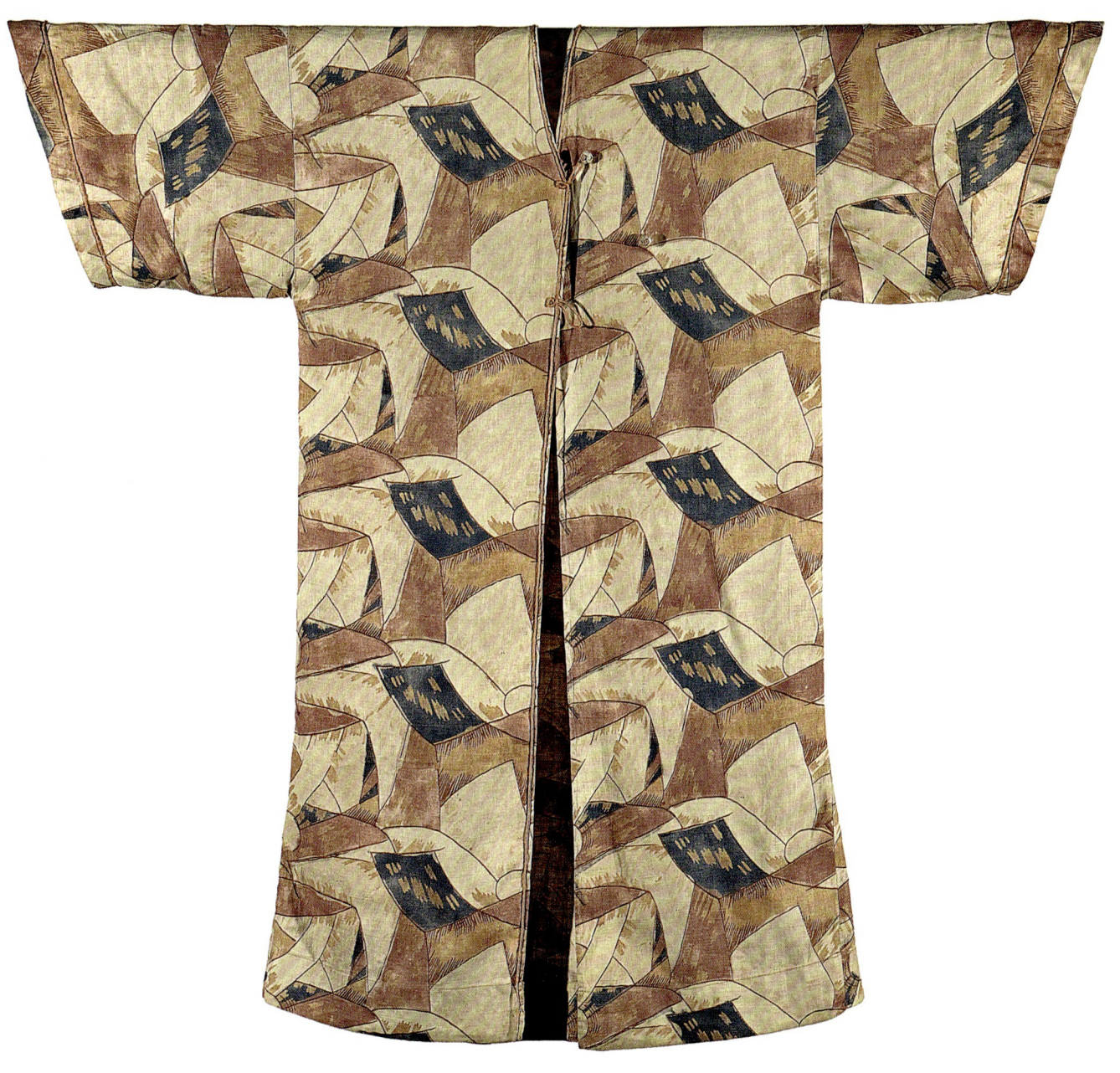

OMEGA DRESS 95

The Omega Workshops sold hand-painted gowns, evening cloaks, and accessories designed to breach boundaries between dress, painting, printing, sculpture, and the decorative arts. Fry's daughter, Pamela, described the artist Henri Doucet on the day of the opening, 'painting the most gorgeous piece of silk. . . . It seemed to have every colour of the Peacock on it and it had people.'[14] The *Daily News and Leader* described a 'Post-Impressionist Gown' in the showroom in August 1913, a radiantly coloured dress of 'gossamery silk' designed by a Post-Impressionist artist with a mass of large foliage and a 'pastoral scene: maidens dancing under the moon, while a philosopher and a peasant stood by'.[15] The journalist questioned whether any English woman would have the courage to wear it. Joy Brown recalled a 'wonderful dress' designed by Duncan Grant, 'made of silks painted in patterns . . . or was it never made up but dressed over a stand so we could see the marvellous painted design at the bottom'.[16] They had hoped, in vain, that Ottoline Morrell would buy it. The Workshops' more extravagant dresses also served as advertisements. One was worn by May Layton to staff the Omega 'room' at the *Ideal Homes Exhibition* in 1913.[17]

Fry described his ambition 'to keep the spontaneous freshness of primitive or peasant work' while appealing to 'modern cultivated' clients in a preface to the Workshops' 1914 catalogue.[18] Omega hand-painted eveningwear, however, was also calculated to attract an elite market. Virginia Woolf described Fry 'escorting now Lady So-and so, now a business man from Birmingham, round the rooms and doing his best to persuade them to buy'.[19] Omega clothing and accessories were dispersed under different headings in the catalogue rather than presented as a collection. In addition to the Omega tunics, listed under 'Printed Linens etc.', orders were also invited, under the heading 'Dress', for 'dresses and evening cloaks made from Omega materials and hand-dyed silk', implying a degree of collaboration between artist and customer.[20] Fry owned a pair of pyjamas and a dressing gown patterned with the *Maud* and *Amenophis* linens, reputedly made up for a Ballets Russes fancy dress party (figs 111 and 112).[21] 'Bead Necklaces', hand-painted silk opera bags and fans, and 'Omega Ladies' Handbags, hand-painted on leather or decorated with beads' were itemized towards the back of the catalogue under the heading 'Miscellaneous'.[22] Bell teased Fry that she was working 'at my bag' in competition with Gill: 'I haven't really got enough colours, & I fear I'm not carrying it out very well. Suppose Winnie's should be better!! Then you would spend all your evenings with her – silly old bumble. Humph.'[23]

Both Winifred Gill and Joy Brown were well known to Fry because they had initially worked in his household at Durbins as governesses for his daughter, Pamela. Like Fry, they were Quakers, and Gill had subsequently been employed by Fry's sister, who lived with him, as her secretary. Roger Fry had encouraged her work as an artist and she trained at the Slade, but she described herself and Nina Hamnett as the Workshops' 'rank and file'. She started as 'a sort of continuity girl', sometimes working in the ground-floor showrooms, sometimes upstairs in the studio, painting, designing, and making Omega products.[24] When Charles Robinson, the Omega business manager, joined the Friends War Victims in Corsica, she was promoted to take his place.[25] She was paid less than the artists, £1.5.0 a week to work full time, and she was given a season ticket for the train: 'Roger Fry came up from Guildford and so did I. We nearly always travelled together . . . we reached the Omega soon after 10.'[26] She calculated her expenditure carefully:

> twenty five shillings did not go far even in those days, when you take off ten shillings paid at home – not so negligible when you realise that five shillings a week covered normal expenditure on food per head in a family. Two shillings a week went on fares from Waterloo to Regents Park, not much remained for clothes, holidays, meals out and so on.[27]

---

111 (p. 94) Roger Fry's pyjamas, designed by Vanessa Bell using the Omega linen *Maud* that she designed in 1913. Art Gallery of South Australia, Adelaide

112 (p. 95) Roger Fry's dressing gown, designed by Vanessa Bell using the Omega linen *Amenophis* that Fry designed in 1913. Art Gallery of South Australia, Adelaide

A ticket to the Ballets Russes, she recalled, was beyond her means, and she described a small stone statuette titled *Sleeping Fawn*, carved by Henri Gaudier-Brzeska, as 'wildly out of my reach'.[28] It was exhibited at the Workshops priced at £2.2.0 – nearly two weeks' salary.

The Workshops' handmade bead jewellery was both distinctive and affordable. It could be commissioned or, like the Workshops' artificial flowers that were made for buttonholes and to be arranged in vases, it could be bought off the shelf to add a dash of colour and style to a simple outfit. Keynes, 'a fairly constant visitor at one time', brought Tamara Karsavina from the Ballets Russes into the showroom and bought her a bracelet made by Jessie Etchells.[29] While the 'Bloomsbury set' was integral to Omega's identity, however, its customers were never limited to an elite 'magic circle'.[30] Bead necklaces were available from three shillings and sixpence, and the Workshops 'got through an enormous quantity of beads' from all over the world. According to Gill, they began with a small muslin sack of beads that she bought from Woolworths.[31] She strung them together, mixing the pure colours, 'pale primrose, mid- and orange chrome, light emerald, sky blue, venetian red and a rather dull viridian green'. When Fry noticed them on the train home, 'he exclaimed . . . "It's like a Picasso."'[32] Long necklaces were fashionable and in the press photographs both Gill and Hamnett wear long strings of Omega beads. These were often finished with a tassel. Gill describes a specialist bead shop in Endell Street in London, lined with 'tiny chests of drawers', where she found 'bunches of curious shaped beads, white, with points around them touched with dark blue'.[33] Her necklaces combined beads in unconventional arrangements. She describes a necklace of roughly made sky-blue beads with inconveniently large holes, 'no doubt made to allow for threading on coarse string or rope of a camel or asses harness', which she combined with dark-blue glass beads to partially block the holes on either side.[34] These and other beads were imported directly from abroad before the war took hold: 'fat little linen-wrapped parcels, tightly stitched and addressed and docketed in purple ink . . . would arrive about every six months' filled with beads and hand-spun silk and muslin squares.[35] The squares were dyed exotic colours and sometimes block-printed or tie-dyed and were joined together to make Omega curtains and clothes.

The idea of drawing together Omega's experiments in dress and launching an Omega collection was led by Vanessa Bell. It was developed collaboratively, and again it was designed to trade on the reputations of Bloomsbury and their friends as artists and intellectuals. She wrote to Fry in the spring of 1915, 'I have an idea . . . which I should like to know whether you think practicable, about dressmaking.'[36] She was staying at the Hutchinsons' Sussex home, Eleanor House in West Wittering, and making a dress for Marjorie Strachey. 'The idea is that I should make or at least superintend the making of several dresses. Ottoline heard from Duncan that I was going to make one for Marjorie and was anxious that she should have one too.'[37] Additional dresses would be made for the poet and actress Iris Tree, for the playwright Constance Marie Beerbohm, and 'perhaps one or two others' in their circle. They would model them at 'a sort of dress parade, perhaps in Ottoline's drawing-room and have a party to see them'.[38] The dresses were to be made of inexpensive fabrics and be less outlandish than Omega's early gowns. 'I believe one could make dresses that would use the fashions and yet not be like dressmaker's dresses', Bell wrote.[39] She was keen to make a start as soon as she returned to London and to have her collection ready for 'the beginning of the season'. She was considering using Lady Ottoline's dressmaker, 'who drinks but is otherwise capable' and could work under her direction.[40]

❋ ❋ ❋

Bell's closest working relationship was with Grant rather than Fry by this time, and her letters draw him in to her interest in dress. Initially they were designed to pique his sexual interest. She described a new evening dress, 'of very bright coral velvet. Don't you think that's exciting?' and, on another occasion, 'a very low shouldered top – where that will get to in the course of the evening I cant think. What a pity you wont be there to appreciate it.'[41] She wrote to Grant in March 1914, describing a trip to Paris with Clive Bell, Roger Fry, and Molly MacCarthy that included visits to Matisse's studio, Jacques Copeau's new theatre, and Michael Stein's collection, and a visit

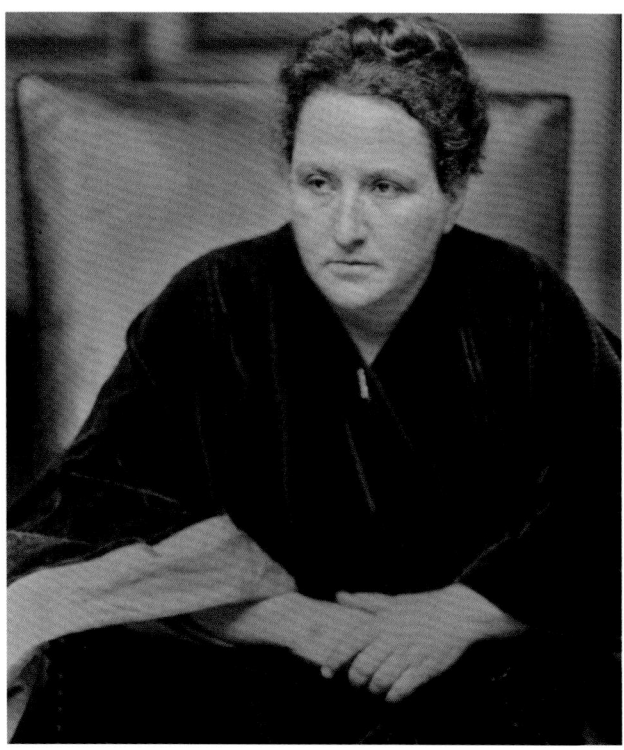
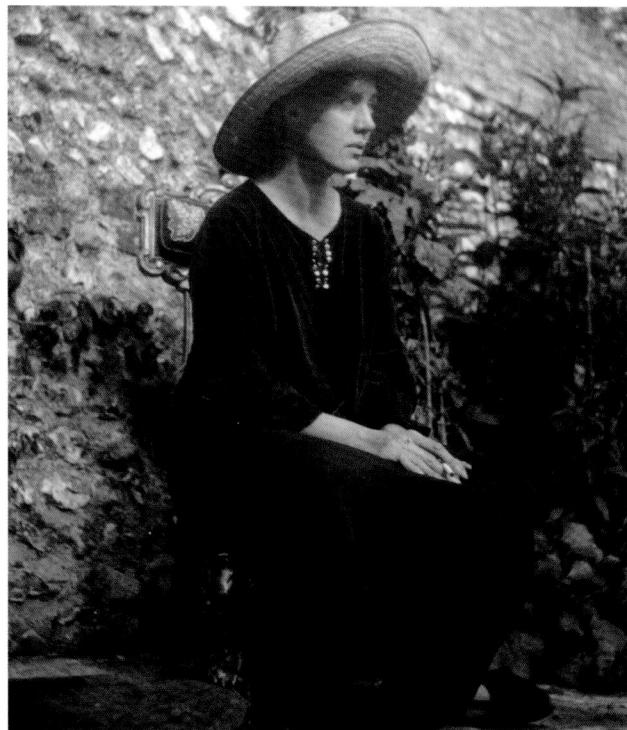

with Gertrude Stein to see Picasso: 'We went to see Gertrude and she took us to Picasso's studio.'[42] The letter is also enthusiastic about a shopping expedition with MacCarthy to the fashionable department store Galeries Lafayette: 'She and I are going to revolutionize our dress. . . . I have already ordered a black velvet dress for £1-8- and we hope to have a large stock of the Paris dresses of the latest cut.'[43] Paris fashions were still nipped in at the waist with ankle-length skirts, and Bell wrote that she and MacCarthy 'had our measurements taken and told them to send us catalogues from which we are to choose models and have dresses made to fit us'.[44]

Bell's choice of black velvet may have been influenced by Gertrude Stein's distinctive, artistic dress. Alvin Langdon Coburn had photographed her at her salon the previous year, wearing one of the long corduroy gowns for which she was renowned (fig. 113).[45] Bringing an intellectual gravitas to the image of the Bohemian, Stein's gowns were spacious and straight, fastened at the neck with a pin. Their stark simplicity and the rich texture of the corduroy were often relieved by a long string of lapis beads with a red bead tassel, and in the Coburn photographs the wide sleeves to Stein's gown are turned back to show a contrasting lining.[46] Bell wrote to her, on her return to England, wishing to return her hospitality and offering to find Stein and her partner, Alice Toklas, a house and servants in London.[47] Fry had involved Stein in the original planning of Omega and when they did visit London he took her to see the Workshops. 'Can you remember', Gill wrote to Grant, 'the vogue there was for Gertrude Stein? . . . People imitated her or tried to.'[48] The Omega artists, she recalled, impersonated Stein's voice. The enduring influence of her style on Bell's dress can be seen some years later in a photograph taken at Charleston in which Bell wears a simple velvet dress with an embellished slit neckline and straight, bracelet sleeves (fig. 114).[49]

Bell's letters to Grant assume a shared interest in dress and a degree of collaboration. She complained of spending a gloomy Christmas at Seend and then Durbins in 1914:

> I couldn't even cheer myself up by wearing my red dress for Clive took against it &

---

113 Alvin Langdon Coburn, Gertrude Stein, 1913. George Eastman Museum, New York

114 Vanessa Bell, Vanessa Bell at Charleston, undated. Tate, London. She is seated on one of the Prie Dieu chairs acquired by Duncan Grant in 1917

I didn't dare face scorn on all sides. . . . However I shall wear the red when you're there to support me. I daresay you're right about the vermilion edge to the coat. I'll try it.[50]

The 'vermilion edge' suggests either an addition or an alteration by Bell to an existing garment. A photograph of her taken at Asheham soon after her return from Paris shows her wearing fashionable clothes that may also have been altered to her own designs (fig. 115).[51] It is unusual as an image in Woolf's albums because it depicts Bell's standing figure in full, as if to show off her dress, with one foot pointing slightly outwards to reveal a polished shoe. Still designed to be worn with corsets, the fashion in 1914 was for matching blouses and full-length, straight, tiered skirts. Bell's long, button-through, straight skirt conforms to shop-bought fashions but there is no evidence of a corseted profile. The effect of a short overskirt is created by an asymmetrical wrap in a different fabric, finished with a wide silk or satinized front band. The black-and-white

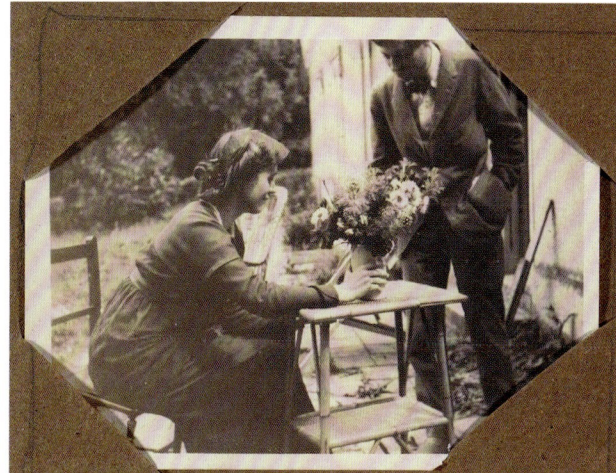

photograph shows only that the colours are dark. It is tempting to assume, however, that the long-sleeved top with which the skirt was worn would have been made of a matching fabric and that its asymmetrical buttoned front-band, again silk or satinized, was another of Bell's adaptations. A stylized artificial flower, offset by folds of fabric, fastens the contrasting shawl collar, and Bell wears a short length of assorted beads. In Woolf's album, the photograph is paired with a slightly later photograph of Bell wearing the same top but a different skirt (fig. 116).[52] The terrace borders at Asheham with their wallflowers date the first photograph to April. They have been cleared in the second photograph, and Bell arranges late-summer flowers, dahlias and chrysanthemums, in a vase while a smartly dressed Duncan Grant looks on. In this photograph, Bell's top, with its distinctive pleat concealing seams to the yoke and drop-shoulder, and its turn-back cuffs, is shown from the side.

By April 1915, when Bell wrote to Fry proposing a dress collection for the Omega Workshops, the First World War was gathering momentum. Bell's interest in making and adapting clothes had practical as well as artistic implications, but her letters also contextualize the Omega dress collection within Bloomsbury's political and intellectual responses to the war. They describe the war's effects on her own family and financial circumstances. Clive Bell's pacifist pamphlet *Peace at Once*, which argued for a settlement with Germany, had become the subject of a court case

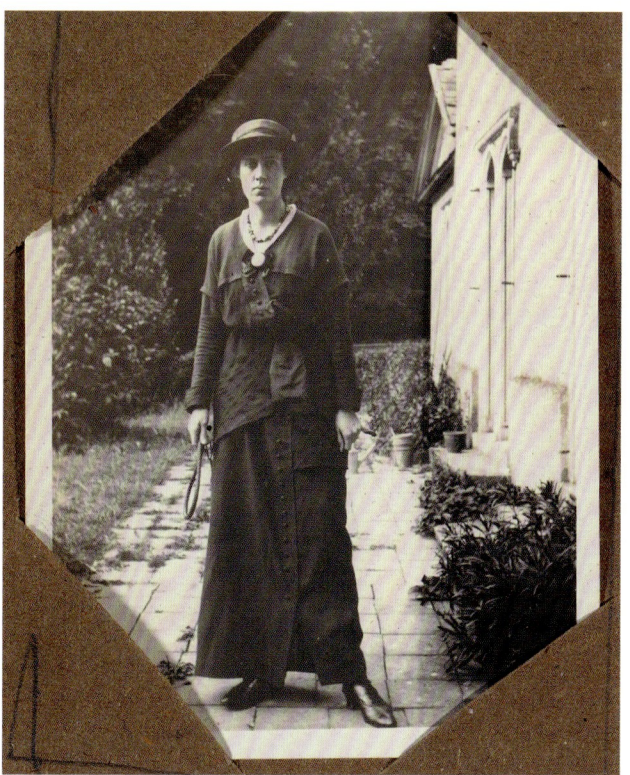

115 Virginia Woolf, Vanessa Bell at Asheham, c.1914–15. Houghton Library, Harvard University

116 Virginia Woolf, Vanessa Bell and Duncan Grant at Asheham, c.1914–15. Houghton Library, Harvard University

OMEGA DRESS 99

when he and Vanessa went to stay at the Hutchinsons' Sussex home, where the collection was developed. Mary Hutchinson's husband, St John, known as Jack, was a barrister and held a seat on the London County Council. 'I fear we shall have Jack's company', Bell wrote to Fry, 'but he wants to see Clive about his pamphlet case which is coming on this week.'[53] The case was lost and the pamphlet was publicly destroyed. Vanessa Bell was also concerned that a rift with Clive's family threatened their income and their potential inheritance. She decided to sublet 46 Gordon Square so as to ease their financial commitments. (Though she did not know it at the time, the lease would be taken by Keynes.) The Omega Workshops was beginning to struggle financially, too. Gill recalled that in 1913 'orders came in, and everything was buzzing and we were just getting on fine until it came to the War in 1914 . . . the War shut down on everything . . . days went by and nobody came in at all'.[54] Bell expressed her concerns in a letter to Fry, who by this time had left Guildford for Paris. Relaying a conversation with Robinson, the Workshops' manager, she reported that there were orders for Omega rugs in prospect but no profits.[55]

Bell's proposal for a dress collection coincided with an intensely difficult period in her relationship with Fry and his departure, as a consequence, for France to undertake war relief work with the Quakers. 'You write as if I had come to an end of all feeling for you & only wanted to get rid of you', she wrote in April 1915. Fry complained to Clive Bell:

> I feel a good deal less in the centre of things than I did. Nessa and Duncan have taken to working so entirely together and not to want me . . . so that I can't see life in London very easily just now. But exactly what and how and where I shall exist isn't clear to me.[56]

Evidently the future of their friendship and, as a consequence, their business relationship at the Workshops was in jeopardy. Vanessa wrote to Fry, ominously: 'You forget that no one, except Duncan, realizes that you are doing more than just going away for a short time.'[57] Although she remained at Eleanor House with Grant and David Garnett for much of April and May, the dress collection marked a stepping up of Bell's responsibilities as one of the Workshops' co-directors. It was conceived in defiance, against the war and the uncertainties and instabilities that she faced. The collection would make manifest a distinctive Bloomsbury aesthetic that Bell and her friends had cultivated in private, but it was also developed as a business proposition.

The availability of new clothing and materials would become increasingly limited during the war, yet Bell was resourceful. She wrote to Grant from Gordon Square in May 1915: 'If you feel inclined to perhaps if youre back in time tomorrow we could go & poke about for odd stuffs to make coats & waistcoats out of. I think we might use all sorts of cheap stuffs, but you & I would have to choose them.'[58] ('Stuffs' was in common use as a word for fabrics.) She concluded the letter with a dig at Grant's relationship with Garnett (whose nickname among close friends was Bunny): 'I daresay you'll stay away till the afternoon & that horrid rabbit will occupy your evening . . . so I shall have to go & stuff hunt alone.'

She worked collaboratively, too, with the artist Kate Lechmere, who had been involved with Wyndham Lewis and the Rebel Art Centre.[59] 'Miss L. is making a dress for me – one to her own measurements & I hope one for Iris', she wrote to Fry. 'She has also given us patterns for coats & waistcoats which Winnie & Miss Shearer will make from stuffs Duncan & I have bought.'[60] In the event, however, Lechmere was 'a complete failure'. Bell wrote to Fry, 'She has spoilt my dress by adding absurd details & the dress she made after her own ideas is too awful they say. So I am telling her we cant employ her now. I see she'd be hopeless & would want constant looking after.'[61] After the war Lechmere established her own hat business, Rigolo, and produced headwear for the theatre and for clients including Edith Sitwell.[62]

Bell's letters to Fry are filled with praise for 'Miss Joy'. She favoured Joy Brown because, unlike the artists working for Omega, she was 'much more in sympathy with us about colour & very anxious to carry out my ideas about cut'.[63] She may have been involved with the Workshops even before the collection was conceived; Gill wrote that friends would be called in to help when there was a 'special job', and Joy had connections to Omega through her cousin May and her work for

Fry at Durbins.[64] Certainly, she was at some point persuaded to take on the making of Bell's dress for Marjorie Strachey and the Iris Tree dress that Lechmere abandoned, thus becoming an important contributor to the first Omega show. 'Also she is going to make a blouse', Bell wrote, '& I said she could exhibit a dress she made for herself out of Turkish stuffs. . . . She has as much as she can do now till she leaves Durbins.'[65] Brown recalled that in fact another seamstress, Isabel Walker, had made this dress for her:

> with the skirt part pleated of tussore silk dyed to tone with one of the Broussa silk squares which Roger brought back from a holiday he had with the Bells and Duncan Grant – when Vanessa had got so ill . . . The Brussa Square [sic] made the top of the dress, just a hole in the middle for the neck and the edges joined at the under arms and beads attached at the corners.[66]

To establish a professional basis for the dress collection, Bell proposed that Joy Brown should combine professional training as a dressmaker with part-time employment at the Workshops. Robinson disagreed: she should 'remain in the background to carry out orders when they're given'.[67] Bell, however, was insistent: 'we must have someone on the spot with stuffs & specimen dresses & I believe Miss Joy with a little more training would be just what we want.' She concluded: 'If the show in June succeeds I think we ought to risk it.'[68]

Bell's exhibition of evening cloaks, coats, dresses, waistcoats, and parasols launched the collection just two months after it was initially proposed, on 10 June 1915. It was combined with a show of woodcuts by Roald Kristian. Fry remained in France and Bell's letters to him describe a frenetic two weeks leading up to the opening, culminating in advance orders the day before the show. 'Mrs MacLaren has ordered a coat. Mary Hutch has promised to get a dress so has Miss Cunard.'[69] Bell wrote to Fry from her sickbed two days after the opening with a degree of disappointment: 'The exhibition was not much of a success the first day but I think more people have been since.'[70] She was determined that 'as soon as I can get about again I shall get people to come & order dresses'. Miss Cunard and Mrs MacLaren are likely to have been a younger generation of society figures, Nancy Cunard and Christabel MacLaren, both known to the Workshops. Bell confided in Fry, however, that despite her earlier ambitions to cultivate a wealthy clientele 'I think really our public ought to be not the very smart but people like myself who just know where to get clothes that aren't too expensive or too ordinary.'[71] At least five 'specimen dresses' were made up for the show. Lechmere produced the dress for Vanessa Bell, and one 'made after her own ideas'. Brown made the dresses for Iris Tree and Marjorie Strachey, and showed the 'one old one of her own'. Setting out her plans in a letter to Fry two weeks before the show, Bell wrote: 'Also we shall have several coats & waistcoats & two old evening cloaks to show & parasols. There is a great difficulty over the dyes of course, but we shall have a good many printed stuffs too.'[72]

By showing dresses that had already been commissioned by Iris Tree and Marjorie Strachey, both independent, Bohemian women known for their intelligence and good families, Bell's collection was designed to appeal to a particular demographic. Even so, 'Marjorie Strachey is very ugly', Bell wrote, '(perhaps that's too harsh but you have seen her)'.[73] 'Vanessa Bell', however, was not a marketing brand for the collection. She wrote to Roger Fry in confusion: 'I had a telegram from Robinson . . . asking for my dress for Miss Joy to be photographed in. I have sent it, but what is happening? Won't the one of me do?'[74] Judith Collins describes a photograph of Bell in an Omega dress with a cut-out of Joy Brown's face stuck over Bell's.[75] She also reproduces an undated press photograph in which a melancholy Bell poses in front of a screen draped with printed fabrics (fig. 117).[76] The dress she wears is likely to have been made of one of the plain Chinese silks that the Workshops bought in and block-printed by hand.[77] However, either the identity of the artist was incompatible with the Workshops' policy of creative anonymity or the characteristic expression that Bell had adopted for formal photographs since her teens was deemed inappropriate. The Omega collection rejected conventional ideals of prettiness. It capitalized, nevertheless, on the Bohemian and intellectual distinction for which Bloomsbury and its wider circle were renowned.

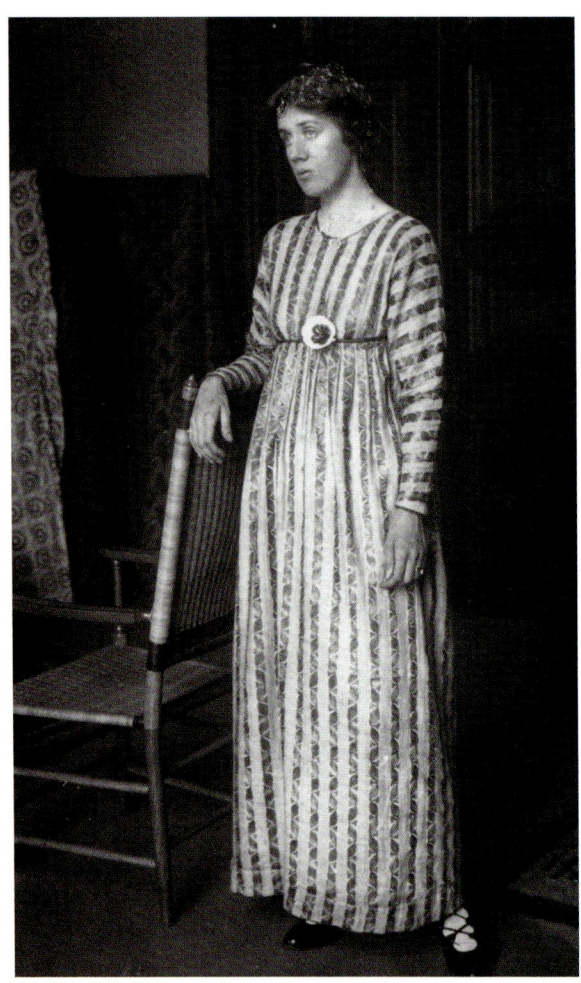

been one of the older items of Workshops stock that were exhibited alongside Bell's new designs in 1915. *Cracow* is one of the fabrics draped over the screen in the press photograph of Bell. Gill also designed long straight waistcoats made up in Omega linens, lined with a plain material matching one of the colours in the pattern, and she recalled that these sold well.[79]

❈ ❈ ❈

In 1915 Bell was savvy in negotiating a business agreement with one of the Workshops' existing suppliers to enable Brown to 'spend her afternoons at the Omega ready to see people or fit them' without covering the cost of her salary. She was to be employed, at a salary of £100 per year, as a dressmaker for Douglas Pepler, and the Workshops would pay him 'the same that he asks other people for every dress she makes for us'.[80] This was a good salary. Bell recruited a new servant for Charleston two years later for £22 a year.[81] In addition, the Workshops would pay Brown a percentage of their profit on the dresses. Bell reasoned that Omega 'should risk nothing as we only pay when we have an order'.[82] Douglas Pepler was a Fabian, a Quaker, and a philanthropist. Eric Gill (no relation to Winifred) dubbed him 'Hilario Bottomlessfinance'

Very few items of dress survive from the Omega Workshops. Towards the end of her life Brown gifted a waistcoat made from one of the Omega upholstery fabrics, *Cracow*, to the Victoria and Albert Museum, London (fig. 118). It is catalogued as a design by Fry, made by Brown in 1913.[78] As such it is compatible with the Workshops' early and unconventional determination to use linen curtain material for tunics. Upholstery and dress fabrics are not generally interchangeable, and one of Omega's distinguishing features was the originality with which it put materials together in unlikely combinations. The stark simplicity of the waistcoat's cut, closely fitting with a wide collar but no buttons or welts, is designed to show off the wool-and-linen fabric that Fry also designed. As it remained in Brown's own collection it may well have

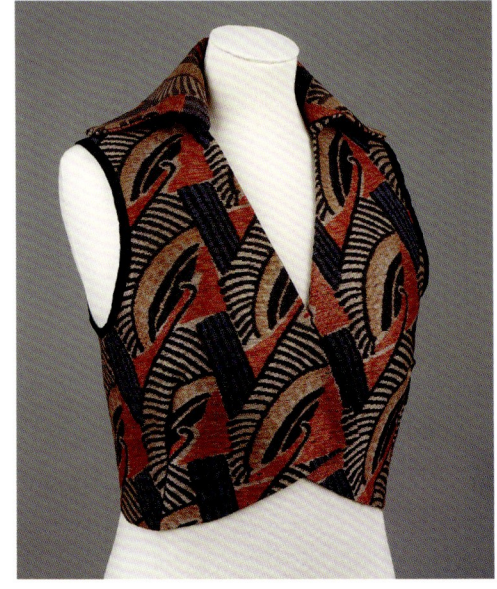

117 Unknown photographer, Vanessa Bell wearing an Omega dress of her own design, undated. From Judith Collins, *The Omega Workshops* (London: Secker and Warburg, 1983), plate 55

118 Roger Fry (designer), *Cracow* waistcoat, 1913. Jacquard-woven and block-printed wool-and-linen waistcoat, 600 × 605 × 605 mm. Victoria and Albert Museum, London

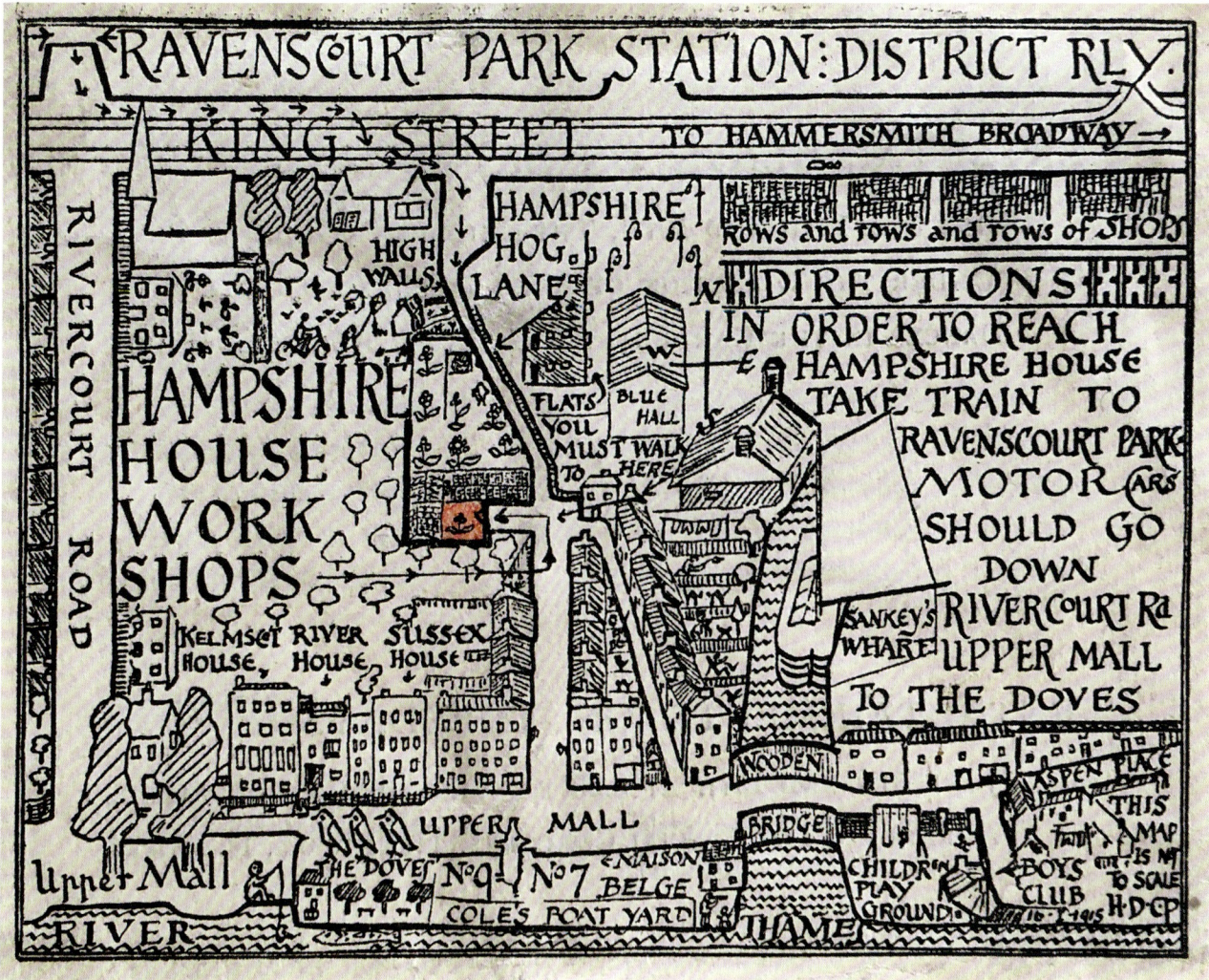

after he moved to Ditchling, changed his name to Hilary, and established his own private press there.[83] His Hampshire House Workshops may have influenced Fry's ideas for Omega. Established in Hammersmith within a few minutes' walk of William Morris's Kelmscott House and the Hutchinsons' London home, they began in 1907 as a club where working men could learn a trade (fig. 119). Edward Carpenter contributed to their lecture series, Ellen Terry gave a guest performance for their dramatic society, and their Annual Picture Exhibition included work by the 'local artists' T. J. Cobden-Sanderson, Frank Brangwyn, and Edward Johnston.[84] As soon as the war broke out the Hampshire House Workshops provided a hostel and employment for some of the first refugees to arrive from Belgium. Pepler recalled that: 'Dressmaking and embroidery, boot making and repairing, "wood work" were carried on in independent rooms or shops.'[85] He described his Workshops, which by the end of 1916 had consolidated into a bakery, a carpenters' shop, and 'The Dressmaking and Embroidery Shop', as 'an attempt to make a positive statement upon some of the things which belong to Peace'.[86] Joy Brown was to join this social enterprise in 1915, drawing the Hampshire House and Omega Workshops more closely together. Pepler wrote that after the Belgian refugees had moved on 'the women's work in dressmaking and embroidery was continued by the English girls who

---

119 Hilary Douglas Pepler, map locating the Hampshire House Workshops close to Kelmscott House and River House, 1915. From *Exhibition of English and Belgian Work by Craftsmen and Artists in Hammersmith*, exh. cat. (Hampshire House Club, Hammersmith, 1915). Ditchling Museum of Art + Craft, Sussex

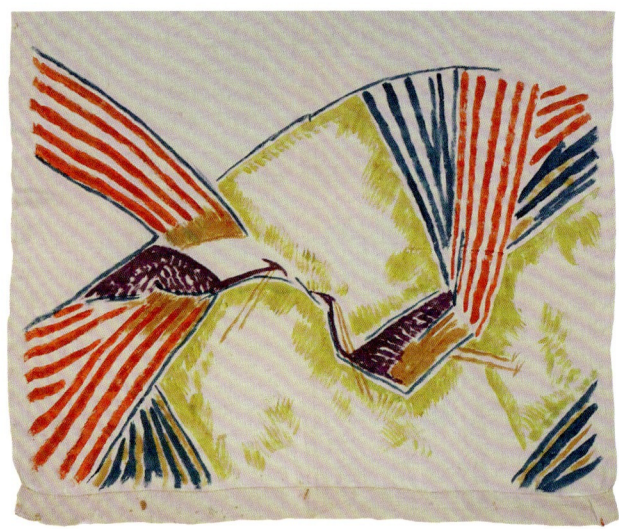

Pepler's exhibitions at the Hampshire House Workshops were distinct from those of the Omega because they were rooted in their local community and its Arts and Crafts affiliations. Although they included sculpture by Eric Gill, who had exhibited in the *Second Post-Impressionist Exhibition*, their focus was on craft skills and the workshop as a centre for training and support. Hampshire House Workshops hosted an exhibition to support its Belgian Refugee and Repatriation Fund in June 1915, for example, which included embroidery, lace, and beadwork by two of its refugees, Gabrielle Goossens and Marie van Aerschott, alongside embroidery by the Hammersmith designer and embroiderer May Morris, the painter Christabel Frampton, and 'the apprentices'.[89] Blouses and dresses by Isabel Walker, who would also make for the Omega Workshops, were included in the show, and five Hammersmith artists contributed to a section of the exhibition dedicated to 'dyeing and stencilling'. It was this technical expertise that proved invaluable to Omega. 'I would say that we "painted" cushion covers, scarves and lampshades in dyes on silk', Winifred Gill wrote. The fabric was prepared at the Omega Workshops by 'being brushed over by some paste or

had been apprenticed', and that by the end of 1919 they were in a position 'to become an independent business on their own'.[87] Omega was already using the specialist skills and facilities at Pepler's workshops to fix the dyes in its hand-painted silk scarves and cushion covers, so an arrangement over dressmaking in 1915 was beneficial for both organizations.[88] Bell would also have been confident that Fry, who was still working with the Quakers in France, would approve of the arrangements.

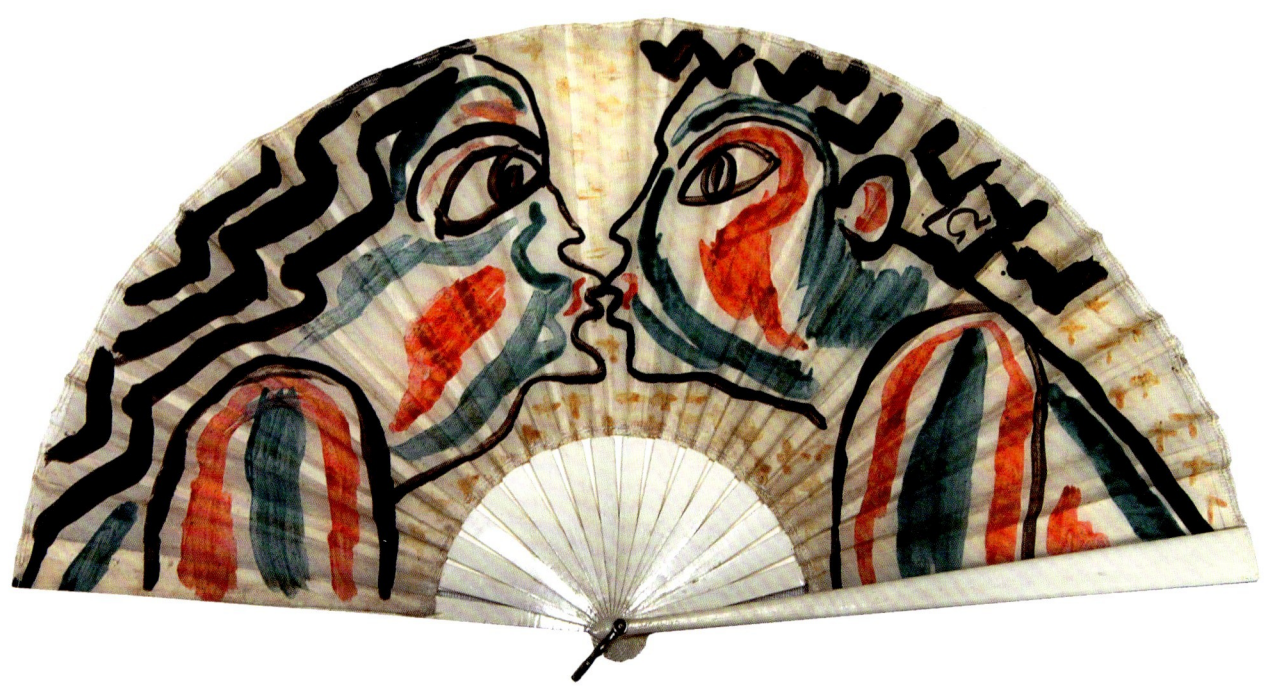

120 (*top*) Roger Fry, hand-painted Omega Workshops shawl, 1913–14. Painted silk, 600 × 650 mm. Victoria and Albert Museum, London

121 (*bottom*) Attributed to Duncan Grant, decorated Omega Workshops fan, c.1913–16. Painted silk and ivory, 310 × 580 mm. David Herbert Collection

104 THE BLOOMSBURY LOOK

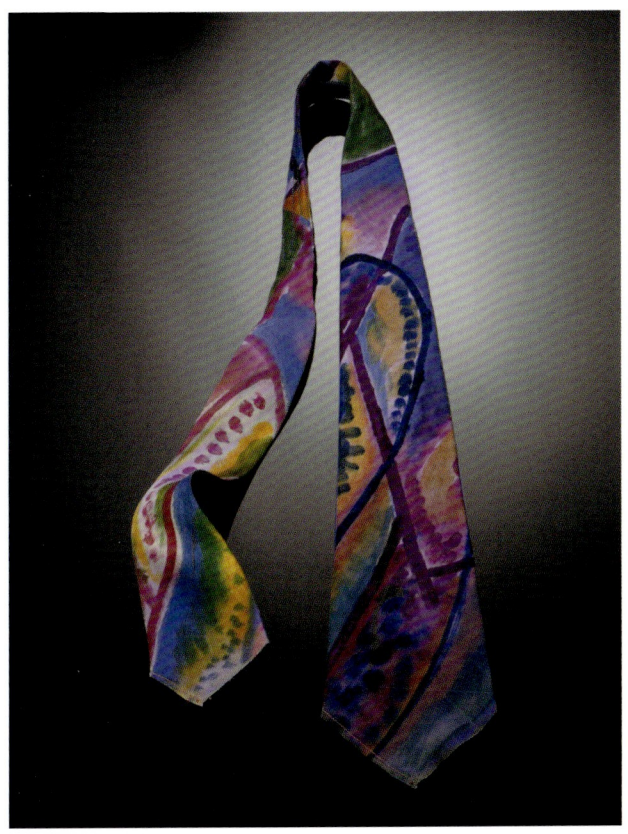
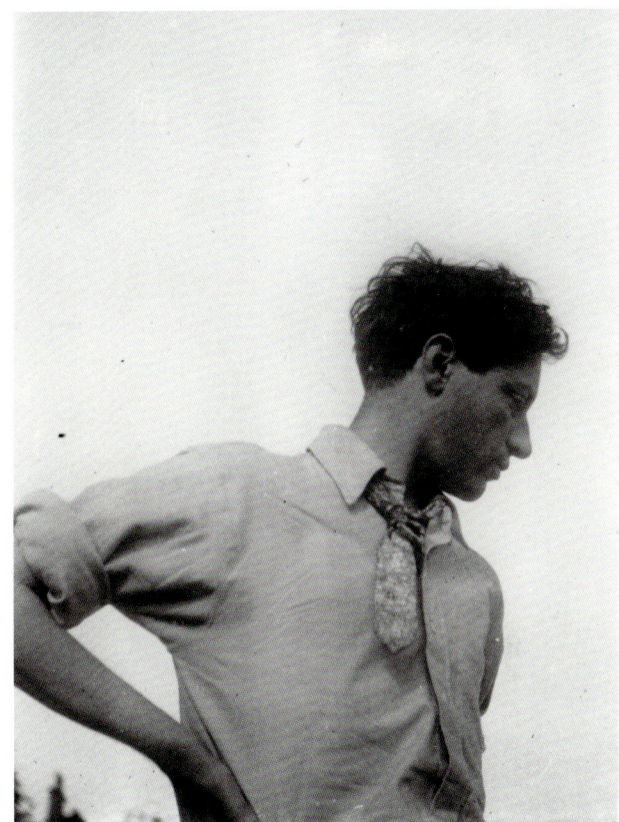

starch mixture brewed by Miles the caretaker. . . . This treatment rendered the silk as safe to paint on as paper.'[90] The dyes were subsequently 'fixed' at the Hampshire House Workshops.

An Omega silk stole given by Fry as a wedding present to Joy Brown and hand-painted with his design of peacocks is evidence of this practice of painting onto silk (fig. 120).[91] Omega fans, scarves, parasols, and cloaks also took advantage of the process to blur the boundaries between art and design and to explore dress as a vehicle for vibrant and innovative Post-Impressionist designs (fig. 121). They offered the Workshops' clients anti-fashion statements that signalled a stylish and cosmopolitan familiarity with new directions in avant-garde painting. A hand-painted silk tie by Gill, for example, reflects the influence of Wassily Kandinsky, whose work she would have seen in London at the Allied Artists Salon in 1913 and at an exhibition of the Grafton Group, when Kandinsky paintings were shown together with those of the Omega artists (fig. 122). It was one of two ties that she made for the brother of one of her fellow workers at the Omega.[92] Grant also appears to have owned at least one Omega tie (fig. 123).[93] Bell's 1915 collection was designed to complement and extend these initial experiments. The Omega Workshops' policy that individual artists should remain anonymous, and the lack of dedicated press coverage for Bell's show, however, make it difficult to differentiate the visual evidence for her 1915 collection from earlier Omega stock.

One of the liveliest images of Omega dress, an undated press photograph, shows Gill and Hamnett standing in front of Bell's screen *Bathers in a Landscape* (see fig. 106), surrounded by Omega rugs and furnishing fabrics (fig. 124). The two women are laughing, facing one another to show off the bold, abstract lines of a Post-Impressionist painted-silk evening cloak and the more subtle design of a skirt and blouse, worn by Gill, with a waistcoat patterned with sunflowers. As a motif, the vivid sunflowers on the waistcoat pay tribute to the Aesthetic and Arts

122 Winifred Gill (designer and maker), Omega Workshops tie, 1915. Painted silk, 1025 × 90 mm. Victoria and Albert Museum, London

123 Vanessa Bell, Duncan Grant wearing a painted tie, undated. The Charleston Trust

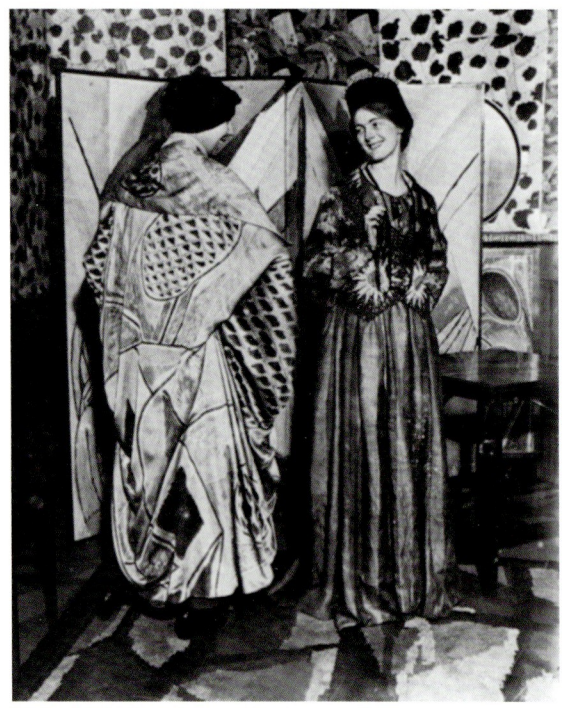

and Crafts movements that paved the way for Omega. They are compatible in style with Omega's earliest interior decorations.[94] Hamnett's painted cloak is also patterned with stylized sunflower seed-heads and this is echoed in the design of one of the Workshops' embroidered firescreens, which can just be seen in the background to the photograph. Gill described the cloak as 'oyster coloured satin', painted in greens and browns either by Doucet or Grant.[95] Both women wear exotic hats made by the Workshops. Hamnett wears a turban and Gill a fez with a row of Omega beads decorating its crown. Gill later recalled posing for the photographs at a 'press pre-view'. 'Nina and I put on the clothes to show them off better than on a stand, for the photograph.'[96] She recalled that the fabric for her waistcoat had been bought in, rather than designed by Omega, and was also used for curtains, and for cushion covers at the *Second Post-Impressionist Exhibition*.[97] The blouse, she wrote, 'would have been made by us', again in a commercially printed fabric 'that Roger approved'. She described her puddle-length striped skirt as makeshift, 'simply made up of a length of plain material . . . tied round the waist with a piece of tape'.

This, she believed, was likely to have been one of the heavy striped silks that the Workshops stocked in several colour ranges, including 'a ground of yellow ochre with a greenish tinge, and black stripes'.[98]

The photograph of Gill and Hamnett, and another of Gill standing on her own in her outfit, were published in the *Illustrated Sunday Herald* in October 1915, together with four others showing artists and staff at work in the Omega studios (fig. 125). Stylistically, however, these two press photographs, and the clothing they depict, appear to be earlier. Gill related them to the *Ideal Homes Exhibition* in October 1913.[99] They represent Omega dress as integral to a broader design agenda and may have been stock photographs offered to the *Sunday Herald* to support the other photographs, which have been staged in the first-floor 'back showroom' at the Workshops. Gill describes this as 'largely devoted to storing our stock of printed linens. These occupied about three quarters of the room, the front part, divided from the rest by curtains, served as a small sitting room where we sometimes had tea.' In the top left image, captioned 'Your hostesses, Miss Gill and Miss Hamlet [*sic*], at work', the figure with his back to the camera, facing Nina Hamnett, appears to be not Gill but Duncan Grant, holding his painted tray *Trojan Women* (fig. 126).[100] Hamnett and Gill, in her long smock, pretend to paint the ceiling in the central image in the

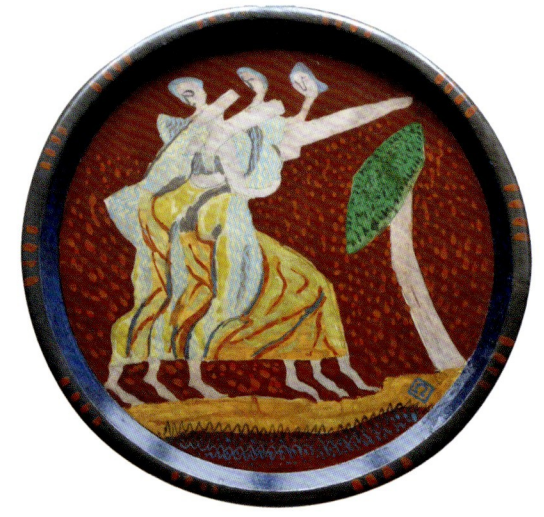

124 Unknown photographer, press photograph of Nina Hamnett (*left*) and Winifred Gill (*right*) modelling Omega Workshops cloak, dress, waistcoat, and hats, c.1913. From Isabelle Anscombe, *Omega and After* (London: Thames & Hudson, 1981), plate 12

125 (*opposite*) Unknown photographer, 'Women Who Do the Most Original War Work of All', *Illustrated Sunday Herald*, 24 October 1915, p. 17
126 (*above*) Duncan Grant, *Trojan Women*, c.1913–15. Painted tray, paint and gesso on wood, 34 × 528 mm diameter. Private collection

106 THE BLOOMSBURY LOOK

Illustrated Sunday Herald. October 24, 1915.—Page 17.

WOMEN WHO DO THE MOST ORIGINAL WAR WORK OF ALL.

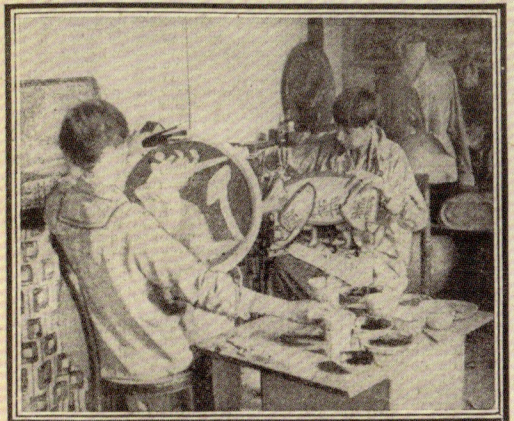
Your hostesses, Miss Gill and Miss Hamlet, at work.

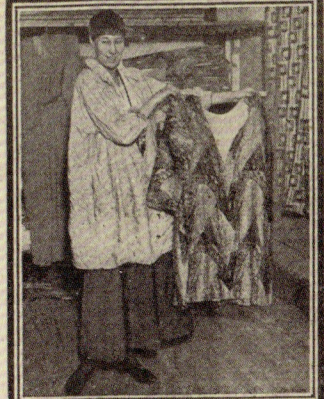
Miss Hamlet shows you her own design.

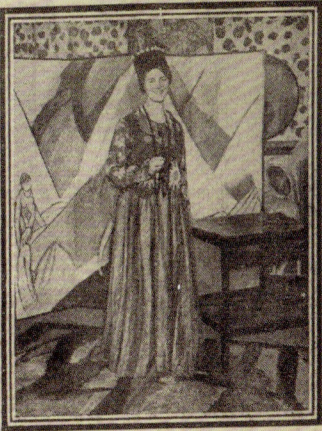
A West End futurist smiles on you.

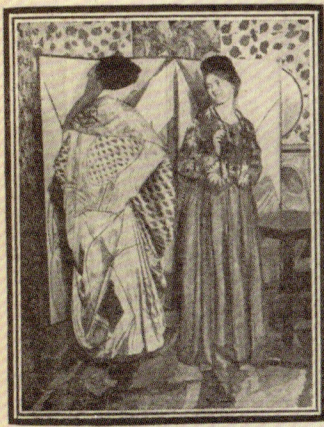
"How do we look?"

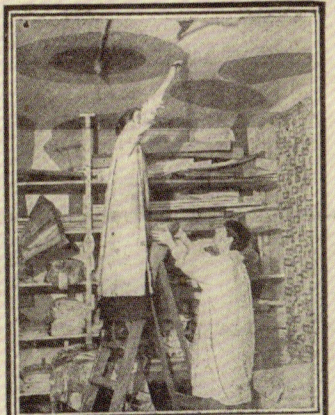
"Sorry we're so busy."

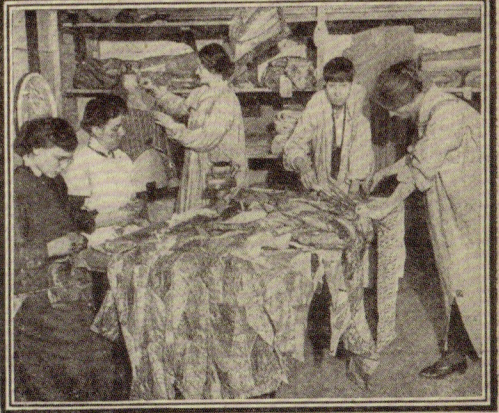
You see the futurist factory in full swing.

These pictures tell the story of half an hour's visit to a futurist studio in the West End of London. Three of the men artists at the Omega workshops have been killed in the war. Three women have taken their places.—(*Sunday Herald* Photographs.)

OMEGA DRESS 107

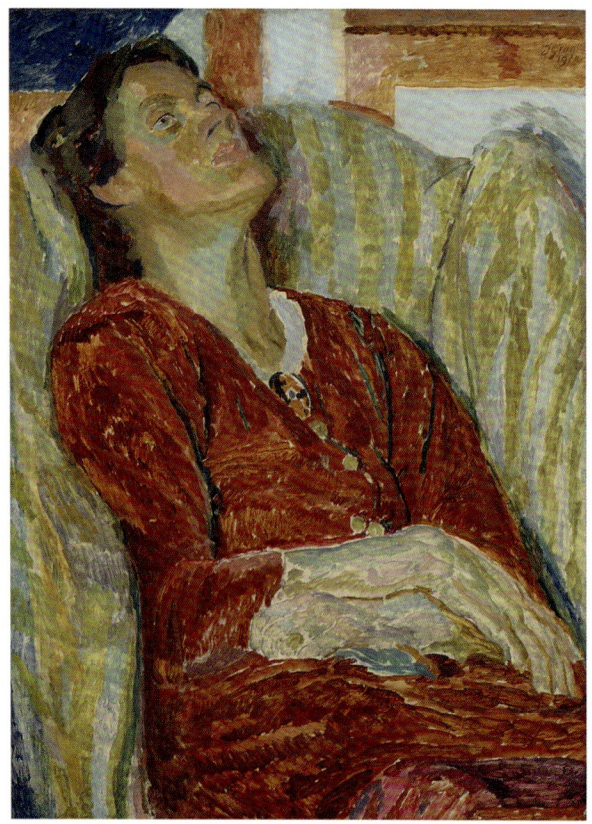

bottom row. In the image to the right of this, they work on Omega textiles, together with three other women. A dress hangs on a coat hanger in the background and one of the women arranges the collar to a jacket on a mannequin. The *Sunday Herald* piece is headlined 'Women Who Do the Most Original War Work of All' and its images are arranged to 'tell the story of half an hour's visit to a futurist studio in the West End of London'. It cannot be assumed, however, that the visit was made in October 1915. The pictures may have been held in readiness as a 'filler'. The paper improvised a topical story that three of Omega's male artists had been killed in the war and their places filled by three women, of whom only the 'hostesses', 'Miss Gill and Miss Hamlet', are named. Henri Doucet and Henri Gaudier-Brzeska had been killed in action in March and June of that year (the third death seems to have been the *Herald*'s invention), and the paper's approach to Omega, ignoring its pacifism to include it in a propagandist narrative, complicates assumptions about its artists as 'outsiders'. The article conflates a celebration of the originality of Omega design with praise for its women artists and their readiness to take on 'men's work' in support of the war effort. Although the story is a nonsense and Omega's policy of anonymity promoted equality for the work of its women long before the outbreak of war, the piece illuminates the patriarchal values that Omega transgressed.

Bloomsbury's painted portraits are more reliable in establishing the chronology of Omega dress. Although they do not detail their sitters' dress, personal attire is significant as a statement of identity in a number of portraits painted in 1915. The paintings consolidate and perpetuate a bold and coherent Bloomsbury image. They are assertively modern in their handling of paint, their use of colour, and their rejection of conventional 'prettiness', as portraits and as paintings. Their female subjects are abstracted and distorted, pressed up against the picture plane in cropped compositions. In Grant's portrait of Bell, *At Eleanor: Vanessa Bell*, her red dress with yellow buttons and an Omega flower fastening a pale shawl collar testify to a shared visual language between the two artists (fig. 127). Grant made a sketch for the painting (fig. 128) when they were working together in Hutchinson's home in West Wittering, and the painting is particularly illuminating because it documents Bell's striking use of colour. The yellow buttons against red and the Omega flower would have broadcast her identity as a Post-Impressionist artist, just as the painting itself broadcast Grant's. The dress may be the one that Clive had condemned at Durbins a few months earlier, or one that Bell had made the previous summer and described in a letter to Fry, anticipating his disapproval.[101] Its simple lines and prominent buttons are replicated in a garment worn by Mary Hutchinson. She posed for Bell for a photograph, perched on a single bed, possibly at Eleanor House in 1915, with an ornament in her hair corresponding in size and shape to an Omega flower (fig. 129).[102]

Bell's portrait of Mary Hutchinson, painted in the same year, has been analysed for its abstract, painterly qualities (fig. 130).[103] The flattening of the composition and the reductive representation of Hutchinson's features, with colours recurring in her skin tones and

127 Duncan Grant, *At Eleanor: Vanessa Bell*, 1915. Oil on canvas, 760 × 556 mm. Yale Center for British Art, New Haven, CT

128 (opposite) Duncan Grant, study for *At Eleanor: Vanessa Bell*, 1915. Pencil on paper, 373 × 275 mm. The Charleston Trust

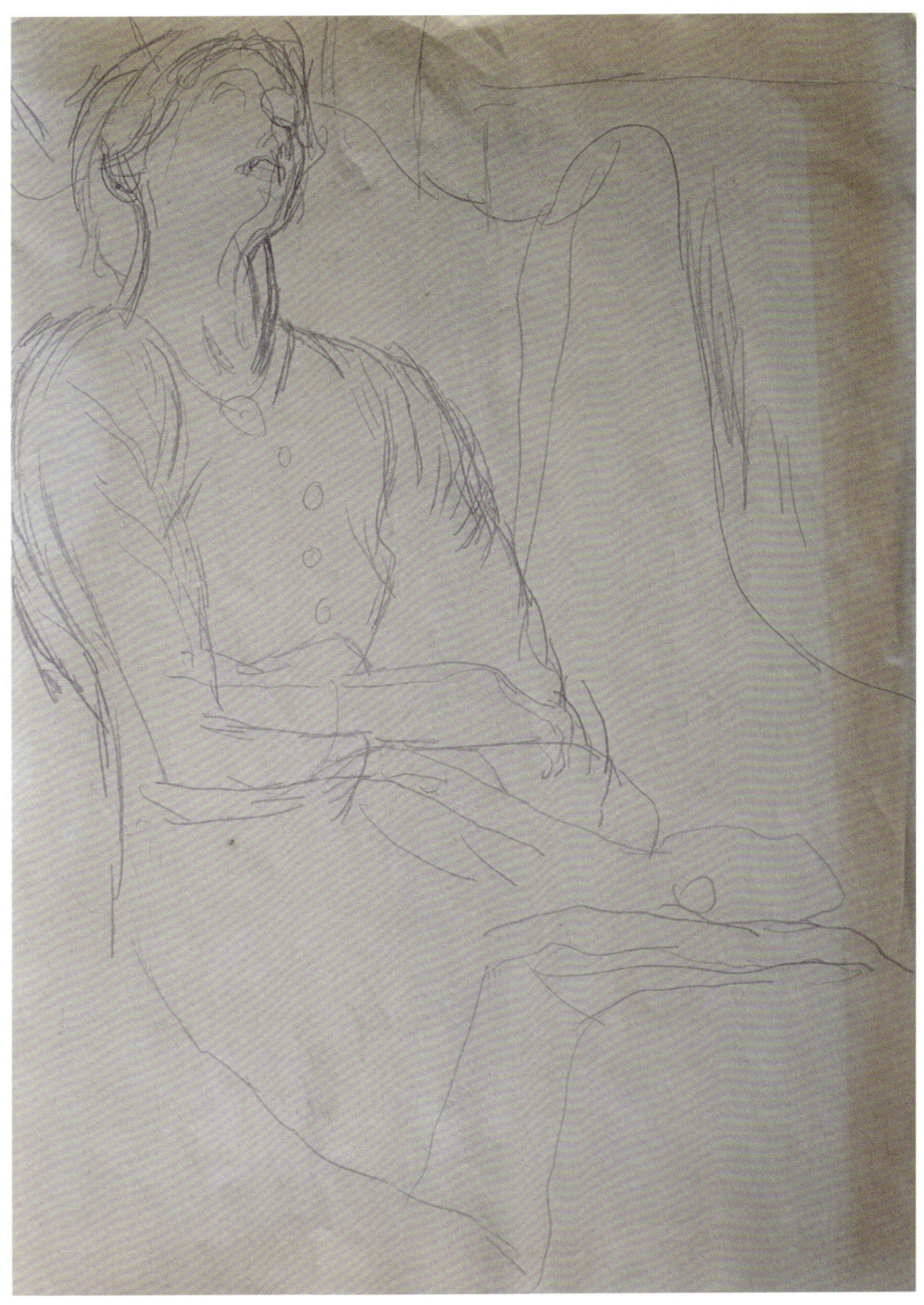

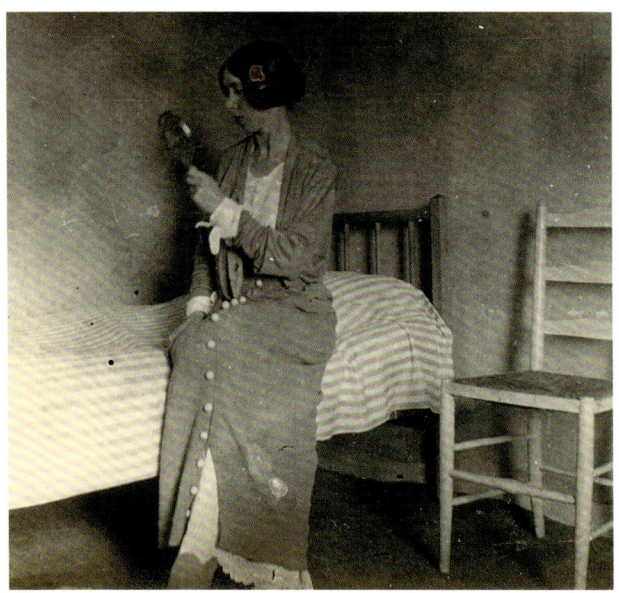

in the abstract painting in the background, challenged the conventions of British portraiture in 1915. Hutchinson's dress, however, has escaped observation. The simple, asymmetrical lines of her top or dress, and her string of yellow beads, may have been identifiable among her contemporaries as an Omega garment and necklace. Bell's use of artistic licence makes such observations speculative. The bold, yellowish-green of Hutchinson's clothing may simply have expressed Bell's exploration of innovative palettes in portraiture, used to contrast against the pink face and background. This is a painting about colour. But it is equally possible that this experimentation extended to Bell's dress collection for Omega. When a version of the portrait was included in Bell's first solo exhibition at the Workshops in 1916, and then in *The New Movement in Art* travelling exhibition the following year, it reinforced Bloomsbury's reputation for distinctive Post-Impressionist dress as well as painting.

Iris Tree also sat for Bell, Grant, and Fry in 1915 (fig. 131).[104] Again her dress is blocked in rather than articulated in detail, and again, in Bell's portrait, the figure and her abstract setting are conceived as a whole. Tree was a 'crop-head', one of a group of young women who included the artists Dora Carrington, Barbara Bagenal, and Nina Hamnett, whose short hair, cut to just below the ears, announced their modernity.

In Bell's portrait the yellow of her hair and her skin tones echo the warm colours of a geometric pattern covering the sofa on which she sits, and those of an abstract screen or painting in the background. As with the Hutchinson portrait, the painting promotes the Omega Workshops' distinctive palette and abstract designs. Tree's dress, however, is almost black, offsetting the vibrant colours of her surroundings. An Omega flower or brooch accentuates the low cut of its 'V' neck, and its empire style suggests that this is the dress designed for Bell's 1915 collection. A band is indicated, in both Bell and Grant's portraits, joining the bodice to the skirt just below the bust, and no attempt is made in either portrait to flatter.

A self-portrait by Bell, again painted in 1915, reinforces this new direction in British portraiture to represent modern women, dressed plainly and unconventionally, in interior settings patterned with abstract paintings or designs (fig. 132). In Bell's portraits of Mary Hutchinson, Iris Tree, and herself, the period ideals of beauty, of figures shaped and defined by corsets, are renounced. Dress, in these portraits, is central to a constructed identity that asserts Bell's seriousness of purpose. If she is clothing her subjects in her own designs, and surrounding them with her abstract works of art, she represents herself, in these portraits, as a polymath and a modernist. Her own features and the bulk of her body are distorted in her *Self Portrait*, as Christopher Reed discusses, to project an assertive and powerful self-image.[105] Her dress may also relate to her collection for Omega. It is cross-hatched, indicating a chequered fabric, and loose fitting. Bell articulates the long line of the shoulder seam for pictorial purposes, to echo the solid, black outline of her shoulder. But the seam also indicates the drop-shouldered cut of her garment, fitted beneath the bust and fastened with yellow buttons.

✤ ✤ ✤

Bell continued to design and make dresses after the opening of her Omega collection. She wrote to Fry suggesting 'an autumn campaign – not making dresses on spec. but sending round notices about

129 Vanessa Bell, Mary Hutchinson perched on a single bed, c.1915. The Charleston Trust

130 (opposite) Vanessa Bell, *Mrs St John Hutchinson*, 1915. Oil on board, 737 × 578 mm. Tate, London

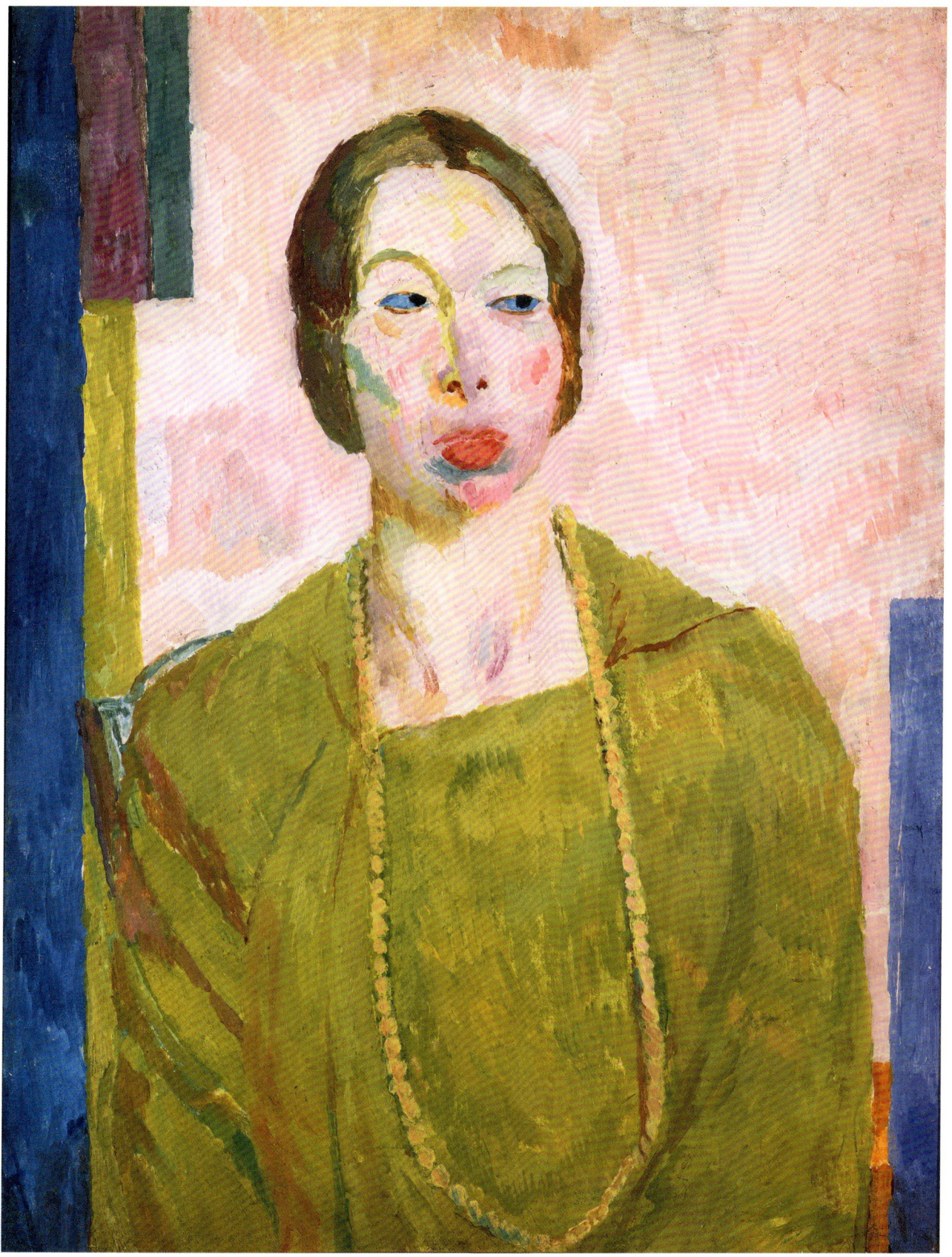

OMEGA DRESS 111

the dressmaking department'.[106] She was designing, too, for her own purposes, writing to Grant from the Sussex village of Bosham in August 1915 about a purple dress she was planning to make out of silk brought back from Broussa: 'I am going to make myself a new dress, and would you mind if you can remember it bringing with you when you come here the yellow waistcoat Lechmere made for me, which I think I can use.'[107] This, presumably, was one of the waistcoats from her show.

The arrangements with Joy Brown, on hand at the Workshops for fittings and supported by the dressmaking facilities at Hampshire House, are documented for a number of prominent commissions. Ottoline Morrell ordered an Omega dress and visited the Workshops with her young daughter, Julian, to choose the fabric in which it would be made up. Gill recalled that she could not decide 'between a golden Chinese silk and a white silk with a pattern of stripes stamped on it in slate grey' that Gill had block-printed herself. 'I hoped she would choose the first, because somewhere in the length I had made a blot, and I was afraid that if she noticed it she would want the price reduced.'[108] Gill's reflections, and those of Brown, are of particular interest because they are written from a maker's perspective, and in Gill's evocative account of the session, which took place in the Workshops' front studio on the first floor, Brown is featured in the anecdote as well as Morrell:

> She was standing in front of a cheval glass . . . while Joy Brown stood near-by with the two lengths of silk. 'I'll consult Julian', she said, 'she has such perfect taste. Julian, dear, come here.' the [sic] child obediently came and stood in front of her mother, facing the glass. 'Now,' said her mother, 'which do you think I should have, darling, the gold,' holding the length against herself and studying the effect in the mirror, 'or . . .' exchanging it with Miss Brown for the other, 'the striped' trying this. 'Well darling, which shall it be?' Julian replied in a disillusioned tone of voice, 'I like the striped best mother.' 'Do you, darling? m.m.m.' . . . trying them both again. Then 'I'll take the gold.' 'And now, darling, you shall have one of these lovely handwoven handkerchiefs for your hat. You choose, either this gold one,' twisting it round the crown, 'or the pink. Well darling which shall it be?' 'I like the gold one, Mother,' she said, without much enthusiasm. 'Do you, darling? m.m.m. I'll take the pink one, Miss Brown.'[109]

When Lady Ottoline returned for her fitting, Gill noted that she did so on her own. She came in August, in the middle of Brown's holiday, even though she had been notified of the dates, and Gill recalled that Brown was called back in specially.

Gill and Brown's recollections of Omega's elite clients are mildly disparaging, reflecting their own class observations. Gill felt able to share these with Grant,

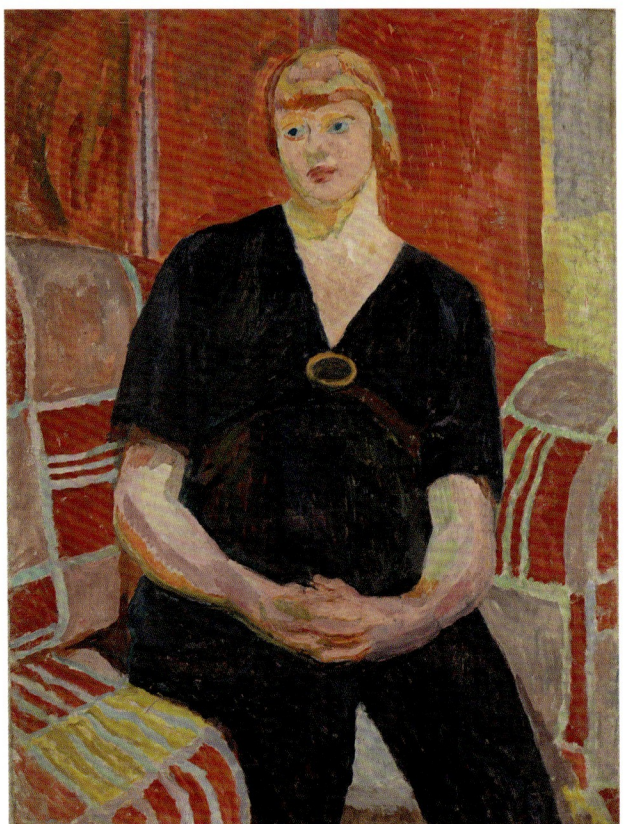

131 Vanessa Bell, *Iris Tree*, 1915. Oil on canvas, 1220 × 915 mm. Private collection

132 (opposite) Vanessa Bell, *Self-Portrait*, c.1915. Oil on canvas, laid on panel, 638 × 459 mm. Yale Center for British Art, New Haven, CT

112 THE BLOOMSBURY LOOK

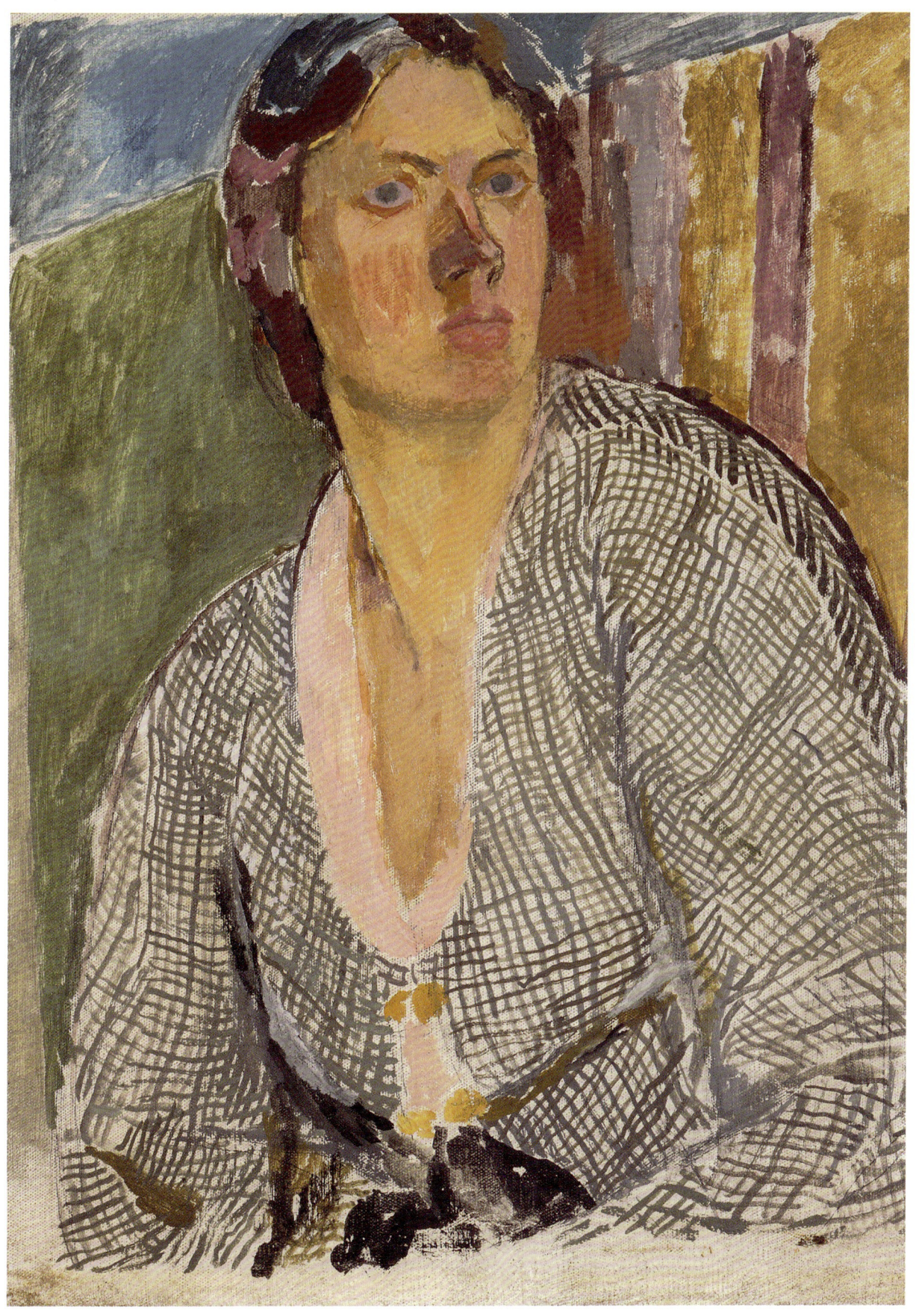

but not until the 1960s, when they were among the last Omega survivors and a combination of age and cultural shifts had diminished the differences between their social backgrounds. At the time she believed Grant would have been unable to distinguish her from the other Workshops 'girls in pinafores', writing 'I don't think you and I exchanged more than a dozen words in all'.[110] She wrote that Lady Ottoline was a great help to Omega: 'She bought our stuff and did much to popularise it', but that her scent was always so strong that she could smell it for at least two days after each visit.[111] Grant agreed: 'how well you describe her manner . . . & the scent how well I remember that'.[112]

Brown recalled that the Workshops produced 'a very ordinary skirt' and 'two bathing dresses' for Iris Tree to wear at a weekend party at Garsington, where there was 'a marvellous swimming-pool'.[113] Both the suits were made up in silk and their cut was unexceptional, but one was patterned with bright blue and yellow squares: 'The squares had to be sewn by hand and she didn't like the bill!' When the Workshops was commissioned to produce a long dress and coat for Tree's mother, the actor Lady Helen Tree, for her forthcoming film, *Still Waters Run Deep*, Brown worked through the night with Isabel Walker and one of the apprentices from Hampshire House to meet the deadline. They took a taxi from Hammersmith in the evening, 'complete with iron-board and all other necessities that would not be found at the Omega. We worked all night round the fire in that back upstairs room, the nice caretaker making tea for us.' Lady Tree had attended the Workshops' 'Art Circles' with her daughters but she had a reputation for 'not paying up'. When the caretaker packed and delivered the costume at 9 a.m. the following morning he was given instructions: 'he must not let go of the box until he had the money! Of course Lady Tree was furious but she had to pay.'[114] The dressmakers went to see the film after it was launched in January 1916, with Lady Tree in the long black silk coat and a pink muslin crinoline dress they had made for her, 'wandering round a lake in the moonlight'.[115]

Although there was a clear social and creative hierarchy within the Workshops, it provided its makers and its artists with a sense of belonging within a working, creative community with shared aesthetics. This was mirrored for its customers by the security that it offered as a brand and as an informal social space. The Bloomsbury Group and its wider circle of artists, authors, intellectuals, and patrons recur in Gill's letters, dropping into the showrooms to browse or to meet one another. Woolf's letters and diaries document the regularity with which she called in. She described herself as an advertisement for the Workshops in the spring of 1916, writing to Bell to say how pleased she was with a blue summer dress that Brown had sent her: 'I think even as an advertisement I should pay the Omega, as I'm always being asked who made my things.'[116] Omega provided Woolf with a touchstone for style. It was a 'family' enterprise and at the same time avant-garde. In the same letter she asked Bell for a design for a summer cloak: 'I bought some grey silk and sent it to Miss Joy, who can't make it for lack of a sketch', Woolf wrote. 'What I want is something light and simple – I should think perhaps a kind of kimono. It is the colour of a young elephant, with a slight crinkle. . . . If you could send the sketch straight to Miss Joy, I should bless your shadow.'[117] The silk is likely to have been from Omega stock and, as Brown had already made a dress for Woolf, no additional, initial fitting would have been necessary. Bell's reply includes a sketch and a reference to the current fashion 'to have it rather straight down to a very low belt and then rather wide but I dont suppose that is what you want. Haven't you an old cloak that Joy could follow the general lines of?'[118] Elizabeth Sheehan has analysed the exchange as illustrative of Bell's processes as a designer, drawing on fashion plates and existing dress to create Omega pieces that could be unobtrusively stylish, combining fashion with originality to suit the individual tastes of her customers. The exchange also reveals Woolf's desire to exercise her own creativity through dress, and shows how the Workshops amalgamated the design authority of a fashion house with the intimacy of working with a dressmaker to enable her to do so.

Woolf records the shock value of her sister's most striking colour combinations for Omega. She wrote to Bell of their sister-in-law, Karin Stephen: 'My God! What colours you are responsible for! Karins clothes almost wrenched my eyes from my sockets – a skirt barred with reds and yellows of the vilest kind, and a pea green blouse on top, with a gaudy handkerchief on her head, supposed to be the very boldest taste.'

Although she teased Bell that she would 'retire into dove colour and old lavender, with a lace collar, and lawn wristlets', she too could be adventurous in the colours she wore.[119] She bought an apricot-coloured Omega coat the following year. Gill claimed that the most revolutionary thing about the Omega was its use of pure colour. She outraged one of the assistants at Liberty's department store at around this time by asking for some emerald-green silk: 'greatly shocked: He said "Emerald, Madam, is a colour we never stock."'[120] Chocolate brown, she recalled, was the predominant colour in most domestic interiors.

The significance of Omega in providing Woolf with a progressive, and at times flamboyant, visual identity within the security of Bloomsbury as a group is illuminated by an incident with a hat and new experiments in identity a decade later. Woolf's insecurities over her appearance in general and her wardrobe in particular have been extensively analysed.[121] Her diaries are peppered with crippling anxieties over 'my clothes complex ... When I am asked out my first thought is, but I have no clothes to go in.'[122] Even in the 1920s, as a successful author and publisher, she likened her distinctive appearance to that of Edith Sitwell: 'I can never look like other people – too broad, tall, flat, with hair hanging.'[123] The Bloomsbury Group exploited this vulnerability revolving around appearance and conformity. Woolf describes being set upon by Clive, Vanessa, Leonard, and Duncan when she brought an evening with the Sitwells to a close by taking Vita Sackville-West to Gordon Square in 1926; 'Clive suddenly said, or bawled rather, what an astonishing hat you're wearing! Then he asked where I got it ... & they pulled me down between them, like a hare.'[124] The hat was symptomatic of Woolf's developing relationships with Sackville-West, the Sitwells, and Dorothy Todd. It identified her with the glamorous, queer, society aesthetics that Todd and Madge Garland were promoting in British *Vogue*.[125] Todd was helping Woolf to explore a more fashionable look to reflect her fame and success as an author.

The attack from her Bloomsbury 'family' was targeted to draw her back in. She recalled that they initially suspected the hat of having been selected by Mary Hutchinson, who was always on the periphery of Bloomsbury and provided one of its links to fashionable society: 'Clive said did Mary choose it? No. Todd said Vita. And the dress? Todd of course.'[126] The conversation, and Leonard's silence, were powerful enough to leave her 'deeply chagrined' and despairing all the following day. The nuanced and fleeting nature of the sting, however, was demonstrated a few days later when Woolf encountered Clive Bell and Mary Hutchinson together by chance, 'in the hat, in the dress', to find the 'dress praised to the skies, hat passed. So that's over.'[127] It was not the hat itself that had provoked ridicule but rather the values and relationships it signalled.

✣ ✣ ✣

Mary Hutchinson was clearly an influence on the original Omega dress collection and its subsequent evolution. Many of Bell's letters regarding dress for the Workshops were written from Hutchinson's home in West Wittering or from Bosham, nearby. Places are often associated with particular activities, and for Bell West Wittering was a place for dressmaking and design, and for painting. In the autumn of 1916, however, Bell wrote to Fry from Charleston proposing a revival of the Omega dress collection. She had recently returned to Sussex with her unconventional household of Grant, Garnett, and her children, and it was here that the next phase of Omega dress was to be developed. Fry, by this time, had returned to Durbins and the future of the Omega Workshops was still uncertain. 'I must tell you now about some business', Bell wrote. Rather than present her proposition as exclusively her own idea she was careful to couch it in the most neutral terms, backed up by expert advice from Hutchinson.[128] She described a social visit to see Faith Henderson (née Bagenal) and her baby, and meeting Henderson's friend Barbara Hiles there. Henderson was one of Karin Stephen's friends, and Bell had considered including her in the 1915 dressmaking team when Brown was employed. She had described her then to Fry as 'Miss Bagginal whom you may have seen at Ottoline's parties dancing, that queer looking creature with no chin'.[129] Henderson was summarily described as unemployed in 1915: 'wants to make a little money & has no job now. It occurred to me she might take up this dress making'. Bell thought she had style. 'She dresses herself with a good deal of idea, & says she is rather good at it.'[130]

By the autumn of 1916, Faith Henderson and Barbara Hiles (who would subsequently marry Faith's brother, Nicholas Bagenal) were both, according to Bell, 'very anxious to do work . . . They both have done a certain amount of dressmaking & asked me whether the Omega would start dressmaking again & let them run it.' Bell had prevaricated, questioning the success of the initial venture, presumably on financial grounds: 'I said I didn't know as it had been a failure before & I thought you couldn't risk anything.'[131]

The letter is illuminating because it documents Bell's ability to work collaboratively and her determination to establish a dress collection for the Workshops without incurring the cost of training and employing the necessary skilled staff. She was ready, however, to revisit her mistakes. She was drawn to Henderson and Hiles as younger women of her own social class. Henderson was a graduate of Newnham College, Cambridge. Hiles was a student at the Slade. Although she wrote of her Omega collection, 'I thought the reason it was a failure was really because Miss Joy didn't make well enough', she was willing to repeat the venture with amateurs of her own social standing rather than tailors and dressmakers established in the trade. She insisted, however, that Henderson should have professional tuition, without which, she argued, 'one can't make for someone like Lala [Vandervelde]'. She wrote that Henderson was inclined to believe 'she could make by instinct', but that she herself had talked with Mary Hutchinson's dressmaker – 'a nice half French & half English woman whom Mary has employed for years, who I am getting to make a dress for me' – and established that she would be willing to provide lessons. 'I am writing to tell Faith this & if she thinks it worth while to risk the cost of training & then finds that perhaps the Omega had collapsed & if you don't have to spend any money on it I suppose it might be worth trying.' This apologetic and somewhat defeatist start to the letter anticipated Fry's objections. It is followed by a detailed account of Hutchinson's recommendations:

> I also consulted Mary about it as I thought her help would be valuable – she was very strongly in favour of our inventing one kind of dress only, something very simple, not fashionable – which would have to be very well cut – which could be made in different stuffs and colours and have all kinds of different borders and edges and embroideries so as to get variety but make it always one dress which would get known as the Omega dress.[132]

Hutchinson agreed with Bell's analysis of the earlier collection's weaknesses:

> She thought the mistake we made before was in trying to be ordinary dressmakers as well as having ones own stuffs etc., as she said any good dressmaker could beat us at that, but that we ought to get this one kind of dress, with our own choice of colour & detail, known & sold for about £3 or £4. She thought that might be very successful.[133]

Bell's letter does not specify the degree to which she would take creative control over the new collection. She and Hutchinson were agreed that 'The difficulty would be to get the really good pattern to start with but that Faith would have to do.' A letter to Fry the following spring, however, clarifies her position as designer. She had asked Gill how to calculate what the Workshops owed her: 'I don't know how people are paid now, whether by time or work & its difficult to know how to charge for things like designing dresses & hats etc.'[134] The economics of Omega's dress collection evidences an interesting fluidity relating to social class. If the dresses were to retail at £4 they would cost more than three weeks' wages for a woman on Gill's salary. They would be more than double the cost of the French department-store dresses that Bell had found 'absurdly cheap' in 1914.[135] Those dresses were designed for an expanding middle-class mass-market of fashionable women. The Omega dresses, by comparison, were designed to appeal to an artistic and intellectual elite. A dressmaker such as Brown, earning £100 a year,

---

133 Roger Fry, *Portrait of Nina Hamnett*, 1917. Oil on canvas, 1372 × 914 mm. University of Leeds Art Collection

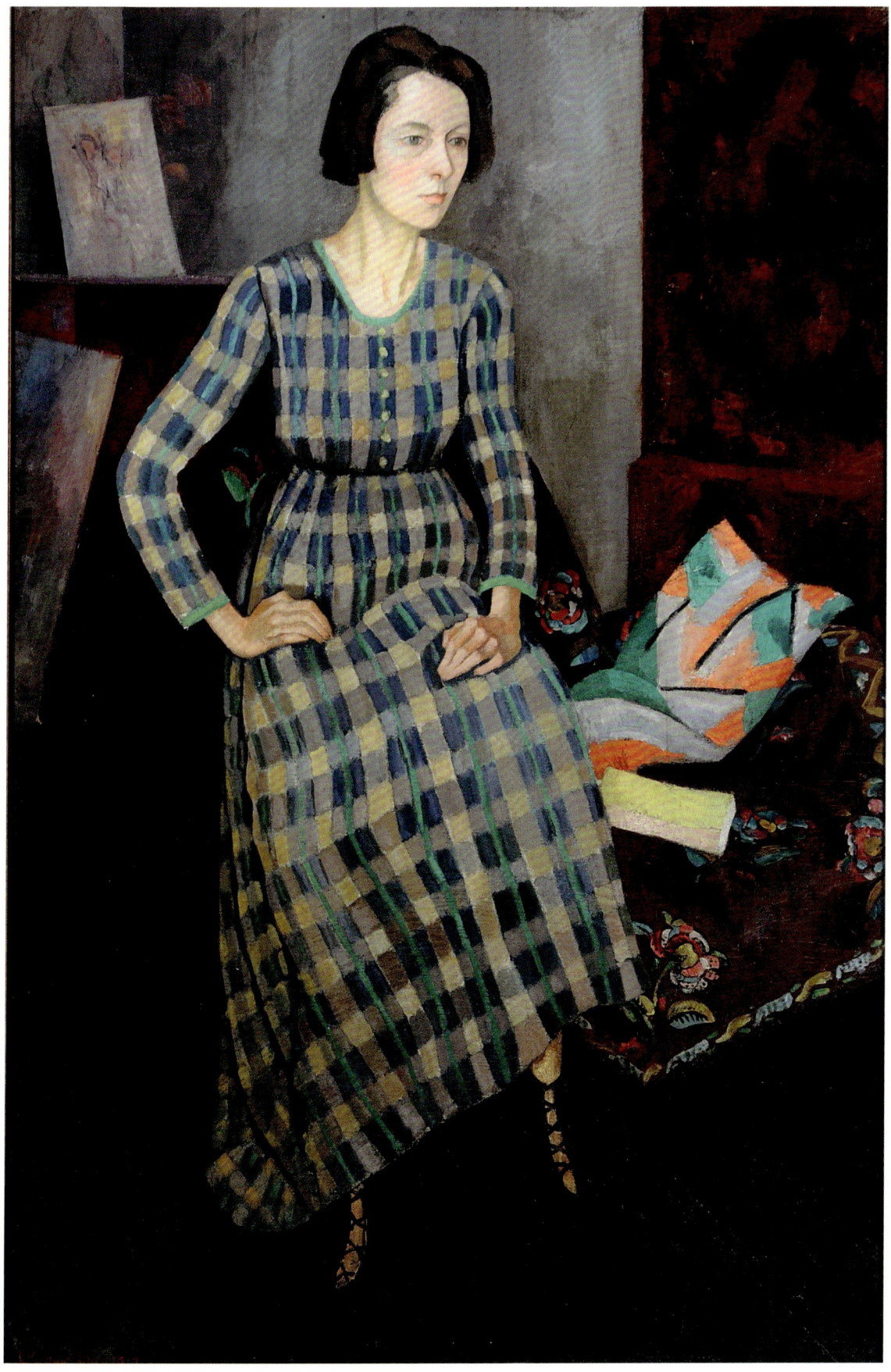

OMEGA DRESS 117

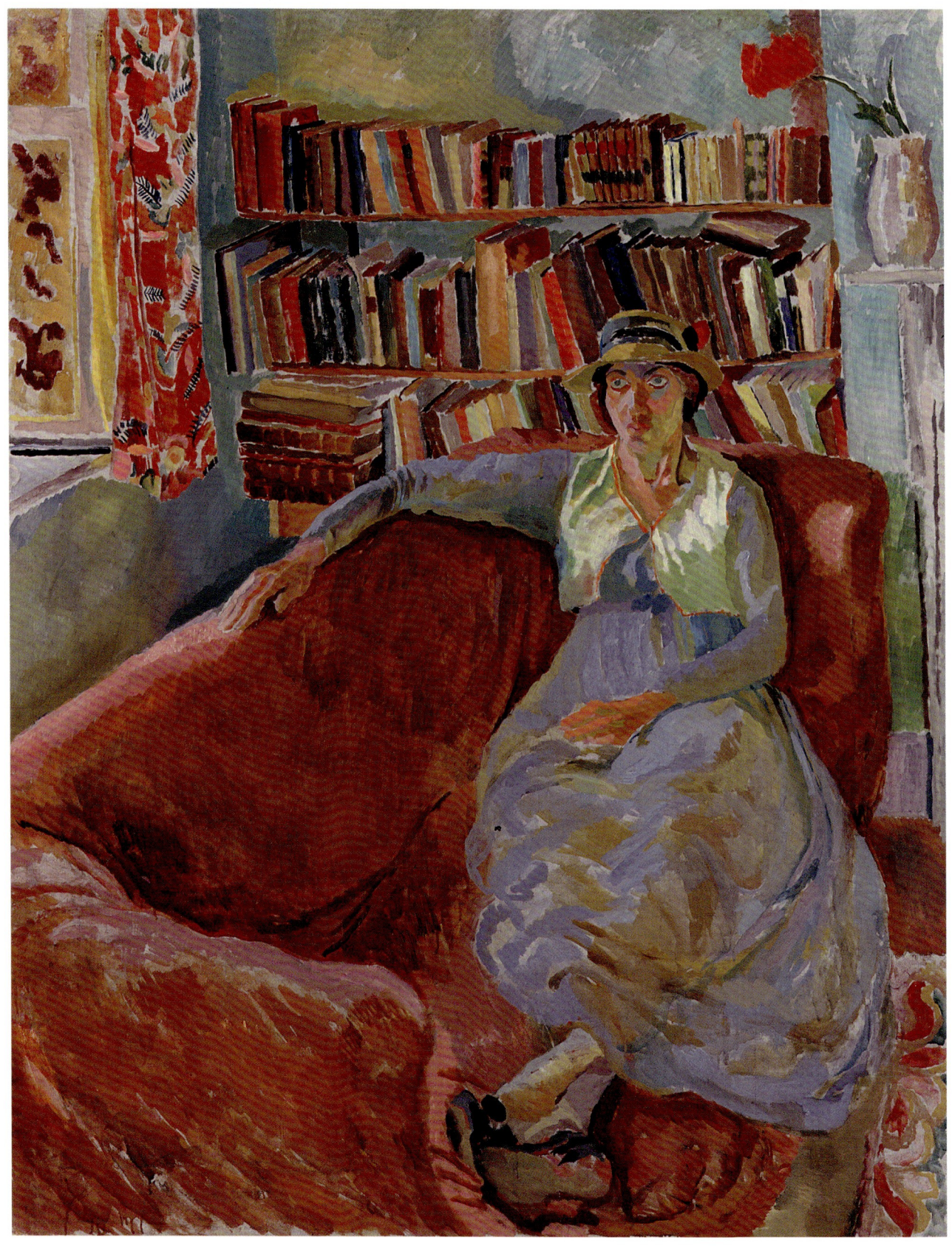

would need to make 25 Omega dresses just to cover the labour costs. Dressmaking and embroidery were fallbacks for many respectable middle-class widows and women of reduced social circumstances. More genteel, and more ambiguous in terms of social categorization than shop work or domestic service, such employment was on a par with the work of a governess. It is no coincidence that Gill, Brown, and Mabel Selwood, all governesses to Fry's and Bell's children, were drawn into dressmaking for the Workshops. But Omega also employed artists and intellectuals in making its products. Bell made her own clothes and would make for others, challenging social classifications. 'Did Faith tell you', she wrote to Fry from Charleston, 'that I have offered to crochet some caps for her to sell at the Omega with ready-made dresses? I am doing some now.'[136] The artist Christine Kühlenthal also describes dressmaking for the Omega Workshops in a letter to her future husband, John Nash: 'What a lot of funny jobs I've done & who ever thought I'd turn into a dressmaker? All the morning I've been making a green, & yellow & black & white & khaki dress for Nina Hamnett.'[137]

The 'artistic dress' of the Arts and Crafts movement, and Parisian couture designers such as Paul Poiret, had combined to make empire-silhouette dresses fashionable. The Workshops and their customers were aware of the trend, and absorbed its influence.[138] Morrell brought her daughter to see the Omega dress exhibition wearing a Kate Greenaway dress down to her ankles, and the dress in Bell's portrait of Iris Tree appears to be cut in this style.[139] It was a profile that Omega customers were already drawn towards. A previously unpublished letter from Hutchinson to Bell, however, indicates that this outline was attractive to Bell because she believed that she was pregnant in the summer of 1917.[140] Omega's empire-line dresses had the subversive effect of making all their owners look pregnant. The feminist author Amber Blanco White, who had given birth to H. G. Wells's illegitimate daughter in 1909, remarked at an Omega fitting that she looked pregnant in her dress, 'but I rather like it even if I'm not going to have a baby!'[141] This accommodating profile formed the basis of the prototype for the standardized 'Omega dress'. Two painted portraits and a number of press and personal photographs document the design replicated in different fabrics. Nina Hamnett wears a blue-and-beige checked version of the empire-line dress with fitted bodice, tapered long sleeves, and long gathered skirt (made by Kühlenthal) in a portrait painted by Fry in 1917 (fig. 133).[142] Duncan Grant's portrait *Vanessa Bell*, painted in the same year at Charleston, represents a blue or lilac version of the dress, worn with a yellow waistcoat (fig. 134). This 'Omega dress' was distinct from wartime fashions. Dresses in *Vogue* and *Les Modes* did become looser-fitting with more comfortable, softer waistlines during the war. Corsets were no longer necessary to achieve a fashionable profile, though they were still favoured by many. The empire silhouette of Omega dresses, however, was conspicuous for obviating the need for restrictive underwear entirely. It was simple, comfortable, practical, and versatile. Because only the bodice was fitted, it could be made to measure or sold 'off the peg' as a ready-made dress.

Hutchinson's surviving letters to Bell make no reference to Omega dresses, but she wrote to her in July 1917 indicating a knowledge of her pregnancy and relating this to a shared interest in dress: 'I am very sorry you are in the sick stage; it is wretched.' Bell had been hoping for a third child and Hutchinson's letter made arrangements to visit her at Charleston: 'It will be delightful to come on the 26th and then we could talk on those clothes.'[143] Hutchinson, whose tailored, fitted clothing indicates the use of corsets, offered Bell 'a wonderful pair of stays made by a Mrs Marion Smith . . . I have been to her all my life & was also recommended by my Doctor to go to her when I had my baby.' She wrote that the stays were expensive, costing around four guineas, and that they laced up on both sides 'so are always the right size; they are clean and ready – would they be any good to you?' She proposed that Bell should have a dress designed for her, 'something loose and grand – it will suit you splendidly and you must have a great coat like a Russian Emperors to go out in'.[144] Whether or not Bell had a failed pregnancy that

134 Duncan Grant, *Vanessa Bell*, 1917. Oil on canvas, 1270 × 1016 mm. National Portrait Gallery, London

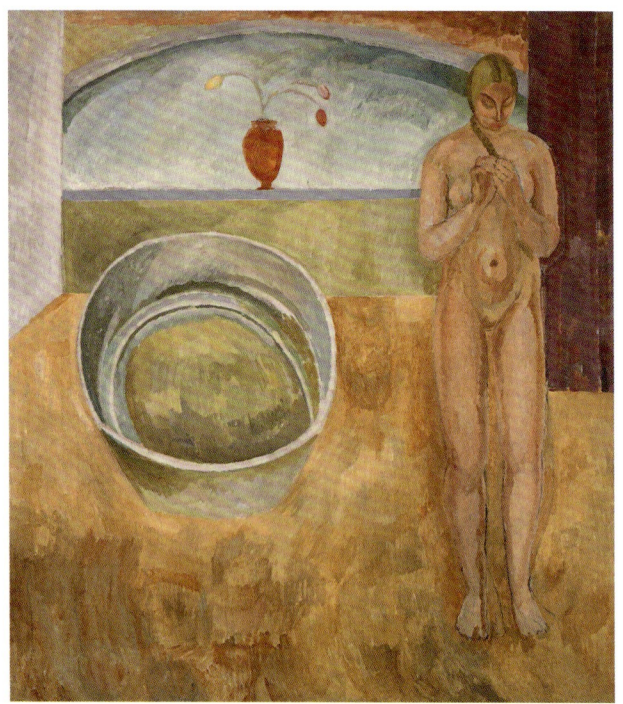

summer, the letter describes an intimacy over dress in the complex relationship between these two women.

Bell's letters from 1917 also describe the challenges of establishing her household in wartime Charleston while Grant and Garnett laboured as conscientious objectors on a neighbouring farm. She complained to Saxon Sydney-Turner that she was 'overwhelmed by Charleston's domestic difficulties and its visitors'. She worried, 'lest I shouldn't provide all the necessary hot water, etc., which Clive's passion demands for his love'.[145] Clive and Mary made frequent visits and water had to be obtained from an outdoor pump and heated on a range. 'We can take in two guests at a time now', Vanessa wrote, 'as though there's room for more, there aren't enough beds, blankets, etc.'[146] It was difficult to recruit servants and their improprieties with soldiers meant that Bell was unable to leave them unsupervised: 'one of them', Bell wrote to Fry, 'was found closeted in an outhouse with a soldier & he pursued the other to a bedroom, & if they get raped of course all the blame will fall on me & I shan't be able to get a girl in the neighbourhood at all'.[147] The additional demands of her two small children made visits to the Omega Workshops and to galleries in London almost impossible. 'I feel I can hardly leave the house even for an hour!'[148] But though concerned to preserve the safety and morals of her servants, Bell applied much looser codes of behaviour to her many visitors. Lytton Strachey brought Dora Carrington. Barbara Hiles visited in July, promised to model in the nude, and then established herself in a tent where she could entertain her own guests. Fry was coaxed back into friendship with Bell and, in October 1917, persuaded to bring Nina Hamnett. They were the subjects of gossip. 'When would you & Nina like to come here?' Bell wrote to him:

> I hope she doesn't think I don't like her or anything of the kind for really I think your arrangement with her perfect . . . Clive says he has no doubt you go to bed with <u>her</u>, but he's not sure about Lala etc. I said nothing. Duncan agreed with him.[149]

The making of the new dress collection thus coincided with an exceptionally experimental period in the evolution of Bloomsbury relationships and in negotiating the memberships of 'in-groups' and 'out-groups'. The dresses are relevant, as well as interesting, because they contextualize Bloomsbury's material culture and highlight the way in which the Group used dress to confer and express progressive identities.

Hutchinson's position within the Group vacillated between acceptance and rejection. Staying at Charleston for over a week in April 1917, she confided in Bell that her relationship with Clive, by now established over several years, had finally been explained to her husband, Jack. Vanessa, in turn, relayed this conversation to Fry. Shared intimacies and triangular relationships were central to the 'in-group' behaviours that bound Bloomsbury together. 'Jack who is much to be pitied poor man . . . became so jealous & uncertain that at last he said he must know the truth, & so she told him.'[150] To avoid a scandal, 'which he wouldn't at all like', Mary proposed that after the war 'she & Clive mean to go abroad together for 6 months. She thinks that Jack will allow this & that she'll be

135 Vanessa Bell, *The Tub*, 1917–18. Oil and gouache on canvas, 1803 × 1664 mm. Tate, London

able to come back to him & the children afterwards & then take them abroad with her for 6 months in the year in future.'[151] Bell thought it unlikely that the plan would succeed. She does not address the personal and financial implications that such an arrangement would have had for her own marriage, but she outlines the consequences for women such as herself and Hutchinson if adulteries were made public. Jack Hutchinson was in a position to ruin his wife, socially and financially, though in doing so his own reputation would have been irreparably damaged. Vanessa wrote that he 'said she wasn't fit to bring up the children', an opinion he was entitled to enforce, and that he had restricted Mary's movements so that 'she has great difficulty in going away or anything'.[152] In the same letter she asks Fry about fabric for the dress collection, 'Do you think I shall ever get that striped stuff?', and describes Hutchinson sitting for her and Grant: 'Duncan & I have been painting her at least doing sketches & drawings from which we mean to paint. One wouldn't have time enough to paint altogether from her.'[153]

Within a few weeks Bell began work on her monumental painting *The Tub*, for which Hutchinson was the inspiration (fig. 135). 'I have started a large picture meant as a decoration for one of the walls in the garden sitting room', she wrote to Fry. 'There's very little in the picture & its mostly one colour, or two. Yellow ochre & a greenish grey. The subject is principally floor, with a bath & a semi nude female rather too like Mary, & the pond seen through the window.'[154] Art historians have analysed Bell's reductive approach to her subject and the evolution of the painting.[155] Watercolour studies show a woman in a chemise standing next to a tub. A photograph depicts Hutchinson in an elaborate white dress, seated in front of a full-scale version of the painting in which the figure is semi-clothed in an open chemise (fig. 136). Bell was reworking the painting in January 1918 when she wrote to Fry, 'I've been working at my big bath picture and am rather excited about that. I've taken out the woman's chemise and in consequence she is quite nude and much more decent.'[156] A woodcut, based on the painting, was also published by the Omega

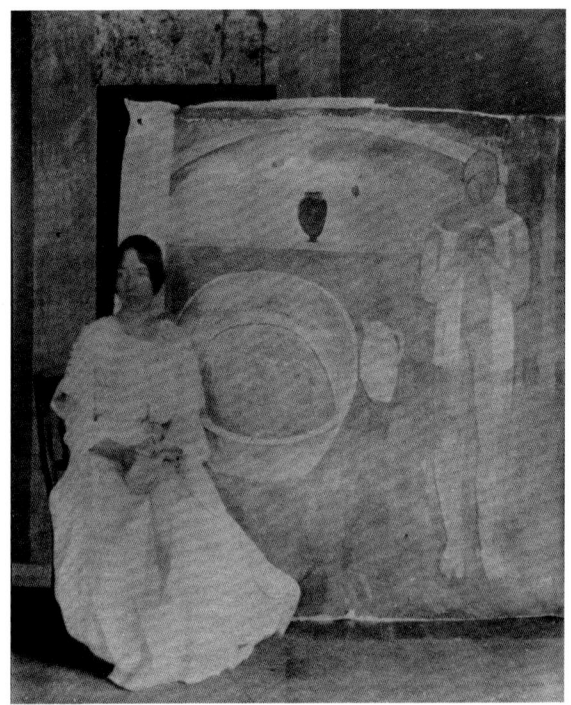

Workshops.[157] The figure remains recognizably that of Hutchinson but the uncomfortable realities of Clive's mistress, of hot water, of Charleston, are superseded in Bell's painting, as Reed concludes, by 'the image's calm ordering of its elements into a formal equilibrium associated with modernist aesthetics'.[158]

Two photographs of Hutchinson, taken by Vanessa Bell at Charleston in 1917, show her wearing an uncharacteristically plain dress in a chequered fabric comparable in its loose, stylish simplicity to the 'Omega dress' (fig. 137).[159] It may have been a prototype. Bell had a suit made up in the same or similar fabric. Photographs of her with Fry and with her two sons at Charleston in 1917 show her wearing a pleated skirt and a jacket with a shawl collar and distinctive, curved hemline (fig. 138).[160] Together, the photographs suggest that the fabric may have been bought in quantity and made up for Hutchinson and Bell in different options as they considered the new Omega collection. Hutchinson's dress has a high, round neckline and front opening fastened with buttons. It has long sleeves and a drop waist. The full, ankle-length skirt joins to the elongated bodice with wide pleats comparable to those of Bell's skirt and the seam is

---

136 Vanessa Bell, Mary Hutchinson posed in front of *The Tub* at Charleston, 1917. The Charleston Trust

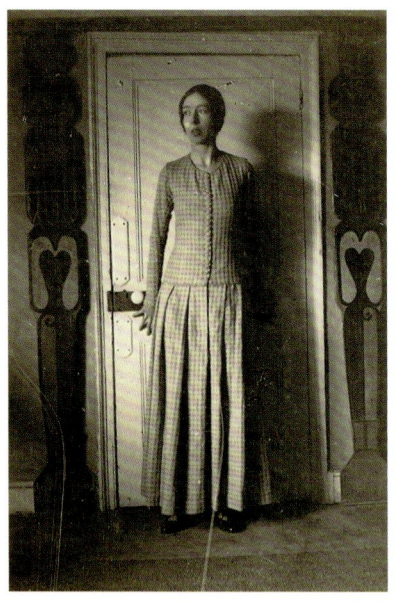 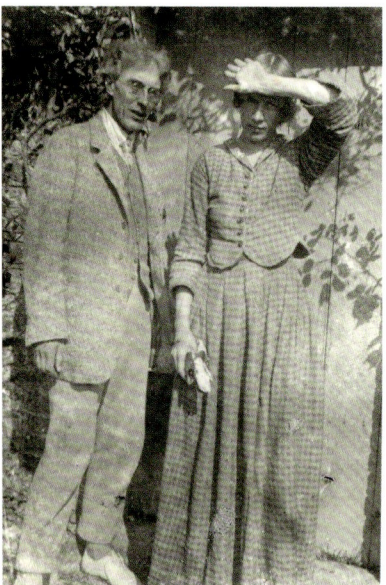 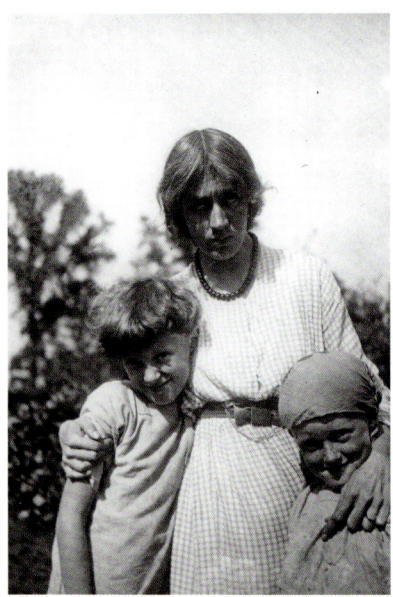

decorated, accentuating the simple, loose, stylish cut of the garment, with a strip of braid. Hutchinson's pose, standing up against a door in both photographs, with her hands behind her back and one toe pointing outwards in one, suggests that they were intended to show off the dress. The shoes, too, may identify this image with Omega's collection. Their low fronts with laces criss-crossed over stockings are comparable to the ankle boots in Fry's portrait of Nina Hamnett (see fig. 133).

In the Hamnett portrait, the style of the 'Omega dress' appears to be resolved and Fry represents her wearing it as an artist, with unframed pictures propped up around the simple interior and a brilliantly coloured Omega cushion at her side. Her hair is cropped and her assertive pose, perched on the arm of a chair, pulls her ankle-length skirt up just enough to show yellow stockings with black ankle boots. Again the dress fabric is chequered, but more boldly patterned this time with a bright green stripe enlivening the beige and black squares. This colour is picked up in a ribbon or tape binding to the high scoop neckline and cuffs. Yellow buttons suggest that the dress was front-fastening. The portrait helps describe Omega dress as a continuum. The empire silhouette, scoop neckline, and the skirt, pleated onto the bodice for Hamnett's dress, replicate the lines of the dress worn by Bell in the Omega press photograph, believed to date from 1915, again worn with laced boots or pumps (see fig. 117). In this dress, too, the scoop neckline and cuffs are finished with a dark bias strip, and a single Omega Workshops flower decorates the thin leather belt that draws in the contours of the dress beneath the bust. Bell had the pattern made up, too, in a summer-weight chequered fabric. Another 1917 photograph shows her, possibly pregnant, wearing this dress with a string of contrasting beads and a wider belt, again fastened just under the bust (fig. 139).[161]

Duncan Grant's *Vanessa Bell* describes a lilac or cornflower-blue version of the 'Omega dress' with a yellow waistcoat trimmed with red (see fig. 134). The painting may not offer an accurate representation of colours but it is plausible that the yellow waistcoat is the one made by Lechmere, worn here with an Omega empire-line summer dress. Grant recalled that this was the first portrait he made of Bell after they moved to Charleston.[162] A single oriental poppy in an Omega vase on the mantelshelf (like the one held aloft by Marjorie Strachey in fig. 80) dates the painting to late May or June 1917. Roger Fry, who shared Bell's

137 (*above left*) Vanessa Bell, Mary Hutchinson at Charleston, 1917. The Charleston Trust

138 (*above middle*) Vanessa Bell, Roger Fry and Vanessa Bell at Charleston, 1917. The Charleston Trust

139 (*above right*) Vanessa Bell, Vanessa Bell with her sons, Quentin and Julian, 1917. The Charleston Trust

interest in gardening, had given her oriental poppies for the garden she was making at Charleston.[163] Bell's pose, reclining with one hand in her lap and the other arm extended along the back of a huge sofa, may suggest early pregnancy. She has her feet up with her ankles crossed, and beneath them it is possible to imagine the features of a bear's face, smiling up at her. The contours of the sofa and this indeterminate form flow into one another. Bell's letters address Grant as 'My Bear' or 'My darling Bear'. Her face and figure are bathed in sunlight. She wears a straw hat, even inside, and Grant locates her in the colourful interior that she was creating at Charleston while he and Garnett laboured in the fields. The walls are distempered turquoise and yellowish green. The patterned curtains at the window are scarlet and lined with yellow.

❦ ❦ ❦

Another 'show of dresses' was organized at the Omega Workshops in November 1917 alongside an exhibition of *Copies and Translations of Old Masters*. Virginia Woolf provides vivid insights into the serious industriousness of Charleston less than a week before the show, and an account of the 'private view day' and party in London. Staying at Charleston, she wrote that it rained all day and so she worked on a review for the *Times Literary Supplement* in the morning and then joined Bell and Grant in the studio in the afternoon:

> Duncan painted a table, & Nessa copied a Giotto. I unpacked all my bits of gossip. They are very large in effect, these painters; very little self-conscious; they have smooth broad spaces in their minds where I am all prickles & promontories. Nevertheless to my thinking few people have a more vigorous grasp or a more direct pounce than Nessa.[164]

Mabel Selwood had been dispatched to London, carrying a painted washstand by Grant, and Woolf, now back in London, describes her in the first-floor back showroom at the Omega Workshops.[165] Attending the private view day, she wrote: 'I went to the Omega where in the semidark Roger was convoying three chattering Frenchwomen round the show . . . The pictures glimmered through the dusk; & I was chiefly impressed by the Gertlers; Vanessa, too, very good: Duncan, I thought, a little pretty or tending to be.' She describes Faith Henderson, too:

> Faith vacillated about, endeavouring to make me see her show of dresses, this being private view day. We had tea in the sewing room – walking up & down munching dry cake, while Mabel stitched lining in a corner, & Roger wrote letters on his knee. Nessa came on top of this & we left, I buying an apricot coloured coat on my way.[166]

Woolf's account locates the new dress collection within the Workshops' activities as a gallery where new work by the Bloomsbury artists and their friends was showcased. She describes Omega as a place where the act of making, 'Mabel stitching lining' in the sewing room, was at least semi-public, and where the prominence that Bell had envisaged for Joy Brown two years earlier was established.

Tellingly, Woolf describes this private view on Wednesday as 'the prelude to a party on Thursday' at 46 Gordon Square. Her account reiterates the interdependence of Bloomsbury's friendships and shared commitment to living by its own values rather than those imposed upon it by society, with Omega's identity as a workshop, retail space, and gallery. She differentiates between the core circle of friends and a younger generation of acolytes:

> The usual people were there, the usual sensation of being in a familiar but stimulating atmosphere, in which all the people one's in the habit of thinking of, were there in the body. A great many mop headed young women in amber & emerald sitting on the floor. Molly, Vanessa & I represented mature matronhood.[167]

Woolf labelled the younger women, who included Faith Henderson, Barbara Hiles, Alix Sargant-Florence, and Dora Carrington, 'Bunnies' and believed that they aspired to be included in 'Bloomsbury', by this time a recognizable phenomenon. She wrote to Bell:

OMEGA DRESS | 123

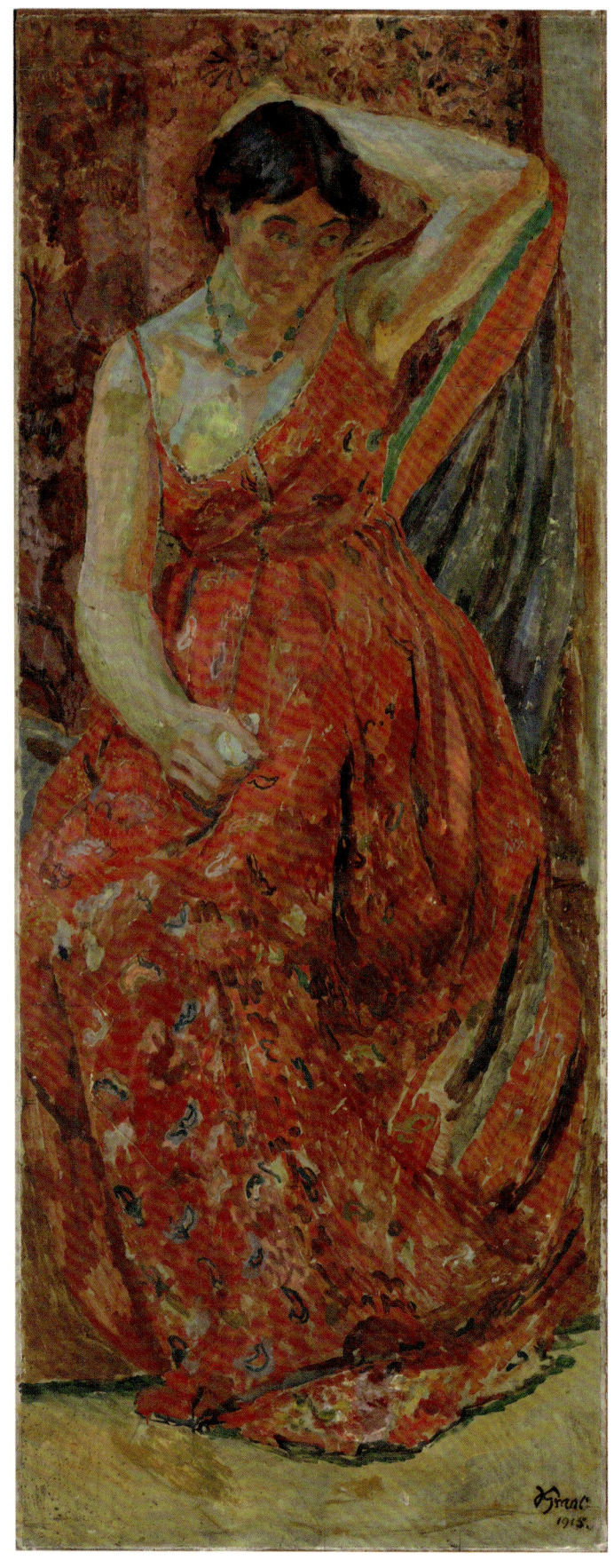

'The Bloomsbury hypnotism . . . is rank, and threatens the sanity of all the poor Bunnies . . . I tried tactfully to explain to Faith that once a Bunny, always a Bunny; and what great Bloomsbury respects is the recognition by the B's that they are B's.'[168] In particular, Bloomsbury and Bunnies alike were enthralled by the complex courtships of their respective members, for example Saxon Sydney-Turner and Barbara Hiles, with Nicholas Bagenal competing for Hiles's affections because, according to Woolf, the 'height of his ambition' was to be associated with Bloomsbury and to have dinner with Keynes. Woolf wittily caricatured the procrastinations of their triangular relationship in a letter to Bell: 'Think of the three of them discussing the question over the stove in her studio, and Nick saying "No, Saxon: you must marry her;" and Saxon refusing to be happy save in their happiness, and Barbara suggesting copulation with each on alternate nights.'[169] This younger generation of crop-heads had their own distinctive style. They wore trousers on occasion and men's sweaters. Carrington was photographed in a fringed, Western-style jacket and trousers, advancing Bloomsbury's experiments in dress in her own expressions of sexual identity.

The Omega Workshops' extreme, Cubist clothing and its unconventional dresses projected a distinctive, public identity for the Bloomsbury circle and its friends. The Workshops served as a crucible as well as a shop-front for a coherent cultural and visual identity for the Group after the *Second Post-Impressionist Exhibition*. During the war years, as the Workshops' finances foundered and the geography and makeup of Bloomsbury households shifted, experimental dress and undress continued to be tested in the country and showcased in London. Within the privacy of their studios and country houses, Bloomsbury members used dress and nudity to affirm their 'in-group' status. The photographs and paintings of Mary Hutchinson are pertinent in this respect because they evidence the ambiguity of her position within the Group, sometimes buying in, sometimes opting out. She wrote to Vanessa Bell in August 1917 that she felt she was 'a spectator and not a member of Bloomsbury'.[170] The marketing of Omega dress alongside paintings and painted furniture by the Group, and the launch

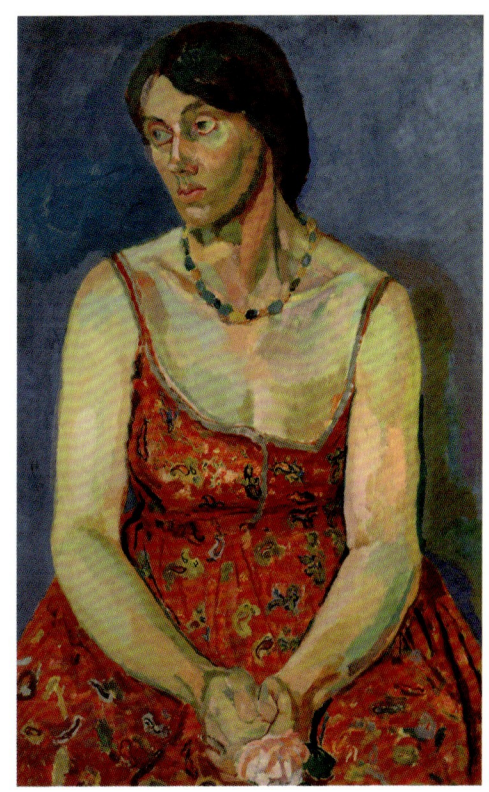

parties, the 'show' of dresses in June 1915 (about which little is recorded), and the Gordon Square party with its younger generation of crop-heads, indicate a calculated determination to trade on Bloomsbury's aesthetic and intellectual capital. The absence of an accurate period perspective – being able to register, for example, the shock-value of Bloomsbury's evident disregard for restrictive underwear and its use of colour – limits understandings of the full significance and impact of Bloomsbury dress and jewellery. If the Omega Workshops expanded Bloomsbury's reputation as a group, however, dress continued to resonate even within its most private and intimate relationships as a signifier of 'difference' and of shared understandings alongside this outward-facing identification.

In Grant's portraits of Bell, dress is integral to her creative potency as a fellow artist and designer, and as a woman. He made a series of three paintings of Bell wearing an extraordinary red dress that document their private visual language. The series positions them within the Bloomsbury Group as makers. In one of them the dress fabric is collaged onto the painted

140 (*opposite*) Duncan Grant, *Vanessa Bell*, 1915. Oil and paper collage on wood, 1590 × 635 mm. The Charleston Trust

141 Duncan Grant, *Vanessa Bell*, c.1918. Oil on canvas, 940 × 606 mm. National Portrait Gallery, London

OMEGA DRESS | 125

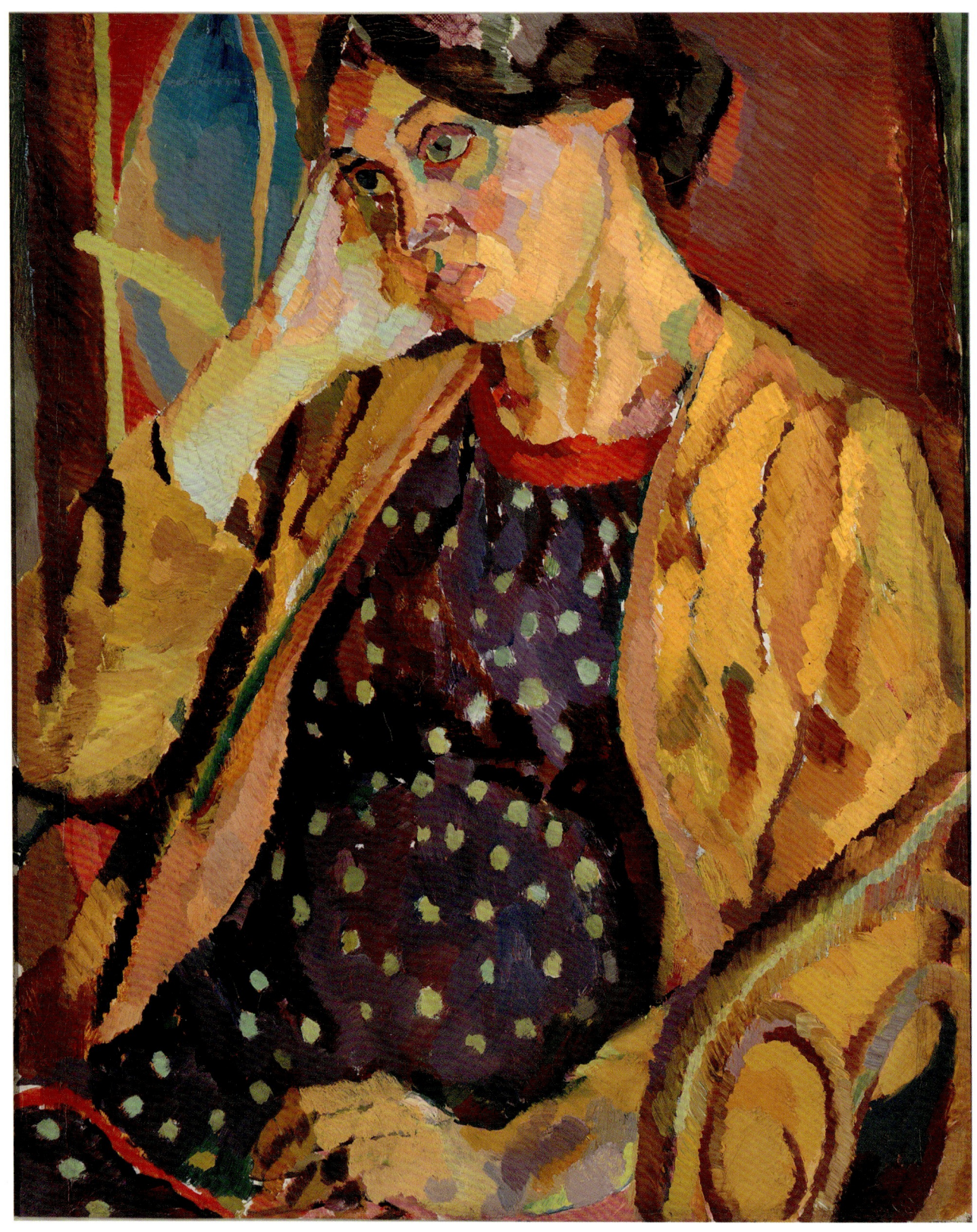

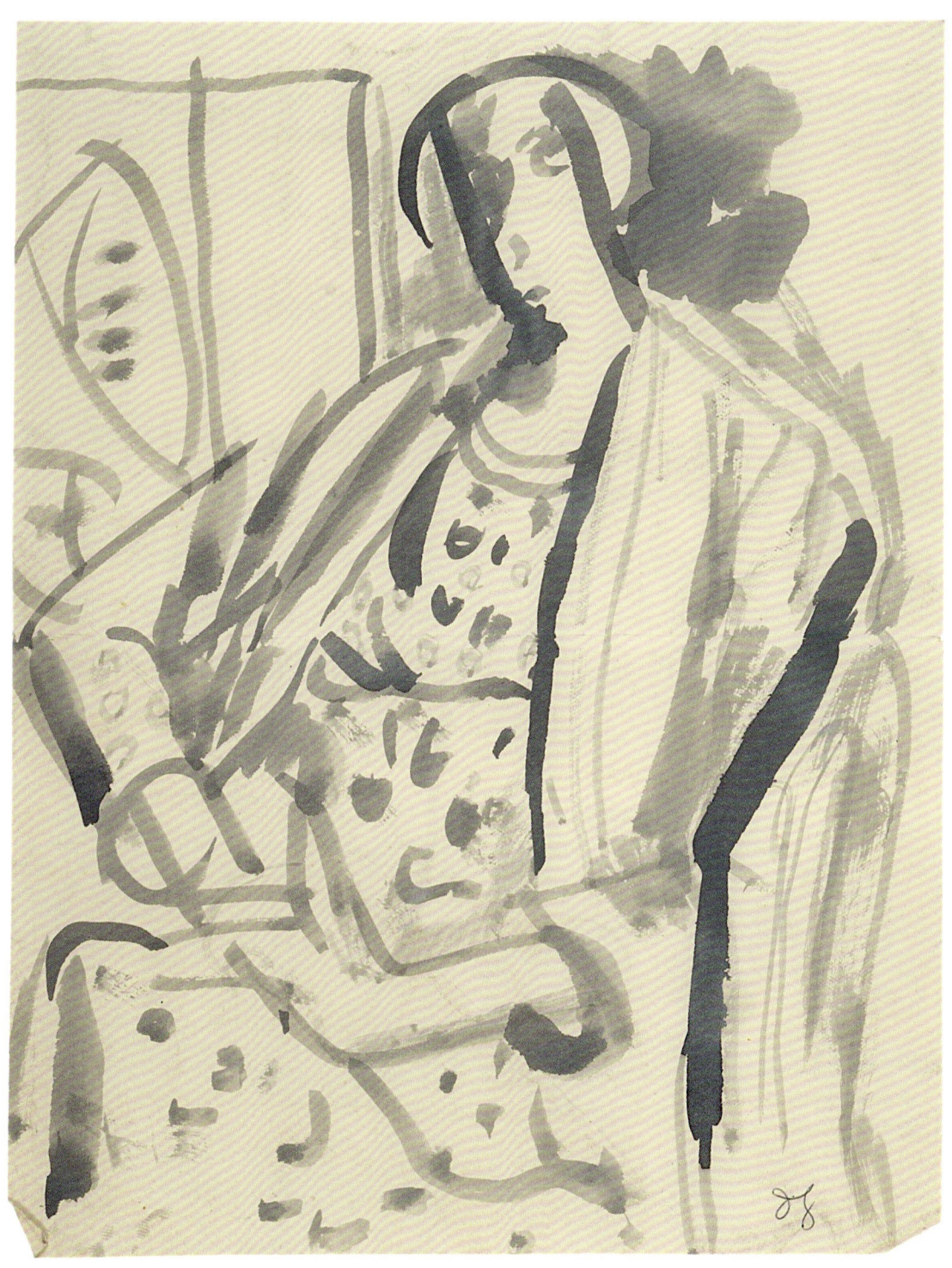

OMEGA DRESS 127

surface, emphasizing the processes of dressmaking and painting as well as the portrait's materiality.[171] In another, the portrait is life-sized and full-length, painted onto a batten-and-ledge door (fig. 140). Scraps of paper are pasted onto the dress and painted over in oil. The portrait captures Bell's audacity as a designer and as a model. It conveys her powerful sexuality and her disregard for respectability. She appears to dance, with one hand raised to the back of her head, looking down to the left as her body twists to the right.[172] In the third, iconic version Bell is seated, holding a single rose with her hands clasped together in her lap (fig. 141). In all three of the portraits in the series, Bell wears a necklace of different-coloured beads. Her red dress is low-cut, slightly gaping in front, with a strip of grey ribbon or binding tape defining the front opening and decorating the shoestring straps. Its empire silhouette corresponds with the Omega dresses, but this insubstantial garment would have been scandalous in the war years. Even evening dresses of the time were modest by comparison.

Grant retained the two portraits pasted with fabric and paper in his collection at Charleston and he exhibited the third, now in the National Portrait Gallery in London, in his first solo exhibition at the Carfax Gallery in 1920.[173] It was sold to the patrons and collectors John Louis and Mary Behrend, who would have known the artists from Ottoline Morrell's parties. They had commissioned Henry Lamb to paint Lytton Strachey's portrait for their collection in 1914.[174] Grant painted Bell again in 1918, heavily pregnant with their daughter, Angelica, wearing a mustard-yellow jacket and an empire-line navy dress, spotted with large yellow or green dots and finished with a contrasting red neckline (figs 142 and 143).[175] The baby was born in December 1918 and the following year Grant painted Bell in the same clothes with a red hat or headscarf (fig. 144).[176] Painted from inside the sitting room at Charleston, with the French doors open into the garden, Bell's reclining figure effectively obstructs the passage from interior to exterior. The portrait was made in springtime, following the armistice, and whatever the psychological implications of its composition, its dappled sunshine and flowering fruit trees express optimism.

Grant's portrait of Bell was given a Bloomsbury title when it was exhibited together with his portrait of her in a red dress at the Carfax Gallery in 1920. It was named in the catalogue *The Room with a View*, chiming with the title of E. M. Forster's 1908 novel *A Room with a View*, and it was bought by the gallery's director, Arthur Clifton. Forster would have seen the painting at Charleston when he visited in August 1919. The title capitalized on a public perception of Bloomsbury as a group, a perception epitomized by Bell in her Bohemian headscarf and colourful clothes. The Omega Workshops had closed down in 1919. Although the dressmaking department was a success, turning a profit of £2 a week by 1918, Omega was not commercially viable as an entity.[177] The Workshops' six trading years, however, marked an important transition in the shaping of Bloomsbury as a named group with a recognizable image. By 1920, when *The Room with a View* was sold, Bloomsbury was collectable.

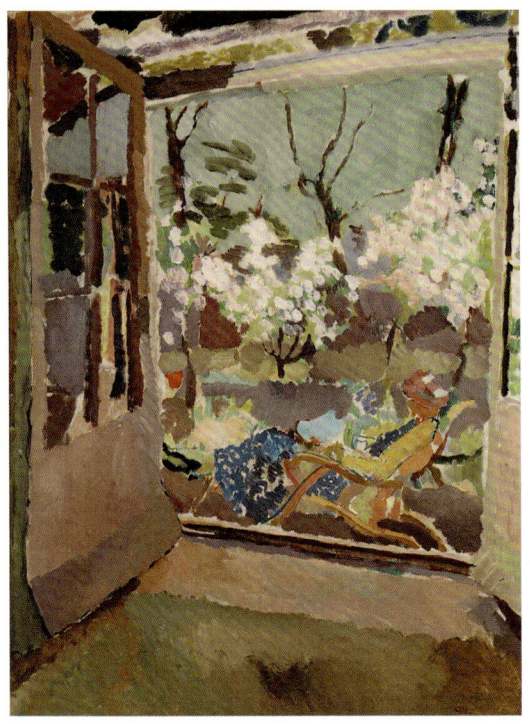

142 (*p. 126*) Duncan Grant, *Vanessa Bell Pregnant*, 1918. Oil on canvas, 660 × 583 mm. Auckland Art Gallery Toi o Tāmaki
143 (*p. 127*) Duncan Grant, study for *Vanessa Bell Pregnant*, 1918. Ink on paper, 227 × 177 mm. The Charleston Trust

144 Duncan Grant, *The Room with a View*, 1919. Oil on canvas, 760 × 570 mm. Private collection

CHAPTER 4

EXHIBITING AND COLLECTING BLOOMSBURY

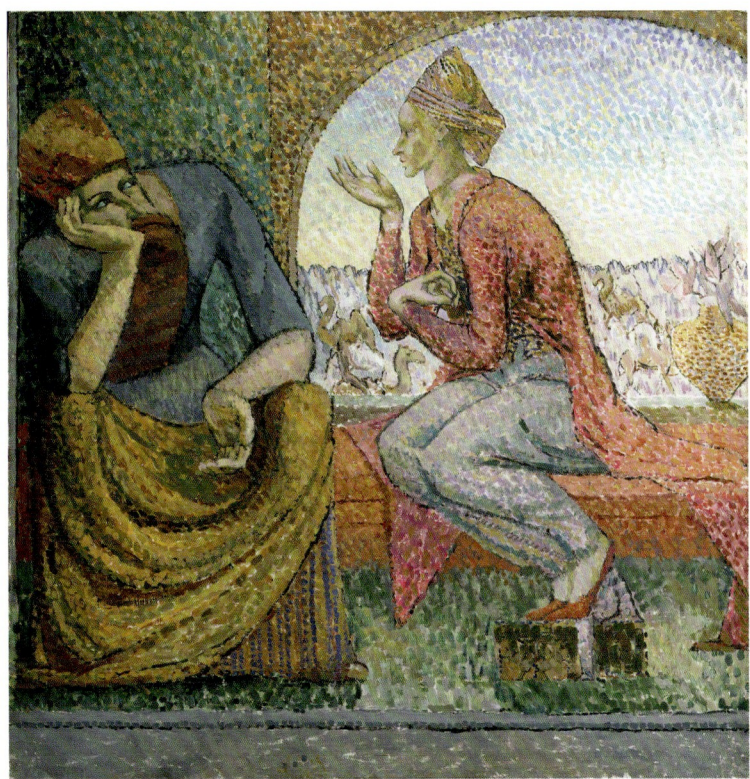

Armed with a screwdriver, in September 1925 Vanessa Bell entered 46 Gordon Square, now the home of Maynard and Lydia Keynes, while they were on their honeymoon in Russia, unscrewed a picture from the bathroom wall, and took it. She had travelled to London from Charleston specifically for the purpose and Lytton Strachey, who was staying with her there, reported the incident to Dora Carrington: 'She now confesses she is terrified. What Maynard will do to her when he returns and discovers the loss, heaven alone knows.'[1] This chapter explores the display of pictures and their ownership as integral to the power dynamics within the Bloomsbury Group. It examines the way in which Bloomsbury operated as a group, from its earliest years through to its maturity, by building and deploying collections and curating exhibitions to promote its collective identity. Bell and Keynes had quarrelled in 1925 over a painting by Grant that they both claimed to own. After the altercation, Keynes had had the picture screwed onto his bathroom wall, in itself a statement about ownership and the relative status of the work within his collection.

Bloomsbury exchanged houses and rooms to accommodate changes in its circumstances and relationships, and Keynes had taken over the running of 46 Gordon Square in 1916. As Clive kept a bedroom and sitting room there throughout the First World War, some of his collection and that of Vanessa probably remained in situ. After the war Vanessa returned to Gordon Square, moving first to no. 50 and then returning to no. 46 before vacating the house for no. 37 so that the Keyneses could live there as man and wife. It was this marriage that had provoked what Strachey described as a 'kind of unofficial war' within Bloomsbury in 1925.[2] The ownership of works of art was seldom shared within the Group. When Bell inventoried the pictures at Charleston, she catalogued the title, artist, and dimensions for each work and the initials of its owner: 'C.B.', 'V.B.', and 'D.G.'[3] The incident with the screwdriver demonstrates the private currency of Bloomsbury pictures and the way in which they codified relationships. Grant's painting and its removal from 46 Gordon Square were emblematic of divisions within the Group.

---

145 Duncan Grant, *The Queen of Sheba*, 1912. Oil on board, 1200 × 1200 mm. Tate, London

Keynes purchased and commissioned work to support his artist friends, almost from his earliest connections with Bloomsbury. As a consequence, his successive homes in Bloomsbury and Cambridge identified him with the Group and boldly declared his status as a progressive patron. Grant decorated Keynes's rooms at King's College, Cambridge, in 1910, and when they moved into a house in Brunswick Square with Adrian and Virginia Stephen and Leonard Woolf the following year, Keynes signed the lease.[4] Grant decorated their ground-floor sitting room with a Post-Impressionist street scene, working collaboratively with Frederick Etchells, whose large, ambitious painting *The Dead Mole* Keynes immediately acquired.[5] He recommended Grant to paint a mural at Newnham College, Cambridge, based on an oil sketch, *The Queen of Sheba*, in his collection and made his own mural at King's College available for inspection.[6] The Newnham commission foundered but Grant produced a large version of *The Queen of Sheba* that was acquired by Fry and then, through the Contemporary Art Society, presented to Tate in 1917 (fig. 145). This enlightened and interlocking patronage had a public interface. *The Dead Mole* and *The Queen of Sheba* were two of the most arresting British paintings in the *Second Post-Impressionist Exhibition*, which was masterminded by Bloomsbury members and ran from 5 October to 31 December 1912 before being extended to 31 January 1913. Both paintings were reproduced in the catalogue. This signalled their importance and enabled comparisons, beyond the confines of the gallery, with other pictures in the catalogue (fig. 146).[7] Their lenders were prominently identified beneath the title of each painting. Fry's reputation as a former curator at the Metropolitan Museum of Art in New York and co-editor of the *Burlington Magazine* would have enhanced that of Grant in 1912; for Keynes, who was as yet little-known, the reputational advantage worked in reverse because it located him within the avant-garde.

✳ ✳ ✳

The context for a painting – when and where it is viewed and its provenance – contributes to its significance. Lytton Strachey and his sister, Pernel, modelled for *The Queen of Sheba*. Grant's conceit in representing his cousins as the wise King Solomon and the Queen of Sheba, who is charged with using her wit and imagination to capture and hold his attention, may have originated in a Strachey family anecdote.[8] With the proposal to work *The Queen of Sheba* up into a mural for Newnham College, the internal references of a family joke expanded to include a wider coterie of academic friends and associates. Both Lytton and Pernel Strachey, who was Director of Modern and Medieval Languages at Newnham and would become the college's Principal, were familiar figures in Cambridge, and their identities and roles within the painting would have been shared as an in-joke. Their exotic costumes and the camels in the background make oblique references to their colonial family background. When the larger version of the painting was shown at the *Second Post-Impressionist Exhibition*, Strachey's likeness, with his unmistakable and unfashionable beard and long hair, cut by Vanessa Bell, was made explicit by the inclusion of a named portrait of him by Henry Lamb in the same Centre Gallery (fig. 147).[9]

Whilst its Bloomsbury subjects were recognizable, the painting was also designed, in scale and technique, as an assertive incursion into modernism. Within the

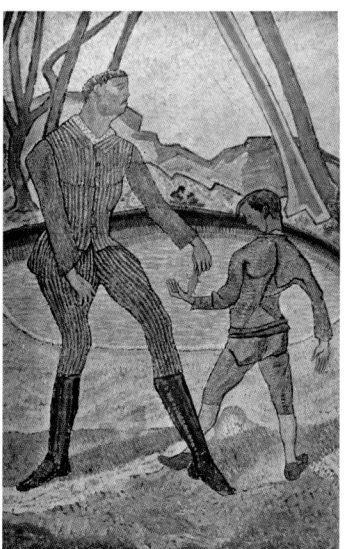

146 Frederick Etchells, *The Dead Mole*, 1912. Reproduced in the catalogue of the *Second Post-Impressionist Exhibition*. The Charleston Trust

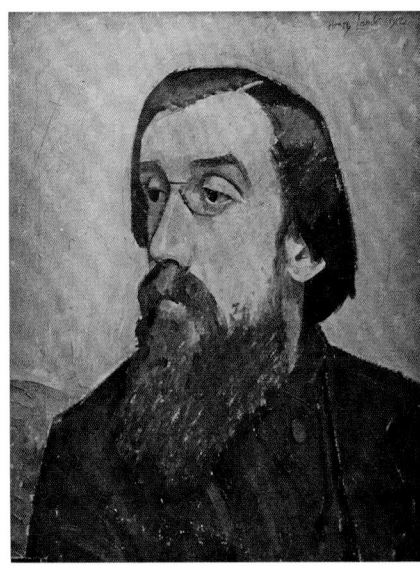

context of the *Second Post-Impressionist Exhibition* its pointillist dashes of colour and the graphic black lines that delineate the figures were clearly responses to the paintings of Van Gogh, Seurat, Matisse, and other European Post-Impressionists. London's culturally sophisticated audiences would have recognized the topicality of *The Queen of Sheba*'s references to the costumes and choreography of the Ballets Russes, which was taking the city by storm. The figures are framed within a shallow picture space, similar to a stage set, and the contorted poses and hand gestures in Grant's painting and in Etchells's *The Dead Mole* mimic the choreography of Mikhail Fokine.

Exhibitions and their reviews were key to the shaping of Bloomsbury's reputation. Reviews were noted and discussed in correspondence. Keynes would include them in his letters to Charleston, 'I enclose a cutting as perhaps you don't get the Times', and Grant pasted reviews into a carefully indexed scrapbook.[10] The *Second Post-Impressionist Exhibition*'s ambition to articulate an English contribution to Post-Impressionism was largely dismissed by the press as feeble, but catalogue essays by Roger Fry and Clive Bell ensured that it was clearly understood.[11] The *Queen of Sheba* was singled out for praise in the *Daily Mail* and *The Times*. The *Mail* reported: 'the group of English artists . . . speak the modern French jargon without, on the whole, attaining to the excessively exhilarating brightness of the Frenchmen's colour. Mr. D. Grant's "The Queen of Sheba" is a work that is remarkable for its loveliness of colour and rhythm of design.'[12] *The Times* described Grant as the most talented of the English artists, again commenting on his use of colour in *The Queen of Sheba* but describing it as 'a very amusing illustration'.[13] Vanessa Bell's *Asheham* was listed in the same article as 'simple and pleasant'. The *Observer* noted, however, that the English paintings were dull and colourless when they were grouped together.[14] Rupert Brooke reviewed the exhibition for the *Cambridge Magazine*, qualifying his praise with a criticism that Grant's painting inclined towards prettiness: 'His genius is an elusive and faithless sprite.'[15] Brooke and Grant had been at school together and when Grant was visiting Cambridge they moved in compatible circles. Grant had stayed with Brooke at the Old Vicarage at Grantchester in 1911 and it is interesting to note that two of the three paintings by Grant that are named in Brooke's review represent their mutual friends; one, indeed, is a portrait of Ka Cox, Brooke's lover. 'There is beauty in *The Seated Woman*', Brooke wrote, 'an exquisite wit and invention in the delightful *The Queen of Sheba*, and a grave loveliness in *The Dancers*.'[16]

As an 'in-group' of radicals, Bloomsbury enabled its artists to withstand criticism and produce their most innovative work. *The Queen of Sheba* exemplifies the ways in which they engaged with Post-Impressionism not only as models and artists, but also as intellectuals, exploring its principles in private as well as in public as a group. It was painted in the shared house in Brunswick Square, and Vanessa Bell describes the intensity of conversations at Asheham when Bloomsbury gathered there in the weeks leading up to the *Second Post-Impressionist Exhibition*. 'Good heavens,' she wrote to the Woolfs, who were in Ravenna on their honeymoon, going on to describe Oliver Strachey and Harry Norton 'in the thick of an aesthetic discussion . . . it does seem odd that that should go on perennially whether one's there or not, and one knows that Norton hasn't and never will have the remotest conception of any of the things he's talking about'.[17] The *Second Post-Impressionist Exhibition* consolidated

147 Henry Lamb, *Portrait of Lytton Strachey*, 1912. Reproduced in the catalogue of the *Second Post-Impressionist Exhibition*. The Charleston Trust

the work of *Manet and the Post-Impressionists* (1910) as a shared project that determined and projected the Group's self-fashioning. The exhibition was directed by Fry, who selected the French work, while Clive Bell chose the English work and introduced the concept of 'significant form' in its catalogue. Leonard Woolf was employed as secretary, Duncan Grant designed the poster, and Vanessa Bell helped Fry with the installation, literally creating a context within which their individual and group identities would shine. The massive simplicity of Matisse's plaster relief *Le dos* in the entrance landing established a context for Grant's monumental figures and his anatomical distortions.[18] His *Seated Woman* was the first British painting that visitors encountered in the next room, surrounded by paintings by Matisse, Cézanne, Derain, and Marchand (fig. 148).[19] Work by the Bloomsbury artists and their friends in the Centre Gallery was interspersed with paintings by Braque, Derain, and Vlaminck and sculpture by Matisse, positioning them within a European avant-garde.

Bloomsbury's ability to determine and to project its own identity through association with the work of artists and writers it admired dates back to the Friday Club, founded by Vanessa Bell in 1905. Some of her earliest letters to Clive Bell and Maynard Keynes draw them into the Club and establish the visual arts as a touchstone for the Group, working in tandem with her siblings' literary and intellectual discussions on 'Thursday evenings'. She involved 'Mr Bell' in a search for rented rooms in which the Club might meet and exhibit in 1905, and wrote to 'Mr Keynes', two years later: 'Can you face another evening at the Friday Club & if so will you dine with us . . . & come on to hear Clive's paper?'[20] Dinner was at 7.45 p.m., the meeting was at 115 Ebury Street, and Keynes was reminded, 'Of course don't trouble to dress.'[21] London was bristling with artists' groups and clubs in the first decades of the twentieth century and Bell's Friday Club enabled her to establish an autonomous artistic identity on her own terms, and to exhibit on an equal footing with male artists as well as other women. Virginia Woolf documented the Club's progress in letters to Violet Dickinson: 'Nessa has fairly got her Club started; and they are to have an exhibition at once, and you will just be in time to go with me to see it. Really that gives me quite a thrill.'[22] She wrote again on 3 December 1905, describing 'Nessa's exhibition' and her sister's evident leadership: 'Old Nessa goes ahead, and slashes about her, and manages all the business, and rejects all her friends pictures, and don't mind a bit. She is said to have a genius for organization.'[23] Ka Cox, Marjorie Strachey, and Bell's siblings were Club members and many of the artists invited to join or to exhibit with the Friday Club were drawn from her connections through the Slade and the Royal Academy Schools.[24]

The Club's annual exhibitions attracted progressive work by young artists. Celebrated French artists, including Pierre-Auguste Renoir, Camille Pissarro, Honoré Daumier, and Pierre Puvis de Chavannes, were also featured in at least three shows to attract visitors and 'as an indication of direction'.[25] Drawings and lithographs by Daumier dominated the 1911 exhibition, making up a third of the exhibits.[26] For emerging artists, including Grant, Hamnett, David Bomberg, C. R. W. Nevinson, Henry Lamb, Paul and John Nash, Frederick and Jessie Etchells, and Mark Gertler, who was still at the Slade and in his

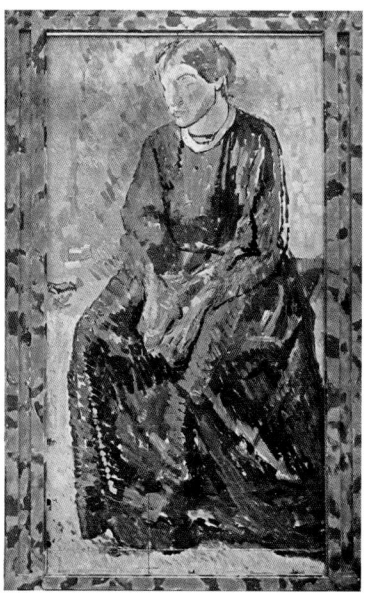

148 Duncan Grant, *Seated Woman*, c.1912. Reproduced in the catalogue of the *Second Post-Impressionist Exhibition*. The Charleston Trust

149 (*opposite*) Duncan Grant, *The Blue Sheep*, c.1913. Folding screen, distemper or gouache on paper stretched over a wooden frame, each panel is 1625 × 683 × 26 mm. Victoria and Albert Museum, London

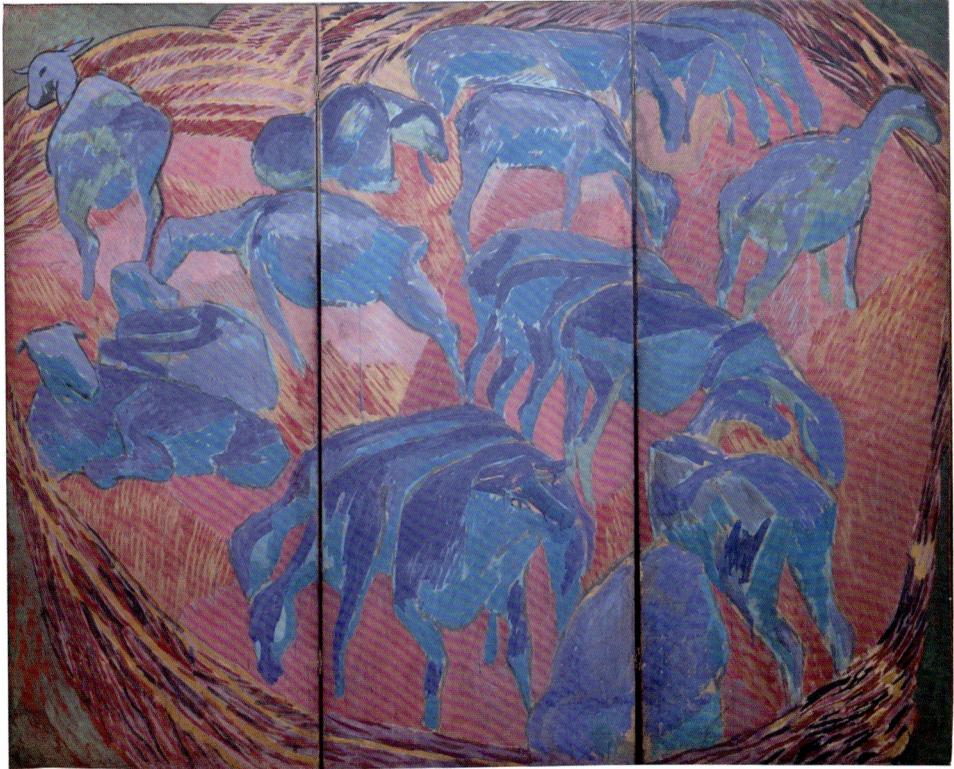

teens when he first showed at the Friday Club, it provided a forum for discussion and an outlet for bold experiments. It quickly gained a reputation for 'very good shows of what were then ultra-modern pictures'.[27] These were subjected to a selection process. Bell describes the rejection of one of her paintings of Studland Beach for the 1910 exhibition, but two of her still lifes were 'hung in the best place' with Grant's *Lemon Gatherers* between them, 'in the principal place of honour'.[28] She bought Grant's painting in anticipation of a gift from Clive Bell's parents of £1,000 on the imminent arrival of her baby, Quentin, and subsequently loaned it to two important exhibitions.[29] These, by their very titles – *Twentieth Century Art* at the Whitechapel Art Gallery in 1914, and *The New Movement in Art* at the Mansard Gallery in Heal's in 1917 – harboured ambitions to define British modernism.[30] The latter, curated by Fry, also included nine of Bell's own paintings.

The Friday Club enabled the Bloomsbury artists to explore their identity as Post-Impressionists and to test the boundaries between fine and applied arts in advance of the *Second Post-Impressionist Exhibition* and the subsequent foundation of the Omega Workshops. The Bloomsbury artists were identified as Post-Impressionists, all 'more-or-less of the same school', in a 1911 review of the Friday Club exhibition.[31] The following year, in February 1912, Bell exhibited a design for a screen with the Friday Club and the exhibition included a design for a menu card by Winifred Gill together with a display of fans, bags, and a screen designed by Constance Lloyd.[32] Although the Club continued until 1922 and its meetings, exhibitions, and annual ball served Bloomsbury as a network, members of the Group did not show with the Club after 1912. In 1913 they formed an alternative exhibition society, the Grafton Group, which emerged out of the *Second Post-Impressionist Exhibition* at the Grafton Galleries. 'The name will be understood', one reporter wrote, documenting their notoriety, 'when I say that Mrs. Bell, Mr. Roger Fry, Mr. Duncan Grant, Mr. P. Wyndham Lewis, and Mr. Frederick Etchells compose the society. The society is Post-Impressionist, and it has invited ten other artists whose work has a general affinity with that of the members to exhibit with them.'[33]

Artists exhibited anonymously in the first Grafton Group show (1913), liberating women in the Group from sexist commentary and anticipating the practice of the Omega Workshops. If this encouraged experiment, however, it failed to impress the critics, who ran through their guesses with the exhibition secretary until they could publish the artists' names: 'It is quite an entertaining game', one critic observed.[34] Grant's screen *The Blue Sheep* (fig. 149) was singled out from the 60 works in their first exhibition as 'essential Post-Impressionism', and Bell was also praised for her *Portrait of a Woman*.[35] Writing in the *Daily Telegraph*, Claude Phillips recognized Grant's debt to Matisse in his flattening of form and the intensity of his palette: 'What if the sheep are blue shot with the green; what if the grass is red and orange! The design, the colour-harmony are all the same beautiful and expressive.'[36]

Wyndham Lewis and Frederick Etchells left the Grafton Group and the Omega Workshops before the second and final Grafton Group show in January 1914. They formed the Rebel Art Centre in opposition to Omega, later becoming known as the Vorticists. In doing so they tacitly acknowledged Bloomsbury's successful strategy for self-fashioning as an avant-garde group. 'Rumour has recently amused a listening world', the *Manchester Courier* wrote, 'with stories of a difference of opinion – and possibly more than one – among our native Post-Impressionists.'[37] The *Daily Telegraph* described Lewis and his colleagues as 'British Cubists' and wryly noted their manipulation of the press and the forging of a distinct identity for their new group through confrontation: 'Mr. Wyndham Lewis and Mr. Nevinson at their head, detached themselves the other day with so portentous a fracas, with so firm a resolve that both supporters of the movement and others should "know all about it," that it is impossible to pass over their secession in silence.'[38] The paper dismissed the cause of the row, without naming it as a disputed commission for the *Ideal Homes Exhibition*, as a 'storm in a tea-cup'.

Bloomsbury's collective engagement with exhibitions as a construction of its own identity located the Group within an international avant-garde and established its artists' reputations in the press as English Post-Impressionists. Paintings by 'two clever foreigners' were included in the first Grafton Group show: two abstract 'Compositions' by Wassily Kandinsky, which Fry borrowed from the collector Michael Sadler, and work by the Russian-born American painter Max Weber.[39] Photographs of Picasso's new constructions and his *Tête d'homme* (1913), recently acquired by Fry, established an avant-garde context for the 1914 exhibition, and Bell was optimistic that Fry might borrow paintings by Cézanne for the following year.[40] French paintings were also borrowed from the poet and dealer Charles Vildrac for the 1914 exhibition, the title of which – *The Grafton Group. Vanessa Bell. Roger Fry. Duncan Grant. Second Exhibition* – clearly identifies the core Bloomsbury artists as the 'diminished Grafton Group'.[41] This relatively small exhibition of 52 works explored a more focused identity for the Group. It combined strikingly innovative paintings with decorative designs, promoting the Omega Workshops and challenging established hierarchies that categorized the decorative arts as inferior to painting and sculpture. Grant showed a piece titled *Design for Needlework*, and Bell again exhibited *Design for Screen*.[42] Prices were given in the catalogue and Bell's screen must have been an elaborate design because it was £25; two further screens by Bell and Fry were on sale at £20 each. Other Omega artists included Doucet, Hamnett, Gill, and Gaudier-Brzeska, who showed six sculptures. There were no further Grafton Group shows after the outbreak of war but the Omega Workshops continued to provide a venue for solo and group exhibitions for its artists, selling work on commission.

✣ ✣ ✣

The exhibitions that Bloomsbury initiated and curated in its formative years, and its example in doing so, form part of its contribution to twentieth-century modernism. The exhibitions stimulated their artists and associates to produce some of their most ambitious work. Bell's painting *Conversation Piece*, locating experimental ideas and Post-Impressionism in Sussex, was shown in Paris in a small exhibition of English art that Fry organized with Vildrac in the spring of 1912 (see fig. 69).[43] She was involved in the installation, together with Fry and Clive Bell, and wrote to Grant at 38 Brunswick Square describing the success of his new painting, *The Dancers*, in the show.[44] It was included that autumn in the *Second Post-Impressionist Exhibition*. Grant wrote to Virginia Woolf that he was still struggling to finish 'some dozen pictures' for the *Second Post-Impressionist Exhibition* just weeks before it opened.[45] Bell recorded the prominence and

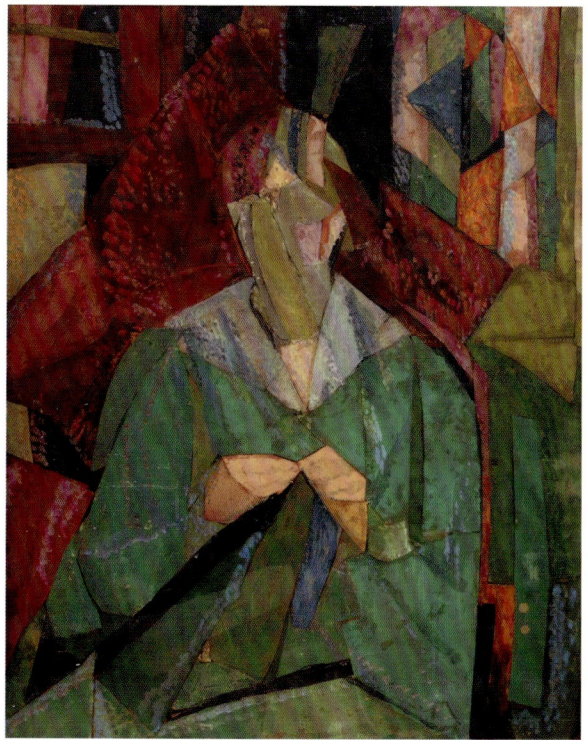

collegiality of artistic practice at Asheham ahead of the show in the summer of 1912 in her paintings as well as her letters. She painted Frederick and Jessie Etchells, and Henri Doucet with Duncan Grant, working together in the studio there.[46] Many of her more exploratory and iconic paintings from this period, including her 'faceless' portraits of Woolf and *Studland Beach*, were not included in the *Second Post-Impressionist Exhibition* or the Grafton Group exhibitions. Their evolution was supported, nevertheless, by this creative environment and by Bell's innate understanding of her own centrality to it.

Bloomsbury exhibited some of its most contentious paintings within the self-curated context of Grafton. Grant's *Adam and Eve* had already been purchased by the recently founded Contemporary Art Society, on Clive Bell's recommendation, when it was shown in the 1914 exhibition, but this was not sufficient to protect it from widespread disapproval by critics and the artists' friends alike.[47] Vanessa wrote to him that the show was 'a great success . . . There have been lots of notices, mostly good', but that 'Of course your Adam and Eve is a good deal objected to, simply on account of the distortion and Adam's standing on his head.' She continued: 'I believe distortion is like Sodomy. People are simply blindly prejudiced against it because they think it abnormal.'[48]

Envisioning the exhibition choices through which Bloomsbury asserted its identity is complicated by ambiguous catalogue entries that give works such general titles as, for example, *Still Life* or *Landscape and Figures*. Bell's *Mrs Desmond MacCarthy* in the Grafton's second exhibition may have been a small, oil-on-panel portrait of her friend in a winged armchair, painted in 1912, which prefigures her iconic portrait of Virginia Woolf.[49] It is possible, however, that this was the later, faceless painting of Molly MacCarthy that challenged portrait conventions with its mixed-media collaged surface, pieced together, its subject's features replaced by a pattern of pasted and painted strips of colour (fig. 150). Other paintings in the exhibition reviews and catalogues cannot be identified. Vanessa Bell's *Tents* in the second Grafton Group exhibition was presumably inspired by the Brandon camping holiday but its current whereabouts, if it survives, are unknown.[50] It was described as a study in an exhibition review by Claude Phillips in the *Daily Telegraph* and his use of language is dismissive, characterizing the picture primarily as the work of a woman: 'Mrs. Bell's study, "Tents," is a composition of original rhythm and genuine charm.' The same review does not attribute 'charm' to the work of Grant and Fry. Rather, this is distinguished by its 'splendid powers . . . the force and the beauty of rhythm' and by its 'brutality . . . ruthless objectivity . . . and deliberate violence'.[51]

Nevertheless, Claude Phillips gave a section of his review the heading 'Mrs. Vanessa Bell and others', signifying her importance in relation to those 'others', Grant and Fry. In doing so he followed Bell's own lead in asserting her independence as an artist and renouncing the conventional use of her married name, 'Mrs Clive Bell'. The exhibition title uses her Christian name and sets her surname in alphabetical order before those of Fry and Grant. Phillips identified Bell as 'the sanest of these post impressionists' because her work had more aesthetic appeal than that of her fellow artists.[52] By implication it was less innovative, and

150 Vanessa Bell, *Portrait of Molly MacCarthy*, c.1914–15. Gouache, oil, and collage on board, 920 × 750 mm. Private collection

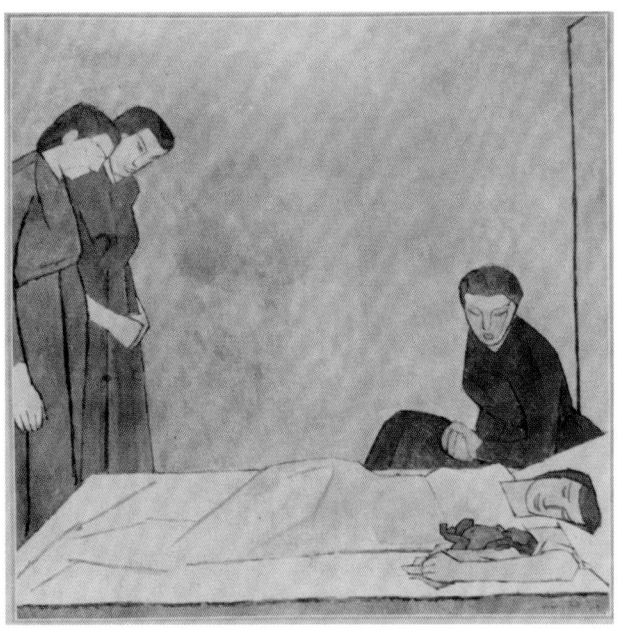

although he described her imposing canvas *Women and Baby* as powerful and expressive, he underestimated its ambition (fig. 151).[53] Reed and Spalding have analysed the seriousness of purpose that Bell brought to this large, experimental, six-foot-square painting.[54] It internalized the influences of Gauguin and Matisse to locate modernist primitivism within a female experience of motherhood. The *Telegraph*, with inherent sexism, described it as a 'decorative composition'. The unnaturally small baby, lying on a cloth in the crook of its mother's arm, the recumbent, pale figure of the mother, whose body, twisted towards the child, is minimally indicated by a few lines, and the sombre figures of three women watching over them may relate to Bell's experience of miscarriage. They are trivialized in Phillips's review: 'the woman who plays with a new-born babe is synthetized with great skill. The smashed noses and formidable aspect generally of the women who look down on her are no doubt a tribute to the requirements of the school.'[55] The *Pall Mall Gazette*, by contrast, recognized the influence of Puvis de Chavannes on the painting and noted its 'primitive passion. . . . None but a woman, none but a great artist, could have so perfectly expressed, with a new sympathy, all the pathos and bewilderment of this time-worn theme.'[56] Bell ignored this commentary when she wrote to Grant about reviews of *Adam and Eve* a few days later, telling him instead that she was grateful to Oliver Strachey, who had 'screwed himself up to write me an enthusiastic letter about my big picture'.[57]

Women and Baby was one of five pictures by Bell selected for the exhibition *Twentieth Century Art: A Review of Modern Movements* at Whitechapel Art Gallery in 1914. It is identified in the exhibition catalogue as belonging to Fry.[58] Although it is one of the many important paintings by Bell to have been lost, it is known from photographs published a few years later in *Vogue*, among which is an image locating it within Fry's collection in the double-height living space at Durbins (fig. 152).[59] In this deliberately curated interior, *Women and Baby* was prominently displayed together with Grant's *Seated Woman*, Fry's own portrait of Nina Hamnett, and a quattrocento Madonna and Child.[60] It was conspicuous, too, as one of the first paintings that visitors to the Whitechapel would have encountered. *Twentieth Century Art* marked a transition for Bloomsbury from the small Grafton Group and Friday Club exhibitions that it had helped to organize and curate in rented rooms at the Alpine Club Gallery to a survey exhibition by a public institution. Nearly 500 works were divided into four groups that the *Daily Telegraph* summarized as 'British Neo-Impressionists, Post-Impressionists, Cubists and Futurists'.[61] The *Telegraph* complained that 'Three-quarters of the exhibits here are old friends (or enemies?)' that had already been reviewed at Grafton Group exhibitions and those of the London Group, which had also been founded as an exhibiting group in 1913.[62] The show's ambition, however, set out in its catalogue, was to identify and categorize modern art by younger contemporary artists working in Britain according to its influences, rather than to showcase new work.[63] Lisa Tickner has analysed the Whitechapel's objectives and its allocation of a separate 'Small Gallery' in the exhibition for work by Jewish artists, curated by Bomberg.[64] The Rebel Art Centre, having established an independent identity through aggressive tactics in a matter of months, was named in the catalogue as part of a group that had 'abandoned representation almost

151 Vanessa Bell, *Women and Baby*, c.1912. No longer extant. Photograph from *Vogue*, early February 1926

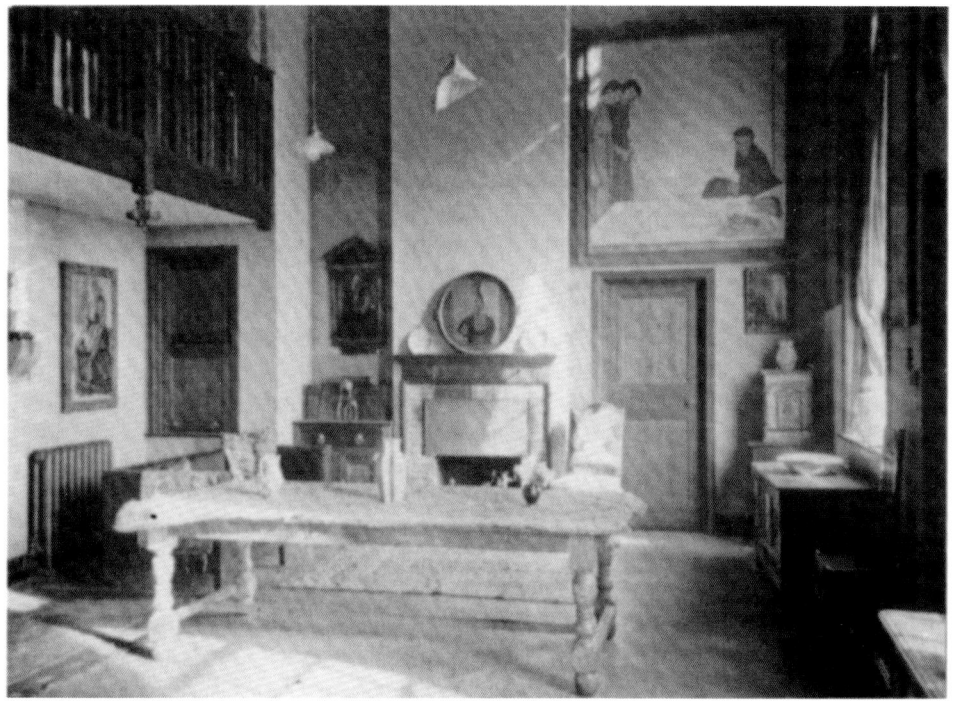

entirely', and work by Lewis, Etchells, Nevinson, William Roberts, Edward Wadsworth, and Helen Saunders was grouped together in the main Lower Gallery. Bell's *Women and Baby* was hung within this 'Cubist' category next to Grant's large painting, *Slops*.[65] The space was dominated by 'A large exhibit of furniture, rugs, wall-hangings, pottery, and objects of art . . . from the Omega Workshops (Ltd.)'.[66] Sixteen pieces of Omega printed linen were displayed on the walls, and over 80 other works – including armchairs, dining chairs, a 'Goldfish Table', screens, ceramics, and a flat case filled with leather bags, fans, and bead necklaces (but no items of dress) – expanded upon the earlier displays at the Friday Club and Grafton Group exhibitions. *Twentieth Century Art* recognized the significance of Bloomsbury's contribution to modernism through the decorative and fine arts and, irrespective of personal differences, its stylistic compatibility with the Rebel Art Centre.

Upstairs in *Twentieth Century Art* the first paintings in the Upper Gallery were also by Bell, Grant, and Fry, including Grant's *Dancers*; further into the space, his *Queen of Sheba* was again hung close to a portrait of Strachey by Henry Lamb, on loan from Morrell's collection, again identifying the sitter.[67] This ability of Bloomsbury painting to span different categories, to sit alongside the 'Cubist' paintings of the Rebel Art Centre and work by Lamb, Walter Sickert, Stanley Spencer, Charles Ginner, and others, is characteristic of the Group's assimilation into different social and artistic networks. The *Daily Telegraph* pointedly noted that 'really distinguished modern artists' included in the exhibition, such as Sickert, 'disdain to advertise themselves by the resounding and persistent banging of the big drum'.[68] The exhibition was not dogmatic, however, in its arrangement. It was applauded in the *Telegraph* as 'a brilliant, if somewhat hazardous, *tour de force*' and the Omega Workshops was designated 'the very stronghold of Post-Impressionism, where the Arch-Priest, Mr. Roger Fry, "rides in the whirlwind and directs the storm"'.[69]

As an emerging group, Bloomsbury was remarkably successful in inventing and establishing the concept of Post-Impressionism in Britain and, in doing so, its own public identity and status within the vanguard of European modernism. It exercised the individual skills

152 A. C. Cooper, the interior of Durbins, home of Roger Fry, photographed in 1917 for *Vogue*, late March 1918, p. 40. Bell's canvas *Women and Baby* hangs above the door

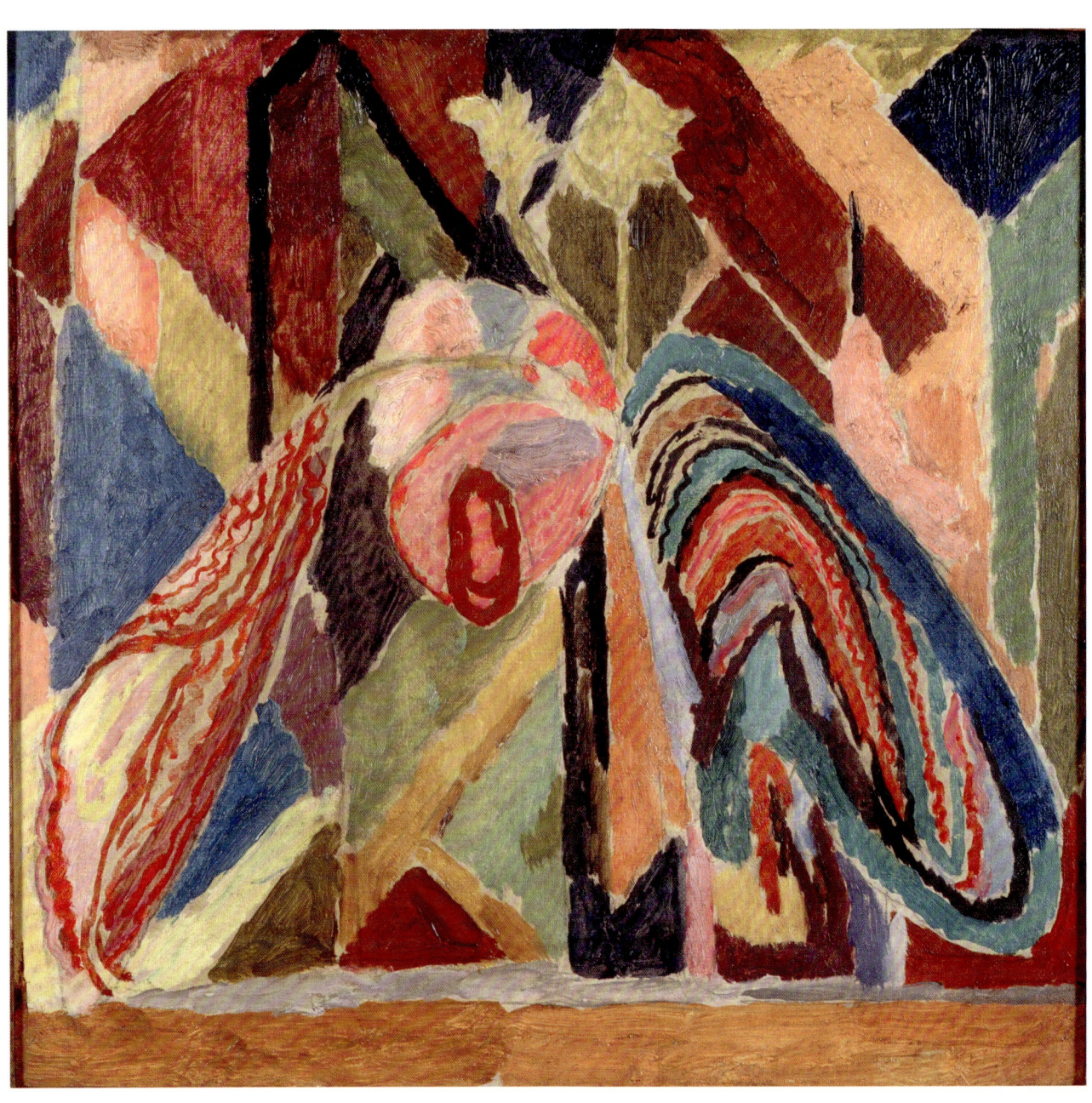

of its members to curate, to manage and organize, and to champion and support. It also stimulated their creative skills to articulate critical theories that were published in catalogues and picked up by the press, and to originate new and experimental work. Although Virginia Woolf described artists as 'an abominable race' and was dismissive of the 'furious excitement' surrounding their exhibitions at the end of 1912, she was fascinated by Post-Impressionism and originated a literary counterpart to it.[70] The Group was not insular in its exhibition choices. Grant exhibited with the Camden Town Group, which was led by Sickert and first exhibited at the Carfax Gallery in 1911, and accepted an invitation to show with the Vorticists.[71]

After the outbreak of the First World War, Bloomsbury continued to showcase experimental work and to introduce the work of new artists from Britain and abroad through its exhibitions at the Omega Workshops. Bell's first solo exhibition was staged in a single room at the Workshops for two weeks in February 1916. Although there was no catalogue and very little correspondence casts light on the exhibition, Omega would have provided Bell with a 'safe space' within which to build on her experience as a curator in a display of her own creative identity. She chose to include her work as a designer and maker alongside her paintings, writing to Fry in January that she was making artificial flowers for the Workshops: 'I thought I might show mine with my pictures.'[72] These were signature Omega products, worn as buttonholes or arranged in vases, and all three of its co-directors painted them in still lifes (fig. 153).[73] They were exotic, sculptural constructions made out of tarlatan, stiffened with size, and decorated with striking patterns and colours. Winifred Gill described the tarlatan, or 'book muslin', as a fine, open-weave cotton commonly used in the ballet skirts of stage fairies. The Workshops brewed its own size, a clear paste that was brushed over fabric to stiffen it, making the fabric 'like paper so that the colours did not run' when it was painted.[74] The inclusion of Omega flowers in Bell's exhibition would thus have complemented the abstract content in her paintings. The show may have assembled an existing body of recent still lifes and portraits, as Judith Collins has suggested, perhaps relating to Bell's Omega dress collection, painted the previous year.[75] Her portrait of Mary Hutchinson, with its extraordinary palette and abstract background, is likely to have been included (see fig. 130). It was praised by Walter Sickert in his 'monthly chronicle' for the *Burlington Magazine* in April 1916. 'Let us have Vanessa Bell's *Portrait of Mrs. Hutchinson*', he wrote, assembling an imaginary list of paintings from recent exhibitions that he found admirable.[76] A review in *The Times*, however, objected that Bell's still lifes and portraits were 'aesthetic experiments' exploring the 'method' of painting: 'the method will seem merely an absurd scribbling with paint . . . in her own way, Mrs. Bell, after the manner of English artists, seems to be aiming too much at beauty, a beauty not of the objects represented, but of calligraphy in paint or of abstract design.'[77]

While some paintings and exhibitions were designed to position their artists' reputations within the complex network of London's groups and clubs, others were undoubtedly made with the market in mind. Sales and commissions were essential to the financial survival of the Omega Workshops as well as to the income and status of its artists. Bell itemized the sales at the second Grafton Group exhibition in a letter to Grant, concluding: 'I don't know if we shall quite cover expenses.'[78] Her letters often negotiated a delicate balance between creative prowess and financial dependence, particularly on Grant's behalf. She wrote to Morrell on Omega Workshops paper soon after her solo show: 'It was most splendid of you to get your brother to buy 3 of Duncan's pictures and I think it will tide him over many difficulties.' She added that it would be 'quite absurd', however, for Morrell to buy one of her own paintings: 'if you really did like any enough to want to have it, I should be so glad to give it to you'.[79] Her offer to gift rather than to sell a painting subverts the conventional relationship between artist and wealthy patron, and the letter might be read as a subtle challenge to the sincerity of Morrell's support: 'I know how pictures accumulate in one's house and if one doesn't like them, they're such a nuisance.'[80]

The Group's letters illuminate the private narratives inherent in owning and displaying one another's work

---

153 Vanessa Bell, *Omega Paper Flowers in a Bottle*, c.1915. Oil on canvas, 305 × 330 mm. Private collection

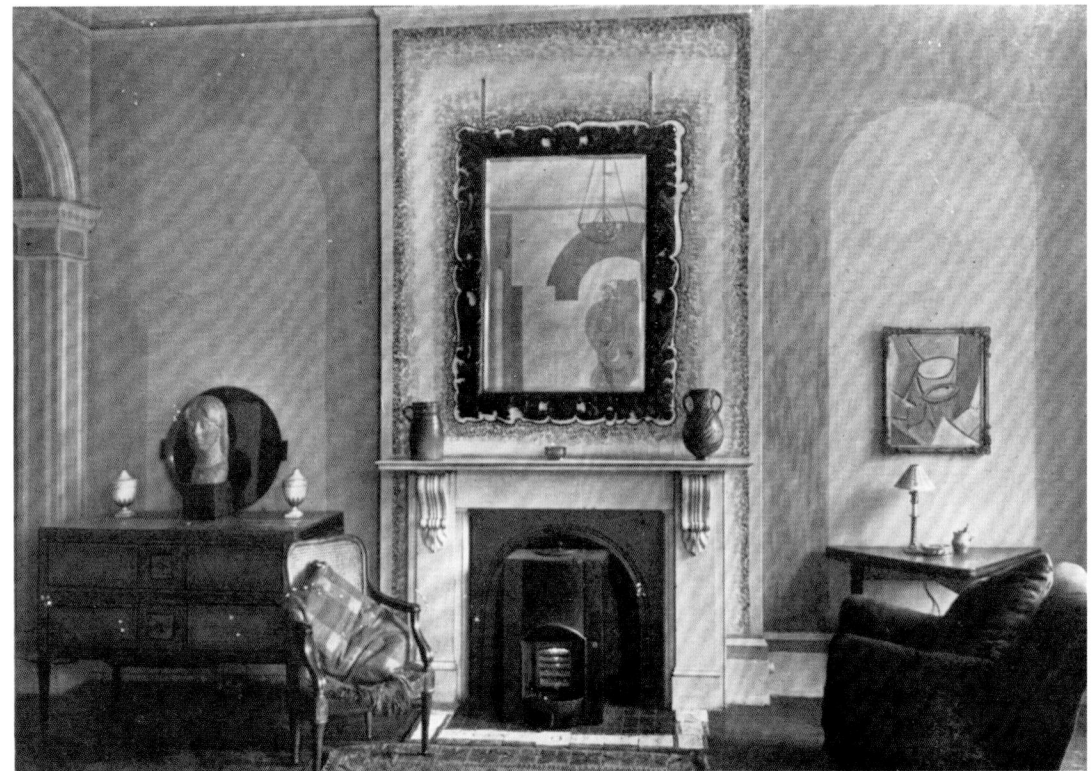

and the complex demonstrations of power relating to gifting and sales. Bell produced two copies after Giotto for an Omega exhibition in 1917. She gave one of them to Keynes and, on Fry's insistence, accepted £10 from him for the second. 'If you want to give me that I will take it as I happen to be rather poor', she wrote to Fry, 'but when I'm not you mustn't pay me for pictures. I think one should give to other artists & sell to people like Mary.'[81] Keynes attended the opening of the exhibition and wrote to Grant:

> Nessa's Giotto (my picture) was greatly admired and also the one of the procession (about which Roger said that Nessa wished to give it him but that he would insist on paying her for it, as he thought it monstrous that she should always be giving her best pictures away!)[82]

This subtle assertion of Keynes's superiority, measured in the quality of his picture and his closeness to the artist, was accompanied by a neat retort to Fry's implied criticism. The exhibition sold only two pictures, both of them to Keynes at the opening. He bought Grant's copy of a work by Piero del Pollaiuolo as a wedding present for his younger brother, Geoffrey Keynes, and Margaret Darwin (granddaughter of Charles Darwin) for £10, giving Fry leave to sell it again for £25 if he could (in which case Grant was to have painted another picture as a wedding gift). His second purchase was Grant's copy of *The Nativity* by Piero della Francesca.[83] In his letter to Grant he describes it as a signifier of the length and depth of their relationship: 'The Piero is so old a friend (I didn't believe you would ever sell it) that I couldn't bear for it to disappear.'[84]

As an experienced curator, Fry used his influence and his own collection beyond the confines of London and the Workshops to promote Bloomsbury as a pioneering force. *An Exhibition of Works Representative of the New Movement in Art* was shown in Birmingham and then at the Mansard Gallery at Heal's in 1917.

154 Unknown photographer, Clive Bell's sitting room at 37 Gordon Square. From Dorothy Todd and Raymond Mortimer, *The New Interior Decoration* (London: B. T. Batsford, 1929), plate 21.

The photograph shows Picasso's *Pots et citron* (1907), framed within its painted niche (*right*), and Grant's decorated vase on the mantelshelf

The catalogue identifies a total of 27 works on loan from Fry's own collection and that of Clive Bell. These paintings represented the Omega artists as well as international painters such as Juan Gris and Maurice de Vlaminck.[85] As published critics and art theorists, the names of Fry and Bell implicitly endorsed the English work and its status among the French modernists. In addition to curating this exhibition, Fry gave a lecture to the press.[86] Bloomsbury was astute in positioning its work in private and public collections. 'I'm so pleased Michael Sadler has bought one of your things at Birmingham, the *Bosham*', Fry wrote to Bell. He bought seven pictures from the show, 'stirred by seeing what a good collection I'd made'.[87] Sadler would add to his Bloomsbury collection a few years later when he bought one of the most striking paintings in Grant's first solo exhibition at the Carfax Gallery, *Venus and Adonis*.[88]

Bloomsbury congregated at exhibition openings, reinforcing perceptions of its cliquishness by the presence, in person, of the individuals represented in so many of its paintings and sculptures. If its portraits reflected and codified enmities and allegiances within the Group, these were on display and open to speculation when they were exhibited. Fry included his own portrait of Nina Hamnett in the *New Movement in Art* exhibition, and a version of Bell's portrait of Mary Hutchinson that he owned, catalogued 'Portrait, M.H.'[89] A second version of the portrait (that shown in fig. 130) remained in Bell's collection; Richard Shone believes that Bell altered this painting before showing it with the London Group two years later, ostensibly as an anonymous portrait.[90] In a letter to Fry she sets out an inner conflict between artistic integrity and knowingly causing offence to Hutchinson:

> I sent my portrait of Mary to the L.G. but I think I shall get into trouble over it. It's perfectly hideous now and yet quite unmistakable. I asked her if she minded and she evidently did – but I had already sent it and I believe it's rather conspicuously hung. However I think it got better in the end.[91]

Bell was acutely aware of the audiences for her images and their dependence, for effect, upon location. She would have understood the indignity that this public display inflicted upon Hutchinson. The letter is ambiguous, however, in locating this unflattering portrait within the complex relationship between the two women. It positions Hutchinson within the Bloomsbury Group as the subject of a boldly original challenge to the conventions of portraiture. But it cruelly caricatures her features, rejecting her from the Group's inner circle and exposing her to derision.

In addition to collecting one another's paintings and portraits, Bloomsbury bonded over progressive, and to some extent competitive, acquisitions. When they were first married, Clive and Vanessa Bell owned *The Childhood of Pyramus* by Augustus John and it was prominently displayed at 46 Gordon Square, filling an entire wall.[92] They were the first private collectors in Britain to buy a Picasso. Bell wrote to her sister from Paris in 1911, 'we're in a huge state of excitement having just bought a Picasso for £4. I wonder how you'll like it.'[93] The painting, *Pots et citron*, was illustrated in Clive Bell's best-selling publication, *Art*, in 1914 and he loaned it to the first major exhibition of Picasso's work in London in 1921.[94] When his

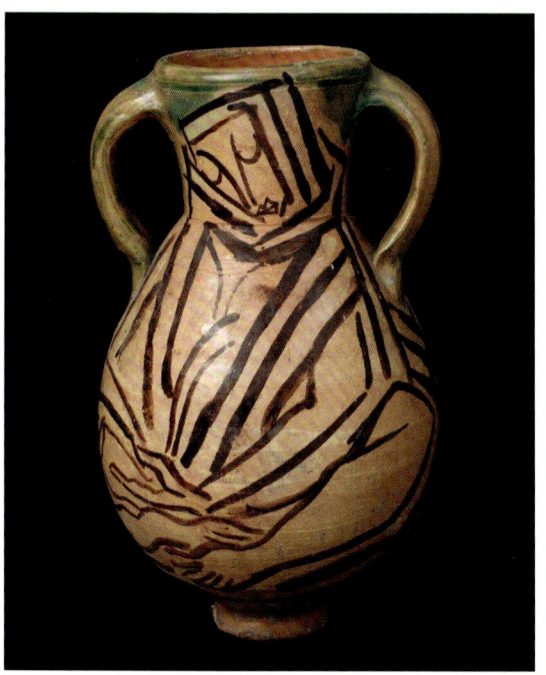

155 Duncan Grant, *Decorated Vase*, 1914. Ceramic, 343 × 200 × 200 mm. The Charleston Trust

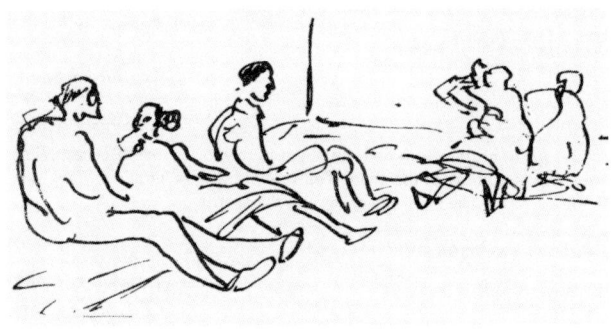

sitting room at 37 Gordon Square, decorated by Bell and Grant, was featured in *The New Interior Decoration* in 1929, the Picasso was displayed in its own painted niche (fig. 154). A ceramic on the mantelshelf to one side, painted by Grant, elegantly presented a Bloomsbury response to Picasso (fig. 155).[95] The photograph thus describes the process of collecting, and the display and purposing of collections, as a shared passion among the Bloomsbury circle.

When the contents of Degas's studio in Paris were auctioned in 1918, the Group collaborated to acquire works for the nation as well as their own private collections. Grant found a catalogue for the sale in Fry's studio and persuaded Keynes that he should use his influence at the Treasury to buy some of the paintings for the National Gallery. Keynes secured 550,000 francs.[96] 'My picture coup was a whirlwind affair', he wrote to Vanessa Bell, adding that the Chancellor of the Exchequer, Bonar Law, was so amused by his plan to cross the Channel with the Director of the National Gallery, Charles Holmes, in the midst of war to buy pictures that he 'eventually let me have my way as a sort of joke'.[97] Keynes went through the catalogue with Bell, Grant, and Fry, declaring his intention to use the journey out to persuade Holmes to buy a Cézanne for the nation 'as a personal reward to me for having got him his money'.[98] The correspondence surrounding the acquisition evidences Bloomsbury's group identity. Its members performed their aesthetic sophistication, more advanced than that of the National Gallery's curators, for their own amusement and for one another. When Holmes could not be convinced to buy a Cézanne, Keynes acquired his *Still Life with Apples* for his own collection and bought a sketch by Delacroix as a gift for Grant to thank him for his involvement in the adventure.[99] Bell took up the story of how he drove back from Folkestone 'in a government motor' with Austen Chamberlain and was dropped at the bottom of the lane to Charleston with the Cézanne in one of his suitcases. 'Maynard came back suddenly and unexpectedly late at night', she wrote to Fry, 'and said he had left a Cézanne by the roadside! Duncan rushed off to get it and you can imagine how exciting it all was.' She described the drawings by Ingres and Delacroix that Keynes had bought for his own collection, and the Cézanne as 'the little one of 7 apples that we liked so much . . . it's most exciting to have it in the house'.[100] The acquisitions for the National Gallery were also itemized but 'Holmes' purchases', she wrote, were 'idiotic considering his chances'.[101] Virginia Woolf described the ceremony surrounding Fry's introduction to the Cézanne at 46 Gordon Square a few days later in a letter to Nicholas Bagenal. 'Nessa left the room and re-appeared with a small parcel about the size of a large slab of chocolate. On one side are painted 6 apples by Cezanne [*sic*]. Roger very nearly lost his senses.'[102] She expanded upon their shared appreciation of the painting – 'I've never seen such a sight of intoxication . . . us all gloating upon these apples' – and observed wryly that Fry knew 'the day, practically the hour, they were done by some brush mark in the background'.[103] The story of 'A Cézanne in the Hedge' became a burnished and celebrated Bloomsbury anecdote.[104]

❇ ❇ ❇

The distinctive interiors and the display of collections through which Bloomsbury performed its identity for itself became part of its public persona. Photographs of its interiors began to appear in *Vogue* from 1918. Bloomsbury's association with Omega was recognizable enough for a stage set and furniture for a new West End play by Israel Zangwill, *Too Much Money*, to be commissioned from the Omega Workshops on

156 Roger Fry, sketch of the Omega Club in a letter to his daughter, 1917. From *The Letters of Roger Fry*, ed. Denys Sutton (London: Chatto & Windus), p. 404

the assumption that its audiences would understand the joke.[105] Vanessa Bell's *Bathers in a Landscape* (see fig. 106) fulfilled the script's requirement for 'a screen of strange hues and symbols', and Fry was responsible for painting scenery for walls 'frescoed with a flamboyant futurist pattern'.[106] Omega's signature cushions and artificial flowers made the origins of the designs unmistakable, and although Fry complained that the lead character's dress had been 'made all horribly more florid and flaunting than my design' he did not take himself too seriously to enjoy the comedy: 'It's really only a farce.'[107] Arnold Bennett included an Omega interior in his bestselling 1918 novel about London during the war, *The Pretty Lady*. It included a cameo appearance by Fry as 'the creative leader of the newest development in internal decoration' and an account of an Omega interior that resembled 'a gigantic and glittering kaleidoscope deranged and arrested'.[108] Bennett was a regular customer at the Workshops and a member of the Omega Club for 'all the more interesting people in London'.[109] This included Clive Bell, Lytton Strachey, W. B. Yeats, George Bernard Shaw, and Max Beerbohm. In 1917, Fry sketched them sitting on the Workshops floor together on 'great pillows of sacking filled with straw' because there were not enough chairs for their first meeting (fig. 156).[110] The Omega interior described in *The Pretty Lady* was commissioned by an independent young woman of means as an antidote to her war-work. Bennett describes the 'excessive brightness, crudity and variety' of its colours:

> every piece of furniture was painted with primitive sketches of human figures, or of flowers, or of vessels, or of animals. On the front of the mantelpiece were perversely but brilliantly depicted, with a high degree of finish, two nude, crouching women who gazed longingly at each other across the impassable semicircular abyss of the fireplace.[111]

The gendering of Bloomsbury's modernity, its acceptance of homosexuality, and its alternative values to the aggressive 'virility' of Wyndham Lewis and his circle have been analysed by Reed and others. Towards the end of the First World War, when Osbert Sitwell encountered Bloomsbury as a group at a party, its public identity was defined and established. It included the Group's authors and intellectuals as well as its artists. Sitwell described the Group's 'great tolerance' and its 'rare and ritualistic' way of speaking. Performances of the 'Bloomsbury voice', he maintained, were 'an outward sign of conversion, a public declaration of faith, like giving the Hitler salute'. He traced its origin to the Strachey family and claimed to have witnessed a moment of conversion when 'one of the Lesser – but now Greater – Bloomsburys took the plunge'.[112] Strachey's innovative and irreverent *Eminent Victorians* was published in May 1918, coinciding with Bloomsbury's wider recognition. Its extraordinary critical and commercial success extended the Group's influence and its renown. It had been written, and passages had been read, to entertain the assembled company at various Bloomsbury strongholds, including Charleston and Durbins. Strachey described the creative simultaneity of writing and painting at Durbins when his family moved into the house, having rented it from Fry in the summer of 1917. He wrote to Carrington, describing Fry's alarming intelligence and admitting to having agreed, with some trepidation, to sit for him:

> I have given way, and agreed to be painted, but it's to be done while I write . . . Oh! The man has begun already! – Planted himself down. With pencil and paper. Oh mon dieu! mon dieu! It's terribly constricting! Shall I ever be able to concoct my sentences? It's like shitting with someone looking on.[113]

The processes of writing and making art, of time designated for thinking and rooms requisitioned for studios and experimental decorations, shaped Bloomsbury's internal sense of its own identity. The Group shared the vivid, tangible, sensory experiences of making: the smell of paint and the squeaky sounds of Strachey reading aloud from his manuscripts. It offered criticism and encouragement before contentious new work was aired in public. Virginia Woolf commented on a draft of *Eminent Victorians* and, although she evaded Strachey's request that she review the book, she empathized with his insecurities, after four years

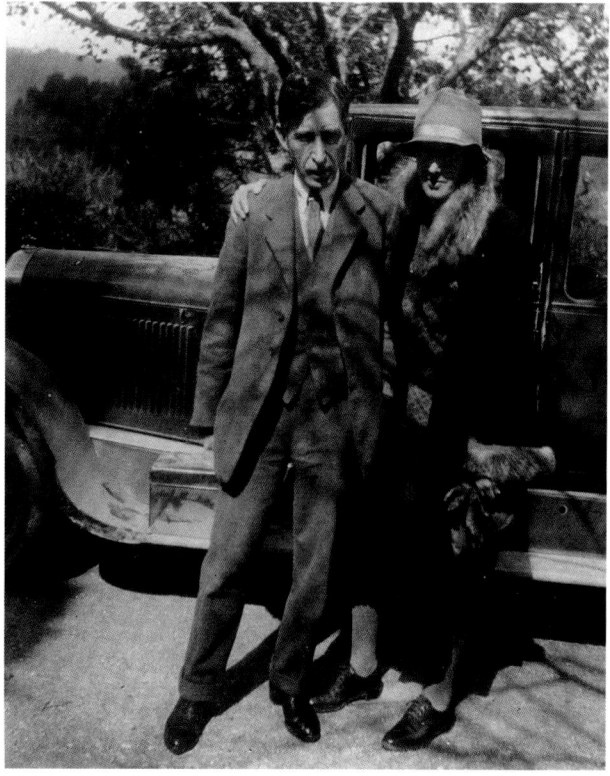

of writing, about whether it was 'quite enough to show for his age, & pretentions'.[114] As the Group became more established in the 1920s, and its members more influential in their respective fields, they continued to support and inspire one another. Visiting Charleston for a week in September 1920, Strachey described the 'general ease and unbuttoned-ness of everything'.[115] 'Duncan and Vanessa painting all days in each other's arms. Pozzo [Keynes] writing on Probability, on the History of Currency, controlling the business of King's, and editing the Economic Journal.'[116] Keynes promised to help with Strachey's new biography, *Queen Victoria*, and he read aloud from the manuscript: 'it was a relief to find that they weren't bored – which was my chief terror'.[117] He went from Charleston to Monk's House. 'While I was there', he wrote, 'a parcel arrived for Leonard: it was Mr Wells's History of the World, from the Author.'[118] Strachey found it dull, detailed, and wordy, and concurred with Clive Bell that it would not compete with the 'great work on civilisation' that he was writing.[119] Bell's *Civilisation: An Essay* was published eight years later.

Within the privacy of her diary Woolf kept an envious record of Strachey's sales, noting in January 1919 that he had dominated a generation at Cambridge: 'Am I jealous? Do I compare the 6 editions of Eminent Victorians with the one of The Voyage Out?'[120] Later in the 1920s she would keep a commentary on the sales for her own books, anticipated and realized, in her diary. When *To the Lighthouse* sold more copies than any of her previous novels, she rewarded herself with the conventional status symbol of a motorcar and was photographed standing in front of it in a coat with a fur collar and cuffs (fig. 157). 'The world gave me this', she wrote triumphantly, 'for writing The Lighthouse.'[121] The coat contributed to a more glamorous image for Woolf's American market. A studio photograph of her wearing it was used for promotional purposes by her American publishers and illustrated reviews of *To the Lighthouse* in the *New York Times* (fig. 158).[122] Earned income from sales was necessary as well as affirming for many of the Bloomsbury members, in spite of their elite family backgrounds. Strachey's royalties brought him a much-needed financial independence. By February 1920, when Grant had his first solo exhibition at the Carfax Gallery, there had been nine printings of *Eminent Victorians*, each of 1,000 copies. Strachey bought one of the largest and most ambitious paintings, *Juggler and Tightrope Walker* (fig. 159), in a display of support that would have been conspicuous as well as characteristic of Bloomsbury's in-group behaviour. 'Lytton laid out £70 on one of the pictures', Woolf noted in her diary, describing a slightly drunken private view lunch at the Café Royal.[123] It was one of 24 paintings to sell, raising over £640 after the gallery's commission.

Bell had written to Keynes that Grant's preparations for his solo exhibition were motivated at least in part by a desire to provide for her and their baby daughter: 'Duncan offers huge shows lavishly & is painting a great many lovely pictures so I daresay he'll really be able to endow me soon.'[124] The exhibition also gave him – released from his farm labouring as a conscientious objector – an opportunity to show a substantial body of new work together for the first time and to establish

157 Vanessa Bell, Virginia and Leonard Woolf in front of their car in Cassis, France, 1928. The Charleston Trust

his reputation. Fry reviewed the exhibition for the *New Statesman* and Clive Bell described Grant as 'the best English painter alive' in a notice for the *Athenaeum*.[125] Woolf tried to buy one of the watercolours at the private view before Grant made her a gift of it. She described the drama of competing with 'an old fur bearing dowager' for the painting, and the ritual performance of the Gallery's owner producing 'a little red seal out of his waistcoat pocket' to mark it as sold.[126] After the crush of the exhibition, full of Bloomsbury familiars and 'well dressed people', she walked with Keynes across to the *Burlington Magazine* offices to have tea with Fry. He told her, en route, that *The Economic Consequences of the Peace*, published less than two months earlier, had already sold over 15,000 copies.[127]

The processes of making and acquiring portraits of one another, with all their inherent complexities of 'ownership' and of shaping and contesting identities,

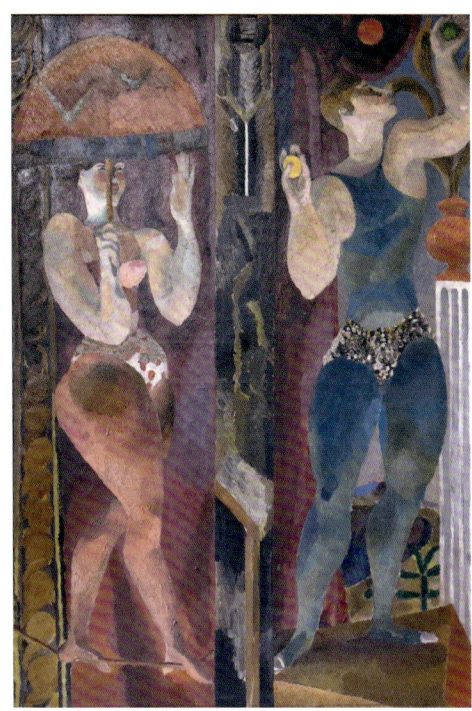

shifted in the 1920s and 1930s as Bloomsbury matured. Its members became recognizable figures of the establishment. Roger Fry and Clive Bell, and the critical theories that they explored in *Art* and *Vision and Design* (published in 1914 and 1920, respectively), had enough common currency by 1921 for Max Beerbohm to exhibit a caricature of them, *Significant Form* (fig. 160).[128] A Strachey caricature was included in the same show and, as an admirer of Beerbohm's work, he enjoyed an invitation to visit the artist at his hotel just weeks before the exhibition so that Beerbohm could 'verify his impressions'.[129] Both Strachey and Keynes used their resources to commission the young sculptor Stephen Tomlin, whom David Garnett introduced into the Group. Grant wrote that he was 'being immortalized in bronze' by Tomlin in November 1924 in a sensuous, slightly larger than life-sized bust (fig. 161). The commission was arranged by Garnett and paid for by Keynes. It celebrates and idealizes Grant's beauty, and both men kept casts of the bust in their private collections for the remainder of their lives. Eddy Sackville-West, a lover of both Grant and Tomlin, acquired the original clay model for the bust and displayed it together with his own bronze bust

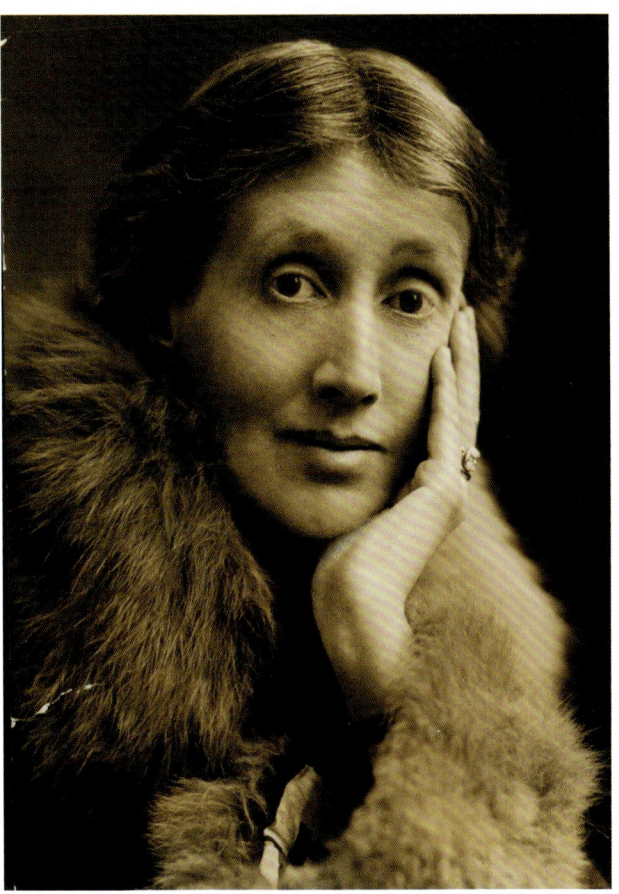

158 Unknown photographer, publicity photograph of Virginia Woolf in her fur-trimmed coat, *c.*1927. Houghton Library, Harvard University

159 Duncan Grant, *Juggler and Tightrope Walker*, *c.*1918–19. Oil on canvas, 1035 × 724 mm. Private collection

by Tomlin in his apartment at Knole in Kent, setting out his sexual identity and history.[130] Tomlin became an intimate of Strachey and Carrington, and Strachey also commissioned and paid for a bust from Tomlin as a means of supporting him (fig. 162). Both men will have recognized, however, that portraits of famous authors, whether by photographers such as George Beresford, painters such as Jacques-Emile Blanche, or aspiring young sculptors, had a market. Strachey arranged a sherry party to show off his new portrait as soon as it was cast and to promote his protégé. 'I thought of asking most of the influential inhabitants of Bloomsbury to come and look at it one day this week', he wrote to Tomlin.[131] Within a few months it was exhibited again at the Leicester Galleries and a cast was sold to the collector Richard Brinsley Ford, an admirer of Strachey's work, who donated it to Tate.[132]

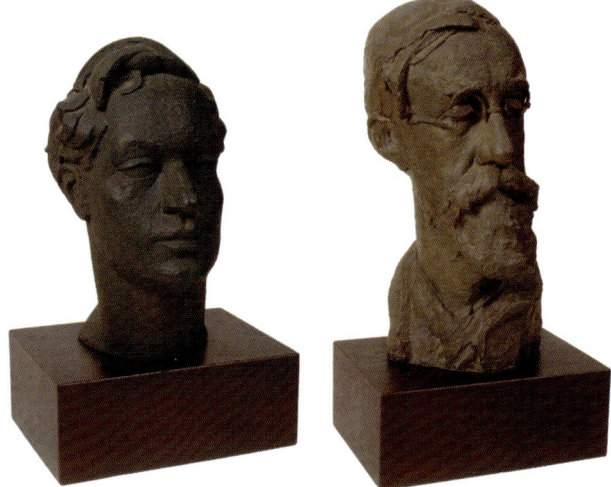

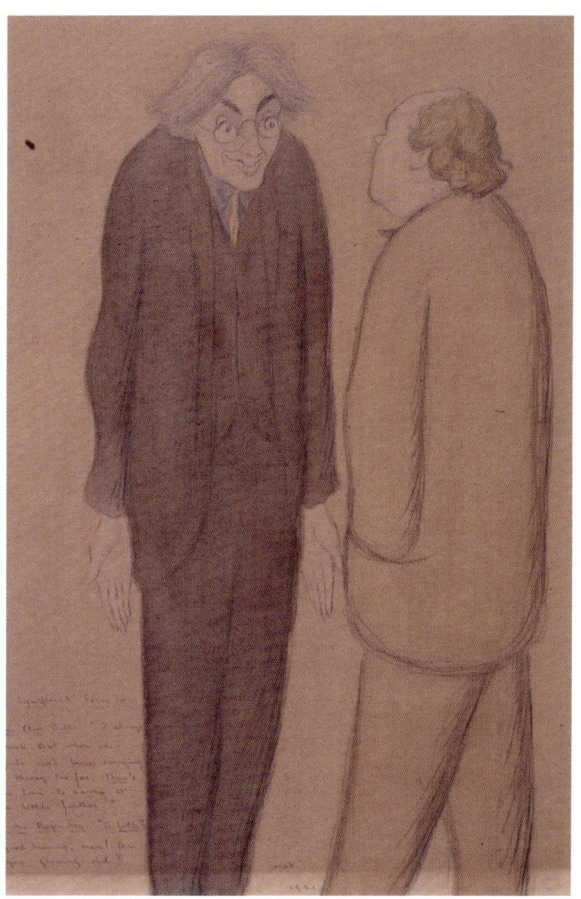

Tomlin was less fortunate in Virginia Woolf as a sitter. Unlike Strachey, she disliked the process of sitting for her portrait, and while Tomlin had stayed with Strachey at his home, Ham Spray, and modelled his bust over a two-week period while Strachey read, Woolf was obliged to take time out of her busy London life to sit. 'Tomlin, has me by the hair: I waste afternoon after afternoon perched in his ratridden and draught-riddled studio: can't escape. If I do, all the bonds of friendship are (he says, and I wish it were true) torn asunder.'[133] The bonds of friendship between Woolf and Tomlin were not strong, the bust was not a commission, and Woolf complained of the sittings to her sister: 'Now that I've tried it for four days I see that it would be sheer idiocy on my part to pretend that I can do this', and yet she was persuaded to continue.[134] Bell shared the sittings with Tomlin and they were timed to coincide with the completion of Woolf's experimental novel, *The Waves* (1931). In her diary she described her nervous exhaustion, 'I don't know that I've ever felt so strained.'[135] This was exacerbated during the course of the sittings when she believed her original typescript to be lost.[136] Although her friend, the composer Ethel Smyth, joined her at Tomlin's studio as a distraction, and Bell described her snorting like an angry bull, 'complaining about her operas and women's rights generally', Woolf recorded the sittings

160 Max Beerbohm, *Significant Form*, 1921. Pencil and watercolour on paper, 325 × 215 mm. The Charleston Trust

161 (*top left*) Stephen Tomlin, *Duncan Grant*, 1924. Bronze, 375 × 230 × 230 mm. Private collection

162 (*top right*) Stephen Tomlin, *Lytton Strachey*, 1929. Bronze, 420 × 240 × 220 mm. Private collection

148   THE BLOOMSBURY LOOK

as a violation: 'what a terrific hemp strong heather root obstinate fountain of furious individuality shoots in me – they tampered with it, Nessa & Tommy – pinning me there, from 2 to 4 on 6 afternoons, to be looked at; & I felt like a piece of whalebone bent.'[137] Tomlin's bust, now recognized as one of the iconic images of Woolf, captures her nervous energy and her vitality. Its blank eyes suggest a creative, inner world and its lips are parted as if in speech. A plaster cast was made of the bust, painted to resemble bronze, but no commissions ensued. It remained in Tomlin's own collection until his early death, when it was given to David Garnett. The National Portrait Gallery had it cast in lead for its own collection in 1953 on his suggestion.[138] Three additional casts were made, for Leonard Woolf at Monk's House, for Vita Sackville-West at Sissinghurst, and for Garnett's own collection (fig. 163).[139] Garnett gave the original plaster to Charleston, where it still presides over the studio (fig. 164).

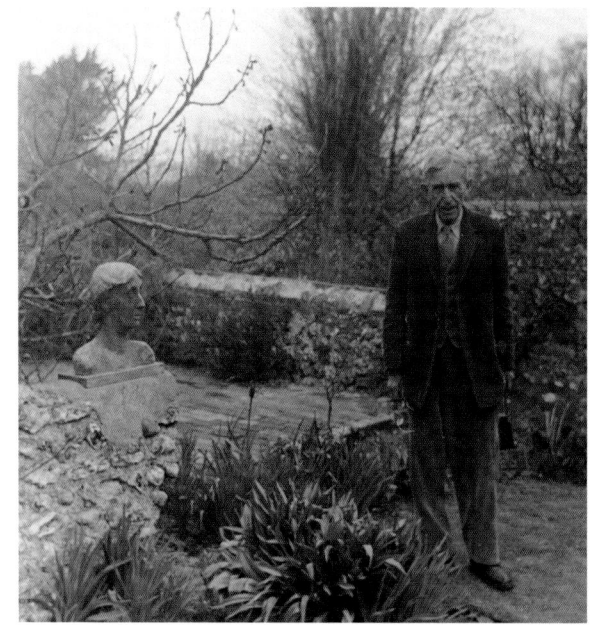

Bell and Woolf were at the centre of Bloomsbury's cohesion as a group throughout their lives and steadfastly supported one another's distinct but related public profiles. Woolf commissioned her sister to design furniture for Monk's House and she sponsored an exhibition of new work by Bell and Grant at the Lefevre Galleries in King Street, St James's, in 1932. It was conceived as a complete interior, a music room devised to promote their reputation as decorative designers and to showcase new rugs and the upholstery fabrics that they had recently designed for Royal Wilton and Allan Walton (fig. 165). The fabrics, including Bell's *Abstract* (1931), could be purchased round the corner at Fortnum & Mason, and the *Architectural Review* included a large illustration of *Abstract* in a double-page spread dedicated to the exhibition and titled 'Orpheus in Bloomsbury'.[140] Reed has analysed the double-edged comments in the review. He designates the exhibition a failure, 'the end of the Amusing era'.[141] It did not generate sales and it was the last complete decorative interior that Bell and Grant designed. However, the *Architectural Review* was the arbiter of taste in modern design. Its lavish coverage of the exhibition documents Bloomsbury's fashionable currency in the 1930s, and images of the music room were subsequently included in Derek Patmore's popular monograph, *Colour Schemes for the Modern Home*.[142] Woolf committed £100 towards the exhibition costs and a glamorous cocktail party for its opening with 'boys in white jackets handing blue green yellow drinks' and music by Debussy played on a harp, according to *Architectural Review*, 'to blend with the surrounding patterns of flowers and falling leaves in a rare union of intellect and imagination, colour and sound'.[143] Nearly twenty years after the Omega Workshops launch, Bloomsbury deployed the same tactics for attracting an 'out-group' of affluent customers, albeit at a more glamorous level. Woolf invited Morrell to the party 'that Nessa and I are giving . . . It's a purely commercial (don't whisper it) affair, to induce the rich to buy furniture.'[144] In her diary she delighted in her collaboration with her sister and 'our party: notable for its peeresses, its chatter, its cocktails . . . Us two hussies entertaining the peerage.'[145]

The Lefevre music room elaborated upon the design of Woolf's own rooms in Tavistock Square. She had unrolled a new carpet there, designed by Grant, just days before the exhibition and shown it off to Morrell, writing to Grant that she hoped this would promote sales: 'I've just had a paean of praise of the

163 Unknown photographer, *Leonard Woolf in the garden at Monk's House, with a cast of Tomlin's bust of Virginia Woolf*, c.1953. Houghton Library, Harvard University

room from Ott: . . . I hope some cash will result.' But her letter also explores a surreal creative engagement with Grant:

> It seems to me a triumphant and superb work of art, and produces in me the sensation of being a tropical fish afloat in warm waves over submerged forests of emerald and ruby. You may well ask what sort of forest that is – I reply it is the sort of fish I am.[146]

The letter playfully asserts that the tropical environment created by the carpet would pervade Woolf's art as well as her life. Bell included the carpet in a full-length portrait of her sister, staged in the interior that she and Grant had created for Woolf at Tavistock Square. In Bell's portrait the spare simplicity of the sitting room, as represented in *Vogue* a decade earlier (see fig. 55), is more fully inhabited. The table has been pushed up against the bookcase (which is now taller), piled with books, and ornamented with a vase of tulips. Woolf's chintz-covered armchair occupies a corner of the room so that her head is framed, in the portrait, by one of the Bell and Grant painted panels. This large, formal portrait represents Woolf as a celebrated author. Her mask-like expression is austere and the low vantage point effectively elevates the sitter. It was painted for Bell's solo exhibition at the Lefevre Galleries in March 1934, for which Woolf wrote the catalogue preface.[147] She describes her supportive role at the private view, encouraging Bell's buyers 'until I had no tongue to praise with left'.[148] The portrait sold immediately to an admirer of Woolf's writing but she retained a photograph of it (fig. 166), and the following year Bell presented Leonard Woolf with her study for the painting as a Christmas present.[149]

❈ ❈ ❈

The visual and intellectual agility with which Bloomsbury was able to adapt to different social, political, and creative contexts was one of its many strengths. Its group identity was deliberately elusive and often playful but its engagement with the events and key figures of its period was wide-ranging and effective. This is illustrated by Woolf's diary in the days immediately preceding Bell's private view. She received a visit from Sickert to thank her for her 1934 article 'Walter Sickert: A Conversation'. As a subscriber for a 75th-birthday celebration concert of Ethel Smyth's work at the Albert Hall, she filled her allocation of seats in the stalls with her Bloomsbury friends and associates. The concert was conducted by Sir Thomas Beecham and attended by the queen and court. Afterwards, Bloomsbury delighted in Smyth's audacity in subverting social conventions by entertaining her aristocratic supporters in a Lyons Corner House, 'a sordid crumby room . . . amid clerks & shop girls eating cream buns'.[150] Bloomsbury assembled at the Arts Theatre Club the following night to watch Lydia Lopokova in her debut as an actor in Ibsen's *A Doll's House*, with Keynes sitting in the stalls 'streaming tears'.[151] The Group's letters and diaries, its memoirs,

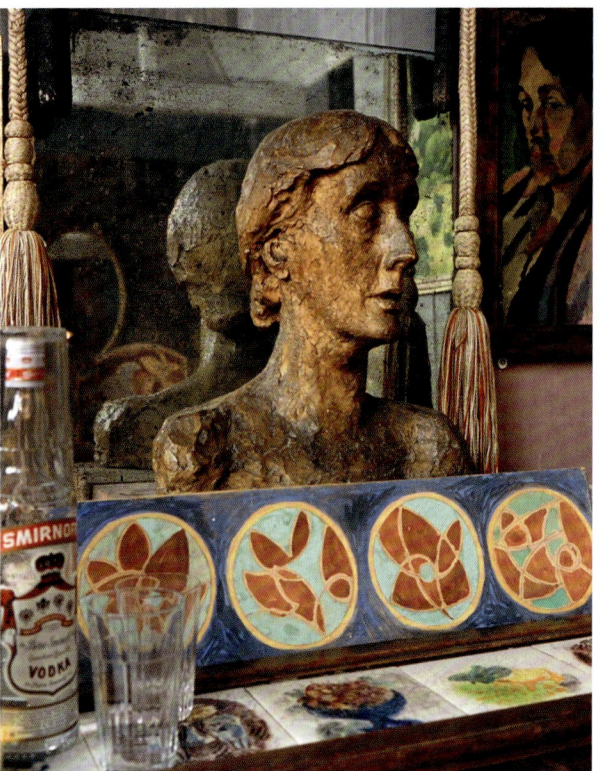

164 Cast of Stephen Tomlin's 1931 bust of Virginia Woolf, photographed in the studio at Charleston by Tony Tree, undated. Painted plaster, 400 × 390 × 220 mm. The Charleston Trust

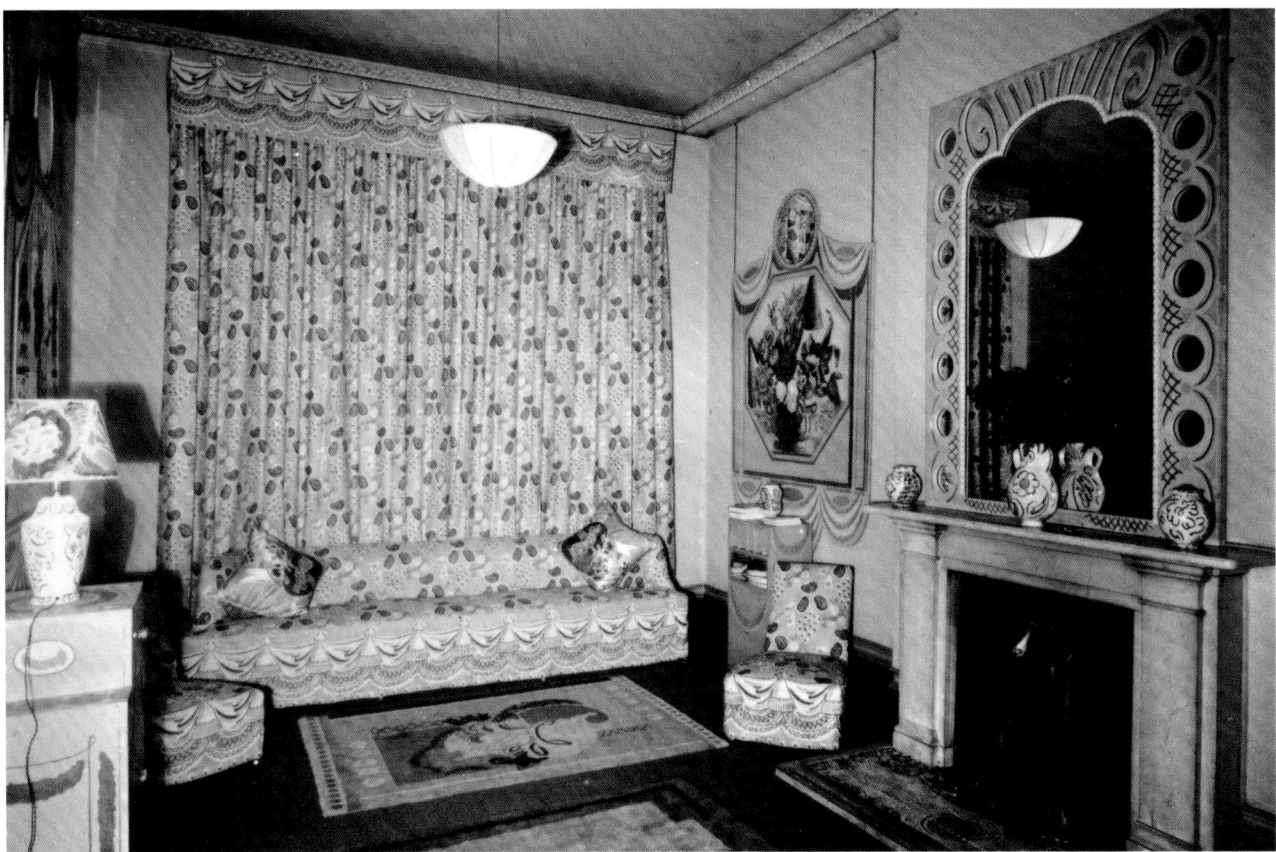

photographs, and portraits provide insights into the extent of its network and the texture of Bloomsbury lives with their complex and varied professional and personal interactions. Their tone, often designed to entertain or to shake out the essentials of a situation, belies the significance of Bloomsbury's contribution to twentieth-century culture, economics, and politics. Keynes remained a committed supporter of the arts throughout his life, using his influence to devise schemes and institutions to fund contemporary practice, ultimately leading to the foundation of the Arts Council. Once they became figures of the establishment, Bloomsbury's authors, artists, publishers, and critics no longer depended upon the robust and protective identity of the Group to frame and explore new ideas. They continued, nevertheless, to subvert conventions and challenge the boundaries of modernity. Bloomsbury's social and artistic porosity, and its rejection of dogma, of formal memberships and manifestos, make its influence and its distinctive identity difficult to chart, as they emerge only through detailed investigation. It was this understated porosity, however, that ensured Bloomsbury's success and its longevity as a group.

Bloomsbury's identity was rooted in the intellectual and colonial family backgrounds that are documented in its childhood snapshots and studio photographs. It kept this visual legacy close. Its framed photographs and family albums served as a set of references in later years. They were reminders of the family narratives and shared identities from school and university years that underpinned Bloomsbury's sense of itself. They informed the memories and publications through which the Group framed its own historiography, but Bloomsbury's Victorian and Edwardian photographs were not confined to the past. Bell and Woolf explored the currency of their bank of Cameron images in interiors, publications, and paintings. Woolf used them as a matrilineal inheritance to impress Vita Sackville-West and as inspiration for her antidote to

165 Vanessa Bell and Duncan Grant, *The Music Room*, installation exhibited at Lefevre Galleries, London, in 1932. The Charleston Trust

fashion, wearing one of her mother's dresses when photographed for *Vogue*. This self-reflective and creative repurposing of material was characteristic of Bloomsbury and it was concurrent with the Group's activities as artists and amateur photographers. Bloomsbury blurred the boundaries between creative practice and transgressive behaviour. Within the privacy of its rural houses and studio spaces it explored the special status accorded to artists. Nakedness, new hairstyles, brilliantly coloured interiors, and unconventional outfits were first tried out within the sequestered security of the Group's private self-fashioning. They then informed its public identity. This was advanced incrementally as the Group positioned itself within an expanding network through its collections and exhibitions, its dress and mannerisms, and its web of social and professional connections. Bloomsbury enjoyed the outrage caused by the *Dreadnought* hoax and *Manet and the Post-Impressionists*, but its effectiveness as a group depended upon a more subtle and sustained cultivation of image and identity – and on the exceptional and enduring resonance of its work.

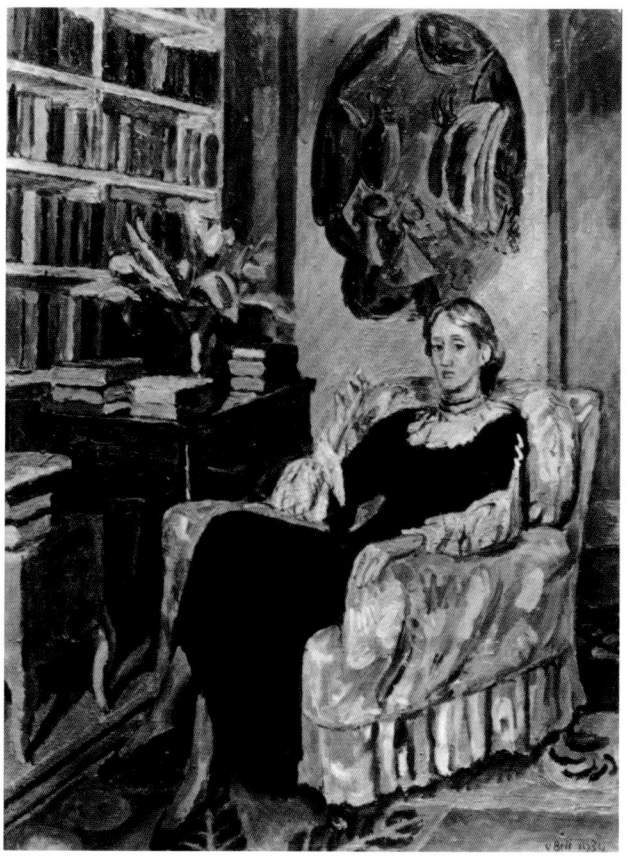

166 Unknown photographer, photograph of Vanessa Bell's *Portrait of Virginia Woolf*, 1934. Houghton Library, Harvard University. The portrait, oil on canvas, measures 943 × 745 mm

ACKNOWLEDGEMENTS

For many years, when I was Curator at Charleston, my daily work included meetings, conversations, and collaborations with Bloomsbury's most eminent authorities. I am fortunate to have worked with Anne Olivier Bell and Angelica Garnett, whose life stories I recorded for the British Library National Sound Archive. We organized birthday parties every year for Anne Olivier and for Jeremy Hutchinson. Their conversations over toasted teacakes in the Charleston kitchen are among my most treasured memories. I am also grateful to the contemporary writers and artists who visited for the Charleston Festival or for their own work, including academics and such celebrated figures as Jeanette Winterson and Patti Smith, for inspiring conversations and for demonstrating Bloomsbury's continuing resonance as a springboard for new work. I am deeply grateful to the late Henrietta Garnett for her kindness, her wisdom, and her irreverent sense of fun. Without her permission and that of Pandora Smith and Sophie Partridge to reproduce images and hitherto unpublished quotations by Vanessa Bell and Duncan Grant, this book would not have been possible. I am grateful, too, to other members of the Bloomsbury family and to Charleston's former trustees, including Richard Shone, Frances Spalding, Simon Watney, Diana Reich, and Virginia Nicholson, for helping to shape my understanding of Bloomsbury. I benefited from the warm friendship and knowledge of my colleagues, in particular Darren Clarke, Jean Birch-Leonard, Colin McKenzie, and Paul Davis, whose cataloguing of Charleston's collection of photographs proved invaluable. It is my great pleasure to thank Charleston for its continuing support. Darren Clarke, Emily Hill, and Nathaniel Hepburn also gave me unrestricted access to Charleston's collections and responded with extraordinary helpfulness to innumerable requests for images and information.

I wish to thank all of the individuals who have supported my research by giving me introductions and access to their private collections over the years, with special thanks to Debo Gage, David Herbert, Sir Christopher and Valda Ondaatje, Jans Ondaatje Rolls, Tony Bradshaw, Lindy Guinness, and Bryan Ferry. I have benefited from the scholarship and insights of many academics but in particular from the work of Christopher Reed, Lisa Tickner, and Maggie Humm. Among the museums, archives, and libraries I have consulted, staff at Tate Gallery Archives; the University of Sussex Library; the British Library; Patricia McGuire, Archivist at the Modern Archive Centre; King's College, Cambridge; and Karen Watson at The Keep in East Sussex have been especially helpful. I am indebted to the Harvard Theatre Collection, Houghton Library, for access to the Monk's House Photographs and Photograph Albums, and to all of those, too numerous to name individually here, who provided me with images and permission to reproduce works in their collections.

I thank my colleagues at the University of Sussex for their support throughout the writing of this book. I have enjoyed working with the excellent team at Yale University Press and am indebted to Mark Eastment, Sophie Neve, Julie Hrischeva, Marianne Fisher, and Georgia Vaux for their enthusiasm for this project, and the consistent care and professionalism that they have brought to it. Finally, I offer my most heartfelt thanks to my family for their love and for the many conversations that have sustained me during the writing of this book.

ABBREVIATIONS

GB181 SxMs University of Sussex Special Collections at The Keep, Brighton

LLS *The Letters of Lytton Strachey*, ed. Paul Levy (London: Penguin, 2006)

MHP & MHPA Virginia Woolf's Monk's House photographs (loose), and Virginia Woolf's Monk's House photograph albums; all housed in the Frederick R. Koch Collection, Harvard Theatre Collection, Houghton Library, Harvard University

MRBC Mortimer Rare Book Collection, Smith College, Northampton, MA

SLVB *Selected Letters of Vanessa Bell*, ed. Regina Marler (New York: Pantheon, 1993)

TDVW *The Diary of Virginia Woolf*, ed. Anne Olivier Bell and Andrew McNeillie, 5 vols (Harmondsworth: Penguin Books, 1977–84)

TGA Tate Archive, London

TLVW *The Letters of Virginia Woolf*, ed. Nigel Nicolson and Joanne Trautmann, 6 vols (London: Hogarth Press, 1975–80)

NOTES

INTRODUCTION

1. In a letter to Dora Carrington, written at Charleston, Lytton Strachey describes 'Maynard . . . weeding in the walled garden with a scarlet knitted wool cap on his head, making him look like some effete Pasha.' L. Strachey to D. Carrington, 25 June 1917, *LLS*, p. 356.
2. For a discussion of the complex relationships between Bloomsbury, Keynes, and pacifism, see J. Ashley Foster, 'Bloomsbury and War', in Derek Ryan and Stephen Ross (eds), *The Handbook to the Bloomsbury Group* (London: Bloomsbury Academic, 2018), pp. 277–93 (at pp. 277–82); Jane Goldman, 'Case Study: Bloomsbury's Pacifist Aesthetics: Woolf, Keynes, Rodker', in Ryan and Ross, *The Handbook to the Bloomsbury Group*, pp. 294–308; and Frances Spalding, *Duncan Grant* (London: Chatto & Windus, 1997), pp. 187–91.
3. Vanessa Bell, 'Memories of Roger Fry', in her *Sketches in Pen and Ink*, ed. Lia Giachero (London: Hogarth Press, 1997), p. 130.
4. Quentin Bell, *Elders and Betters* (London: John Murray, 1995), p. 85.
5. See L. Strachey to D. Carrington, 4 September 1920, *LLS*, p. 469.
6. J. M. Keynes to V. Bell, 3 June 1919, King's College, Cambridge, King's/PP/CHA/341/3.
7. Roy Baumeister and Mark Leary, 'The Need to Belong: Desire for Interpersonal Attachments as a Fundamental Human Motivation', *Psychological Bulletin*, vol. 117, no. 3 (1995), pp. 497–529 (at p. 497).
8. Glen Elder Jr and Elizabeth Clipp, 'Wartime Losses and Social Bonding: Influences across 40 Years in Men's Lives', *Psychiatry*, vol. 51, no. 2 (1988), pp. 177–98.
9. J. M. Keynes to V. Bell, 21 November 1916, GB181 SxMs56/1/124, MKVB 6.
10. Virginia Woolf, 'Old Bloomsbury', in her *Moments of Being: Autobiographical Writings* [1978], ed. Jeanne Schulkind (London: Pimlico, 2002), p. 53.
11. Leonard Woolf, *Beginning Again: An Autobiography of the Years 1911 to 1918* (London: Hogarth Press, 1964), p. 23.
12. Leon Festinger, Stanley Schachter, and Kurt Black, *Social Pressures in Informal Groups: A Study of Human Factors in Housing* (Stanford, CA: Stanford University Press, 1950), pp. 33–59.
13. Margaret Irwin, *Fire Down Below* (London: William Heinemann, 1928), p. 109.
14. M. Hutchinson to V. Bell, 16 August 1917, GB181 SxMs56/1/112, MHVB 21.
15. V. Woolf, 'Old Bloomsbury', p. 56.
16. Ibid., p. 55.
17. E. M. Forster wrote: 'Are you coming to town to hear Virginia read on Old Bloomsbury on Wednesday?' E. M. Forster to L. Strachey, 2 July 1928, quoted in S. P. Rosenbaum, 'Old Bloomsbury', in J. M. Haule (ed.), *The Bloomsbury Group Memoir Club* (London: Palgrave Macmillan, 2014), pp. 151–3 (at p. 151).
18. Ibid.
19. Virginia Woolf, 31 May 1928, *TDVW*, vol. 3, p. 185.
20. S. P. Rosenbaum (ed.), *The Bloomsbury Group: A Collection of Memoirs, Commentary and Criticism* (London: Croom Helm, 1975), pp. ii–iii.
21. R. Fry to V. Bell, 12 December 1917, quoted in ibid., p. 20.
22. Raymond Williams, 'The Bloomsbury Faction', in his *Problems in Materialism and Culture: Selected Essays* (London: Verso, 1980), pp. 148–69 (at p. 151).
23. Michael Billig and Henri Tajfel, 'Social Categorization and Similarity in Intergroup Behaviour', *European Journal of Social Psychology*, vol. 3, no. 1 (1973), pp. 27–52 (at pp. 49–50).
24. Bell included 15 versions of this photograph in her photograph album CH 5 (TGA 9020/6). There are six prints per page on

pages 15 and 16, additional prints on pages 31 and 32, and loose prints.
25. V. Woolf to O. Morrell, 25? November 1932, in *TLVW*, vol. 5, p. 130.
26. V. Woolf, 10 September 1933, *TDVW*, vol. 4, p. 178; L. Strachey to V. Woolf, 19 September 1922, *LLS*, p. 521.
27. L. Strachey diary, quoted in Rosenbaum, *The Bloomsbury Group: A Collection of Memoirs*, p. 4.
28. Vanessa Bell, 'Notes on Bloomsbury' [1951], in Rosenbaum, *The Bloomsbury Group: A Collection of Memoirs*, pp. 74–84 (at p. 77).
29. See Virginia Woolf, *The Platform of Time: Memoirs of Family and Friends*, ed. S. P. Rosenbaum (London: Hesperus Press, 2008), pp. 106–61.
30. Adrian Stephen, *The 'Dreadnought' Hoax* (London: Hogarth Press, 1936), p. 52.
31. See Quentin Bell, *Virginia Woolf: A Biography*, vol. 1: *Virginia Stephen, 1882–1912* (London: Hogarth Press, 1972), p. 214.
32. Jean Kennard, 'Power and Sexual Ambiguity: The "Dreadnought" Hoax, "The Voyage Out", "Mrs Dalloway" and "Orlando"', *Journal of Modern Literature*, vol. 20, no. 2 (1996), pp. 149–64 (at p. 152).
33. V. Bell to C. Bell, 9 October 1910, *SLVB*, p. 96.
34. Virginia Woolf, *Roger Fry: A Biography* (London: Hogarth Press, 1940), p. 153.
35. Ibid., p. 152.
36. V. Woolf, 'Old Bloomsbury', p. 56.
37. Desmond MacCarthy, 'The Post-Impressionist Exhibition of 1910' [1953], in Rosenbaum, *The Bloomsbury Group: A Collection of Memoirs*, pp. 68–73 (at p. 72).
38. V. Woolf, *Roger Fry*, p. 153.
39. Quoted in Rosenbaum, *The Bloomsbury Group: A Collection of Memoirs*, p. 82.
40. V. Bell, 'Memories of Roger Fry', p. 129.
41. Ibid., p. 130.
42. Quentin Bell, *Bloomsbury* (London: Weidenfeld & Nicolson, 1968), p. 50.
43. V. Bell, 'Notes on Bloomsbury', p. 83.
44. Ibid.
45. John Maynard Keynes, 'My Early Beliefs' [1949], in Rosenbaum, *The Bloomsbury Group: A Collection of Memoirs*, pp. 48–64 (at p. 61).
46. Quoted in ibid., p. 337.
47. David Garnett, *The Flowers of the Forest* (London: Chatto & Windus, 1955), pp. 53–4.
48. Christopher Reed, 'Bloomsbury Bashing: Homophobia and the Politics of Criticism in the Eighties', in Brenda Helt and Madelyn Detloff (eds), *Queer Bloomsbury* (Edinburgh: Edinburgh University Press, 2016), pp. 36–63 (at p. 58).
49. See, for example, Helt and Detloff, *Queer Bloomsbury*.
50. V. Bell to L. Woolf, 20 July 1950, *SLVB*, p. 527.
51. Ryan and Ross, *The Handbook to the Bloomsbury Group*, p. 1.
52. Grace Brockington, *Above the Battlefield: Modernism and the Peace Movement in Britain, 1900–1918* (New Haven, CT, and London: Yale University Press, 2010), p. 33.
53. Clive Bell, *Old Friends: Personal Recollections* (London: Chatto & Windus, 1956), p. 127.
54. L. Woolf, *Beginning Again*, p. 23.
55. Quentin Bell, *Virginia Woolf: A Biography* (London: Pimlico, 1996), p. xiii.
56. Regina Marler, *Bloomsbury Pie: The Making of the Bloomsbury Boom* (London: Virago, 1997), p. 35.
57. Michael Holroyd, *Lytton Strachey: A Biography* [1967] (Harmondsworth: Penguin, 1980), p. 14.
58. Ibid., p. 20.
59. See Vanessa Bell's photograph album CH 1 (TGA 9020/1), p. 26; and MHPA, MH-1 (MS Thr 557), (181). See also Charleston Trust Collection, Anne Olivier Bell Gift.
60. Q. Bell, *Elders and Betters*, p. 100.
61. See John Higgens, interviewed by Joyce Duncan, 5 October 2004, British Library National Sound Archive, C466/212/04-05, track 6: tape 4 side A.
62. Roger Fry, 'A Possible Domestic Architecture', *Vogue* [London], late March 1918, pp. 40–41, 66, 68, with photographs by A. C. Cooper (taken in 1917).
63. Anon., 'Modern English Decoration: Some Examples of the Interesting Work of Duncan Grant and Vanessa Bell', *Vogue* [London], early November 1924, pp. 43–5, 106 (for photographs of 52 Tavistock Square); Anon., 'An Economist and Modern Art: The Cambridge Rooms of Mr Keynes', *Vogue* [London], early March 1925, pp. 46–7.
64. Q. Bell, *Bloomsbury*, p. 100.
65. Quentin Bell, 'Foreword: Charleston Preserved', in Quentin Bell, Angelica Garnett, Henrietta Garnett, and Richard Shone, *Charleston Past and Present* (London: Hogarth Press, 1987), pp. 7–16 (at p. 13).
66. Frances Spalding, 'Obituary: Professor Quentin Bell', *Independent*, 18 December 1996 <www.independent.co.uk/news/people/obituary-professor-quentin-bell-1315047.html> (accessed 27 April 2020).
67. Maggie Humm, *Modernist Women and Visual Cultures: Virginia Woolf, Vanessa Bell, Photography and Cinema* (Edinburgh: Edinburgh University Press, 2002); and Maggie Humm, *Snapshots of Bloomsbury: The Private Lives of Virginia Woolf and Vanessa Bell* (London: Tate, 2006).

CHAPTER 1

1. Angelica Garnett, *Deceived with Kindness: A Bloomsbury Childhood* (London: Chatto & Windus/The Hogarth Press, 1984).
2. Ibid., p. 12.
3. Ibid.
4. See Angelica Garnett, *Deceived with Kindness: A Bloomsbury Childhood* (San Diego: Harcourt Trade, 1985). The photograph is in Vanessa Bell's photograph album CH 5 (TGA 9020/6), p. 18.
5. Whilst it is possible that Grant was the photographer for this, and other images in Bell's photograph albums, he did not retain

extensive collections of photographs, as Bell and Woolf did, indicating 'ownership'. Bloomsbury texts invariably identify Bell rather than Grant as an amateur photographer.

6. Carlo Marochetti, *Head of Julia Jackson*, 1856, marble, 390 × 210 × 240 mm, Charleston Trust Collection, CHA/SC/33.

7. The two photographs, captioned 'Bust by Marochetti of her grandmother Julia Jackson. A.V.B.' and 'Q.B. A.V.B. Bust of their grandmother', are arranged together in Vanessa Bell's photograph album CH 5 (TGA 9020/6), p. 30. It is perhaps not a coincidence that the following two album pages are devoted to Angelica dressed as a Russian princess, taken to illustrate Virginia Woolf's novel *Orlando*.

8. Images of the sculpture on a brick plinth in Charleston's garden are in Bell's collection of loose photographs (TGA 9020), neg. nos J19 and J20.

9. Queen Victoria's journal, 15 December 1856, Royal Archives, Windsor, quoted in Philip Ward-Jackson, 'Expiatory Monuments by Carlo Marochetti in Dorset and the Isle of Wight', *Journal of the Warburg and Courtauld Institutes*, vol. 53 (1990), pp. 266–80 (at pp. 277–8).

10. Leslie Stephen, *Sir Leslie Stephen's Mausoleum Book* (Oxford: Clarendon Press, 1977), p. 32.

11. Janet Ross, *The Fourth Generation: Reminiscences by Janet Ross* (London: Constable, 1912), p. 39.

12. Ibid., p. 40.

13. Stephen, *Mausoleum Book*, pp. 99–100.

14. In addition to original prints of this photograph in the Charleston Trust Collection, a print was included in Leslie Stephen's photograph album, plate 39c. The album is now in the Mortimer Rare Book Collection, Smith College, Northampton, MA, cat. no. MRBC-MS-00005.

15. Photographs of Julia and Leslie Stephen were kept in Leslie Stephen's photograph album and in the albums and collections of Virginia Woolf and Vanessa Bell.

16. Janet Vaughan, 'Some Bloomsbury Memories', *Charleston Newsletter*, no. 12 (1985), pp. 20–22 (at p. 20).

17. MHPA, MH-1 (MS Thr 557), leaves 23 and 48.

18. Leslie Stephen's photograph album (MRBC-MS-00005), leaf 39.

19. A. Garnett, *Deceived with Kindness*, p. 12.

20. Ibid.

21. Anne Olivier Bell in conversation with the author, 15 April 2011.

22. Stephen, *Mausoleum Book*, p. 31.

23. Ibid., p. 32.

24. Ibid., p. 97.

25. Ibid.

26. Frederic William Maitland, *The Life and Letters of Leslie Stephen* (London: Duckworth, 1906).

27. The case is now in the Charleston Trust Collection, CHA/PH/576.

28. MHPA, MH-1 through MH-6 (MSS Thr 557 and 559–63).

29. The albums were organized by Quentin and Anne Olivier Bell. Vanessa Bell's photograph album CH 1 (TGA 9020/1),
for example, has their bookplate pasted onto the upper left corner of the cover, over the top of which is written in felt-tip pen 'CH.1'. Angela Garnett gifted the loose negatives and prints to the Tate in 1981, followed by albums CH 1–9 (TGA 9020/1 and 9020/3–9020/10) in 1988, and the earliest album, CH a1 (TGA 9020/2) in 1992.

30. A list inside the front cover of album CH 1, for example, includes photographs of Virginia loaned to Richard Shone, and of Clive Bell loaned to Michael Holroyd, in 1965 and 1966, respectively.

31. Vanessa Bell's photograph album CH 1 (TGA 9020/1), leaf 27.

32. For the illustrations to *A Marriage of True Minds*, see Maggie Humm, *Snapshots of Bloomsbury: The Private Lives of Virginia Woolf and Vanessa Bell* (London: Tate, 2006), p. 187.

33. Quentin Bell and Angelica Garnett, *Vanessa Bell's Family Album* (London: Jill Norman & Hobhouse, 1981).

34. Humm, *Snapshots of Bloomsbury*; and Maggie Humm, *Modernist Women and Visual Cultures: Virginia Woolf, Vanessa Bell, Photography and Cinema* (Edinburgh: Edinburgh University Press, 2002).

35. Leslie Stephen followed Alfred Tennyson as president of the London Library in 1892. The Mausoleum Book is in the Archives and Manuscripts Collection of the British Library, London, Add. MS 57920–57922: 1895–1903.

36. Sotheby's, London, 6 December 1984, lot 289. The Leslie Stephen photograph album, 1856–94, was purchased and presented by Elizabeth Power Richardson and Phyllis Colley Paige to the Mortimer Rare Book Collection, Smith College, Northampton, MA.

37. Anne Olivier Bell recalled that she and Quentin Bell sold the album to a young dealer and believed that he must have removed the Cameron photographs, recognizing their value, before selling the album to Smith College. Anne Olivier Bell in conversation with the author, 3 November 2011.

38. 'Julia with the 4 younger children' is the heading for leaf 36 in the contents page of Leslie Stephen's photograph album (MRBC-MS-00005), c.1895, box 1.

39. Stephen, *Mausoleum Book*, p. 32.

40. Titles in the contents page to the album do not correlate exactly with titles written at the top of each page. The contents page, for example, lists leaves 37 and 38 as 'In the holidays', and leaf 39 as 'In the Alps'; the equivalent page headings are 'At St Ives' and 'In Switzerland taken by Loppé'. Leslie Stephen's photograph album (MRBC-MS-00005), c.1895, box 1.

41. Stella Hills (née Duckworth) album of photographs, Sir Leslie Stephen collection of papers in the New York Public Library, Berg Collection MSS Stephen, portraits. In Sir Leslie Stephen's photograph album (MRBC-MS-00005), see plate 37a, of the Stephen-Duckworth family at Wimbledon; and plates 37f, 38a, 38c, and 38e, of the family at Talland House.

42. Stephen, *Mausoleum Book*, p. 96.

43. Humm, *Modernist Women and Visual Cultures*, pp. 5–7.

44. Ibid., p. 2.

45. MHPA, MH-1 (MS Thr 557), leaf 14 (78) and (77).

46. Charles Dickens, 'The Carte de Visite', *All the Year Round*,

vol. 7 (26 April 1862), pp. 165–8 (at p. 166) <www.djo.org.uk/all-the-year-round/volume-vii/page-166.html> (accessed 27 April 2020).
47. Ibid.
48. Ibid., p. 165.
49. The photograph in Virginia's album is MHP (MS Thr 564), (49). The image is included in Vanessa Bell's photograph album CH 1 (TGA 9020/1), p. 23, and on leaf 37 of Leslie Stephen's photograph album (MRBC-MS-00005), box 1.
50. MHPA, MH-3 (MS Thr 560), (2).
51. Virginia Woolf and Roger Fry, *Victorian Photographs of Famous Men and Fair Women by Julia Margaret Cameron* [1926] (Boston: David R. Gordine, 1973), p. 13.
52. 'The Supreme Indian Council, Simla', c.1864, National Portrait Gallery, London, NPG x1296637; and 'The King's Visit to India', 1875–6, National Portrait Gallery, London, NPG x129649. Both photographs are attributed to Bourne & Shepherd.
53. John Smith Hazard, 'Lytton Strachey', c.1883, National Portrait Gallery, London, NPG x13075.
54. 'Portrait of Bartle Grant', n.d., hand-coloured photograph, 400 × 300 mm, Charleston Trust Collection, CHA/PH/108.
55. 'Portrait of Major Bartle Grant', n.d., Charleston Trust Collection, CHA/PH/9; and 'Portrait of Ethel Grant', c.1883, Charleston Trust Collection, CHA/PH/10.
56. See Charleston Trust Collection, CHA/PH/68a–k.
57. Recording of Duncan Grant in conversation with Quentin Bell, c.1969, British Library National Sound Archive, Charleston Trust Recordings, C1180.
58. Quoted in Humm, *Snapshots of Bloomsbury*, p. 5.
59. V. Woolf, 6 February 1897, in Virginia Woolf, *A Passionate Apprentice: The Early Journals, 1897–1909*, ed. Mitchell Leaska (London: Hogarth Press, 1990), p. 30.
60. They stayed in Bognor from 8 February to 13 February 1897, joined briefly by Leslie Stephen on 9 February.
61. V. Woolf, 12 February 1897, in Woolf, *A Passionate Apprentice*, p. 34.
62. V. Woolf, 12 February 1897, ibid.
63. V. Woolf, 12 February 1897, ibid.
64. V. Woolf, 13 February 1897, ibid., p. 35.
65. V. Woolf, 14 February 1897, ibid.
66. See V. Woolf, 18 February 1897, ibid., p. 38, as well as 14 February 1897.
67. V. Woolf, 10 February 1897, ibid., p. 33.
68. Vanessa Bell's photograph album CH a1 (TGA 9020/2), leaf 1, and its (unnumbered) facing page.
69. V. Stephen to T. Stephen, November 1896, *SLVB*, p. 6.
70. Vanessa Bell's photograph album CH a1 (TGA 9020/2), leaf 9, November 1896.
71. Ibid., leaf 12, November 1896.
72. V. Woolf, *A Passionate Apprentice*, p. 163.
73. Mitchell Leaska, as editor of *A Passionate Apprentice*, wrote that 'Friendship's Gallery' was written at Fritham House (p. 163). Ellen Hawkes has subsequently shown that it was written in 1907: Ellen Hawkes, 'Friendships Gallery', *Twentieth Century Literature*, vol. 25, nos 3–4 (1979), pp. 270–302 (at p. 300).
74. Vanessa Bell's photograph album CH 1 (TGA 9020/1).
75. The image appears in the Charleston Trust Collection and is replicated in ibid., leaf 2.
76. Vanessa Bell's photograph album CH 1 (TGA 9020/1), leaf 6.
77. V. Bell to V. Woolf, 1 November 1904, quoted in Christopher Reed, *Bloomsbury Rooms: Modernism, Subculture, and Domesticity* (New Haven, CT, and London: Yale University Press, 2004), p. 23.
78. V. Bell to D. Grant, 3 August 1921, *SLVB*, p. 252; and V. Woolf to Vita Sackville-West, 6 March 1923, *TLVW*, vol. 3, pp. 18–19.
79. V. Woolf to V. Sackville-West, 3 January 1923, ibid., p. 1.
80. V. Woolf to V. Sackville-West, 7 January 1923, ibid., p. 4.
81. Lisa Tickner, 'Mediating Generation: The Mother–Daughter Plot', *Art History*, vol. 25, no. 1 (2002), pp. 23–46 (at pp. 23–6).
82. J. P. S., 'Cameron, Julia Margaret', in *Oxford Dictionary of National Biography*, ed. Leslie Stephen (London: Smith, Elder & Co., 1888), vol. 8, p. 300.
83. V. Woolf and R. Fry, *Victorian Photographs of Famous Men and Fair Women*, p. 28.
84. Virginia Woolf, *A Room of One's Own* [1929] (Harmondsworth: Penguin, 1973), p. 76.
85. Tickner, 'Mediating Generation', p. 26.
86. Stella Duckworth profile portrait, studio photograph, Rome, MHPA, MH-1 (MS Thr 557), leaf 50 (160).
87. The framed photograph of Stella Duckworth was evidently taken at the same sitting and is almost identical to the print in MHPA, MH-1 (MS Thr 557), leaf 50 (160). The framed photograph is in the Charleston Trust Collection, CHA/PH/210.
88. Humm, *Snapshots of Bloomsbury*, p. 9.
89. Ibid.
90. MHPA, MH-1 (MS Thr 557), leaf 60 (180).
91. Leonard Woolf, *Beginning Again: An Autobiography of the Years 1911 to 1918* (London: Hogarth Press, 1964), p. 27.
92. V. Woolf to M. Vaughan, 17 December 1906, *TLVW*, vol. 1, p. 265.
93. Maitland, *The Life and Letters of Leslie Stephen*, p. 268.
94. George Charles Beresford, 'Virginia Woolf and Sir Leslie Stephen', 1902, National Portrait Gallery, London, NPG x4600.
95. The photograph is numbered NPG P221 in the catalogue of the National Portrait Gallery.
96. V. Woolf to V. Dickinson, early August 1902, *TLVW*, vol. 1, pp. 52–3.
97. Vanessa Bell's photograph album CH 1 (TGA 9020/1), leaves 21 and 27.
98. A number of photographs of the studio taken during Grant's lifetime and when the house was initially restored show the image of Bell on display. This one is item PH.88 in the Charleston Trust Collection. The photograph of Bell is item CHA/PH/5.
99. V. Bell to D. Grant, 31 December 1927, TGA 20078/1/44/151.
100. Lisa Tickner, 'Vanessa Bell: Studland Beach, Domesticity, and "Significant Form"', *Representations*, no. 65 (1999), pp. 63–92 (at pp. 63–8).
101. Fifteen photographs of male and female nudes were given by

102. See, for example, Cecil Beaton, 'Ottoline Morrell', 1927, National Portrait Gallery, London, NPG x14149.
103. Madge Garland, 'Recollections of Virginia Woolf', in Joan Russell Noble (ed.), *Recollections of Virginia Woolf* (London: Peter Owen, 1972), pp. 171–4 (at p. 173).
104. Ibid., p. 172.
105. V. Woolf to L. Pearsall Smith, [28 January 1925]; and V. Woolf to V. Sackville-West, [29 January 1925] and [1 September 1925]; all in *TLVW*, vol. 3, pp. 158, 159, and 200. Her article is Virginia Woolf, 'Indiscretions', *Vogue* [London], late November 1924, pp. 47, 88.
106. In her recollections, Garland describes this as 'one of the most successful pictures of Virginia' and claims responsibility for its styling: 'I arranged for this to be taken … and went to the[ir] studio to greet her there.' Garland, 'Recollections of Virginia Woolf', p. 173. For a detailed discussion of this photograph, see Reed, *Bloomsbury Rooms*, pp. 24–5.
107. Roger Fry, 'A Possible Domestic Architecture', *Vogue* [London], late March 1918, pp. 40–41, 66, 68, with photographs by A. C. Cooper.
108. Anon., 'An Economist and Modern Art: The Cambridge Rooms of Mr Keynes', *Vogue* [London], early March 1925, pp. 46–7; Anon., 'Modern English Decoration: Some Examples of the Interesting Work of Duncan Grant and Vanessa Bell', *Vogue* [London], early November 1924, pp. 43–5, 106.
109. V. Woolf to V. O'Campo, 27 November 1934, *TLVW*, vol. 5, p. 349.
110. Reed, *Bloomsbury Rooms*, pp. 223–4.
111. Ibid., p. 227.
112. Ibid., pp. 242–4.
113. V. Woolf to V. Sackville West, [30 October 1927], *TLVW*, vol. 3, p. 434.
114. 'Orlando on her Return to England' is reproduced in Virginia Woolf, *Orlando* (London: Hogarth Press, 1928). The poster is reproduced in Nino Strachey, *Rooms of Their Own* (London: Pitkin, 2018), p. 64.
115. MPH (MS Thr 564), (94).
116. V. Woolf to V. Sackville-West, 29 January 1929, *TLVW*, vol. 4, p. 9. Sackville-West's copy of the photograph is in the National Trust Collection at Sissinghurst Castle, Kent, NT 8030622. Woolf's copy is MHP (MS Thr 564), (75).
117. V. Woolf to D. Brace, 21 October 1929, *TLVW*, vol. 4, p. 101.
118. V. Woolf to V. Sackville-West, [9 September 1932], ibid., vol. 5, p. 102.
119. Virginia Woolf, 16 September 1932, *TDVW*, vol. 4, p. 124. Leonard Woolf's photograph was used as the frontispiece in Winifred Holtby, *Virginia Woolf* (London: Wishart, 1932).
120. Humm, *Snapshots of Bloomsbury*, pp. 34–5.
121. MHPA, MH-3 (MS Thr 560), (92), (93), and (94).
122. The image is MHP (MS Thr 564), (63). See also 'Virginia Woolf seated in armchair at Monk's House (Rodmell, England) holding reading glasses and a book', 20 August 1932, MHP (MS Thr 564), (59) <https://id.lib.harvard.edu/ead/c/hou02507c00063/catalog> (accessed 27 April 2020).
123. MHP (MS Thr 564), (76).
124. MHP (MS Thr 564), (53). The image appeared on the cover of *Time. The Weekly Magazine*, vol. 29, no. 15 (12 April 1937).

CHAPTER 2

1. Jeremy Hutchinson, interview recorded with the author, 19 May 2009, Charleston Trust Collection, Sound Archive.
2. Virginia Woolf, *Moments of Being: Autobiographical Writings* [1978], ed. Jean Schulkind (London: Pimlico, 2002), p. 36.
3. Ibid.
4. Leonard Woolf, *Sowing: An Autobiography of the Years 1880 to 1904* (London: Hogarth Press, 1960), p. 183.
5. Leonard Woolf, *Beginning Again: An Autobiography of the Years 1911 to 1918* (London: Hogarth Press, 1964), pp. 74–5.
6. Ibid., p. 74.
7. Duncan Grant, *James Strachey*, c.1910, oil on canvas, 640 × 760 mm, Tate N05765.
8. Cecil Hartley, *The Gentlemen's Book of Etiquette and Manual of Politeness* (Boston: Cottrell, 1860), p. 144.
9. MHPA, MH-2 (MS Thr 559), leaf 24, (68).
10. Hartley, *The Gentlemen's Book*, p. 118.
11. Photographs of Lytton Strachey after his haircut, and of Adrian Stephen having his hair cut by Bell, are arranged next to each other in Vanessa Bell's photograph album CH 3 (TGA 9020/4), p. 2. The page is titled 'Asheham 1913'. Bell's dress indicates that the photographs were taken on the same occasion. The photograph in figure 68 is National Portrait Gallery, London, NPG Ax160974; see also NPG x21196, and photographs in the Charleston Trust Collection, Anne Olivier Bell Gift.
12. V. Bell to D. Grant, 28 August 1915, TGA 20078/1/44/35.
13. V. Bell to J. M. Keynes, [August 1915], GB181 SxMs56/1/30, VBMK 12.
14. Virginia Woolf, 12 February 1927, *TDVW*, vol. 3, p. 127.
15. V. Woolf to V. Sackville-West, 16 February 1927, *TLVW*, vol. 3, p. 330.
16. V. Woolf, *TDVW*, vol. 3, note 3, p. 127.
17. V. Woolf to V. Sackville-West, 16 February 1927, *TLVW*, vol. 3, p. 331.
18. V. Woolf, 12 February 1927, *TDVW*, vol. 3, p. 127.
19. V. Bell to V. Woolf, 22 February 1927, *SLVB*, p. 309.
20. V. Bell to J. M. Keynes, 1 April 1927, GB181 SxMs56/1/30, VBMK 83.
21. V. Woolf to V. Sackville-West, 16 February 1927, *TLVW*, vol. 3, p. 331.
22. See 'Clive Bell', c.1909, Vanessa Bell's photograph album CH 1 (TGA 9020/1), p. 31; Henry Lamb, *Clive Bell*, c.1909–10, pencil on paper, 340 × 240 mm, Charleston Trust Collection, CHA/P/13.
23. Virginia Woolf, 'Old Bloomsbury', in her *Moments of Being*, p. 49.

24. Clive Bell, *Old Friends: Personal Recollections* (London: Chatto & Windus, 1956), p. 50.
25. S. P. Rosenbaum (ed.), *The Bloomsbury Group: A Collection of Memoirs, Commentary and Criticism* (London: Croom Helm, 1975), pp. 8–15; and L. Strachey to D. Carrington, 1 August 1916, *LLS*, p. 317.
26. Christopher Reed, *Bloomsbury Rooms: Modernism, Subculture, and Domesticity* (New Haven, CT, and London: Yale University Press, 2004), pp. 54–7.
27. Ibid., pp. 56–7.
28. Richard Shone, *The Art of Bloomsbury: Roger Fry, Vanessa Bell and Duncan Grant*, exh. cat. (Tate Gallery: London, 1999), p. 66; and Frances Spalding, *Duncan Grant* (London: Chatto & Windus, 1997), p. 95.
29. J. M. Keynes to D. Grant, 30 May 1910, quoted in ibid., p. 95.
30. D. Grant to J. M. Keynes, 10 June 1910, quoted in ibid., p. 95.
31. J. M. Keynes to D. Grant, 6 June 1910, British Library, London, Add. MS 57930B.
32. See Reed, *Bloomsbury Rooms*, pp. 60–62.
33. The paintings are Duncan Grant, *The Lemon Gatherers*, 1910, oil on millboard, 565 × 813 mm, Tate N03666; and Duncan Grant, *Two Nudes on a Beach*, c.1910, oil on panel, 420 × 270 mm, Yale Center for British Art B1984.31.1. See also Reed, *Bloomsbury Rooms*, pp. 56–9.
34. C. Bell, *Old Friends*, p. 43.
35. V. Bell to R. Fry, 23 November 1911, *SLVB*, pp. 111–12.
36. V. Bell to D. Grant, 29 September 1913, TGA 20078/1/44/15.
37. V. Bell to V. Woolf, 22 August 1915, *SLVB*, p. 186.
38. V. Woolf to V. Dickinson, 10 April 1917, *TLVW*, vol. 2, p. 147.
39. Ibid.
40. Lady Ottoline Morrell, 'Dora Carrington', 1917, National Portrait Gallery, London, NPG x144309, NPG x144310, and NPG x144311.
41. John Greenland, interview recorded with the author, 28 April 2003, Charleston Trust Collection, Sound Archive.
42. Maggie Humm, *Snapshots of Bloomsbury: The Private Lives of Virginia Woolf and Vanessa Bell* (London: Tate, 2006), p. 21.
43. V. Bell to D. Grant, c.1914, TGA 20078/1/44/26.
44. Vanessa Bell, 'Julian Bell, Asheham', 1913, Vanessa Bell's photograph album CH 2 (TGA 9020/2), p. 37. The photograph was also included in Virginia Woolf's Monk's House photograph album as 'Julian Bell nude as a child, leaning on the outside of a window', 1913, MHPA, MH-1 (MS Thr 557), (158). 'Photograph of Julian and Quentin Bell, Asheham', Vanessa Bell, 1913, was included in Vanessa Bell photograph album CH 2 (TGA 9020/2), p. 34. See also Charleston Trust Collection, Anne Olivier Bell Gift. Thirteen pages of photographs of the two boys naked at Asheham, with page titles 'Asheham 1914', are included in Vanessa Bell's photograph album CH 3 (TGA 9020/4).
45. See also 'Molly MacCarthy and Vanessa Bell posing nude in Vanessa Bell's studio', c.1913, TGA 9020, AD27; and 'Molly MacCarthy posing nude in Vanessa Bell's studio', c.1913, TGA 9020, AD5.
46. Frances Spalding, *Vanessa Bell* (London: Weidenfeld & Nicolson, 1983), p. 185.
47. Eugène Druet, 'Vaslav Nijinsky in the Siamese Dance from *Les orientales*', 1911, Charleston Trust Collection, CHA/PH/2.
48. Ottoline Morrell, *Ottoline: The Early Memoirs of Lady Ottoline Morrell*, ed. Robert Gathorne-Hardy (London: Faber & Faber, 1963), p. 228.
49. Duncan Grant, *Tennis Player*, 1913, pencil, gouache, and oil on paper, 250 × 159 mm, Pamela Diamond Collection, Courtauld Gallery, London, D.1958.PD.60.
50. See Vanessa Bell, *Design for a Folding Screen: Adam and Eve*, c.1913–14, gouache and pencil on paper, 357 × 509 mm, Courtauld Gallery, London, given by Pamela Diamond in 1958.
51. See Duncan Grant, *Vanessa Bell*, 1917, oil on canvas, 1270 × 1016 mm, National Portrait Gallery, London, NPG 5541. The vase is in the Charleston Trust Collection, CHA/C/542.
52. See 'Nude photograph of Molly MacCarthy with her hair down in Vanessa Bell's studio', c.1914, Charleston Trust Collection, Anne Olivier Bell Gift.
53. See Reed, *Bloomsbury Rooms*, p. 151.
54. Ibid.
55. Edward Alfred Martin, *Dew Ponds* (London: King, Sell and Olding, 1907), pp. 1–12.
56. See also TGA AD11 and TGA AD18. The photograph may have been taken in preparation for Duncan Grant, *Adam and Eve*, 1913, oil on canvas, approx. 2130 × 3350 mm, lost or destroyed. Illustrated in Shone, *The Art of Bloomsbury*, p. 29.
57. The photograph taken on Studland Beach also appears in Vanessa Bell's photograph album CH 1 (TGA 9020/1), leaf 39.
58. Lisa Cohen, '"Frock Consciousness": Virginia Woolf, the Open Secret, and the Language of Fashion', *Fashion Theory*, vol. 3, no. 2 (1999), pp. 149–74 (at p. 162).
59. See Vanessa Bell's photograph album CH 1 (TGA 9020/1), leaves 35 to 41. St Ives and Asheham, as seaside and rural places, each had their own distinctive dress codes, but they are comparable in their relative informality as locations away from London and its society gatherings.
60. V. Bell to R. Fry, 5 June 1912, *SLVB*, p. 120.
61. The self-portrait is Vanessa Bell, *Self-Portrait at the Easel*, 1912, oil, private collection, reproduced in Reed, *Bloomsbury Rooms*, p. 86.
62. The photograph is missing from Vanessa Bell's photograph album CH 1 (TGA 9020/1), p. 45, where it was paired with an image of Fry with the same wall in the background. The page is titled 'Guildford 1911'. See also Charleston Trust Collection, Anne Olivier Bell Gift.
63. The photograph is also included on page 10 of Vanessa Bell's photograph album CH 3 (TGA 9020/4), titled 'Guildford 1914'.
64. See also Augustus John, *Dorelia*, 1908, graphite and watercolour on paper, 501 × 354 mm, Tate N05158.
65. Morrell, *Ottoline*, p. 163.
66. Bedspread, n.d., linen with silk embroidery, 2560 × 1640 mm, Charleston Trust Collection, CHA/T/25.
67. Two pages of photographs are devoted to the process of

painting Strachey's portrait in Vanessa Bell's photograph album CH 3 (TGA 9020/4), pp. 4–5.
68. The portrait in figure 95 is Smith College Museum of Art, cat. no. SC2002.21. The other portraits are Roger Fry, *Virginia Woolf*, c.1912, oil on board, 402 × 310 mm, Leeds Museum and Galleries, PCF1 (on loan from a private collection); Vanessa Bell, *Virginia Woolf*, c.1912, oil on board, 550 × 450 mm, National Trust, Monk's House, 768417; and Vanessa Bell, *Virginia Woolf*, 1912, oil on board, 400 × 340 mm, National Portrait Gallery, London, NPG5933.
69. This photograph is MHPA, MH-1 (MS Thr 557), (202). For others that feature this jacket, see figures 97 and 98, and 'Leonard Woolf, Roger Eliot Fry, and Virginia Woolf sitting outdoors', 1912, MHPA, MH-1 (MS Thr 557), leaf 68 (201) <https://id.lib.harvard.edu/ead/c/hou02067c00418/catalog> (accessed 27 April 2020).
70. Woolf concluded her letter, 'D'you like this photograph? – rather too noble, I think. Here's another.' V. Woolf to L. Woolf, 1 May 1912, *TLVW*, vol. 1, p. 497. The 'noble' photograph of Virginia is GB181 SxMs18/1/A/2/2.
71. The photograph is MHPA, MH-1 (MS Thr 557), leaf 69 (203).
72. Duncan Grant, *Seated Woman*, c.1912, oil on panel, 948 × 530 mm, Courtauld Gallery, P.1935.RF.183.
73. V. Woolf, 25 May 1938, *TDVW*, vol. 5, p. 143.
74. Ibid., pp. 143–4.
75. V. Woolf to C. Bell, 23 January 1911, *TLVW*, vol. 1, p. 450.
76. V. Woolf to C. Bell, 18 April 1911, ibid., p. 460.
77. V. Woolf to C. Bell, 18 April 1911, ibid., p. 462.
78. V. Woolf to V. Bell, 19 April 1911, ibid.
79. See Shone, *The Art of Bloomsbury*, p. 96, for the argument that this portrait was painted at Brunswick Square in 1912. Vanessa Bell described her painting (whereabouts unknown) in a letter to Roger Fry, complaining of a doctor's appointment: 'it will just cut up my morning's painting Ka, about which I'm rather excited in spite of Duncan.' V. Bell to R. Fry, 6 March 1912, TGA 8010.8.99. Grant's painting is item A2155 in the collection of the National Museum of Wales.
80. V. Woolf to M. MacCarthy, March 1911, *TLVW*, vol. 1, p. 455.
81. V. Woolf to V. Bell, 21 July 1911, ibid., p. 470.
82. Gill Lowe, '"Wild Swimming", Rupert Brooke and Virginia Woolf', paper delivered at 'Virginia Woolf and the Natural World', the 20th International Virginia Woolf Conference, held at Georgetown College, Georgetown, KY, 3–6 June 2010, available at <http://oars.uos.ac.uk/id/eprint/111> (accessed 27 April 2020); Christopher Hassall, *Rupert Brooke: A Biography* (London: Faber & Faber, 1964), p. 280.
83. Virginia Woolf, 'Rupert Brooke', in her *Collected Essays*, vol. 2: *1912–1918* (London: Hogarth Press, 1966), p. 279.
84. Ibid.
85. The photograph is National Portrait Gallery, London, NPG x13124.
86. Ibid.
87. V. Woolf to O. Morrell, end-January 1911, *TLVW*, vol. 1, p. 451.
88. V. Woolf to Violet Dickinson, 24 January 1911, ibid.
89. V. Woolf to M. MacCarthy, April 1911, ibid., p. 456.
90. For a discussion of the setting of this portrait at Little Talland House or at Asheham, see Shone, *The Art of Bloomsbury*, pp. 84–5.
91. V. Woolf to C. Bell, 18 April 1911, *TLVW*, vol. 1, p. 462.
92. V. Woolf to Ka Cox, November? 1912, ibid., vol. 2, p. 11.
93. V. Woolf to L. Woolf, November 1912, ibid., p. 12.
94. V. Woolf to L. Woolf, 14 September 1911, ibid., vol. 1, p. 478.
95. V. Woolf to V. Dickinson, 24 December 1912, ibid., vol. 2, pp. 14–15.
96. See photographs 'Virginia Woolf at Asheham with Leonard Woolf and Vanessa Bell', MHPA, MH-1 (MS Thr 557), (202) <https://id.lib.harvard.edu/ead/c/hou02067c00420/catalog> (accessed 27 April 2020); and Vanessa Bell's photograph album CH 2 (TGA 9020/3), leaf 1.
97. V. Woolf to K. Cox, 2 May 1912, *TLVW*, vol. 1, p. 497.
98. Pages 29–33 of Vanessa Bell's photograph album CH 2 (TGA 9020/3) are devoted to images of the camp.
99. Pippa Harris (ed.), *Song of Love: The Letters of Rupert Brooke and Noel Olivier: 1909–1915* (London: Bloomsbury, 1991), p. 248.
100. V. Bell to J. M. Keynes, 16 August [1913], GB181 SxMs56/1/30, VBMK 7.
101. The screen was initially known as 'Tents and Figures'.
102. See Shone, *The Art of Bloomsbury*, p. 145; and Hana Leaper, 'Between London and Paris', in S. Milroy and I. A. C. Dejardin (eds), *Vanessa Bell* (London: Philip Wilson, 2017), pp. 41–53 (at p. 50).
103. N. Olivier to R. Brooke, 25 September 1913, in Harris, *Song of Love*, p. 250.
104. See Sherrill Schell, 'Olivier sisters on the beach at Cornwall', c.1912, photograph reproduced in Paul Delany, *Fatal Glamour: The Life of Rupert Brooke* (Montreal: McGill-Queens University Press, 2015), following p. viii.

CHAPTER 3

1. V. Bell to R. Fry, 6 February 1913, *SLVB*, p. 135.
2. V. Bell to R. Fry, 6 February 1913, *SLVB*, p. 135. The *Second Post-Impressionist Exhibition* at the Grafton Galleries closed on 31 January 1913.
3. The card is item CHA/P/402 in the Charleston Trust Collection.
4. V. Bell to R. Fry, 6 March 1913, TGA 8010.8.99.
5. Winifred Gill and Pamela Diamand, interview with Stephen Chaplin, n.d. [1958–9]. Transcripts of the interview with manuscript additions by Pamela Diamand (Roger Fry's daughter) are in the Courtauld Gallery Archives and in the Quentin Bell Papers, GB181 SxMs74/1/76.
6. W. Gill to Q. Bell, 15 April 1967, Quentin Bell Papers, GB181 SxMs74/1/7/6. Gill added that after the Workshops' manager, Mr Robinson, started, 'money was only paid out on Fridays'.
7. Omega Workshops, *Omega Workshops Ltd, Artist Decorators*, descriptive cat. (London: Omega Workshops, n.d. [autumn

1914]), p. 9. There is a copy of the catalogue in the National Art Library, Victoria and Albert Museum, acc. no. L.2209-1955.

8. Letter from J. Brown, quoted in W. Gill to D. Grant, Letter XI, 30 March 1967 (Tate Archive TAM 24M). That Brown and Layton were cousins is stated on page 4 of Gill's letter.

9. V. Bell to R. Fry, 24 August 1914, *SLVB*, p. 170; Virginia Woolf, 7 January 1915, *TDVW*, vol. I, p. 11.

10. For an analysis of Bohemian style in London and its popularity in the first decades of the twentieth century, see Elizabeth Wilson, 'Bohemian Dress and the Heroism of Everyday Life', *Fashion Theory: The Journal of Dress, Body and Culture*, vol. 2, no. 3 (1998), pp. 225–44 (at pp. 233–6).

11. W. Gill to D. Grant, Letter VII, 10 October 1966, p. 2 (Tate Archive TAM 24M).

12. For an account of 'Art Circle' evenings, see W. Gill to D. Grant, Letter VIII, 13 December 1966 (Tate Archive TAM 24M).

13. W. Gill to D. Grant, Letter III, 4 July 1966, p. 3 (Tate Archive TAM 24M).

14. W. Gill and P. Diamand, transcript, GB181 SxMs74/1/76.

15. M. M. B., 'Post-Impressionist Furniture', *Daily News and Leader*, 7 August 1913, p. 10.

16. Joy Brown recalled that '(I think that was made by the Cavendish Square Dressmaker – or was it never made up . . .)'; quoted in W. Gill to D. Grant, Letter XI, 30 March 1967, p. 2 (Tate Archive TAM 24M).

17. Joy Brown recalled, 'I can remember the dress May (Layton) wore at the Ideal Home. I don't know who made it, it might have been the Cavendish Square one. (i.e. Dressmaker.).' This may have been the 'wonderful dress made of silks' designed by Duncan Grant. Quoted in W. Gill to D. Grant, Letter XI, 30 March 1967, p. 1 (Tate Archive TAM 24M). Gill recalled that the Omega caretaker 'took over the "manning" of our "room" replacing our Miss Layton' after 6 p.m. at the *Ideal Homes Exhibition*. W. Gill to D. Grant, Letter X, 20 February 1967, p. 7 (Tate Archive TAM 24M).

18. Roger Fry, 'Preface', to Omega Workshops, descriptive cat., p. 4.

19. Virginia Woolf, *Roger Fry: A Biography* (London: Hogarth Press, 1940), p. 190.

20. Omega Workshops, descriptive cat., p. 6.

21. The design of these garments is attributed to Vanessa Bell and dated c.1918 on the assumption that they were made from surplus Omega stock. The full details are: *Pair of Pyjamas in Maud Design*, Omega Workshops, Bloomsbury, London, Britain, 1913–20, Vanessa Bell, designer, fabric and garment, Britain, 1879–1961, 1918, fabric designed 1913, Bloomsbury, London, printed linen, 1054 mm (trousers, outer leg), 1200 mm (trousers, centre back length), 840 mm (jacket, centre back length), 1500 mm (jacket, cuff to cuff), South Australian Government Grant 1984, Art Gallery of South Australia, Accession No. 849A98 (a&b); and *Dressing Gown in Amenophis VI Design*, Omega Workshops, Bloomsbury, London, Britain, 1913–20, Roger Fry, designer of fabric, Britain, 1866–1934, Vanessa Bell, designer of garment, Britain 1879–1961, attributed to Besselièvre Cie, Maromme, France, working 19th–20th century, fabric designed 1913, designed London, printed France, printed linen, garment designed 1918, 1310 mm (centre back), 1580 mm (cuff to cuff), South Australian Government Grant 1984, Art Gallery of South Australia, Accession No. 849A99. See also the catalogue description, 'Worn for a Russian Ballet Fancy Dress Party', in Richard Shone, *Vanessa Bell, 1879–1961: A Retrospective Exhibition*, exh. cat. (Davis & Long Company, New York, 1980), cat. no. 83, p. 42.

22. Omega Workshops, descriptive cat., p. 14.

23. V. Bell to R. Fry, n.d., TGA 8010.8.101.

24. Gill describes herself as 'a sort of continuity girl' in W. Gill and P. Diamand, transcript, GB181 SxMs74/1/76.

25. W. Gill to D. Grant, Letter XII, 18 April 1967, p. 5 (Tate Archive TAM 24M). See also the Winifred Gill archive in the Bodleian Library, Oxford, MSS 6241/1–70.

26. W. Gill and P. Diamand, transcript, GB181 SxMs74/1/76.

27. W. Gill to D. Grant, Letter VII, 10 October 1966, p. 4 (Tate Archive TAM 24M).

28. Gill describes *Sleeping Fawn* as 'a tiny sleep-in [sic] fawn, about five inches long, carved in brown stone'. W. Gill to D. Grant, Letter IX, 29 December 1966, p. 6 (Tate Archive TAM 24M). For a cast of the original statuette, see Henri Gaudier-Brzeska, *Sleeping Fawn*, 1913, painted plaster, 114 × 254 × 216 mm, Tate T03728.

29. W. Gill to D. Grant, Letter VII, 10 October 1966, p. 4 (Tate Archive TAM 24M).

30. W. Gill to Q. Bell, 14 May 1967, Quentin Bell Papers, GB181 SxMs74/1/7/6. See also W. Gill to N. Pevsner, 3 March 1941, TGA 8022.8.

31. Necklaces are listed 'from £0.3.6' in Omega Workshops, descriptive cat., p. 14. Winifred Gill describes the bead sources in detail and the Woolworths beads as 'the size and shape of a quarter inch section of raw macaroni' in W. Gill to D. Grant, Letter VII, 10 October 1966, pp. 3–7 (Tate Archive TAM 24M).

32. Ibid., p. 3.

33. Ibid., p. 5.

34. W. Gill to D. Grant, Letter VI, 12 September 1966, p. 4 (Tate Archive TAM 24M).

35. Ibid.

36. V. Bell to R. Fry, 9(?) April 1915, *SLVB*, p. 173.

37. Ibid.

38. Ibid., p. 174.

39. Ibid.

40. Ibid.

41. V. Bell to D. Grant, 30 November 1913, TGA 20078/1/44/16; and V. Bell to D. Grant, c.5 December 1913, TGA 20078/1/44/17.

42. V. Bell to D. Grant, 25 March 1914, *SLVB*, p. 160.

43. Ibid.

44. Ibid., p. 160.

45. The George Eastman Museum, New York, holds 11 images of Stein by Alvin Langdon Coburn, acquisition numbers 1967.0156.0016, 1967.0156.0017, 1978.0050.0040, and 1979:4010:0001 through 1979:4010.008.

46. The combination of brown corduroy gown, fastening pin,

and lapis beads is also represented in Félix Edouard Vallaton, *Gertrude Stein*, 1907, oil on canvas, 1000 × 813 mm, Baltimore Museum of Art.

47. V. Bell to G. Stein, 13 June 1914, *SLVB*, pp. 165–6.
48. W. Gill to D. Grant, Letter IV, 18 August 1966, pp. 1–2 (Tate Archive TAM 24M).
49. Duncan Grant acquired the Prie Dieu chairs in 1917, dating the photograph to 1917 or later. The photograph is neg. no. R18 among the loose photographs of TGA 9020.
50. V. Bell to D. Grant, n.d. [December 1914], TGA 20078/1/44/27.
51. MHPA, MH-1 (MS Thr 557), leaf 69 (198).
52. MHPA, MH-1 (MS Thr 557), leaf 69 (200). The photograph is also included in Vanessa Bell's photograph album CH 3 (TGA 9020/4), p. 39.
53. V. Bell to R. Fry, n.d. [April 1915], TGA 8010.8.159.
54. W. Gill and P. Diamand, transcript, GB181 SxMs74/1/76.
55. V. Bell to R. Fry, 27 May 1915, TGA 8010.8.168.
56. R. Fry to C. Bell, 9 May 1915, in *Letters of Roger Fry*, ed. Denys Sutton (London: Chatto & Windus), p. 385.
57. V. Bell to R. Fry, April 1915, TGA 8010.8.161.
58. V. Bell to D. Grant, 6 May 1915, TGA 20078/1/44/33.
59. See Jeffrey Meyers, 'Kate Lechmere's "Wyndham Lewis from 1912"', *Journal of Modern Literature*, vol. 10, no. 1 (1983), pp. 158–66.
60. V. Bell to R. Fry, Monday, n.d. [1915], TGA 8010.8.169.
61. V. Bell to R. Fry, 12 June 1915, TGA 8010.8.172.
62. See Meyers, 'Kate Lechmere's "Wyndham Lewis"'.
63. V. Bell to R. Fry, Monday, n.d. [1915], TGA 8010.8.169.
64. W. Gill to D. Grant, Letter VII, 10 October 1966, p. 5 (Tate Archive TAM 24M).
65. V. Bell to R. Fry, Monday, n.d. [1915], TGA 8010.8.169.
66. Quoted in W. Gill to D. Grant, Letter XI, 30 March 1967, pp. 1–2 (Tate Archive TAM 24M).
67. Quoted in V. Bell to R. Fry, n.d., TGA 8010.8.173.
68. Ibid.
69. V. Bell to R. Fry, 9 June 1915, TGA 8010.8.171.
70. V. Bell to R. Fry, 12 June 1915, TGA 8010.8.172.
71. Ibid.
72. V. Bell to R. Fry, 27 May 1915, TGA 8010.8.168. Bell's letters indicate that Brown was initially to have produced two new dresses and Lechmere was to have produced the dresses for Bell and Tree.
73. V. Bell to Margery Snowden, 21 October 1908, *SLVB*, p. 77.
74. V. Bell to R. Fry, [c. July 1915], GB181 SxMs56/1/28, VBRF 178. Bell goes on to write: 'I shouldn't think she would be very good in my dress as it wont fit in the least, & its rather important in that dress that the shoulders at any rate should be closely fitted.'
75. See Judith Collins, *The Omega Workshops* (London: Secker and Warburg, 1983), pp. 108–9.
76. In Collins's list of plates in *The Omega Workshops* (p. 298) this image is identified as 'Vanessa Bell wearing an Omega dress of her own design, summer 1915, Omega publicity photograph'.
77. Gill recalled the technique in detail and wrote: 'Unfortunately we had a passion for stripes at the time, the most unsuitable scheme for the process, since a slight irregularity which would have passed unnoticed in a floral or more complicated geometrical pattern was horribly obvious in this case.' W. Gill to N. Pevsner, 3 March 1941, TGA 8022.8.
78. The waistcoat is item CIRC.640-1964 in the catalogue of the Victoria and Albert Museum. See also Alexandra Gerstein (ed.), *Beyond Bloomsbury: Designs of the Omega Workshops, 1913–19*, exh. cat. (Courtauld Gallery, London, 2009), cat. no. 41, p. 130.
79. See Winifred Gill, 'Two sketches of a sleeveless tunic or waistcoat', pen on letter paper, 180 × 90 mm, Winifred Gill Papers, Bodleian Library, Oxford. The sketches are reproduced in Gerstein, *Beyond Bloomsbury*, p. 57.
80. Bell wrote that 'Mr Douglas Pepler has offered her £100 per year to start with to work for him at dress making. He will let her spend her afternoons at the Omega ready to see people & fit them.' V. Bell to R. Fry, 12 June 1915, TGA 8010.8.172.
81. 'I have actually secured a very nice girl, fresh from making 40 beds daily at a Y.M.C.A. in Brighton, anxious to be here & near her home & jumping at £22 a year.' This, however, would have included her 'keep'. V. Bell to R. Fry, n.d. [19 October 1917], GB181 SxMs56/1/28, VBRF 243.
82. V. Bell to R. Fry, 12 June 1915, TGA 8010.8.172.
83. E. Gill, MS letter, 8 August 1928, private collection, quoted in Lotti Hoare, 'Pepler, Harry Douglas Clarke [Hilary]', *Oxford Dictionary of National Biography* <https://doi.org/10.1093/ref:odnb/66287> (accessed 27 April 2020).
84. H. D. C. Pepler, 'Hampshire House Workshops', *Blackfriars*, vol. 31, no. 359 (1950), pp. 70–74 (at p. 70).
85. Ibid., p. 71.
86. Ibid., p. 72.
87. Ibid., pp. 71–3.
88. Collins, *The Omega Workshops*, p. 108.
89. *Exhibition of English and Belgian Work by Craftsmen and Artists in Hammersmith*, exh. cat. (Hampshire House Club, Hampshire Hog Lane, Hammersmith, 3–20 June 1915), unpaginated. A copy of the catalogue is housed in the Ditchling Museum of Art + Craft, Sussex, cat. no. 1991.1305.1. Christabel Frampton trained at the Royal Academy Schools and was married to the sculptor George Frampton. By 1910 they were living in St John's Wood in a house designed by him.
90. W. Gill to D. Grant, Letter II, June 1966, p. 2 (Tate Archive TAM 24M).
91. See Gerstein, *Beyond Bloomsbury*, pp. 84–5, cat. no. 4.
92. Although the Victoria and Albert Museum gives a date of 1915 for the tie, Gill provided an earlier date when she recalled that she made the ties for Hugh Hynes, the brother of Gladys Hynes, who 'came to the Omega in perhaps 1913 or 1914 before he sailed for India'. W. Gill to D. Grant, 12 January 1967, covering letter to Letter IX (Tate Archive TAM 24M).
93. The negative is among Vanessa Bell's loose photographs (TGA 9020), neg. no. J14.
94. Sunflowers feature prominently in 'Wall Decorations in

Antechamber', late 1913/early 1914, tempera on plaster?, whereabouts unknown; see Collins, *The Omega Workshops*, p. 35.

95. W. Gill to Q. Bell, 26 September 1967, Quentin Bell Papers, GB181 SxMs74/1/7/6.

96. Ibid.

97. Gill recalled that the fabric was manufactured by Foxton and that 'a pattern of it is now in the Victoria and Albert'. No corresponding W. Foxton Ltd. fabric is catalogued in the V&A Collection. W. Gill to Q. Bell, 26 September 1967, Quentin Bell Papers, GB181 SxMs74/1/7/6.

98. Ibid.

99. Quentin Bell sent a copy of the photograph to Gill with a note, 'It was at the S. Kensington Omega exhibition.' Q. Bell to W. Gill, 14 September 1967. She replied, 'I am glad too to know where the photograph was taken, I could not quite make it fit any of the showrooms.' W. Gill to Q. Bell, 26 September 1967, Quentin Bell Papers, GB181 SxMs74/1/7/6. Bell was referring to a 1963 exhibition at the Victoria and Albert Museum in 'S. Kensington', but Gill misunderstood and presumably thought he was referring to the 1913 *Ideal Homes Exhibition*, which was held at Olympia in Kensington.

100. See also Duncan Grant, *Design (known as 'Trojan Women')*, 1913–15, gouache and pencil on paper, 205 × 284 mm, Courtauld Gallery Collection, D.1958.PD.59. This is one of the original Omega designs given to the Courtauld by Pamela Diamand in 1958. The figure in the press photograph is clearly not Gill, who had long hair, and it is unlikely that another artist would have been working on Grant's painted tray. Moreover, the figure in the press photograph resembles Grant in other photographs from this time and in Bell's painting *The Studio: Duncan Grant and Henri Doucet at Asheham*, 1912.

101. Bell wrote: 'I have made myself a dress, price 3/6. I wonder if you'll think it too awful.' V. Bell to R. Fry, 24 August 1914, *SLVB*, p. 170.

102. The original print is comparable in size to the 1915 photograph of Clive Bell and Mary Hutchinson outside Eleanor House (figure 75) and has the appearance of having been taken on the same visit.

103. See Christopher Reed, *Bloomsbury Rooms: Modernism, Subculture, and Domesticity* (New Haven, CT, and London: Yale University Press, 2004), pp. 151–2; and Richard Shone, *The Art of Bloomsbury: Roger Fry, Vanessa Bell and Duncan Grant*, exh. cat. (Tate Gallery, London, 1999), pp. 103–5.

104. See also Duncan Grant, *Iris Tree*, 1915, oil on board, 760 × 630 mm, Reading Museum & Town Hall, REDMG: 1965.227.1. Tree had already sat for William Nicholson and subsequently sat for Augustus John, Roger Fry, Jacob Epstein, Henry Lamb, Alvaro Guevara, Man Ray, and Cecil Beaton.

105. Reed, *Bloomsbury Rooms*, p. 172.

106. V. Bell to R. Fry, Monday n.d., TGA 8010.8.179.

107. V. Bell to D. Grant, 6 August 1915, *SLVB*, p. 185. The Omega Workshops were importing textiles from Broussa by this time.

108. W. Gill to D. Grant, Letter X, 20 February 1967, p. 4 (Tate Archive TAM 24M).

109. Ibid., pp. 4–5.

110. W. Gill to D. Grant, Letter III, 4 July 1966, p. 5 (Tate Archive TAM 24M).

111. W. Gill to D. Grant, Letter X, 20 February 1967, pp. 4–5 (Tate Archive TAM 24M).

112. D. Grant to W. Gill, 7 March 1967 (Tate Archive TAM 24M).

113. J. Brown, quoted in W. Gill to D. Grant, Letter XI, 30 March 1967, p. 2 (Tate Archive TAM 24M).

114. J. Brown, quoted in ibid., p. 3.

115. J. Brown, quoted in ibid., p. 2. Gill describes the pink muslin dress and attributed its design, with some uncertainty, to Vanessa Bell, in W. Gill to D. Grant, Letter X, 20 February 1967, p. 6 (Tate Archive TAM 24M).

116. V. Woolf to V. Bell, 23 April 1916, *TLVW*, vol. 2, p. 92.

117. Ibid.

118. V. Bell to V. Woolf, 10 May, 1916, Berg Collection, New York Public Library; quoted, reproduced, and discussed in Elizabeth M. Sheehan, 'Dressmaking at the Omega: Experiments in Art and Fashion', in Gerstein, *Beyond Bloomsbury*, pp. 50–59 (at pp. 55–6).

119. V. Woolf to V. Bell, 16 August 1916, *TLVW*, vol. 2, p. 111.

120. Gill recalled, 'it was the middle of the war'; W. Gill and P. Diamand, transcript, GB181 SxMs74/1/76.

121. See Lisa Cohen, '"Frock Consciousness": Virginia Woolf, the Open Secret, and the Language of Fashion', *Fashion Theory*, vol. 3, no. 2 (1999), pp. 149–74.

122. V. Woolf, 9 May 1926, *TDVW*, vol. 3, p. 81.

123. V. Woolf, 21 March 1927, ibid., p. 132.

124. V. Woolf, 30 June 1926, ibid., p. 91.

125. See Reed 2006.

126. V. Woolf, 30 June 1926, *TDVW*, vol. 3, p. 91.

127. V. Woolf, 1 July 1926, ibid., p. 91.

128. V. Bell to R. Fry, n.d. [23 October 1916], GB181 SxMs56/1/28, VBRF 212.

129. V. Bell to R. Fry, 30 April 1915, TGA 8010.8.163.

130. Ibid.

131. V. Bell to R. Fry, n.d. [23 October 1916], GB181 SxMs56/1/28, VBRF 212.

132. Ibid.

133. Ibid.

134. V. Bell to R. Fry, n.d. [2–4 June 1917], GB181 SxMs56/1/28, VBRF 226.

135. V. Bell to R. Fry, n.d. [25 March 1914], *SLVB*, p. 160.

136. V. Bell to R. Fry, 23 April 1917, GB181 SxMs56/1/28, VBRF 225.

137. C. Kühlenthal to J. Nash, n.d., written on lined notepaper with 'The Omega Workshops' written in Kühlenthal's autograph, top right of paper (TGA 8022.6).

138. See Patricia Cunningham, *Reforming Women's Fashion, 1850–1920* (Kent, OH: Kent State University Press, 2003), pp. 203–22; and Sheehan, 'Dressmaking at the Omega'.

139. See J. Brown, quoted in W. Gill to D. Grant, Letter XI, 30 March 1967, p. 2 (Tate Archive TAM 24M). Brown does not specify whether this was the exhibition in 1915 or that of 1917,

discussed further below.

140. M. Hutchinson to V. Bell, 11 July 1917, GB181 SxMs56/1/112, MHVB 20.

141. Amber Blanco White was a Fabian and a Newnham graduate. Joy Brown described the fitting for her Omega dress, which was made by Isabel Walker at the Hampshire House Workshops and fitted by Brown; quoted in W. Gill to D. Grant, Letter XI, 30 March 1967, p. 2 (Tate Archive TAM 24M). Fry painted Blanco White's portrait in 1917; see R. Fry to P. Fry, 7 March 1917, in *Letters of Roger Fry*, ed. Sutton, p. 406.

142. Lytton Strachey described the portrait as 'a frightful arrangement of Nina Hamnett – just done by him – full length in blue check, with carefully disposed red and yellow still life, and a still life face. Le pauvre homme.' L. Strachey to D. Carrington, 22 June 1917, *LLS*, p. 359.

143. M. Hutchinson to V. Bell, 11 July 1917, GB181 SxMs56/1/112, MHVB 20.

144. Ibid.

145. V. Bell to S. Sydney Turner, 19 January 1917, *SLVB*, p. 202.

146. Ibid.

147. V. Bell to R. Fry, n.d. [1917], GB181 SxMs56/1/28, VBRF 220.

148. Ibid.

149. V. Bell to R. Fry, n.d. [October 1917], GB181 SxMs56/1/28, VBRF 242.

150. V. Bell to R. Fry, 23 April [1917], GB181 SxMs56/1/28, VBRF 225.

151. Ibid.

152. Ibid.

153. Ibid.

154. V. Bell to R. Fry, [May 1917], GB181 SxMs56/1/28, VBRF 221.

155. See Richard Shone, *Bloomsbury Portraits: Vanessa Bell, Duncan Grant and Their Circle* (Oxford: Phaidon, 1976), p. 176; Frances Spalding, *Vanessa Bell* (London: Weidenfeld & Nicolson, 1983), pp. 170–71; Reed, *Bloomsbury Rooms*, pp. 193–5; and Mary Ann Caws, *Women of Bloomsbury: Virginia, Vanessa, and Carrington* (New York: Routledge, 1990), p. 171.

156. V. Bell to R. Fry, [January 1918], *SLVB*, p. 209.

157. 'The Tub', in Roger Fry, Duncan Grant, and Vanessa Bell, *Original Woodcuts by Various Artists* (London: Omega Workshops, 1918), edition of 75.

158. Reed, *Bloomsbury Rooms*, p. 195.

159. The other photograph is 'Mary Hutchinson in profile at Charleston', Anne Olivier Bell Gift, Charleston Trust Collection, uncatalogued. The door furniture in the photograph and the warped door frame indicate that the photograph was taken in the room now known as Clive Bell's Study, before the door was painted by Duncan Grant.

160. See also 'Vanessa, Quentin and Julian Bell at Charleston', c.1917, Anne Olivier Bell Gift, Charleston Trust Collection, uncatalogued.

161. The photograph is included in Vanessa Bell's photograph album CH 4 (TGA 9020/5), p. 3, with heading 'Charleston 1917'.

162. Shone, *The Art of Bloomsbury*, cat. no. 115, p. 193.

163. Bell wrote, 'It has got quite cold again . . . Your poppies looked rather withered but I don't think theyre really dead. The middles are green. Some of your tulips are only just dying now & the white blossom was lovely for a long time.' V. Bell to R. Fry, [May 1917], GB181 SxMs56/1/28, VBRF 221.

164. V. Woolf, 2 November 1917, *TDVW*, vol. 1, p. 69.

165. Bell wrote to Fry, 'When do you want pictures for the Omega show? I am trying to get my red haired woman finished & I shall send Duncan's wash stand & perhaps that up by Mabel on Monday if possible.' V. Bell to R. Fry, n.d. [19 October 1917], GB181 SxMs56/1/28, VBRF 243.

166. V. Woolf, 10 November 1917, *TDVW*, vol. 1, pp. 72–3.

167. Ibid., p. 73.

168. V. Woolf to V. Bell, 17 January 1918, *TLVW*, vol. 2, pp. 211–12.

169. V. Woolf to V. Bell, 29 January 1918, ibid., p. 214.

170. M. Hutchinson to V. Bell, 16 August 1917, GB181 SxMs56/1/112, MHVB 21.

171. Duncan Grant, *Vanessa Bell*, c.1916, oil and fabric collage, 915 × 610 mm, private collection of Mark Lancaster; reproduced in Shone, *The Art of Bloomsbury*, p. 193.

172. There are similarities between this pose and a photograph of *Reclining nude 1 (Aurora)*, a small Matisse bronze exhibited in the 1910 exhibition *Manet and the Post-Impressionists* and photographed for a review, 'Not Horrible Result of Golfing Swing but "Reclining Woman." By Matisse', in 'Anarchy in High Art', *Tatler*, 23 November 1910, p. 228.

173. The painting was listed in October 1919 as 'Portrait'; see Shone, *The Art of Bloomsbury*, cat. no. 114, p. 192.

174. Henry Lamb, *Portrait of Lytton Strachey*, 1914, oil on canvas, 2445 × 1784 mm, Tate T00118.

175. In this painting Bell appears to be wearing a similar dress to that in figure 52.

176. See Shone, *The Art of Bloomsbury*, cat. no. 122, pp. 201–3.

177. Fry wrote, 'the dressmaking is really a profit to the Omega now – we get nearly £2 a week out of it (which is really too much only it makes up for past deficiencies).' R. Fry to V. Bell, 21 February 1918, GB181 SxMs56/1/83, RFVB 130.

CHAPTER 4

1. L. Strachey to D. Carrington, 24 September 1925, *LLS*, p. 549.

2. Ibid.

3. Vanessa Bell, manuscript inventory of Charleston, c.1950, copy in Charleston Trust Collection, archive store box 1. When Bloomsbury artworks were exhibited the lenders were often recorded, as in *Duncan Grant: A Retrospective Exhibition*, exh. cat. (Tate Gallery, London, 1959).

4. Keynes and Grant had rooms at 21 Fitzroy Square from 1909 and moved to 38 Brunswick Square together in November 1911.

5. Frederick Etchells, *The Dead Mole*, 1912, oil on canvas, 1670 × 1060 mm, Fitzwilliam Museum, Cambridge, PCF13,

on loan from the Provost and Fellows of King's College, Cambridge (Keynes Collection).

6. See Richard Shone, *The Art of Bloomsbury: Roger Fry, Vanessa Bell and Duncan Grant*, exh. cat. (Tate Gallery, London, 1999), cat. no. 20, p. 83.

7. See *Second Post-Impressionist Exhibition: British, French and Russian Artists*, exh. cat. (Grafton Galleries, London, 1912); *The Queen of Sheba* was cat. no. 74, p. 32, and *The Dead Mole* cat. no. 103, p. 35. A copy of the catalogue is held in the Charleston Trust Collection, archive store box 12.

8. See Frances Spalding, *Duncan Grant* (London: Chatto & Windus, 1997), p. 121.

9. The portrait is in the *Second Post-Impressionist Exhibition* catalogue as cat. no. 107, p. 35. For a related portrait by the same artist, see Henry Lamb, *Lytton Strachey*, c.1913–14, oil on canvas, 590 × 460 mm, Fitzwilliam Museum, Cambridge, acc. no. 2748.

10. J. M. Keynes to V. Bell, 13 May 1921, GB181 SxMs56/1/124, MKVB 33; and scrapbook containing cards, press cuttings, and correspondence relating to Duncan Grant, 1910–31, Duncan Grant Collection, TGA 7243.

11. P. G. Konody, 'Art & Artists: English Post-Impressionists', *Observer*, 27 October 1912, p. 10.

12. P. G. Konody 'The Comic Cubists: Laughable Pictures at the Grafton Galleries', *Daily Mail*, 5 October 1912, p. 6.

13. Anon., 'The Post-Impressionists', *The Times*, 21 October 1912, p. 10.

14. Konody, 'Art & Artists: English Post-Impressionists.'

15. Rupert Brooke, 'The Post-Impressionists – II', *Cambridge Magazine*, 30 November 1912.

16. Ibid.

17. V. Bell to L. Woolf, 21 September [1912], *SLVB*, p. 127.

18. See *Second Post-Impressionist Exhibition*, cat. no. 1, pl. 1. A bronze cast of Henri Matisse's *Nu de dos I*, c.1909–10, 1899 × 1168 × 184 mm, is in the Tate Collection, no. T00081.

19. *Second Post-Impressionist Exhibition*, cat. no. 8, p. 24.

20. V. Bell to C. Bell, n.d. [September 1905], *SLVB*, p. 36; and V. Bell to J. M. Keynes, 5 December [1907], GB181 SxMs56/1/30, VBMK 2.

21. Ibid.; and V. Bell to J. M. Keynes, 7 December [1907], GB181 SxMs56/1/30, VBMK 1a.

22. V. Woolf to V. Dickinson, 9 November [1905], *TLVW*, vol. 1, p. 210.

23. V. Woolf to V. Dickinson, [3 December 1905], ibid., p. 213.

24. Richard Shone, 'The Friday Club', *Burlington Magazine*, vol. 117, no. 866 (1975), pp. 279–84 (at p. 280).

25. Work by Renoir and Pissarro was shown in 1908, drawings by Puvis de Chavannes in 1910, and drawings and lithographs by Daumier in 1911. See ibid., p. 280; and *Catalogue of an Exhibition of Pictures by Members of the Friday Club and of a Collection of Drawings and Lithographs by Honore Daumier* (Alpine Club Gallery, London, 1911). A copy of the catalogue is in the National Art Library, Victoria and Albert Museum, call no. 200.B.168. The purpose of these displays is discussed in Anon., 'Daumier's Lithographs and the Exhibition by Members of the Friday Club', *Athenaeum*, no. 4349 (4 March 1911), p. 255.

26. *Catalogue of an Exhibition of Pictures by Members of the Friday Club*, cat. nos. 68–118.

27. Randolph Schwabe, 'Reminiscences of Fellow Students', *Burlington Magazine*, vol. 82, no. 478 (1943), pp. 6–9 (at p. 9).

28. V. Bell to C. Bell, [23 June 1910], *SLVB*, pp. 92–3. Bell's rejected Studland Beach painting is Vanessa Bell, *Studland Beach*, c.1912, oil on canvas, 762 × 1016 mm, Tate T02080 <www.tate.org.uk/art/artworks/bell-studland-beach-verso-group-of-male-nudes-by-duncan-grant-t02080> (accessed 27 April 2020).

29. V. Bell to C. Bell, 24 June 1910, GB181 SxMs56/1/25, VBCB 29. Bell wrote, 'It's a birthday present for you', and that she 'considered the matter carefully for 2 days & 2 nights & thought that most likely Clarissa will bring in £1000'. Clarissa was her name for the baby. She compared the price (not given) with 'enough to buy a handsome dress, enough to buy a drawing by John'.

30. Duncan Grant, *The Lemon Gatherers*, 1910, oil on millboard, 565 × 813 mm, Tate N03666. The painting was exhibited at the *Friday Club*, Alpine Club Gallery, June 1910; *Twentieth Century Art*, Whitechapel Art Gallery, May–June 1914, cat. no. 329; and *The New Movement in Art*, Mansard Gallery, October 1917, cat. no. 35. Tate purchased it from Clive Bell in 1922.

31. Anon., 'Daumier's Lithographs', p. 255.

32. *Catalogue of an Exhibition of Pictures by Members of the Friday Club*. Gill exhibited with the Club for the first time in 1911 as a 'non-member'.

33. Anon., 'Our London Letter: The Grafton Group', *Manchester Courier*, 21 March 1913, p. 6.

34. Ibid.

35. Vanessa Bell, *Portrait of a Woman*, has not been identified. Though the screen shown in figure 149 is likely to be that exhibited in the Grafton Group exhibition of 1913 (named in the review as *Sheep*), the Victoria and Album Museum dates it slightly later, to 1915 (cat. no. CIRC.806-1966).

36. Claude Phillips, 'The Grafton Group', *Daily Telegraph*, 22 March 1913, p. 6.

37. Anon., 'Our London Letter: Dissension amongst Impressionists', *Manchester Courier*, 6 January 1914, p. 6.

38. Claude Phillips, 'More Post-Impressionism', *Daily Telegraph*, 5 January 1914, p. 8.

39. Phillips, 'The Grafton Group', p. 6. For a discussion of Kandinsky in this exhibition, see Anna Gruetzner Robins, 'The Company of Strangers: Max Weber and the First Grafton Group Exhibition', in Sarah MacDougall (ed.), *Max Weber: An American Cubist in Paris and London 1905–15* (London: Lund Humphries, 2014), pp. 58–105 (at p. 68).

40. See V. Bell to D. Grant, [5 March 1914], *SLVB*, p. 157.

41. 'The diminished Grafton Group' was defined by Phillips, 'More Post-Impressionism', p. 8. Exhibitors were listed as Vanessa Bell, Roger Fry, Duncan Grant, Winifred Gill, Nina Hamnett, William Roberts, Charles Tabley, Henri Doucet, C. Vibette, J. Marchand, O. Friesz, Henri Gaudier-Brzeska, and Picasso (whose works were on loan), in Anon., 'Our London Letter: Dissension amongst Impressionists', p. 6.

42. *The Grafton Group: Vanessa Bell, Roger Fry, Duncan Grant; Second Exhibition*, exh. cat. (Alpine Club Gallery, London, 1914), cat. nos. 22 and 26A. A copy of the catalogue is in the National Art Library, Victoria and Albert Museum, call no. 200.B.5.15.
43. The painting is inscribed on the back, 'Galerie Barbazanges . . . par Vanessa Bell (Mme)'. It was shown in *Exposition de quelques indépendants anglais*, Galerie Barbazanges, Paris, 1912.
44. Duncan Grant, *The Dancers*, 1912, oil on canvas, 710 × 920 mm, private collection. This is a later and larger version of the painting now in the Tate's collection, N06181. Bell described the installation in a postcard to Grant: V. Bell to D. Grant, [French postmark 30 April 1912, English postmark 2 May 1912], TGA 20078/1/44/7.
45. D. Grant to V. Woolf, 23 September 1912, Monk's House Papers, GB181 SxMs18/1/D/62/1.
46. Vanessa Bell, *Frederick and Jessie Etchells Painting*, 1912, oil on board, 511 × 530 mm, Tate T01277; and Vanessa Bell, *The Studio: Duncan Grant and Henri Doucet at Asheham*, 1912, oil on board, 572 × 445 mm, private collection, reproduced in Christopher Reed, *Bloomsbury Rooms: Modernism, Subculture, and Domesticity* (New Haven, CT, and London: Yale University Press, 2004), p. 89.
47. Duncan Grant, *Adam and Eve*, 1913, oil on canvas, approx. 2130 × 3350 mm, lost or destroyed; illustrated in Shone, *The Art of Bloomsbury*, p. 29.
48. V. Bell to D. Grant, 14 January [1914], SLVB, pp. 153–4. Her description includes an account of Jacques and Gwen Raverat's response to the painting.
49. Vanessa Bell, *Portrait of Molly MacCarthy*, 1912, oil on panel, 584 × 432 mm, private collection. Vanessa Bell, *Mrs Desmond MacCarthy*, was exhibited in the second Grafton Group exhibition as cat. no. 34. The portrait was 'Not for Sale'.
50. Vanessa Bell, *Tents*, is listed in the catalogue for the second Grafton Group exhibition as cat. no. 19, for sale at £10. No further details about this painting are known.
51. Phillips, 'More Post-Impressionism', p. 8.
52. Ibid.
53. The painting's title comes from the catalogue for the second Grafton Group exhibition, where it is listed as cat. no. 33. The painting was 'Not for Sale'.
54. Reed, *Bloomsbury Rooms*, pp. 31–4; and Frances Spalding, *Vanessa Bell* (London: Weidenfeld & Nicolson, 1983), pp. 124–5 and 127.
55. Phillips, 'More Post-Impressionism', p. 8.
56. G. R. H., 'The Grafton Group at the Alpine Gallery', *Pall Mall Gazette*, 8 January 1914, p. 5.
57. V. Bell to D. Grant, 14 January [1914], SLVB, p. 153.
58. *Twentieth Century Art: A Review of Modern Movements; Summer Exhibition*, exh. cat. (Whitechapel Art Gallery, London, 8 May–20 June 1914), p. 26. Vanessa Bell, *Women and Baby* (lender Roger Fry, Esq.) is cat. no. 12. The painting's subject may have had resonance for Fry because of his time caring for Bell after her miscarriage in Broussa.
59. *Women and Baby* was the lead image for Roger Fry, 'The Work of a Woman Painter: Vanessa Bell', *Vogue* [London], early February 1926, pp. 33–5, 78. It is also visible in photographs of the interior of Durbins in Roger Fry, 'A Possible Domestic Architecture', *Vogue* [London], late March 1918, pp. 40–41, 66, 68 (photographs by A. C. Cooper).
60. For an analysis of this display of Fry's collection, see Reed, *Bloomsbury Rooms*, pp. 43–6.
61. Claude Phillips, 'Art in Whitechapel: Twentieth Century Exhibition', *Daily Telegraph*, 12 May 1914, p. 14.
62. Ibid.
63. For an analysis of the positioning of the Whitechapel exhibition as a survey of British modernism, see Lisa Tickner, *Modern Life and Modern Subjects: British Art in the Early Twentieth Century* (New Haven, CT, and London: Yale University Press, 2000), pp. 1–9.
64. Ibid., pp. 143–83.
65. Duncan Grant, *Slops*, 1913, oil on canvas, dimensions unknown, private collection.
66. Phillips, 'Art in Whitechapel', p. 14.
67. See Whitechapel Gallery, *Twentieth Century Art*, p. 26. Duncan Grant, *The Queen of Sheba*, is cat. no. 364; Henry Lamb, *Portrait of Lytton Strachey*, is cat. no. 366.
68. Phillips, 'Art in Whitechapel', p. 14.
69. Ibid.
70. V. Woolf to V. Dickinson, 24 December [1912], *TLVW*, vol. 2, pp. 14–15. For an analysis of Woolf and Post-Impressionism, see Ann Banfield, 'Time Passes: Virginia Woolf, Post-Impressionism, and Cambridge Time', *Poetics Today*, vol. 24, no. 3 (2003), pp. 471–516.
71. Duncan Grant, *Parrot Tulips*, 1911, oil on canvas, 520 × 490 mm, was exhibited at the Second Camden Town Group Exhibition, Carfax Gallery, 1911; it is now in Southampton Art Gallery. Grant also exhibited three works at the Vorticist Exhibition, Doré Galleries, London, 1915.
72. V. Bell to R. Fry, 4 January [1916], GB181 SxMs56/1/28, VBRF 189.
73. Bell made a gift of this painting to Joy Brown; see Shone, *The Art of Bloomsbury*, cat. no. 47, p. 119.
74. W. Gill to A. Bowness, 4 February 1959, TGA 8022.6. For a detailed account of Omega flowers, see Wendy Hitchmough, 'Omega Flowers', *Charleston Press*, no. 3 (2019), pp. 72–9.
75. See Judith Collins, *The Omega Workshops* (London: Secker and Warburg, 1983), pp. 125–7.
76. W. Sickert, 'A Monthly Chronicle: O Matre Pulchrâ', *Burlington Magazine for Connoisseurs*, vol. 29, no. 157 (April 1916), p. 35.
77. Anon., 'The Omega Workshops', *The Times*, 11 February 1916, p. 9.
78. V. Bell to D. Grant, 25 March 1914, SLVB, p. 162.
79. V. Bell to O. Morrell, [17 March 1916], ibid., p. 192.
80. Ibid.
81. V. Bell to R. Fry, n.d. [2–4 June 1917], GB181 SxMs56/1/28, VBRF 226.
82. J. M. Keynes to D. Grant, 13 May 1917, GB181 SxMs56/1/125, JMKDG 2.
83. Grant's *Detail from Piero della Francesca*, c.1906, Keynes

Bequest, King's College, Cambridge. *Exhibition of Copies and Translations*, Omega Workshops, May 1917, is discussed in Richard Howells, 'Copies and Translations: Roger Fry, Old Masters and the Omega Workshops', *The British Art Journal*, vol. 16, no. 1 (2015), pp. 47–57.
84. J. M. Keynes to D. Grant, 13 May 1917, GB181 SxMs56/1/125, JMKDG 2.
85. See Collins, *The Omega Workshops*, p. 152.
86. Fry described this as 'a terrific pie-jaw which kept 'em quiet for a bit'; R. Fry to V. Bell, 20 July 1917, in *Letters of Roger Fry*, ed. Denys Sutton (London: Chatto & Windus, 1972), p. 414.
87. R. Fry to V. Bell, 27 August 1917, ibid., p. 415.
88. Duncan Grant, *Venus and Adonis*, c.1919, oil on canvas, 635 × 940 mm, Tate T01514.
89. Shone, *The Art of Bloomsbury*, cat. no. 35, pp. 103–5.
90. Quoted in Shone, *The Art of Bloomsbury*. See also the Tate catalogue entry for this painting, <www.tate.org.uk/art/artworks/bell-mrs-st-john-hutchinson-t01768> (accessed 27 April 2020).
91. V. Bell to R. Fry, 29 October [1919], SxMs56/1/28 VBRF 296.
92. Augustus John, *The Childhood of Pyramus*, c.1908, oil on canvas, 1206 × 1505 mm, Johannesburg Art Gallery.
93. V. Bell to V. Woolf, [19 October 1911], SLVB, p. 109.
94. Pablo Picasso, *Pots et citron*, 1907, oil on canvas, 550 × 460 mm, Albertina Museum, Vienna, Batliner Collection, GE96DL; reproduced in Clive Bell, *Art* (London: Chatto & Windus, 1914), p. 294. See James Beechey and Chris Stephens, *Picasso and Modern British Art* (London: Tate, 2012), cat. no. 2, p. 55.
95. The vase is item CHA/C/185 in the Charleston Trust Collection.
96. This 550,000 francs, then the equivalent of approximately £20,000, was transferred to the British Embassy account in Paris. Bell complained that the Director of the National Gallery, Charles Holmes, returned with £5,000 unspent, although his acquisitions included paintings by Delacroix, Ingres, Corot, Gauguin, and Manet. See V. Bell to R. Fry, [3 April 1918], SLVB, p. 213. The National Gallery Acquisitions File for works purchased at the sale, with hand-written notes by Holmes, is archive reference number NG14/25/1.
97. J. M. Keynes to V. Bell, 23 March 1918, GB181 SxMs56/1/124, MKVB 14.
98. Ibid.
99. Paul Cézanne, *Still Life with Apples*, c.1878, oil on canvas, 190 × 270 mm, Fitzwilliam Museum, Cambridge, PCF6, on loan from the Provost and Fellows of King's College, Cambridge (Keynes Collection).
100. V. Bell to R. Fry, [3 April 1918], SLVB, p. 213.
101. Ibid.
102. V. Woof to N. Bagenal, 15 April 1918, TLVW, vol. 2, p. 230. Woolf miscounted the apples.
103. Ibid.
104. The facts of the anecdote are outlined in V. Bell to R. Fry, [3 April 1918], SLVB, p. 213. See also Q. Bell, 'A Cézanne in the Hedge', in Hugh Lee (ed.) *A Cézanne in the Hedge* (London: Collins & Brown, 1992), pp. 136–9.

105. *Too Much Money* opened at the Royal Theatre, Glasgow, before transferring to the Ambassadors Theatre, London, on 9 April 1918. See *Letters of Roger Fry*, ed. Sutton, pp. 424–5.
106. Israel Zangwill, *Too Much Money: A Farcical Comedy in Three Acts* (London: William Heinemann, 1924), p. 1.
107. R. Fry to P. Fry, 16 February 1918, in *Letters of Roger Fry*, ed. Sutton, p. 425.
108. Arnold Bennett, *The Pretty Lady* (London: Cassell, 1918), pp. 168–71. Fry is also named as the designer proposed for a First Aid Station at a pageant: 'I shall get Roger Fry to design the Station and the costumes of my attendants' (p. 234).
109. Fry wrote: 'We've started a sort of evening club at the Omega; it meets once a week and is a great success . . . Yeats and Arnold Bennett came last night.' R. Fry to P. Fry, 2 March 1917, in *Letters of Roger Fry*, ed. Sutton, p. 404. He described the Club and its members to Max Beerbohm, too: R. Fry to M. Beerbohm, 11 May 1917, ibid., p. 411.
110. R. Fry to P. Fry, 2 March 1917, ibid., p. 404.
111. Bennett, *The Pretty Lady*, p. 170.
112. Osbert Sitwell, *Laughter in the Next Room* (London: Macmillan, 1949), p. 18.
113. L. Strachey to D. Carrington, 22 July 1917, LLS, p. 360.
114. V. Woolf, 5 April 1918, TDVW, vol. 1, p. 131.
115. L. Strachey to D. Carrington, ? September 1920, LLS, p. 471.
116. L. Strachey to J. Strachey, 10 September 1920, ibid., p. 473.
117. L. Strachey to D. Carrington, ? September 1920, ibid., p. 471.
118. L. Strachey to J. Strachey, 10 September 1920, ibid., p. 473.
119. Ibid.
120. V. Woolf, 31 January 1919, TDVW, vol. 1, p. 238.
121. V. Woolf, 23 July 1927, ibid., vol. 3, p. 147.
122. MHP (MS Thr 564), (55). See also Louis Kronenberger, 'Virginia Woolf Explores an English Country Home', *New York Times Book Review*, 8 May 1927, p. 2. The photograph was also published in C. S. and M. A., 'The Bookshelf', *Bookshelf Review*, June 1927, p. 37 <www.woolfonline.com/?node=content/contextual/> (accessed 27 April 2020).
123. V. Woolf, 13 February 1920, TDVW, vol. 2, p. 18.
124. V. Bell to J. M. Keynes, 19 March [1919], GB181 SxMs56/1/30, VBMK 52.
125. See Spalding, *Duncan Grant*, pp. 224–5.
126. V. Woolf to D. Grant, 11 February 1920, TLVW, vol. 2, pp. 421–2. 'Mr Clifton' in Woolf's letter was Arthur Bellamy Clifton, owner of the Carfax Gallery.
127. V. Woolf, 13 February 1920, TDVW, vol. 2, p. 18.
128. The watercolour is inscribed: <u>Significant Form</u> Mr Clive Bell: "I always think that when one feels one's been carrying a theory too far, <u>then</u>'s the time to carry it a little further." Mr Roger Fry: "A <u>little</u>? Good heavens man! Are you growing old?"' It is item CHA/P/314 in the Charleston Trust Collection.
129. L. Strachey to J. Strachey, 14 April 1921, LLS, p. 485.
130. See Nino Strachey, *Rooms of Their Own* (London: Pitkin, 2018), pp. 26–8.
131. L. Strachey to S. Tomlin, 1 December 1929, quoted in Oliver Garnett, 'The Sculpture of Stephen Tomlin', unpublished

undergraduate thesis presented at the University of Cambridge, 1979, p. 31.
132. Stephen Tomlin, *Lytton Strachey*, bronze, 420 × 240 × 220 mm, Tate N04616. One of three casts, it was accepted soon after Strachey's death in 1932. Strachey's own cast of the bust and a lead cast are both in private collections.
133. V. Woolf to D. Bussy, 22 July 1931, *TLVW*, vol. 4, p. 360.
134. V. Woolf to V. Bell, 23 July 1931, ibid.
135. V. Woolf, 17 July 1931, *TDVW*, vol. 4, p. 35.
136. See V. Woolf to E. Smyth, 28 July 1931, *TLVW*, vol. 4, pp. 362–3.
137. V. Bell to J. Bell, 29 July 1931, *SLVB*, p. 366; and V. Woolf, 7 August 1931, *TDVW*, vol. 4, p. 37.
138. Stephen Tomlin, *Virginia Woolf*, 1953, based on a work of 1931, lead, 400 × 390 mm, National Portrait Gallery, London, NPG 3882.
139. The photograph is MHP (MS Thr 564), (6).
140. Cyril Connolly, 'Orpheus in Bloomsbury: A Music Room Decorated, Furnished and Painted by Vanessa Bell and Duncan Grant', *Architectural Review*, vol. 73 (February 1933), pp. 74–5.
141. Reed, *Bloomsbury Rooms*, p. 272.
142. See Derek Patmore, *Colour Schemes for the Modern Home* (London: The Studio, 1933), pl. 15, reprinted in a new edition as *Colour Schemes and Modern Furnishing* in 1945.
143. V. Woolf, 4 December 1932, *TDVW*, vol. 4, p. 131; Connolly, 'Orpheus in Bloomsbury', p. 75.
144. V. Woolf to O. Morrell, [25 November 1932], *TLVW*, vol. 5, p. 130.
145. V. Woolf, 4 December 1932, *TDVW*, vol. 4, p. 131.
146. V. Woolf to D. Grant, [24 November 1932], *TLVW*, vol. 5, p. 129.
147. The painting is signed and dated 1934. Vanessa Bell wrote to Quentin Bell on 5 March 1934, just before the exhibition opened, that her studio was 'now beautifully empty, and I feel free to do whatever I like', making it likely that the portrait was painted specifically for the Lefevre Galleries exhibition that opened on 7 March; V. Bell to Q. Bell, 5 March [1934], *SLVB*, p. 379.
148. V. Woolf to Q. Bell, 8 March 1934, *TLVW*, vol. 5, p. 281.
149. The purchase of the painting at the private view was explained by the current owner to the author. She inherited the painting from its original owner, her grandmother. Woolf's photograph of the painting is MHP (MS Thr 564), (77).
150. V. Woolf, 4 March 1934, *TDVW*, vol. 4, p. 203.
151. V. Woolf to Q. Bell, 8 March 1934, *TLVW*, vol. 5, p. 282.

BIBLIOGRAPHY

Alpine Club Gallery, *Catalogue of an Exhibition of Pictures by Members of the Friday Club and of a Collection of Drawings and Lithographs by Honore Daumier*, exh. cat., London: Alpine Club Gallery, 1911 (National Art Library, Victoria and Albert Museum, call no. 200.B.168)

———, *The Grafton Group*, exh. cat., London: Alpine Club Gallery, 1913

———, *The Grafton Group: Vanessa Bell, Roger Fry, Duncan Grant; Second Exhibition*, exh. cat., London: Alpine Club Gallery, 1914 (National Art Library, Victoria and Albert Museum, call no. 200.B.5.15)

Anand, Mulk Raj, *Conversations in Bloomsbury*, London: Wildwood House, 1981

Anon., 'Anarchy in High Art', *Tatler*, 23 November 2010, p. 228

———, 'The Art of Duncan Grant', *Vogue* [London], late February 1923, pp. 50–51, 70

———, 'A Bachelor Flat in Bloomsbury', *Vogue* [London], late April 1925, pp. 44–5

———, 'The Contemporary Style of Decoration', *Vogue* [London], early January 1924, pp. 50–51, 74

———, 'Daumier's Lithographs and the Exhibition by Members of the Friday Club', *Athenaeum*, no. 4349 (4 March 1911), p. 255

———, 'An Economist and Modern Art: The Cambridge Rooms of Mr Keynes', *Vogue* [London], early March 1925, pp. 46–7

———, 'The Father of Post-Impressionism', *Pall Mall Gazette*, 4 October 1912, p. 10

———, 'The Grafton Group', *Pall Mall Gazette*, 27 March 1913, p. 4

———, 'The Grafton Group', *The Times*, 20 March 1913, p. 4

———, 'The Grafton Group at the Alpine Club Gallery', *Athenaeum*, 10 January 1914, p. 70

———, 'A Harmony of the Furnishing of Two Centuries at River House', *Vogue* [London], early February 1919, pp. 40–41

———, 'Manet and the Post-Impressionists', *Athenaeum*, 12 November 1910, pp. 598–9

———, 'Modern Embroidery', *Vogue* [London], late October 1923, pp. 66–7, 78

———, 'Modern English Decoration: Some Examples of the Interesting Work of Duncan Grant and Vanessa Bell', *Vogue* [London], early November 1924, pp. 43–5, 106

———, 'A New Venture in Art: Exhibition at the Omega Workshops', *The Times*, 9 July 1913, p. 4

———, 'The Omega Workshops', *The Times*, 11 February 1916, p. 9

———, 'The Omega Workshops: Decorative Form and Colour', *The Times*, 10 December 1913, p. 13

———, 'Our London Letter: Dissension amongst Impressionists', *Manchester Courier*, 6 January 1914, p. 6

———, 'Our London Letter: The Grafton Group', *Manchester Courier*, 21 March 1913, p. 6

———, 'The Post-Impressionists', *The Times*, 21 October 1912, p. 10

Anscombe, Isabelle, *Omega and After: Bloomsbury and the Decorative Arts*, London: Thames & Hudson, 1981

Anthony d'Offay Gallery, *The Omega Workshops: Alliance and Enmity in English Art, 1911–1920*, exh. cat., London: Anthony d'Offay Gallery, 1984

———, *Vanessa Bell: Paintings from Charleston*, exh. cat., London: Anthony d'Offay Gallery, 1979

Arts Council, *Vanessa Bell, 1879–1961: A Memorial Exhibition of Paintings*, exh. cat., London: Arts Council Gallery, 1964

Banfield, Ann, 'Time Passes: Virginia Woolf, Post-Impressionism, and Cambridge Time', *Poetics Today*, vol. 24, no. 3 (2003), pp. 471–516

Baron, Wendy, *The Camden Town Group*, London: Scolar Press, 1979

———, *Sickert: Paintings and Drawings*, New Haven, CT, and London: Yale University Press, 2006

Baumeister, Roy, and Mark Leary, 'The Need to Belong: Desire for Interpersonal Attachments as a Fundamental Human Motivation', *Psychological Bulletin*, vol. 117, no. 3 (1995), pp. 497–529

Beechey, James, and Chris Stephens, *Picasso and Modern British Art*, London: Tate, 2012

Bell, Clive, *An Account of French Painting*, London: Chatto & Windus, 1932

———, *Art*, London: Chatto & Windus, 1914

———, *Civilization: An Essay*, London: Chatto & Windus, 1928

———, 'Duncan Grant', *New Statesman and Athenaeum*, 19 May 1934, pp. 763–4

———, 'The English Group', introduction to the *Second Post-Impressionist Exhibition*, exh. cat., London: Grafton Galleries, 1912

———, 'The French Pictures at Heal's', *Nation*, 16 August 1919, pp. 586–8

———, 'Inside the "Queen Mary"', *The Listener*, 8 April 1936, pp. 658–60

———, 'The London Group and Sargent', *Vogue* [London], late February 1926, pp. 54–5, 80

———, *Old Friends: Personal Recollections*, London: Chatto & Windus, 1956

———, *Peace at Once*, London: National Labour Press, 1915

———, *Pot-Boilers*, London: Chatto & Windus, 1918

———, *Since Cézanne*, London: Chatto & Windus, 1922

Bell, Quentin, *Bloomsbury*, London: Weidenfeld & Nicolson, 1968

———, *Elders and Betters*, London: John Murray, 1995

———, 'Foreword: Charleston Preserved', in Quentin Bell, Angelica Garnett, Henrietta Garnett, and Richard Shone, *Charleston Past and Present*, London: Hogarth Press, 1987, pp. 7–16

———, 'The Omega Revisited', *The Listener*, 30 January 1964, pp. 200–01

———, *Virginia Woolf: A Biography*, London: Pimlico, 1996

———, *Virginia Woolf: A Biography*, vol. 1: *Virginia Stephen, 1882–1912*, London: Hogarth Press, 1972

———, *Virginia Woolf: A Biography*, vol. 2: *Mrs Woolf, 1912–41*, London: Hogarth Press, 1973

Bell, Quentin, and Stephen Chaplin, 'The Ideal Home Rumpus', *Apollo*, October 1964, pp. 284–91

Bell, Quentin, and Angelica Garnett, *Vanessa Bell's Family Album*, London: Jill Norman & Hobhouse, 1981

Bell, Quentin, and Virginia Nicholson, *Charleston: A Bloomsbury House and Garden*, London: Frances Lincoln, 1997

Bell, Vanessa, *Catalogue of Recent Paintings by Vanessa Bell*, with a foreword by Virginia Woolf, London: Alex, Reid and Lefevre, 1934

———, 'Notes on Bloomsbury' [1951], in S. P. Rosenbaum (ed.), *The Bloomsbury Group: A Collection of Memoirs, Commentary and Criticism*, London: Croom Helm, 1975, pp. 74–84

———, *Selected Letters of Vanessa Bell*, ed. Regina Marler, New York: Pantheon, 1993

———, *Sketches in Pen and Ink*, ed. Lia Giachero, London: Hogarth Press, 1997

Benjamin, Walter, 'A Short History of Photography', *Screen*, vol. 13, no. 1 (1972), pp. 5–26

Bennett, Arnold, *The Pretty Lady*, London: Cassell, 1918

Billig, Michael, and Henri Tajfel, 'Social Categorization and Similarity in Intergroup Behaviour', *European Journal of Social Psychology*, vol. 3, no. 1 (1973), pp. 27–52

Blair, Sara, 'Local Modernity, Global Modernism: Bloomsbury and the Places of the Literary', *English Literary History*, vol. 71, no. 3 (2004), pp. 813–38

Blythe, Robert J., Andrew Lambert, and Jan Rüger, *The Dreadnought and the Edwardian Age*, Farnham: Ashgate, 2011

Bowman, Sara, and Michel Molinare, *A Fashion for Extravagance: Art Deco Fabrics and Fashions*, New York: E. P. Dutton, 1985

Boyd, Elizabeth French, *Bloomsbury Heritage: Their Mothers and Their Aunts*, London: Taplinger, 1976

Boyd Haycock, David, *A Crisis of Brilliance: Five Young British Artists and the Great War*, London: Old Street Publishing, 2009

Breward, Christopher, 'Cultures, Identities, Histories: Fashioning a Cultural Approach to Dress', *Fashion Theory*, vol. 2, no. 4 (1998), pp. 301–13

Brewer, John, *The Pleasures of the Imagination: The Emergence of English Culture in the Eighteenth Century*, London: Harper Collins, 1997

Brockington, Grace, *Above the Battlefield: Modernism and the Peace Movement in Britain, 1900–1918*, New Haven, CT, and London: Yale University Press, 2010

———, '"A Lavender Talent" or "The Most Important Woman Painter in Europe"? Reassessing Vanessa Bell', *Art History*, vol. 36, no. 1 (2013), pp. 128–53

———, 'Relationships: Formal, Creative and Political', in her *In Focus: 'Abstract Painting' c.1914 by Vanessa Bell*, Tate Research Publications (2017) <www.tate.org.

uk/research/publications/in-focus/abstract-painting-vanessa-bell/relationships> (accessed 27 April 2020)

Brooke, Rupert, 'The Post-Impressionists – II', *Cambridge Magazine*, 30 November 1912

Bullen, J. B. (ed.), *Post-Impressionists in England: The Critical Reception*, London: Routledge, 1988

Bywater, William G., *Clive Bell's Eye*, Detroit: Wayne State University Press, 1975

Caine, Barbara, 'Bloomsbury Masculinity and Its Victorian Antecedents', *Journal of Men's Studies*, vol. 15, no. 3 (2007), pp. 271–81

———, *Bombay to Bloomsbury: A Biography of the Strachey Family*, Oxford: Oxford University Press, 2005

Carrington, Dora, *Carrington's Letters*, ed. Anne Chisholm, London: Vintage Digital, 2017

Caughie, Pamela (ed.), *Virginia Woolf in the Age of Mechanical Reproduction*, New York: Garland, 2000

Caws, Mary Ann, *Women of Bloomsbury: Virginia, Vanessa, and Carrington*, New York: Routledge, 1990

Caws, Mary Ann, and Sarah Bird Wright, *Bloomsbury and France: Art and Friends*, Oxford: Oxford University Press, 2000

Cecil, Hugh, and Mirabel Cecil, *Clever Hearts: Desmond and Molly MacCarthy, A Biography*, London: Victor Gollancz, 1990

Chisholm, Anne, *Frances Partridge: The Biography*, London: Weidenfeld & Nicolson, 2009

Clarke, Darren, 'Some Contemporary Responses to the Omega', in A. Gerstein (ed.), *Beyond Bloomsbury: Designs of the Omega Workshops, 1913–19*, exh. cat., London: Courtauld Gallery, 2009, pp. 78–9

Clarke, Meaghan, and Francesco Ventrella, 'Women's Expertise and the Culture of Connoisseurship', *Visual Resources*, vol. 33, nos 1–2 (2017), pp. 1–10

Clutton-Brock, Alan, 'Mr Roger Fry', *Athenaeum*, 18 June 1920, pp. 805–6

Cohen, Lisa, '"Frock Consciousness": Virginia Woolf, the Open Secret, and the Language of Fashion', *Fashion Theory*, vol. 3, no. 2 (1999), pp. 149–74

Collins, Judith, *The Omega Workshops*, London: Secker and Warburg, 1983

Collins, Judith, and Fiona MacCarthy, *The Omega Workshops, 1913–19: Decorative Arts of Bloomsbury*, exh. cat., London: Crafts Council, 1984

Colmer, John, *E. M. Forster: The Personal Voice*, London: Routledge & Kegan Paul, 1975

Connolly, Cyril, 'Orpheus in Bloomsbury: A Music Room Decorated, Furnished and Painted by Vanessa Bell and Duncan Grant', *Architectural Review*, vol. 73, February 1933, pp. 74–5

Constable, W. G., 'Lotiron, Duncan Grant and Vanessa Bell', *The Burlington Magazine for Connoisseurs*, vol. 37, no. 213 (1920), pp. 325–7

Cork, Richard, *Art Beyond the Gallery in Early Twentieth-Century England*, New Haven, CT: Yale University Press, 1985

———, *A Bitter Truth: Avant-Garde Art and the Great War*, New Haven, CT: Yale University Press, 1994

Cox, Julian, and Colin Ford, *Julia Margaret Cameron: The Complete Photographs*, London: Thames & Hudson in association with the J. Paul Getty Museum, 2003

Cunningham, Patricia, *Reforming Women's Fashion, 1850–1920*, Kent, OH: Kent State University Press, 2003

Davies, Randall, 'The Grafton Group', *New Statesman*, 10 January 1914, pp. 436–7

Delany, Paul, *Fatal Glamour: The Life of Rupert Brooke*, Montreal: McGill-Queens University Press, 2015

———, *The Neo-Pagans: Rupert Brooke and the Ordeal of Youth*, New York: Free Press, 1987

Di Bello, Patrizia, *Women's Albums and Photographs in Victorian England: Ladies, Mothers and Flirts*, Aldershot: Ashgate, 2007

Dickens, Charles, 'The Carte de Visite', *All the Year Round*, vol. 7 (26 April 1862), pp. 165–8 <www.djo.org.uk/all-the-year-round/volume-vii/page-166.html> (accessed 27 April 2020)

Dickie, George, 'Clive Bell and the Method of *Principia Ethica*', *British Journal of Aesthetics*, vol. 5, no. 2 (1965), pp. 139–43

Dunn, Jane, *A Very Close Conspiracy: Vanessa Bell and Virginia Woolf*, London: Jonathan Cape, 1990

Edel, Leon, *Bloomsbury: A House of Lions*, New York: Avon Books, 1980

Edwards, Elizabeth, and Christopher Morton, *Photographs, Museums, Collections: Between Art and Information*, London: Bloomsbury, 2015

Elder, Glen Jr, and Elizabeth Clipp, 1988, 'Wartime Losses and Social Bonding: Influences across 40 Years in Men's Lives', *Psychiatry*, vol. 51, no. 2, pp. 177–98

Elkin, Lauren, 'Bloomsbury and Feminism', in Derek Ryan and Stephen Ross (eds), *The Handbook to the Bloomsbury Group*, London: Bloomsbury Academic, 2018, pp. 109–20

———, *Flâneuse: Women Walk the City*, London: Chatto & Windus, 2016

Falkenheim, Jacqueline, *Roger Fry and the Beginnings of Formalist Art Criticism*, Ann Arbor: UMI Research Press, 1980

Fassler, Barbara, 'Theories of Homosexuality as Sources for Bloomsbury's Androgyny', *Signs*, vol. 3, no. 2 (1979), pp. 237–51

Festinger, Leon, Stanley Schachter, and Kurt Black, *Social Pressures in Informal Groups: A Study of Human Factors in Housing*, Stanford, CA: Stanford University Press, 1950

Forster, E. M., *Virginia Woolf*, Cambridge: Cambridge University Press, 1942

Foster, J. Ashley, 'Bloomsbury and War', in Derek Ryan and Stephen Ross (eds), *The Handbook to the Bloomsbury Group*, London: Bloomsbury Academic, 2018, pp. 277–93

Frost, Abigail, 'Omega Anonymous', *Crafts*, vol. 66 (1984), pp. 40–44

Froula, Christine, *Virginia Woolf and the Bloomsbury Avant-Garde: War, Civilization, Modernity*, New York: Columbia University Press, 2005

Fry, Roger, *Catalogue of an Exhibition of Works Representative of the New Movement in Art, Selected and Arranged by Mr. Roger Fry*, exh. cat., London: Mansard Galleries, [1917]

———, *Cézanne: A Study of his Development* [1927], Chicago: University of Chicago Press, 1989

———, *Characteristics of French Art*, London: Chatto & Windus, 1932

———, *Duncan Grant*, London: Hogarth Press, 1923

———, *Exhibition of Omega Copies and Translations*, London: Omega Workshops, 1917

———, *Flemish Art: A Critical Study*, London: Chatto & Windus, 1927

———, 'The Friends' Work for War Victims in France', *Charleston*, no. 12, Autumn/Winter 1995, pp. 22–4

———, *Last Lectures*, Cambridge: Cambridge University Press, 1939

———, *Letters of Roger Fry*, ed. Denys Sutton, London: Chatto & Windus, 1972, 2 vols

———, 'Mr. Duncan Grant's Pictures at Patterson's Gallery', *New Statesman*, 21 February 1920, pp. 586–7

———, 'A Possible Domestic Architecture', *Vogue* [London], late March 1918, pp. 40–41, 66, 68

———, *Reflections on British Painting* [1934], Freeport, NY: Books for Libraries Press, 1969

———, *Transformations: Critical and Speculative Essays on Art*, London: Chatto & Windus, 1926

———, *Vision and Design*, London: Chatto & Windus, 1920

———, 'What To Do with Our Artists', *The Bystander*, 10 December 1913, p. 608

———, 'The Work of a Woman Painter: Vanessa Bell', *Vogue* [London], early February 1926, pp. 33–5, 78

Fry, Roger, Duncan Grant, and Vanessa Bell, *Original Woodcuts by Various Artists*, London: Omega Workshops, 1918

Fry, Roger, et al., *Georgian Art (1760–1820): An Introductory Review of English Painting, Architecture, Sculpture, Ceramics, Glass, Metalwork, Furniture, Textiles and Other Arts during the Reign of George III*, London: Batsford, 1929

Furbank, Philip N., *E. M. Forster: A Life*, New York: Harvest/Harcourt Brace Jovanovich, 1978

G. R. H., 'The Grafton Group at the Alpine Gallery', *Pall Mall Gazette*, 8 January 1914, p. 5

Gallery Edward Havane, *A Homage to Duncan Grant*, exh. cat., London: Gallery Edward Havane, 1975

Garland, Madge, 'Recollections of Virginia Woolf', in Joan Russell Noble (ed.), *Recollections of Virginia Woolf*, London: Peter Owen, 1972, pp. 171–4

———, 'A Room Decorated by Duncan Grant and Vanessa Bell', *The Studio*, vol. 100, no. 449 (1930), pp. 142–3

Garnett, Angelica, *Deceived with Kindness: A Bloomsbury Childhood*, London: Chatto & Windus/The Hogarth Press, 1984

Garnett, David, *The Familiar Faces*, London: Chatto & Windus, 1962

———, *The Flowers of the Forest*, London: Chatto & Windus, 1955

———, *The Golden Echo*. London: Chatto & Windus, 1953

———, 'War Victims' Relief', in Julian Bell (ed.), *We Did Not Fight: 1914–1918 Experiences of War Resisters*, London: Cobden-Sanderson, 1935, pp. 129–40

Garnett, Henrietta, 'Visits to Charleston: Vanessa', in Quentin Bell, Angelica Garnett, Henrietta Garnett, and Richard Shone, *Charleston Past and Present*, London: Hogarth Press, 1987, pp. 135–160

Garnett, Richard, *Constance Garnett: A Heroic Life*, London: Sinclair-Stevenson, 1991

Garrity, Jane, 'Selling Culture to the "Civilized": Bloomsbury, British *Vogue*, and the Marketing of National Identity', *Modernism/Modernity*, vol. 6, no. 2 (1999), pp. 29–58

———, 'Virginia Woolf and Fashion', in Maggie Humm (ed.), *The Edinburgh Companion to Virginia Woolf and the Arts*, Edinburgh: Edinburgh University Press, 2010, pp. 195–211

———, 'Virginia Woolf, Intellectual Harlotry, and 1920s British *Vogue*', in Pamela Caughie (ed.), *Virginia Woolf in the Age of Mechanical Reproduction*, New York: Garland, 2000, pp. 185–218

Gerstein, Alexandra (ed.), *Beyond Bloomsbury: Designs of the Omega Workshops, 1913–19*, exh. cat., London: Courtauld Gallery, 2009

Gerzina, Gretchen Holbrook, *Carrington: A Life*, New York: W. W. Norton, 1989

Gillespie, Diane, *The Sisters' Arts: The Writing and Painting of Virginia Woolf and Vanessa Bell*, Syracuse, NY: Syracuse University Press, 1991

Glendinning, Victoria, *Leonard Woolf: A Biography*, New York: Free Press, 2006

———, *Vita: The Life of V. Sackville-West*. London: Weidenfeld & Nicolson, 1983

Goldman, Jane, 'Case Study: Bloomsbury's Pacifist Aesthetics: Woolf, Keynes, Rodker', in Derek Ryan and Stephen Ross (eds), *The Handbook to the Bloomsbury Group*, London: Bloomsbury Academic, 2018, pp. 294–308

———, *The Feminist Aesthetics of Virginia Woolf: Modernism, Post-Impressionism and the Politics of the Visual*, Cambridge: Cambridge University Press, 2001

Goodwin, Craufurd, 'The Bloomsbury Group as Creative Community', *History of Political Economy*, vol. 43 (2011), no. 1, pp. 59–82

Grafton Galleries, *Manet and the Post-Impressionists*, exh. cat., London: Grafton Galleries, 1910

———, *Second Post-Impressionist Exhibition: British, French and Russian Artists*, exh. cat., London: Grafton Galleries, 1912

Grant, Duncan, 'Virginia Woolf', *Horizon*, vol. 2, no. 18 (1941), pp. 403–4

Green, Christopher (ed.), *Art Made Modern: Roger Fry's Vision of Art*, London: Merrell Holberton, 1999

Green-Lewis, Jennifer, *Victorian Photography, Literature, and the Invention of Modern Memory: Already the Past*, London: Bloomsbury Academic, 2017

Hamnett, Nina, *Laughing Torso*, New York: Ray Long & Richard R. Smith, 1932

Hampshire House Club, *Exhibition of English and Belgian Work by Craftsmen and Artists in Hammersmith*, exh. cat., Hammersmith: Hampshire House Club, 1915 (Ditchling Museum of Art & Craft, Sussex, cat. no. 1991.1305.1)

Harris, Pippa (ed.), *Song of Love: The Letters of Rupert Brooke and Noel Olivier: 1909–1915*, London: Bloomsbury, 1991

Harrison, Charles, *English Art and Modernism, 1900–1939*, London: Allen Lane, 1981

Harrod, R. F., *The Life of John Maynard Keynes*, London: Macmillan, 1952

Hartley, Cecil, *The Gentlemen's Book of Etiquette and Manual of Politeness*, Boston: Cottrell, 1860

Hassall, Christopher, *Rupert Brooke: A Biography*. London: Faber & Faber, 1964

Haule, James (ed.), *The Bloomsbury Group Memoir Club*, Basingstoke: Palgrave Macmillan, 2014

Hawkes, Ellen, 'Friendships Gallery', *Twentieth Century Literature*, vol. 25, no. 3–4 (1979), pp. 270–302

Helt, Brenda, and Madelyn Detloff (eds), *Queer Bloomsbury*, Edinburgh: Edinburgh University Press, 2016

Hitchmough, Wendy, 'Omega Flowers', *Charleston Press*, no. 3 (2019), pp. 72–9

Hoare, Lottie, 'Pepler, Harry Douglas Clarke [Hilary]', *Oxford Dictionary of National Biography* (2004), available at <https://doi.org/10.1093/ref:odnb/66287> (accessed 27 April 2020)

Hollander, Anne, *Seeing Through Clothes*, New York: Penguin, 1988

———, *Sex and Suits: The Evolution of Modern Dress*, New York: Knopf, 1994

Holroyd, Michael, *Augustus John: A Biography*, Harmondsworth: Penguin, 1976

———, *Lytton Strachey: A Biography* [1967], Harmondsworth: Penguin, 1980

Hooker, Denise, *Nina Hamnett: Queen of Bohemia*, London: Constable, 1986

Howells, Richard, 'Copies and Translations: Roger Fry, Old Masters and the Omega Workshops', *The British Art Journal*, vol. 16, no. 1 (2015), pp. 47–57

Hudgins, Nicole, 'A Historical Approach to Family Photography: Class and Individuality in Manchester and Lille, 1850–1914', *Journal of Social History*, vol. 43, no. 3 (2010), pp. 559–86

Hulme, T. E., 'Modern Art – I: The Grafton Group', *The New Age*, 15 January 1914, pp. 341–2

Humm, Maggie (ed.), *The Edinburgh Companion to Virginia Woolf and the Arts*, Edinburgh: Edinburgh University Press, 2010

———, *Modernist Women and Visual Cultures: Virginia Woolf, Vanessa Bell, Photography and Cinema*, Edinburgh: Edinburgh University Press, 2002

———, *Snapshots of Bloomsbury: The Private Lives of Virginia Woolf and Vanessa Bell*, London: Tate, 2006

Irwin, Margaret, *Fire Down Below*, London: William Heinemann, 1928

Janes, Dominic, 'Eminent Victorians, Bloomsbury Queerness and John Maynard Keynes' *The Economic Consequences of the Peace* (1919)', *Literature and History*, vol. 23, no. 1 (2014), pp. 19–32

Johnston, Georgia, 'Virginia Woolf's Talk on the Dreadnought Hoax', *Woolf Studies Annual*, vol. 15 (2019), pp. 1–45

Johnstone, J. K., *The Bloomsbury Group: A Study of E. M. Forster, Lytton Strachey, Virginia Woolf, and Their Circle*, New York: Noonday Press, 1963

Jones, Enid Huws, *Margery Fry: The Essential Amateur*, Oxford: Oxford University Press, 1966

Joyce, Simon, 'On or About 1901: The Bloomsbury Group Looks Back at the Victorians', *Victorian Studies*, vol. 46, no. 4 (2004), pp. 631–54

Kennard, Jean, 'Power and Sexual Ambiguity: The "Dreadnought" Hoax, "The Voyage Out", "Mrs Dalloway" and "Orlando"', *Journal of Modern Literature*, vol. 20, no. 2 (1996), pp. 149–64

Keynes, John Maynard, *The Collected Writings of John Maynard Keynes*, London: Macmillan, 1971

———, 'My Early Beliefs' [1949], in S. P. Rosenbaum (ed.), *The Bloomsbury Group: A Collection of Memoirs, Commentary and Criticism*, London: Croom Helm, 1974, pp. 48–64

Keynes, Milo (ed.), *Essays on John Maynard Keynes*, Cambridge: Cambridge University Press, 1975

Knights, Sara, *Bloomsbury's Outsider: A Life of David Garnett*, London: Bloomsbury, 2015

Konody, P. G., 'Art & Artists: English Post-Impressionists', *Observer*, 27 October 1912, p. 10

———, 'The Comic Cubists: Laughable Pictures at the Grafton Galleries', *Daily Mail*, 5 October 1912, p. 6

———, 'Post-Impressionism in the Home', *Observer*, 14 December 1913, p. 8

———, 'Post-Impressionists at the Grafton Galleries', *Observer*, 13 November 1910, p. 9

Laing, Donald, *Roger Fry: An Annotated Bibliography of the Published Writings*, New York: Garland, 1979

Laurence, Patricia, *Lily Briscoe's Chinese Eyes: Bloomsbury, Modernism and China*, Columbia: University of South Carolina Press, 2003

Leaper, Hana, 'Between London and Paris', in S. Milroy and I. A. C. Dejardin (eds), *Vanessa Bell*, London: Philip Wilson, 2017, pp. 41–53

Lee, Hermione, *Virginia Woolf*, London: Chatto & Windus, 1996

Lee, Hugh (ed.), *A Cézanne in the Hedge*, London: Collins & Brown, 1992

Lehmann, John, *Virginia Woolf* [1975], London: Thames & Hudson, 1999

Lewis, Wyndham, *Apes of God*, London: Arthur Press, 1930

———, *Wyndham Lewis on Art: Collected Writings, 1913–1956*, ed. Walter Michel and C. J. Fox, New York: Funk and Wagnalls, 1969

Light, Alison, *Mrs Woolf and the Servants: The Hidden Heart of Domestic Service*, London: Penguin, 2007

Lowe, Gill, '"Wild Swimming", Rupert Brooke and Virginia Woolf', paper delivered at 'Virginia Woolf and the Natural World', the 20th International Virginia Woolf Conference, held at Georgetown College, Georgetown, KY, 3–6 June 2010, available at <http://oars.uos.ac.uk/id/eprint/111> (accessed 27 April 2020)

Luckhurst, Nicola, *Bloomsbury in Vogue*, London: Cecil Woolf, 1998

M. M. B., 'Post-Impressionist Furniture', *Daily News and Leader*, 7 August 1913, p. 10

[MacCarthy, Desmond] [unsigned], 'The Post-Impressionists', introduction to *Manet and the Post-Impressionists*, exh. cat., London: Grafton Galleries, 1910, pp. 7–13

MacCarthy, Desmond, *Portraits*. London: MacGibbon and Kee, 1949

———, 'The Post-Impressionist Exhibition of 1910' [1953], in S. P. Rosenbaum (ed.), *The Bloomsbury Group: A Collection of Memoirs, Commentary and Criticism*, London: Croom Helm, 1975, pp. 68–73

MacGibbon, Jean, *There's the Lighthouse: A Biography of Adrian Stephen*, London: James and James, 1997

Maitland, Frederic William, *The Life and Letters of Leslie Stephen*, London: Duckworth, 1906

Marcus, Jane (ed.), *Virginia Woolf and Bloomsbury: A Centenary Celebration*, London: Macmillan, 1987

Marcus, Laura, 'Virginia Woolf and the Hogarth Press', in Iain Willison, Warwick Gould, and Warren Chernaik (eds), *Modernist Writers and the Marketplace*, Basingstoke: Macmillan, 1996, pp. 124–50

Marler, Regina, *Bloomsbury Pie: The Making of the Bloomsbury Boom*, London: Virago, 1997

Marsh, Edward, *A Number of People: A Book of Reminiscences*, London: William Heinemann, 1939

Martin, Edward Alfred, *Dew Ponds*, London: King, Sell and Olding, 1907

Meyers, Jeffrey, 'Kate Lechmere's "Wyndham Lewis from 1912"', *Journal of Modern Literature*, vol. 10, no. 1 (1983), pp. 158–66

Milroy, Sarah, and Ian A. C. Dejardin (eds), *Vanessa Bell*, London: Philip Wilson, 2017

Moore, G. E., *Principia Ethica*, Cambridge: Cambridge University Press, 1966

Morrell, Ottoline, *Ottoline: The Early Memoirs of Lady Ottoline Morrell*, ed. Robert Gathorne-Hardy, London: Faber & Faber, 1963

———, *Ottoline at Garsington: Memoirs of Lady Ottoline Morrell, 1915–1918*, ed. Roger Gathorne-Hardy, London: Faber & Faber, 1974

Mortimer, Raymond, *Duncan Grant*, Harmondsworth: Penguin, 1944

———, 'Duncan Grant at the Independent Gallery', *Vogue* [London], late June 1923, pp. 56–7

———, 'Lively Portraits: The Bloomsbury Set from the Inside', *Sunday Times*, 11 November 1956, p. 4

———, 'Modern Furniture and Decoration', *Architectural Review*, December 1930, pp. 252–3

Naylor, Gillian, *Bloomsbury: The Artists, Authors and Designers by Themselves*, London: Pyramid, 1990

Nead, Lynda, *The Female Nude: Art, Obscenity and Sexuality*, London and New York: Routledge, 1992

Nicholson, Virginia, *Among the Bohemians: Experiments in Living, 1900–1939*, London: Penguin, 2003

———, *An Artists' Home: Charleston*, Lewes: Charleston Trust, 1999

Nicolson, Benedict, 'Post-Impressionism and Roger Fry', *Burlington Magazine*, vol. 93, no. 574 (1951), pp. 11–15

Nicolson, Juliet, *The Great Silence, 1918–1920: Living in the Shadow of the Great War*, London: John Murray, 2009

———, *A House Full of Daughters*, London: Vintage, 2016

Nicolson, Nigel, *Portrait of a Marriage*, London: Weidenfeld & Nicolson, 1973

——— (ed.), *Vita and Harold: The Letters of Vita Sackville-West and Harold Nicolson*, London: Weidenfeld & Nicolson, 1992

Noble, Joan Russell (ed.), *Recollections of Virginia Woolf*, London: Peter Owen, 1972

Olive, Guillaume, 'Pour une anthropologie du groupe de Bloomsbury', in *Conversation anglaise: Le Groupe de Bloomsbury*, exh. cat., Musée La Piscine, Roubaix, Paris: Gallimard, 2009, p. 37

Omega Workshops, *Omega Workshops Ltd, Artist Decorators*, descriptive cat., London: Omega Workshops, [1914] (National Art Library, Victoria and Albert Museum, acc. no. L.2209-1955)

Ondaatje Rolls, Jans, *The Bloomsbury Cookbook: Recipes for Life, Love and Art*, New York: Thames & Hudson, 2014

Patmore, Derek, *Colour Schemes for the Modern Home*, London: The Studio, 1933

Pepler, H. D. C., 'Hampshire House Workshops', *Blackfriars*, vol. 31, no. 359 (1950), pp. 70–74

Pevsner, Nikolaus, 'Omega', *Architectural Review*, vol. 90, August 1941, pp. 45–8

———, *Pioneers of the Modern Movement*, London: Faber & Faber, 1936

Phillips, Claude, 'Art in Whitechapel: Twentieth Century Exhibition', *Daily Telegraph*, 12 May 1914, p. 14

———, 'The Grafton Group', *Daily Telegraph*, 22 March 1913, p. 6

———, 'More Post-Impressionism', *Daily Telegraph*, 5 January 1914, p. 8

Poiret, Paul, *En habillant l'époque*, Paris: Bernard Grasset, 1930

Pollock, Griselda, *Differencing the Canon: Feminist Desire and the Writing of Art's Histories*, London: Routledge, 1999

———, *Vision and Difference: Femininity, Feminism, and the Histories of Art*, London: Routledge, 1988

Porter, David H., *The Omega Workshops and the Hogarth Press: An Artful Fugue*, London: Cecil Woolf, 2008

A Post-Impressionist Scribbler, 'Pictorial Art in South London', *National Review*, no. 58, December 1911, pp. 648–56

Potts, Gina, and Lisa Shahriari (eds), *Virginia Woolf's Bloomsbury*, Basingstoke: Palgrave Macmillan, 2010, 2 vols

Powers, Alan, 'Roger Fry and the Making of Durbins', *Charleston*, no. 13 (1996), pp. 14–22

Randall, Bryony, and Jane Goldman, *Virginia Woolf in Context*, Cambridge: Cambridge University Press, 2012

Reed, Christopher, 'Bloomsbury Bashing: Homophobia and the Politics of Criticism in the Eighties', in Brenda Helt and Madelyn Detloff (eds), *Queer Bloomsbury*, Edinburgh: Edinburgh University Press, 2016, pp. 36–63

———, *Bloomsbury Rooms: Modernism, Subculture, and Domesticity*, New Haven, CT, and London: Yale University Press, 2004

———, *Roger Fry's Durbins: A House and Its Meanings*, London: Cecil Woolf, 1999

——— (ed.), *A Roger Fry Reader*, Chicago: Chicago University Press, 1996

———, 'A *Vogue* that Dare not Speak Its Name: Sexual Subculture during the Editorship of Dorothy Todd, 1922–26', *Fashion Theory*, vol. 10, no. 1–2 (2006), pp. 39–72

Ribeiro, Aileen, *The Gallery of Fashion*, London: National Portrait Gallery, 2000

Richardson, Elizabeth P., *A Bloomsbury Iconography*, Winchester: St Paul's Bibliographies, 1989

Robins, Anna Gruetzner, 'The Company of Strangers: Max Weber and the First Grafton Group Exhibition', in Sarah MacDougall (ed.), *Max Weber: An American Cubist in Paris and London 1905–15*, London: Lund Humphries, 2014, pp. 58–105

———, *Modern Art in Britain, 1910–1914*, exh. cat., London: Barbican Art Gallery, 1997

Rodker, John, 'The New Movement in Art', *Dial Monthly*, May 1914, pp. 184–8

Rose, Clare, *Clothing, Society and Culture in Nineteenth-Century England*, London: Picking & Chatto, 2011

Rosenbaum, S. P., (ed.), *The Bloomsbury Group: A Collection of Memoirs, Commentary and Criticism*, London: Croom Helm, 1975

———, *Edwardian Bloomsbury: The Early Literary History of the Bloomsbury Group*, New York: St Martin's Press, 1994

———, *Georgian Bloomsbury: The Early Literary History of the Bloomsbury Group*, London: Palgrave Macmillan, 2003

———, 'Old Bloomsbury', in J. M. Haule (ed.), *The Bloomsbury Group Memoir Club*, London: Palgrave Macmillan, 2014, pp. 151–3

———, *Victorian Bloomsbury: The Early Literary History of the Bloomsbury Group*, New York: St Martin's Press, 1987

Rosner, Victoria (ed.), *The Cambridge Companion to the Bloomsbury Group*, Cambridge: Cambridge University Press, 2014

Ross (née Duff Gordon), Janet, *The Fourth Generation: Reminiscences by Janet Ross*, London: Constable, 1912, available at <https://archive.org/stream/fourthgeneration00rossiala#page/38> (accessed 27 April 2020)

Rothenstein, John, *Modern English Painters* [1952], London: Macdonald, 1984, 3 vols

Rutter, Frank, *Revolution in Art: An Introduction to the Study of Cézanne, Gauguin, Van Gogh, and Other Modern Painters*, London: Art News Press, 1910

Ryan, Derek, and Stephen Ross (eds), *The Handbook to the Bloomsbury Group*, London: Bloomsbury Academic, 2018

Sackville-West, Vita, *The Edwardians*, London: Hogarth Press, 1930

———, *The Letters of Vita Sackville-West to Virginia Woolf*, ed. Louise DeSalvo and Mitchell A. Leaska, London: Papermac, 1985

Sadleir, Michael, *Michael Ernest Sadler*, London: Constable, 1949

Schwabe, Randolph, 'Reminiscences of Fellow Students', *Burlington Magazine*, vol. 82, no. 478 (1943), pp. 6–9

Scrase, David, and Peter Croft, *Maynard Keynes: Collector of Pictures, Books and Manuscripts*, Cambridge: Fitzwilliam Museum, 1983

Sheehan, Elizabeth M., 'Dressmaking at the Omega: Experiments in Art and Fashion', in Alexandra Gerstein (ed.), *Beyond Bloomsbury: Designs of the Omega Workshops, 1913–19*, exh. cat., London: Courtauld Gallery, 2009, pp. 50–59

Shone, Richard, *The Art of Bloomsbury: Roger Fry, Vanessa Bell and Duncan Grant*, exh. cat., London: Tate Gallery, 1999

———, *Bloomsbury Portraits: Vanessa Bell, Duncan Grant and Their Circle*, Oxford: Phaidon, 1976

———, 'The Friday Club', *Burlington Magazine*, vol. 117, no. 866 (1975), pp. 279–84

———, *Vanessa Bell, 1879–1961: A Retrospective Exhibition*, exh. cat., New York: Davis & Long Company, 1980

———, 'Vanessa Bell's Late Self-Portraits', in S. Milroy and I. A. C. Dejardin (eds), *Vanessa Bell*, London: Philip Wilson, 2017, pp. 179–83

[Sickert, Walter] [unsigned], 'A Monthly Chronicle: Roger Fry', *The Burlington Magazine for Connoisseurs*, vol. 28, no. 153 (1915), p. 117

Sickert, Walter, 'A Monthly Chronicle: O Matre Pulchrâ', *The Burlington Magazine for Connoisseurs*, vol. 29, no. 157 (April 1916), p. 35

———, 'Vanessa Bell', *The Burlington Magazine for Connoisseurs*, vol. 41, no. 232 (1922), pp. 32–5

Silver, Brenda, *Virginia Woolf Icon*, Chicago: University of Chicago Press, 1999

Sitwell, Osbert, *Laughter in the Next Room*, London: Macmillan, 1949

Skidelsky, Robert (ed.), *The Essential Keynes*, London: Penguin, 2015

Snaith, Anna, 'Conversations in Bloomsbury: Colonial Writers and the Hogarth Press', in Lisa Shahriari and Gina Potts (eds), *Virginia Woolf's Bloomsbury*, vol. 2: *International Influence and Politics*, Basingstoke: Palgrave Macmillan, 2010, pp. 138–57

Sohaili, Vajdon, '"The Mirror-Like Sea": A Bloomsbury Vision of Same-Sex Desire In Duncan Grant's *Bathing*, 1911', *British Art Studies*, issue 4 (2016) <https://doi.org/10.17658/issn.2058-5462/issue-04/vsohaili> (accessed 27 April 2020)

Southworth, Helen (ed.), *Leonard and Virginia Woolf, the Hogarth Press and the Networks of Modernism*, Edinburgh: Edinburgh University Press, 2010

Spalding, Frances, *The Bloomsbury Group*, London: National Portrait Gallery, 2013

———, *Duncan Grant*, London: Chatto & Windus, 1997

———, 'Obituary: Professor Quentin Bell', *Independent*, 18 December 1996 <www.independent.co.uk/news/people/obituary-professor-quentin-bell-1315047.html> (accessed 27 April 2020)

———, *Portraits by Roger Fry*, London: Courtauld Institute Galleries, 1976

———, *Roger Fry: Art and Life*, London: Granada, 1980

———, *Vanessa Bell*, London: Weidenfeld & Nicolson, 1983

Spink Gallery, *Duncan Grant and Vanessa Bell: Design and Decoration, 1910–1960*, exh. cat., London: Spink Gallery, 1991

Stansky, Peter, *Bloomsbury as Publisher: Virginia and Leonard Woolf and the Hogarth Press*, San Francisco: Arion Press, 2008

———, *On or About 1910: Early Bloomsbury and its Intimate World*, London and Cambridge, MA: Harvard University Press, 1996

Stansky, Peter, and William Abrahams, *Julian Bell: From Bloomsbury to the Spanish Civil War*, Stanford, CA: Stanford University Press, 2011

Steele, Valerie, *Paris Fashion: A Cultural History*, New York: Oxford University Press, 1988

Stephen, Adrian, *The 'Dreadnought' Hoax*, London: Hogarth Press, 1936

Stephen, Leslie, *Sir Leslie Stephen's Mausoleum Book*, Oxford: Clarendon Press, 1977

Strachey, Lytton, *Eminent Victorians* [1918], ed. Michael Holroyd, London: Penguin, 1986

———, *The Letters of Lytton Strachey*, ed. Paul Levy, London: Penguin, 2006

———, *Lytton Strachey, by Himself: A Self-Portrait*, ed. Michael Holroyd, London: Heinemann, 1971

———, *The Really Interesting Question, and Other Papers*, ed. Paul Levy, London: Weidenfeld & Nicolson, 1972

Strachey, Nino, *Rooms of Their Own*, London: Pitkin, 2018

Tate Gallery, *Duncan Grant: A Display to Celebrate His 90th Birthday*, exh. cat., London: Tate Gallery, 1975

———, *Duncan Grant: A Retrospective Exhibition*, exh. cat., London: Tate Gallery, 1959.

Tatlock, R. R., 'The London Group', *The Burlington Magazine for Connoisseurs*, vol. 43, no. 248 (1923), pp. 250, 253

Tickner, Lisa, 'Mediating Generation: The Mother–Daughter Plot', *Art History*, vol. 25, no. 1 (2002), pp. 23–46

———, 'Men's Work? Masculinity and Modernism', in Norman Bryson, Michael Ann Holly, and Keith Moxley (eds), *Visual Culture: Images and Interpretations*, Hanover, NH: Wesleyan University Press, 1994, pp. 42–82

———, *Modern Life and Modern Subjects: British Art in the Early Twentieth Century*, New Haven, CT, and London: Yale University Press, 2000

———, *The Spectacle of Women: Imagery of the Suffrage Campaign, 1907–14*, Chicago: University of Chicago Press, 1988

———, 'Vanessa Bell: Studland Beach, Domesticity, and "Significant Form"', *Representations*, no. 65 (1999), pp. 63–92

Tillyard, Stella, *The Impact of Modernism, 1900–1920: Early Modernism and the Arts and Crafts Movement in Edwardian England*, London and New York: Routledge, 1988

Todd, Avery, *Saxon Sydney-Turner: The Ghost of Bloomsbury*, London: Cecil Woolf, 2015

——— (ed.), *Unpublished Works of Lytton Strachey: Early Papers*, London: Pickering & Chatto, 2011

Todd, Dorothy, and Raymond Mortimer, *The New Interior Decoration: An Introduction to Its Principles, and International Survey of Its Methods*, London: B. T. Batsford, 1929

Todd, Pamela, *Bloomsbury at Home*, London: Pavilion, 1999

Vaughan, Janet, 'Cousin Virginia', in J. H. Stape (ed.), *Virginia Woolf: Interviews and Recollections*, Basingstoke: Macmillan, 1995, pp. 9–12

———, 'Some Bloomsbury Memories', *Charleston Newsletter*, no. 12 (1985), pp. 20–22

Ward-Jackson, Philip, 'Expiatory Monuments by Carlo Marochetti in Dorset and the Isle of Wight', *Journal of the Warburg and Courtauld Institutes*, vol. 53 (1990), pp. 266–80

Watling, Sarah, *Noble Savages: The Olivier Sisters; Four Lives in Seven Fragments*, London: Vintage Digital, 2019

Watney, Simon, *The Art of Duncan Grant*, London: John Murray, 1990

———, *English Post-Impressionism*, London: Studio Vista, 1980

Weld-Blundell, C. J., 'Manet and the Post-Impressionists', *The Times*, 7 November 1910, pp. 11–12

Whitechapel Art Gallery, *Twentieth Century Art: A Review of Modern Movements; Summer Exhibition*, exh. cat., London: Whitechapel Art Gallery, 1914

Wilcox, Denys J., *The London Group, 1913–1939: The Artists and Their Works*, Aldershot: Scolar Press, 1995

Williams, Raymond, 'The Bloomsbury Faction', in his *Problems in Materialism and Culture: Selected Essays*, London: Verso, 1980, pp. 148–67

———, *The Country and the City*, London: Chatto & Windus, 1973

———, 'The Significance of "Bloomsbury" as a Social and Cultural Group', in Derek Crabtree and A. P. Thirlwall (eds), *Keynes and the Bloomsbury Group: The Fourth Keynes Seminar Held at the University of Kent at Canterbury, 1978*, London: Macmillan, 1980, pp. 40–57

Williams, Val, 'Carefully Creating an Idyll: Vanessa Bell and Snapshot Photography, 1907–46', in Jo Spence and Patricia Holland (eds), *Family Snaps: The Meanings of Domestic Photography*, London: Virago, 1991, pp. 186–98

Wilson, Elizabeth, 'Bohemian Dress and the Heroism of Everyday Life', *Fashion Theory: The Journal of Dress, Body and Culture*, vol. 2, no. 3 (1998), pp. 225–44

Wolfe, Jesse, *Bloomsbury, Modernism and the Reinvention of Intimacy*, Cambridge: Cambridge University Press, 2011

Woolf, Leonard, *Beginning Again: An Autobiography of the Years 1911 to 1918*, London: Hogarth Press, 1964

———, *Downhill All the Way: An Autobiography of the Years 1919 to 1939*, London: Hogarth Press, 1967

———, *Economic Imperialism*, New York: H. Fertig, 1970

———, *Empire and Commerce in Africa*, London: Allen & Unwin, 1968

———, *Growing: An Autobiography of the Years 1904 to 1911*, London: Hogarth Press, 1961

———, *Imperialism and Civilization*, New York: Garland, 1972

———, *The Journey Not the Arrival Matters: An Autobiography of the Years 1939 to 1969*, London: Hogarth Press, 1969

———, *The Letters of Leonard Woolf*, ed. Frederick Spotts, San Diego: Harcourt Brace Jovanovich, 1989

———, *Sowing: An Autobiography of the Years 1880 to 1904*, London: Hogarth Press, 1960

Woolf, Virginia, *Collected Essays*, London: Hogarth Press, 1966–7, 4 vols

———, *The Complete Shorter Fiction*, ed. Susan Dick, London: Triad Grafton Books, 1985

———, *The Diary of Virginia Woolf*, ed. Anne Olivier Bell and Andrew McNeillie, Harmondsworth: Penguin Books, 1977–84, 5 vols

———, *The Essays 2, 1912–1918*, ed. Andrew McNeillie, London: Hogarth Press, 1987

———, *Freshwater: A Comedy*, ed. Lucio P. Ruotolo, London: Hogarth Press, 1976

———, 'Indiscretions', *Vogue* [London], late November 1924, pp. 47, 88

———, *Jacob's Room*, Richmond: Hogarth Press, 1922

———, *Kew Gardens*, Richmond: Hogarth Press, 1919

———, *Killing the Angel in the House*, London: Penguin, 1995

———, *The Letters of Virginia Woolf*, ed. Nigel Nicolson and Joanne Trautmann, London: Hogarth Press, 1975–80, 6 vols

———, *Moments of Being: Autobiographical Writings* [1978], ed. Jeanne Schulkind, London: Pimlico, 2002

———, *Mrs Dalloway*, London: Hogarth Press, 1925

———, *Night and Day*, London: Duckworth, 1919

———, 'Old Bloomsbury', in her *Moments of Being: Autobiographical Writings* [1978], ed. Jeanne Schulkind, London: Pimlico, 2002, pp. 43–61

———, *Orlando*, London: Hogarth Press, 1928

———, *A Passionate Apprentice: The Early Journals, 1897–1909*, ed. Mitchell Leaska, London: Hogarth Press, 1990

———, *The Platform of Time: Memoirs of Family and Friends*, ed. S. P. Rosenbaum, London: Hesperus Press, 2008

———, *Roger Fry: A Biography*, London: Hogarth Press, 1940

———, *A Room of One's Own* [1929], Harmondsworth: Penguin, 1973

———, *Three Guineas*, London: Hogarth Press, 1938

———, *To the Lighthouse*, London: Hogarth Press, 1927

———, *The Voyage Out*, London: Duckworth, 1915

———, *Walter Sickert: A Conversation*, London: Hogarth Press, 1934

———, *The Waves*, London: Hogarth Press, 1931

———, *The Years*, London: Hogarth Press, 1937

Woolf, Virginia, and Leonard Woolf, *Two Stories*, Richmond: Hogarth Press, 1917

Woolf, Virginia and Roger Fry, *Victorian Photographs of Famous Men and Fair Women by Julia Margaret Cameron* [1926], Boston: David R. Gordine, 1973

Zangwill, Israel, *Too Much Money: A Farcical Comedy in Three Acts*, London: William Heinemann, 1924

INDEX

Page numbers in *italics* refer to illustrations

Asheham House, East Sussex 9, 17, 45, 63, *63*, 69, 70, 72–4, *73*, 76, 77, *77*, 80, *80*, *81*, 83–4, 83n90, 99, *99*, 136–7

Bagenal, Barbara (née Hiles) 11, 110, 115–16, 120, 123–5
Bagenal, Nicholas 116, 125, 144
Ballets Russes 70, 91, 96–7, 133
Beaton, Cecil 50, 110n104
Beerbohm, Max 17, 145, 145n109, 147
  Significant Form 147, *148*
Behrend, John Louis and Mary 128
Bell, Anne Olivier 18, 19, 23, 27, 28, 29
Bell, Clive 49, 63, *63*, *64*, 69, 74, 84, 131, 137, *142*, *148*
  appearance of 65
  and Bloomsbury 12, 16, 147, 149
  and Charleston 8, 65, 120, 131
  collection of 143–4
  death of 17
  and Memoir Club 10, *11*
  and Omega Workshops 91, 93, 145
  and Post-Impressionism 13, 133–4
  relationship to: Angelica Garnett 23; Duncan Grant 8, 11, 147; Lytton Strachey 12; Mary Hutchinson 10, 59, 72, 100, 115, 120–01; Pablo Picasso 70; Roger Fry 11, 100, 120; Thoby Stephen 9; Vanessa Bell 8, 9, 10, 11, 13, 49, 65, 68–9, 76, *76*, 97–8, 100, 108, 120–01, 134, 136–7; Virginia Woolf 63–4, 69, 81, 83, 115
  and *Vogue* 50
  works: *Art* 143, 147; *Civilisation: An Essay* 146; *Old Friends* 16, 65n24, 68n34; *Peace at Once* 99
Bell, Quentin *11*, 17, 29, 47, 68, 70, 92n6, 135
  and Bloomsbury scholarship 18–19, 29
  and Charleston 7, 17, 18, 23, 27, *122*
  and professional and amateur photographs 17, 28, 36, 45, 106n99
  relationship to: Angelica Garnett 24, *25*; Duncan Grant 18, 39n57; Leonard Woolf 8, 16; Virginia Woolf 13, 16
  works: *Bloomsbury* 17, 18; *Virginia Woolf: A Biography* 13, 16, 28
Bell, Julian 45, 49, 68, 70, 76, *122*, 149n137

Bell, Vanessa (née Stephen)
  and Asheham 9, 136–7
  and Bloomsbury Group 9-10, 12, 15, 16, 73, 125, 133–4
  and Charleston 5, 9, 27, 49, 72, 98, *118*, 119–23, *122*, 128, *128*, 131, 144, 146
  collection of 135, 143
  death of 17, 23, 27
  and disinhibited 68–71, 128
  and dress 59, 61, 74, 76–81, 97–9, 108, 119, 121, 125–8, *124–8*
  and exhibitions 18, 110, 133–43, 136n41, 149–50
  and The Friday Club 16, 80, 134–5
  and Grafton Group 135
  and hair 63–4, 132
  and Hogarth Press 12, 51–2
  and interior design 9, 18, 42, 51, *51*, 83, 123, *142*, 144, 150
  and Julia Margaret Cameron 28, 30, 42–4, *43*, *44*, 151
  and Memoir Club 10, *11*, 15
  memoir: 'Notes on Bloomsbury' 15
  and Omega Workshops 5, 84, 88, *88*, 91, *91*, 93, 100, 110, 116, 120–21, 123, 135, *140*, 141–2
  and Omega Workshops dress collection 5, 59, 97, 99–123, *102*, *106–18*, 125–8, 141–42
  photographs by 12, 24, *25*, 36, *36*, 69, 71, *73*, 74, 76, 80, *80*, 98, *98*, *105*, 108n102, *110*, 121–2, *122*, 136, *146*
  photographs of 24, *32*, *34*, *35*, *36*, *41*, *43*, 47, *47*, 49, *49*, 59, *63*, *71*, 74, *75*, *79*, 84, *85*, *98*, *99*, *99*, 101–02, *102*, *122*
  and Post-Impressionism 7, 13, 15, 70, 108, 134–7
  and professional and amateur photographs 11, *12*, 12, 16, 17, 18, 19, 23, 24, *24*, 25, *25*, 26–31, 39–46, *41*, 49–50, *49*, 52, 56, 70–74, 108, 121, 138
  relationship to: Adrian Stephen 8, 9; Angelica Garnett 23, 24, 64, 128; Clive Bell 8, 9, 10, 11, 13, 49, 65, 68–9, 76, *76*, 97–98, 100, 108, 120–01, 134, 136–7; Duncan Grant 42, 49, 64, 68–70, 72–3, 76, 91, 97–101, *99*, 112, 115, 121, 123–8, *124–8*, 131, 136–8, 141, 146; John Maynard Keynes 7, 9, 51, 63–4, 68, 84, 131–2, 134, 142, 144, 146; Julia Jackson Stephen 8, 23, 42, 44, 49; Leonard Woolf 16, 61, 133, 150; Leslie Stephen 8, 28, 31, 42; Lytton Strachey 10, 12, 76, 77, *77*, 120, 131–2; Mabel Selwood 47, 63, 119, 123; Mary Hutchinson 10, 12, 76, 77, *77*, 97, 100, 108, 112, 116, 119–22, 125, 131–2, 142–3; Ottoline Morrell 76, 97, 141; Pablo Picasso 70, 143–4; Roger Fry 11, 15, 68–9, 74, 76, *76*, 81, 84, *85*, 91, 93–7, *94–5*, 99–101, 104, 108, 110, 115–23, *122*, 134, 137, 141–4; Stella Duckworth 8, 28, 40–42, 45, 50; Thoby Stephen 8–9, 17, 31, 40, 47; Virginia Woolf 8–10, 12, 31, 36, 40, 42, 46, 49, 51, 56, 64, 69, 73, 77–81, *78*, 84, 99, 114–15, 123–5, 133–4, 143–4, 148–50
  and *Vogue* 51, 150
  works: *Abstract* textile design 55, 149; *Adam and Eve* folding screen 72; *Bathers in a Landscape* folding screen 84–8, *88*, 105, 145; *Conversation Piece* 64, 65, 83, 136; Decoration Clive Bell's rooms, 37 Gordon Square *142*, 143–4; Decoration Keynes's rooms, King's College Cambridge 18, 51; Decoration 52 Tavistock Square 18, 51, *51*, 150; Dressing gown reputed to have been for Roger Fry *95*, 96; *Iris Tree* 110, *112*, 119; *Landscape with Haystack, Asheham* 73, *73*; *Lytton Strachey* 77, *77*; *Maud* Omega Workshops linen 92, *94*; Menu card 91, *91*; *Mrs Desmond MacCarthy* 137, 137n49; *Mrs St John Hutchinson* 108–10, *111*, 141, 143; *The Music Room* installation, Lefevre Galleries 149, *151*; *Omega Paper Flowers in a Bottle 140*, 141, 141n73; *Pamela* Omega Workshops linen 92, *93*; *Portrait of Molly MacCarthy* 137, 137n49, *137*; *Portrait of Virginia Woolf*

150, 150n147, 150n149, *152*; *Portrait of a Woman* 136, 136n35; Pyjamas reputed to have been for Roger Fry 94, 96; *The Red Dress* 44, *44*; *Seated Figure* 84, *86*; *Self Portrait*, 110, *113*; Sketch for *The Memoir Club* 11, *11*; *Studland Beach* 49–50, 135n28, 137; *Summer Camp* 84–8, *87*; *The Tub* 72, *120*, *121*; *Virginia Woolf* 77, *78*, 137; *Women and Baby* 137–9, 138n58, 138n59, *138–9*

Bennett, Arnold 145
Beresford, George, *18*, *27*, 27, 29, 45–49, *45–47*, *49*, 61, 63, 148
Blanche, Jacques-Emile 44, *44*, 46, 148
Blanco White, Amber 119, 119n141
Bloomsbury Group
  and Charleston Farmhouse 5, 9, 18
  and collections 131, 141–4, 152
  and colonialism 37–9, 68, 132, 151
  and dress 5–8, 13, 20, 50, 59–65, 74, 76–7, 84, 88, 99–100, 108–10, 115, 120, 125, 152
  and exhibitions 20, 128, 131, 132–41, 143, 146, 152
  and First World War 11, 15, 99, 141, 144–5
  group identity 5, 7, 8, 9, 10, 11, 12, 13, 15, 16, 17, 19, 20, 26–30, 39, 49–51, 61, 65, 70, 88, 101, 108, 115, 120, 125, 128, 131, 133–34, 136–37, 143–7, 150–52
  influence of 16, 19, 151
  and London residences: 21 Fitzroy Square 9, 132n4; 22 Hyde Park Gate 9, 26–7, *26*, 45, 46; 29 Fitzroy Square 9, 10, 12; 38 Brunswick Square 7, 9, 132, 132n4, 133, 136; 46 Gordon Square *8*, 8, 9, 10, 12, 13, 17, 30, 42, 44, 61, 68, 70, *71*, 73, 91, 100, 115, 123–5, 131, 143–4; 52 Tavistock Square 50–51, *51*, 149
  and marriage 9, 10
  membership of 5, 7, 8, 9, 10, 11, 12, 123–5, 147, 149, 151
  memoirs 9, 10, 15, 23, 150–01
  and modernity 7, 10, 13, 15, 17, 20, 30, 50–02, 92, 132–4, 136, 139, 142–3, 145, 151–2
  and nudity 20, 50, 59–61, 65, 68–71, 73, 88, 125, 152
  and Omega Workshops 5, 15, 88, 91–2, 97, 108, 114–15, 123–28, 141, 144
  and photographs 8, 13, 18, 19, 20, 23, 24, 26, 28, 29, 30, 36, 39, 49–52, 55, 65, 68, 144, 151
  see also *Dreadnought* Hoax
  see also entries for individual members
  and sexuality 15–16, 17, 50, 52, 88, 145

Bomberg, David 134, 138
Brooke, Rupert 17, 38, 80–84, *83*, 88n103, 133
Brown, Joy 93, 96, 100–03, *104*, 105, 112–19, 119n141, 123, 141n73

Camden Town Group 10, 141
Cameron, Julia Margaret (née Pattle) 16, 19, 24, 27, 28, 30, *30*, 37, 42–6, *43–4*, 50, 56, 151
Carfax Gallery 12, 128, 141, 143, 146–7
Carrington, Dora 5n1, 7n5, 11, 17, 63, 65n25, 69, 110, 119n142, 120, 123, 125, 131, 145
Cézanne, Paul 13, 15, 70, 88, 134, 136, 144
Charleston Albums 18–19, 23n4, 26n15, 29, 29n29, 30, 36, 40–44, *41*, *43*, 47, 49–50, 63n11, 65, 70, 74n57, 74n59, 74n62–63, 77n67, 84, 84n96, 84n98, *85*, 122n160
Charleston Farmhouse, East Sussex *62*, *120*, *121*, 145
  and Angelica Garnett 23
  and Bloomsbury Group 5, 9, 18
  'Charleston Time' 7
  and Clive Bell 8, 65, 120, 131
  collection at 18, 24, 26–9, 49, 149, *150*
  and David Garnett 9, 120
  and Duncan Grant 5, 7, 9, 18, 27, 70, 72, *118*, 119–20, 122–3, 128, *128*, 131, 144, 146
  and E. M. Forster 128
  and First World War 5, 7, 120, 128
  house museum 18, 19, 27
  and John Maynard Keynes, 5, *5*, 6, 7, 133, 144, 146
  and Lytton Strachey 5n1, 7, 120, 131, 145–6
  and Quentin Bell 7, 17, 18, 23, 27, *122*
  and Roger Fry 5
  store for paintings, photographs and archives 7, 13, 18, *19*, 28–9, 38
  and Vanessa Bell 5, 9, 27, 49, 72, 98, *118*, 119–123, *122*, 128, *128*, 131, 144, 146
  and Virginia Woolf 9, 123, 146
Clifton, Arthur 128, 147, 147n126
Coburn, Alvin Landon 98, *98*
Cole, Horace de Vere 13, *14*

Contemporary Art Society 132, 137
Cox, Katherine (Ka) 69, *69*, 80–84, *80–82*, 133–4, *134*
  see also Neo-Pagans
Cunard, Maud 92

Degas, Edgar 70, 144
Delacroix, Eugène 144, 144n96
Derain, André 88, 134
Dickens, Charles 31, 36
Dickinson, Violet 41, 45–7, 69n38, 83–4, 134
Doucet, Henri 96, 106, 108, 136–7, 136n41
Dreadnought hoax 12–13, *14*, 68, 152
Druet, Eugène 70, 72
Duckworth, George 28, *28*, 30, *32*, 36, 40, *41*, 46–7, 61
Duckworth, Gerald 30, *32*, 42, *42*, 61
Duckworth, Stella 8, 28–9, 30, 31, *32*, 36, 40–42, *41*, *43*, 44, *44*, 45, 49–50
Durbins, Guildford 18, 51, 74, *75*, 76, 96, 98, 101, 108, 115, 138, 138n59, *139*, 145

Eleanor House, West Wittering 69, *69*, 97, 100, 108, *108*, *109*, 115
Eliot, T. S. 12, 17
Etchells, Frederick 92, 132–3, 132n5, 132n7, *132*, 134–7, 139
Etchells, Jessie 92, 97, 134, 137
An Exhibition of Works Representative of the New Movement in Art 142–3

First World War 84, 103, 131
  conscientious objectors 7, 15, 120, 146
  see also Bloomsbury Group; Charleston Farmhouse; Omega Workshops
Fokine, Mikhail 70, 72, 133
Forster, E. M. 10, 10n17, *11*, 13, 16, 62–3, *62*, 128
Freud, Sigmund 10, 17
Friday Club 16, 80, 134–5, 135n30, 138–9
Fry, Pamela *93*, 96
Fry, Roger 63, *63*, *75*, 77, 84, *85*, 110n104, 119n141, 145, 147, *148*
  biography by Virginia Woolf 13
  and Bloomsbury Group 5, 134, 147
  and Charleston 5
  collection of 132, 136, 138, 142–3
  Durbins, Guildford 18, 51, 74, 76, 96, 115, 138, *139*
  and exhibitions 135, 136n41, 137, 139
  and Grafton Group 135

and Memoir Club 10
and Omega Workshops 72, 91, 93–9, *93–5*, 99–103, 106, 123, 135, 139, 144–5, 145n108
and Post-Impressionism 13, 15, 133–6
relationship to: Clive Bell 11, 100, 120; Desmond MacCarthy 13; Duncan Grant 11, 101, 120, 147; John Maynard Keynes 7, 142, 144; Joy Brown 96, 101, *104*, 105, 119; Vanessa Bell 11, 15, 68–9, 74, 76, *76*, 81, 84, *85*, 91, 93–7, *94–5*, 99–101, 104, 108, 110, 115–23, *122*, 134, 137, 141–4; Virginia Woolf 81, 84, 123, 144, 147; Winifred Gill 96–7, 119
and *Vogue* 50–01
works: Omega Workshops shawl *104*, 105; Omega Workshops vase 72, *122*; *Portrait of John Maynard Keynes* 6, 7; *Portrait of Nina Hamnett* 117, 119, 119n142, 122, 138, 143; *Portrait of Vanessa Bell* 74, *75*; *Sketch of the Omega Club* 144, *145*; *Victorian Photographs of Famous Men and Fair Women* 16, 37, 42, 44

Garland, Madge 50, 115
Garnett, Angelica (née Bell) 11, *11*, 12, *12*, 17, 18, 23–8, *24*, *25*, 30, 49, 51, 64, 69, 128, 146
Garnett, David 7, 9, 11, *11*, 16, 23, 100, 115, 120, 147, 149
Garsington Manor 16, 65, 69, 114
Gaudier-Brzeska, Henri 92, 97, 108, 136, 136n41
Gauguin, Paul 15, 138, 144n96
Gertler, Mark 123, *124*
Gill, Eric 102, 104
Gill, Winifred 91–3, 93n8, 96–8, 100, 102, 104–8, *105–7*, 112–19, 135 135n32, 136, 136n41, 141
Grafton Gallery 13, 135
Grafton Group 105, 135–41
Grant, Bartle 38, 38n55, *38*, *39*
Grant, Duncan
  and Bloomsbury Group 5, 125
  and Charleston 5, 7, 9, 18, 27, 70, 72, *118*, 119–20, 122–3, 128, *128*, 131, 144, 146
  childhood of 38
  and colonialism 38–9, 68
  death of 23
  and dress *62*, 105, *105*
  and exhibitions 12, 18, 133–4, 136–41,

136n41, 143, 146–7, 149
  and Grafton Group 135–6
  and hair 63
  and Memoir Club 10, *11*
  and Omega Workshops, 5, 59, 72, 96, 98, *104*, 105–6, 112–14, 123, 135
  photographs of *14*, 38, *38*, *39*, *62*, *63*, 65–6, 93n8, *99*, *105*, 106, *107*
  and Post-Impressionism 47, 70, 80, 108, 132–6
  and professional and amateur photographs 24n5, 52, 65, 70, 73
  relationship to: Adrian Stephen 9, 132; Angelica Garnett 23–4, 49, 69, 128, 146; Clive Bell 8, 11, 147; David Garnett 9, 23, 100, 120; Frederick Etchells 132; Gerald Shove 9; Jacques-Emile Blanche 44; James Strachey 38, 61; John Maynard Keynes 7, 9, 61, 65–8, 131–2, 142, 144, 147; Leonard Woolf 9, 132; Lytton Strachey 10, 11, 77, *77*, 132, 146; Mary Hutchinson 10, 108; Pippa Strachey 38; Quentin Bell 18, 39n57; Roger Fry 11, 101, 120, 147; Rupert Brooke 133; Stephen Tomlin 147–8, *148*; Vanessa Bell 42, 49, 64, 68–70, 72–3, 76, 84, 91, 97–101, *99*, 112, 115, 121, 123–8, *124–8*, 131, 136–8, 141, 146; Virginia Woolf 9, 12, 40, 115, 123, 132, 136, 147, 149–50
  and *Vogue* 51, *51*, 150
  works: *Adam and Eve* 73n56, 137–8, 137n47; *At Eleanor: Vanessa Bell* 108 *108*; *At Eleanor: Vanessa Bell*: study for 108, *109*; *The Blue Sheep* folding screen *135*, 136, 136n35; *The Dancers* 133, 136, 136n44, 139; *Decorated Vase* 142, *143*, 144; Decoration Clive Bell's rooms, 37 Gordon Square *142*, 144; Decoration Keynes's rooms, King's College Cambridge 18, 51, 68, 132; Decoration Keynes's rooms, King's College Cambridge: study for *65*, 68; Decoration 52 Tavistock Square 18, 51, *51*, 150; *Iris Tree* 110, 110n104; *James Strachey* 61, 61n7; *John Maynard Keynes* 61, *62*; *John Maynard Keynes's Hat, Shoes and Pipe* 60, 61–2; *Juggler and Tightrope Walker* 146, *147*; *Katherine Cox* 80–01, *82*; *The Lemon Gatherers* 68, 68n33, 135, 135n30; *Lytton Strachey in the Garden at Asheham* 77, *77*; Menu card

91, *91*; *The Music Room* installation, Lefevre Galleries 149, *151*; Omega Workshops fan *104*; *Pamela* Omega Workshops linen 92, *93*; *Portrait of John Maynard Keynes* 5, *5*, 7; *Portrait of Vanessa Bell c. 1915* 47, *48*; *The Queen of Sheba* 131, 132–3, 132n7, 139; *The Room with a View* 128, *128*; *Seated Woman* 80, 133–4, *134*, 138; *Self-Portrait in a Turban* 67, 68; *Sketch of Vanessa Bell when pregnant* 69, *69*; *Study for Composition (Self-Portrait in a Turban)* 66, 68; *Trojan Women* Omega Workshops tray, 106, 106n100, *106*, *107*; *Two Nudes on a Beach* 68, 68n33; *Vanessa Bell* *118*, 119, 122–3; *Vanessa Bell* 124, 125–8; *Vanessa Bell* 125–8, *125*; *Vanessa Bell Pregnant* 126, 128; *Vanessa Bell Pregnant*, study for *127*
Grant, Ethel 38, 38n55, *39*
Grindelwald, Switzerland 23, 26, *27*, 33

Hamnett, Nina 92–3, 96–7, 105–8, *106–7*, 110, *117*, 119, 119n142, 120, 122, 134, 136, 136n41, 138
Hampshire House Workshops 103–5, 103n84, *103*, 112–14, 119n141
Henderson, Faith (née Bagenal) 115–19, 123–5
Hills, Jack 40–01, *41*
Hogarth Press 10, 12–13, 16–17, 51, 55
Hutchinson, Jeremy 59
Hutchinson, Mary 51, 69, 110, 120–22, 141
  and Bloomsbury Group 10, 11, 59, 115, 120, 125, 143
  and dress 59, 97, 101, 108, 110, 115–19
  and Omega Workshops 101, 103, 110–11, 115–16
  paintings of 50, 72, 108-10, *111*, 143
  relationship to: Clive Bell 10, 59, 72, 100, 115, 120–01; Duncan Grant 10, 108; Lytton Strachey 10; St John Hutchinson 100, 120–01; Vanessa Bell 10, 12, 76, 77, *77*, 97, 100, 108, 112, 116, 119–22, 125, 131–2, 142–3
Hutchinson, St John 100, 103, 108, 120–01

Ideal Homes Exhibition 96, 106, 136
Irwin, Margaret 9n13

Jackson, Maria (née Pattle) 29, *29*, 37
John, Augustus 46, *75*, 76, *76*, 80, 93, 110n104, 135n29, 143

Kandinsky, Wassily 105, 136, 136n39
Keynes, Geoffrey 80–01, 142
Keynes, John Maynard
   and Bloomsbury Group 5, 15, 125, 132, 150
   and Charleston 5, *5*, *6*, *7*, 133, 144, 146
   collection of 7, 131–2, 142, 144, 147
   and Degas studio sale 144
   and dress 5, 7, *60*, *61*, *61*, 134
   The Economic Consequences of the Peace 7, 147
   and Gordon Square, 9, 100, 131
   and Memoir Club 10, *11*
   and Omega Workshops 97
   portraits of 5, *5*, *6*, *7*, *61*, *61*
   and professional and amateur photographs 55, 65, 68
   relationship to: Adrian Stephen 9, 132; Duncan Grant 7, 9, 61, 65–8, 131–2, 142, 144, 147; Leonard Woolf 9, 132; Lydia Keynes 17, 64, 70, 131, 150; Pablo Picasso 70; Roger Fry 7, 142, 144; Thoby Stephen 9, 31; Vanessa Bell 7, 9, 31, 63–4, 68, 84, 131–2, 134, 142, 144, 146; Virginia Woolf 9, 132, 147
   rooms in Cambridge 17
   and Treasury 5, 7
Keynes, Lydia (née Lopokova) *11*, 17, 55, 64, 70, 131–2, 150

Lamb, Henry 65, 128, 134, 139, 110n104
   Portrait of Lytton Strachey 128n174, 132, *133*, 139
Layton, May 93, 96, 100
Lechmere, Kate 100–01, 112, 122
Lefevre Galleries 12, 149–50, 150n147, *151*
Lenare 52–53, *52*, *53*, 55
Lewis, Wyndham 15–16, 92, 100, 135–6, 139, 145
Little Talland House, Firle 9, *64*, 83–4, 88
Lloyd, Constance 135
London Group 138, 143
Loppé, Gabriel *23*, 26–8, *27*, 30, *33*, 56

MacCarthy, Desmond 10, *11*, 13, 15, 74
MacCarthy, Molly 10, *11*, 13, 15, 70, *71*, 72, 74, *74*, 81, 83–4, 97–8, 123, 137, *137*
Maitland, Frederic William 28, 28n26, 46n93
Manet, Édouard 70, 144n96

Manet and the Post-Impressionists exhibition 13, 15, 128n171, 133, 152
Man Ray 56, *56*, 110n104
Marchand, Jean 134, 136n41
Marochetti, Carlo 24–6, *25*
Matisse, Henri 7, 13, 68, 70, 73, 88, 97, 128n172, 133–4, 136, 138
McNeill, Dorelia *75*, 76, *76*, 93
Memoir Club 10, 11, *11*, 13, 15
Monk's House 9, 17, 18, 28, *54–5*, 55–6, *62*, 73, 146, 149, *149*
Monk's House Albums 19, 26n15, 29–30, 36, 42, 44–5, 49–50, *54–5*, 70, 72, 79, 84, 84n96, 99, *99*
Moore, G. E. 9
Morrell, Lady Ottoline 12, 13, 16, 50, 65, 69, 70, 76, *76*, 83–4, 96–7, 112–15, 119, 128, 139–41, 149–50
Morris, May 104
Morris, William 45, 92, 103

Nash, Christine (née Kühlenthal) 92, 119
Nash, John 119, 134
Nash, Paul 92, 134
Neo-Pagans 59, 69, 81–4
Nevinson, C. R. W. 134, 136, 139
The New Movement in Art exhibition 110, 135, 135n30, 143
Nijinsky, Vaslav 70, 72
Norton, H. T. J. 11, 76, 133

Olivier, Noel 83–8, *83*, *85*
Olivier sisters 84–8, *85*
Omega Workshops 13, 15–16, 70, 72, 72, 73, *88*, 96, 100, 112, 135–36, 144–5, 149
   and Clive Bell 91, 93, 145
   closure of 128
   Copies and Translations exhibition 123, 142, 142n83
   dress collection 5, 59, 88, 91–7, *94*, *95*, 99–123, *102*, *104–18*, 125–8, 139–42, 145
   and Duncan Grant 5, 59, 72, 96, 98, *104*, 105–6, 112–14, 123, 135
   and exhibitions 123n164, 136, 139, 141–42
   and First World War 92, 99–100, 108
   foundation of 5, 76, 84, 88, 91, *91*
   and Hampshire House Workshops 103–4, 112–14, 119n41
   and John Maynard Keynes 97
   and Mary Hutchinson 101, 103, 110–111, 115–16

   and Ottoline Morrell 96–97, 112–14, 119
   and press photographs 92, 93, 105–6, *106*, *107*, 122
   and Roger Fry 72, 91, 93–9, *93–5*, 99–103, 106, 123, 135, 139, 144–5, 145n108
   see also Bloomsbury Group
   showroom at 33 Fitzroy Square 5, 88, 91, *92*, 93, *93*, 106, *107*
   textiles 92–7, *93–5*, 101–2, 104–8, *104*, *105*, 112–14, 121–2, 139–41
   and Vanessa Bell 5, 84, 88, *88*, 91, *91*, 93, 100, 110, 116, 120–21, 123, 135, *140*, 141–2
   and Virginia Woolf 84, 93, 96, 114–15, 123

Partridge, Ralph 11, 17
Pattle sisters 27, 29, 37
Pepler, Hilary Douglas 102–4, 103n84, *103*
Picasso, Pablo 13, 70, 98, 136, 136n41, *142*, 143–4, 143n94
Poiret, Paul 119
Post-Impressionism 7, 13, 15, 47, 70, 72, 80–83, 88, 92–6, 105, 108, 110, 132–41
Puvis de Chavannes, Pierre 134, 138

Rebel Art Centre 100, 136, 138–9
River House, Hammersmith 59, 103, *103*
Robinson, Charles 92n6, 96, 100–01

Sackville-West, Eddy 147–8
Sackville-West, Vita 42, 50n105, 52–55, *52*, *54*, 63–5, 115, 149, 151
Sadler, Michael 136, 143
Sargant-Florence, Alix 11, 123
Second Post-Impressionist Exhibition 80, 91n2, 92, 104, 106, 125, 132–4, 132n7, *132–3*, *135*, 136–7
Selwood, Mabel 47, 63, 119, 123
Shaw, George Bernard 17, 145
Shove, Gerald 9–10, 84
Sickert, Walter 11, 17, 139–141, 150
Sitwell, Edith 17, 100, 115
Sitwell, Osbert 115, 145
Smyth, Ethel 148, 148n136, 150
Stein, Gertrude 98, *98*
Stephen, Adrian 8–10, 13, *14*, 28, 30, *32*, *34*, 36, *36*, 49, 63n11, *64*, 84, *85*, 132, 134
Stephen family archive 13, 16, 24, 30–31
Stephen, Julia Jackson 8, 13, 23, *23*, 24–30, *25–29*, *32–34*, 36, *36*, 37, 40–42, *42*,

INDEX 181

44, *44*, 46, 49, 50–01, 56, 152
Stephen, Karin (née Costelloe) 10, 11, 114–15
Stephen, Laura 42, *43*
Stephen, Leslie 8, 25–7 *26–7*, 30, *32*, *33*, 36, *36*, 41–2, 45–47, *45*, 61
   Dictionary of National Biography 28, 42
   Mausoleum Book 18, 28, 30
   photograph album 16, 26n14, 26n15, 27n17, 28, 30, 31, *32–4*, 36, 40, 42, 44
Stephen, Thoby 8–9, *8*, 17, *18*, 28, 30–31, *32*, *34*, *35*, 40, 45, *45*, 47, 49, 61, 65
Strachey family 13, 37–8, *37*, 61, 65, 132, 145
Strachey, James 10, 17, *37*, 38, *38*, 61
Strachey, Lytton 10, *37*, 70, 119n142, 128, *131*, *133*, 139, 145–7
   appearance of 63, *63*, 65, 77, 132
   and biography 10, 17
   and Bloomsbury 12
   and Charleston 5n1, 7, 120, 131, 145–6
   collection of 146–7
   Eminent Victorians 11, 37, 145–6
   and homosexuality 17
   and Memoir Club 10
   photographs of 37–8, *37*, *63*, 76
   relationship to: Clive Bell 12; Duncan Grant 10, 11, 77, *77*, 132, 146; Mary Hutchinson 10; Ottoline Morrell 12; Stephen Tomlin 147–8, *148*; Vanessa Bell 10, 12, 76, 77, *77*, 120, 131–2; Virginia Woolf 12, 145–6
   and *Vogue* 50
Strachey, Marjorie *37*, 70–72, *71*, 74, *74*, 97, 101, 134
Strachey, Oliver *37*, 73, 133, 138
Strachey, Pernel *37*, *131*, 132
Strachey, Pippa *37*, 38, *39*
Strachey, Sir Richard *37*, 37, 38
Sydney-Turner, Saxon 8, 10, *63*, 120, 125

Talland House, St Ives 30, 36, *36*, 49, 83
Todd, Dorothy 50, 52, 115, *142*, 144
Tomlin, Stephen 50, 147–9, 148n132, *148–50*
Tree, Iris 97, 101, 110, 110n104, *112*, 114, 119
Twentieth Century Art: A Review of Modern Movements exhibition 135, 135n30, 138–9

University of Cambridge 8, 9, 16–17, 49, 61, 65–66, 68, 80–01, 116, 132–3

Van Gogh, Vincent 7, 15, 133
Vaughan, Madge 26–7, 45, 49
Vlaminck, Maurice de 134, 143
Vogue 18, 50–52, *50–51*, 138, 138n59, *138–9*, 144, 150, 152
Vorticists 136, 141, 141n71

Wadsworth, Edward 92, 139
Walker, Isabel 101, 104, 114, 119n141
Waterlow, Sydney and Margery 10–11, 80, *81*
Watts, George Frederick 13, 25, 29, *29*
Wells, H. G. 119, 146
Woolf, Leonard, 64, 146, *146*, 149
   autobiography 8, 9, 10, 16, 29, 61
   and Bloomsbury Group 16
   and Charleston 9
   death of 16
   and Memoir Club 10, *11*
   and Monk's House 8, 9, 18, 149
   and photographs 29, 45, 51, 55, *55*, 62, *79*, 80
   and Post-Impressionism 134
   relationship to: Adrian Stephen 9, 132; Duncan Grant 9, 132; Gerald Shove 9; John Maynard Keynes 9, 132; Quentin Bell 8, 16; Thoby Stephen 9, 45, 61; Vanessa Bell 16, 61, 133, 150; Virginia Woolf 8, 9, 61, 73, 77, 83–4, 115, 132–3, 149
   see also Hogarth Press
   works: *Beginning Again: An Autobiography of the Years 1911 to 1918* 9n11, 16n54, 45n91, 61n5; *Sowing: An Autobiography of the Years 1880 to 1904* 29, 61n4
Woolf, Virginia (née Stephen)
   and Asheham 9
   and Bloomsbury Group 9–10, 115, 123–5, 149, 152
   and Charleston 9, 123, 146
   and dress 50–01, 61, 74, 77–81, 84, 114–15, 123, 146, 152
   and exhibitions 134, 149–50
   and hair 63–5
   and Little Talland House 9, 83–4, 88
   and Memoir Club 10, 13
   memoir: 'Old Bloomsbury' 9, 10, 65n23

   and mental illness 10
   and Monk's House 9, 149
   and Omega Workshops 84, 93, 96, 114–15, 123
   photographs by *62*, 84, *99*
   photographs of *14*, *32*, *34*, *36*, *41*, *45*, 46–47, *46*, *50*, *51–3*, *52*, 55, *56*, *56*, 77, *79*, *80*, *83*, 146, *146*, *147*, 150
   and Post-Impressionism 13, 15, 81, 88, 141, 144
   and professional and amateur photographs 13, *14*, 16, 19, 26–36, 39–40, 45, 49–55, *54*, 70
   relationship to: Adrian Stephen 8, 9, 10, 36, 132; Clive Bell 63–4, 69, 81, 83, 115; Dorothy Todd 115; Duncan Grant 9, 12, 40, 115, 123, 132, 136, 147, 149–50; George Duckworth 36, 46–7; Gerald Shove 9; John Maynard Keynes 9, 132, 147; Julia Jackson Stephen 8, 36, 42, 44, 50–01, 56, 152; Julia Margaret Cameron 16, 37, 42–4, 50, 56, 151; Julian Bell 13; Katherine Cox 80–84; Leonard Woolf 8, 9, 61, 73, 77, 83–4, 115, 132–3, 149; Leslie Stephen 8, 28, 31, 36, 45–6; Lytton Strachey 12, 145–6; Ottoline Morrell 12, 83, 149–50; Quentin Bell 13, 16; Roger Fry 81, 84, 123, 144, 147; Rupert Brooke 80–83, *83*; Stella Duckworth, 40, 45; Stephen Tomlin 148–9, *149*, *150*; Thoby Stephen 8, 9, 17, 36, 40, 45; T. S. Eliot 12; Vanessa Bell 8–10, 12, 31, 36, 40, 42, 49, 51, 56, 64, 69, 73, 77–81, *78*, 84, 99, 114–15, 123–5, 133–4, 143–4, 148–50; Violet Dickinson 41, 45–7, 69n160, 83–4, 134; Vita Sackville-West 42, 50n105, 52–5, 63–5, 115, 149, 151
   see also Hogarth Press
   and *Vogue* 50–51, *50*, *51*, 115, 150, 152
   works: *Freshwater* 44; *Orlando* 10, *12*, 24n7, 52, *52*; *Roger Fry: A Biography* 13, 16, 96n19; *A Room of One's Own* 44n84, 52; *To the Lighthouse* 42, 63, 146; *Victorian Photographs of Famous Men and Fair Women* 16, 37, 42, 44

Zangwill, Israel 144–5

PICTURE CREDITS

Images that have been provided by the owners or custodians of the works, as indicated in the figure captions, are reproduced with their permission. Images for which further credit is due are listed below by figure number.

Art by Vanessa Bell © The Estate of Vanessa Bell

Art by Duncan Grant © The Estate of Duncan Grant, DACS

Art Gallery of South Australia, Adelaide, South Australian Government Grant 1984: 111, 112

Auckland Art Gallery Toi o Tāmaki, Mackelvie Trust Collection, purchased with the assistance of the National Art Collection Fund, 1992. Frame sponsored by the Portrait Group: 142

By kind permission of the family of Pamela Diamond: 156

The Charleston Trust: 3, 8, 9, 11, 14, 15, 16, 17, 18, 19, 20, 21, 22, 30, 34, 35, 36, 37, 40, 45, 47, 49, 51, 52, 53, 63, 66, 72, 73, 74, 75, 76, 77, 78, 79, 80, 81, 83, 84, 85, 87, 88, 91, 92, 93, 97, 99, 100, 107, 108, 123, 128, 129, 136, 137, 138, 139, 140, 143, 146, 147, 148, 155, 157, 165

The Charleston Trust, acquired with the assistance of the National Heritage Memorial Fund, The Art Fund and the MLA/V&A Purchase Grant Fund: 1

The Charleston Trust © the Estate of Max Beerbohm: 160

The Charleston Trust © Tony Tree: 164

Collection of Bryan Ferry: 105

David Herbert Collection: 121

Ditchling Museum of Art + Craft: 119

George Beresford via Getty Images: 50

Harvard Theatre Collection, Houghton Library, Harvard University: 7, 27, 28, 29, 46, 57, 58, 59, 60, 61, 67, 96, 98, 115, 116, 158, 163, 166

Harvard Theatre Collection, Houghton Library, Harvard University © Man Ray 2015 Trust/ADAGP, Paris and DACS, London 2019: 62

Ivor Braka Collection: 94

Metropolitan Museum of Art, Gilman Collection, Purchase, Alfred Stieglitz Society Gifts, 2005: 23

© Mortimer Rare Book Collection: 24, 25, 26

© National Portrait Gallery, London: 6, 31, 32, 33, 48, 68, 90, 102, 141

Philip Mould & Company, London: 104

Photo © National Museum of Wales: 101

Photo © National Portrait Gallery, London 2019. Image © The Estate of Duncan Grant. All rights reserved, DACS/Art Image: 134

Photo © Tate, London 2019: 10, 12, 38, 39, 41, 103, 114, 130, 135

Photo © Tate, London 2019. Image © The Estate of Augustus John/Bridgeman Images: 89

Photo © Tate, London 2019. Private collection: 131

Private Collection, courtesy Robert Travers (Works of Art) Ltd.: 150

Private Collection, London: 64, 153

The Royal Pavilion and Museums, Brighton and Hove: 42

Smith College Museum of Art, Northampton, Massachusetts: purchased with the gift of Anne Holden Kieckhefer, class of 1952 in honor of Ruth Chandler Holden, class of 1926: 82; Gift of Ann Salford Mandel, class of 1953: 95

© Tate, London 2019: 145

UK Government Art Collection, photo © Crown Copyright: 44

© The Universal Order: 113

University of Hull Art Collection: 69

University of Leeds Art Collection: 133

Victoria and Albert Museum, London: 106, 109, 149

© Victoria and Albert Museum, London: given by Mrs Margaret Southam, 1941: 43; given by Mrs Joy Hedger: 118, 120

Victoria and Albert Museum, London © Bodleian Libraries, University of Oxford: 122

With the permission of the Provost and Scholars of King's College, Cambridge: 2, 65

Yale Center for British Art, Paul Mellon Fund: 127, 132

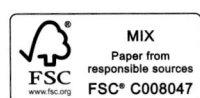

First published by Yale University Press 2020
302 Temple Street, P. O. Box 209040, New Haven CT 06520–9040
47 Bedford Square, London WC1B 3DP
yalebooks.com | yalebooks.co.uk

Copyright © 2020 Wendy Hitchmough

All rights reserved. This book may not be reproduced or transmitted in any form or by any means, electronic or mechanical, including photocopy, recording or any other information storage and retrieval system (beyond that copying permitted by Sections 107 and 108 of the US Copyright Law and except by reviewers for the public press), without prior permission in writing from the publisher.

ISBN 978–0-300–24411–3 HB
Library of Congress Control Number: 2020932051

10 9 8 7 6 5 4 3 2 1
2024 2023 2022 2021 2020

Designed by Georgia Vaux

Printed in China

Front cover: Vanessa Bell, *Mrs St John Hutchinson* (detail), 1915. Oil on board, 737 × 578 mm. Tate, London

Frontispiece: Duncan Grant, *Vanessa Bell Pregnant*, 1918. Oil on canvas, 660 × 583 mm. Auckland Art Gallery Toi o Tāmaki